THE VICTIM

She came from a close-knit Catho
good and honest life. But then Ann
one fatal mistake—and began a
wrong man . . .

THE KILLER

Married and the father of four youn
Capano was the picture of success.
customed to power, he hid his darkes
rage . . .

THE WITNESS

After Capano killed his lover, he need
his own troubled younger brother. As
Marie's lifeless body sink into the Atla
out: "This is wrong. This is wrong!"

THE TRIAL

Tom Capano's powerful family rallie
while Capano had political connecti
stunned courtroom would learn the
who used it all to destroy the life of
woman . . .

FATAL EMBR

FATAL EMBRACE

CRIS BARRISH
and
PETER MEYER

St. Martin's Paperbacks

To the memory of
Anne Marie Sinead Fahey

Acknowledgments

I am indebted to dozens of people for their assistance, counsel, and support over the last three years while I was reporting this story as a staff writer for the *Wilmington News Journal* and writing this book with Peter Meyer.

At my newspaper I had the pleasure of collaborating with three fine reporters who at various times served as partners on the story—Terry Spencer, Valerie Helmbreck, and, especially, Jerry Hager. I want to also thank John Mura, the editor who initially assigned me to investigate the mystery of Anne Marie Fahey's disappearance, in July of 1996, and who provided immeasurable inspiration and guidance; and his fellow editors Al Mascitti, E. J. Mitchell, and Merritt Wallick.

I would like to express my great appreciation to members of the Fahey family—especially Robert, Kathleen, Brian, Mark, and Kevin, all of whom were gracious and accommodating, despite the loss of their sister, throughout this long ordeal.

I also appreciate the help of former assistant U.S. attorney Colm Connolly, the man most responsible for bringing Tom Capano to justice, who gave freely of his time and insight. Also, this project would not have been possible without the help of prosecutor Ferris Wharton; FBI agents Eric Alpert and Tim Munson; Wilmington police detective Bob Donovan; Delaware state trooper Mark Daniels; IRS agent Ron Poplos; Gov. Tom Carper; Delaware secretary of state Ed Freel; gubernatorial chief of staff Jeff Bullock; Superior Court judge William Swain Lee; Annie's friends Kim Horstmann, Jackie Steinhoff, and Beth Barnes; former Wilmington mayors Bill McLaughlin and Tom Maloney; attorneys David Weiss, Dan Lyons, Katie Recker, Tom Bergstrom, Joseph Oteri, Mike Modica, Charles Butler, and Joe diGenova; juror Erin Reilly; and Ken Chubb, Ron Smith, Bud Freel, Kevin Freel, Michael Scanlan, Shaw Taylor, Kristi Pepper, Joe Smagala, Brian Murphy, Mike Harkins, Robert Long, Theresa Jordan, Heather Brand, Donna

Rizzo, Loretta Farkas, Carol Vannicola, Kathi Carlozzi, Warren Trent, CynDee Royle, Natasha Lebedeva, and a host of sources who choose to remain anonymous. I owe you all.

Last, special thanks to Peter Meyer, a writer of immense talent who brought me on to his project; and to my lovely wife, Mary, and our precious little boy, Luke, for tolerating me while I spent fourteen hours a day shackled to a computer screen.

June 7, 1999
Cris Barrish

I recall my amazement, surveying the crowd outside Courtroom 302 on the first day of Thomas Capano's murder trial, when I realized that this book was, literally, standing in front of me. Friends and family of the accused, friends and family of the victim, witnesses, prosecutors, defense attorneys, reporters, members of the general public—everyone was there. The nearness—my jaw dropped when I saw several jurors follow Tom Capano's mother and two of his daughters off the elevator—was a reminder of the complexity of this case. And I knew that I would need a guide through the crowd, someone who knew the players and the playing field, someone who could appreciate and explain the volatile yet subtle relationships that were, at bottom, what this story was all about.

That's when, as if he had sprung from my musings, I noticed a man, legal pad cradled in his right arm, weaving through the crowd. He would stop to talk briefly with a Fahey family member or a relative of Tom Capano, scribbling on his pad as he went. Clearly, he was a reporter; but unlike the journalists who stood in a group chatting with one another beside the metal detector at the courtroom door, this guy was working. Whoever he was, I knew immediately that he was Sherpa material.

It turned out better than I could have imagined. Cris Barrish, a writer for the *Wilmington News Journal*, had been covering the case almost from the day that Anne Marie Fahey was first reported missing. And as I would come to learn, after we decided to collaborate on this book, Cris knew the people of this story better than anyone else did, not by luck but through hard and constant work. I also discovered that he was possessed of the endurance of a marathoner, an obdurate and ferocious respect for facts, and an exhilarating curiosity—the Holy Trinity of journalism. Best of all, especially for a project like this, he could write like prairie fire. I am grateful to have met Cris and am especially thankful to him for carrying me across the finish line.

I must also express my sincere thanks to Charles Spicer, our editor, for his encouragement, patience, and good cheer in helping bring this book into being.

June 7, 1999
Peter Meyer

Contents

Prologue: A Strange Discovery   1

Book One: Annie
1. Missing   7
2. A Jealous Maniac   21
3. Searching for Annie   26
4. Falling Too Hard   70

Book Two: Tom
5. Crazy for You   91
6. Eye of the Storm   118
7. A Dangerous Dance   142
8. A Cold Summer Wind   152
9. Business as Usual   163

Book Three: Colm
10. Chasing the Spin   179
11. Tom Turned Inside Out   191
12. Be a Man   214
13. One Hell of a Burden   224
14. Stripped of Privilege   237

Book Four: Justice
15. Bail Denied   247
16. A Liar, a Junkie, a Stone-cold Bum   272
17. To Tell the Truth   279
18. The Greater Evil   316

Book Five: The End
19. A Verdict   347
20. A Malignant Force   358

Epilogue   371

Prologue: A Strange Discovery

Ken Chubb counted his blessings. Reclining in the captain's chair of his twenty-seven-foot fishing boat late in the afternoon on Independence Day, 1996, the retired navy submariner and prison maintenance boss surveyed the placid green Atlantic ocean beneath a beaming sun and cloudless blue sky.

The day's catch—about three dozen sea bass, flounder, and trout—packed his oversize cooler. Three of his grandchildren nibbled cookies and lounged on the deck. His wife, Gay, chatted with their son, David, and David's wife, Carol.

It had been a splendid Fourth of July.

The sixty-three-year-old Chubb, a burly, easygoing man who lived near Harrisburg, Pennsylvania, 175 miles away from the sea, had found his ocean hideaway fifteen years earlier. He and Gay had spent a week every summer in nearby Ocean City, Maryland. During those visits, Chubb often went crabbing at the inlet, a dozen miles north, with a guy who worked for him at the jail and had a summer home in Ocean City. Ken and Gay decided to get one, too, picking up an old thirty-five-foot trailer that they renovated and expanded.

Chubb found comfort in the tranquil, timeless pace of Bay City, a blue-collar sanctuary midway between the bustling resorts of Delaware's Rehoboth Beach, the summer playground for Washington preppies, and Ocean City's glitzy skyscraper strip. The ex–navy man couldn't imagine a more peaceful place.

The Chubb clan woke up early on the Fourth, donned shorts and swimsuits, and loaded up Ken's prize possession, *Morningstar 3,* a sleek white $60,000 Tiara fishing boat, equipped with twin 350cc engines. Gay fixed a cooler full of goodies—turkey, ham, and sweet baloney sandwiches, fruit, cookies, Tastycakes, and sodas. And by 8:30 the party set off for Chubb's "secret spot."

Most fishermen at the inlet gravitated to Buoy B, about ten miles out in the Atlantic. But years earlier Chubb had discovered another, more private site about two miles away. Only a rare fishing party ever stopped there. He logged the place as Number 55 on his loran navigation system, almost always fished there, and never divulged his location. "Oh, I'm at my secret spot," he was fond of telling other anglers on the short-wave radio.

Drift fishing was his game. He'd cut the engine and drop reels heavy with squid and minnow to the ocean floor, some seventy feet below, and let the boat drift with the tide for an hour or so. Then he'd haul up the catch, toss the fish in the cooler, motor back to Number 55, and start again.

The routine worked wonders that Fourth of July. The ocean was still, barely a ripple, with just a hint of a breeze. Each stop netted a cache that eventually filled the battered, 40.5-gallon warhorse of a cooler Chubb kept meaning to replace. His teenage grandchildren—Jared, Christina, and Rachel—howled delightedly as each fish emerged, wriggling for freedom, from the ocean.

About three-thirty, Chubb decided to call it a day. As he started the engine, David called from the deck below, "What's that floating over there?"

Following David's pointing hand, Chubb spied something white some one hundred yards away, sparkling in the late-afternoon sun, bobbing a few inches above the surf. Accustomed to finding bait buckets, logs, buoys, and other waterborne junk, he usually ignored the ocean debris. But for some reason, on this day, he was drawn to the shimmering speck.

"Let's go over and take a look at it," he told his son.

David directed his dad to the spot. The women and kids watched as he pulled alongside the floating object.

"It's a cooler. A fishing cooler!" David shouted.

"Well, grab hold of it and pull it in," said Ken, leaning down from his pilot's perch.

David lifted the cooler from the ocean. It was the same size as the one his dad owned but brand-new. Oddly enough, however, the new one didn't have a lid and was missing a handle. He poured out the salt water and set the cooler on the deck.

Ken scrambled down from his chair and studied the discovery.

"Man, that looks like a brand-new cooler," he said.

He looked closer and now noticed two holes, each a perfect half-inch in diameter, on either side of the hard plastic container. "Looks like bullet holes," Ken said, stumped. "Who in the hell would shoot a brand-new cooler?"

He inspected the rest of the cooler, noticing a pinkish-red stain on the bottom that he figured for blood from someone's bleeding fish.

He was still mystified by the bullet holes and the missing lid but was already thinking about how he could patch the sides, replace the lid, and have a decent cooler.

A new top-of-the-line Igloo like this one would have cost about two hundred dollars. Forty-four inches long, nearly two feet deep and wide, it was the granddaddy of coolers.

An hour later, Chubb pulled into his slip and saw his buddy Ron Smith changing the spark plugs on his own twenty-five-foot boat, *Grady Lady*.

Chubb lugged the cooler onto the old wooden dock.

"Hey, Ron. Come and see," said Chubb. "Take a look at this. It looks like it's brand-new. Doesn't have a lid on it. Looks like somebody was using it for target practice."

Smith, an experienced deer hunter, approached the cooler and stuck his finger in one of the holes. "Yeah, it's a bullet hole. I'd say it was from a 12-gauge shotgun."

"You know what?" Chubb told Smith. "The old cooler I have is the same size as this one. And it's worn out from dragging across the dock. I'm just going to take lid off my old one, patch the holes on this one, and I'll have a new cooler."

That weekend, using his power screw gun, Chubb moved the weathered and discolored lid from his old cooler to the new one. He mixed up a batch of fiberglass patch and filled the bullet holes. Satisfied with his handiwork, Chubb slid the new cooler into his unlocked shed.

BOOK ONE

It makes me feel good to know
that I can provide him with such happiness.
—ANNE MARIE FAHEY,
diary entry, March 1994

1 *Missing*

Her mind racing, Kathleen Hosey pushed open the door to her sister's apartment and took a deep, fretful breath.

It was ten o'clock at night, and the room, at the top of the stairs in the old brick house on the fringe of Wilmington's gritty Market Street strip, was quiet and dark. Anne Marie, according to Carl Olliver, the landlord, was not there. Olliver, who lived on the first floor of the house, said he hadn't seen Ms. Fahey for several days.

For Kathleen that news was no more reassuring than the unreturned messages, the skipped dinner date, the unanswered phone—none of it made any sense. It was not like her kid sister, appointments secretary to the governor of Delaware, to just disappear.

The alarm had come from Michael Scanlan, Anne Marie's boyfriend, an hour earlier, interrupting a restful summer Saturday barbecue at the Hosey house. Annie's older sister, a trim thirty-six-year-old physical therapist, lived in Brandywine Hundred, a bedroom community of middle-class and affluent families a few miles north of Wilmington, Delaware's largest city. Kathleen had grown up in the district's working-class section with her five siblings, including Annie, the youngest and six years Kathleen's junior. Kathleen had just put her two young boys to bed and her husband, Patrick, was pulling a plate of chicken off the grill when the phone rang. It took a few moments to focus on what Mike was telling her.

"Annie hasn't returned any of my calls and we were supposed to go to dinner at Robert's," said the young banker, who had been dating Anne Marie for almost a year. "Have you seen her?"

Kathleen had known about the dinner with Robert Fahey, Annie and Kathleen's brother, one of four boys in the big Irish-Catholic family. "I left a message on her machine," Kathleen told Mike, "asking her to pick up one of the boys' shoes from Robert's house when you stopped there tonight."

The Faheys were a tight-knit family in a town of tight-knit families. Kathleen and Annie, the only girls, talked on the phone almost every day, sharing secrets, dreams, and disappointments. In fact, just two weekends earlier, at the Fahey family beach home in New Jersey, Annie, who had turned thirty the previous January, had told Kathleen which friends she wanted for bridesmaids at the wedding of her and Scanlan, a rising star at MBNA, the giant financial institution headquartered in banking-friendly Wilmington. As director of the bank's community affairs department, Scanlan often worked with the governor's office coordinating MBNA grants to worthy charities. And it was the governor himself who had played matchmaker, suggesting to the eligible, handsome Scanlan that he might like to meet the governor's intelligent and pretty appointments secretary. Both single, both Catholic (Scanlan took Annie to see the pope a month after their first date), both young, smart, and ambitious, their relationship, casual at first, had steadily blossomed. And although Annie was outgoing and Scanlan reserved, she had confided to Kathleen and her girlfriends that he was "the guy." Now hearing that Annie had missed a date with Michael, Kathleen was alarmed. Annie loved the guy. She would not have blown him off.

On the phone Mike told Kathleen he had even driven by Annie's apartment earlier that day and seen her green Jetta parked on the street in front of the building. But, polite to a fault, the young banker had been too reserved to knock, unannounced, on her door. When the hour for their dinner date came and went and he still hadn't heard from Annie, he knew something was wrong.

And so, now, did Kathleen. "Let me make a few calls and I'll get back to you," she said and hung up. Kathleen knew Annie had taken Friday off work, and though it wasn't like her not to check in, perhaps she had gone to the beach with friends, had car trouble, and was late getting back.

Kathleen called Ginny Columbus, a childhood friend of Annie's who also worked in the governor's office. But Columbus said she didn't know where Annie was or what her plans were.

Kathleen then called her brother Robert, who she knew was probably still with his wife, Susan, at the Overbrook Golf Club in Newtown Square, Pennsylvania—no doubt waiting for Annie and Mike, even though it was after nine. The couples' dinner reservations had been for 7:30, on the patio overlooking a valley and woods that led to the eighteenth hole, a perfect setting, Robert had figured, to get to know Scanlan better. Robert, a commercial real estate broker, had only spoken casually with the young MBNA executive at family functions. He considered Mike, a New England native and Georgetown University graduate, restrained and a little aloof but enjoyed his dry wit and sense of humor. It was much like his own.

But on this evening he was not especially impressed with Scanlan's punctuality. Annie and Mike had been due at Robert and Susan's house at 6:30—and didn't show. Figuring they had had a flat (or a spat), Robert left messages on both of their phones, saying he and Susan would meet them at the Club. Mike hadn't called Robert because Annie had set up the dinner.

"Something's not right here," Kathleen told Robert. "Mike hasn't heard from Annie. She hasn't called you. I called her Thursday at work, and she didn't call back. The last time I saw her was Wednesday, when we picked up Patrick's car and she came over to do her laundry and have dinner."

Robert immediately paid the bill and rushed home. Tall, balding, and rugged, Robert, at thirty-eight, was the family leader, though only the third oldest of the six Fahey children. He wore wire-rim glasses and a stern expression and, eight years older than Annie, had been more parent than sibling to his youngest sister, especially since their mother had died in 1975, when Annie was only nine, and their father took to drinking. Though Annie was closest to Kathleen, it was Robert to whom she confided her struggles with anorexia and bulimia, the eating disorders that had recently sent her weight plummeting from 150 to 125 pounds, a worrisome weight for Annie's five-foot, ten-inch frame—and the reason for Kathleen's comment on Annie's ribs when she was trying on a blouse the previous Saturday. Robert knew Annie was having some personal problems, but she would not disappear like this.

Kathleen, meanwhile, called Scanlan back and suggested they go to Annie's apartment. Ginny Columbus then called

Kathleen to say that Jill Morrison, another aide to the governor and close friend of Annie, had told her she hadn't heard from Annie, either. Anyone who knew the outgoing and gregarious Annie knew that if none of her closest friends had heard from her, something was wrong. Ginny said she was going to the apartment as well.

Kathleen called the Wilmington police while waiting for Scanlan. "I want to report a missing person," she told the dispatcher.

During the ten-minute drive from Kathleen's suburban home to Annie's third-floor walk-up, Mike and Kathleen quietly reviewed their last contacts with Annie. Kathleen knew how thin her sister looked. But on Wednesday, the last time either Kathleen or Mike had talked to Annie, they agreed she had been in fine spirits. Still, Wednesday was three days ago.

And as they pulled up to the rambling brick house on the corner of 17th and Washington Streets, Mike and Kathleen were mindful of another peril. "The hood," as Annie jokingly called her block, whose once-proud homes had begun the descent into decay, wasn't dangerous. Still, while the tree-lined street looked peaceful, Kathleen and Mike knew Annie wouldn't walk alone at night, that armed crack dealers worked the corners of the dingy strip just six blocks away, that Wilmington was in the midst of a crime wave. Over the past several weeks, the *Wilmington News Journal* had run several lengthy stories about the shooting wars by rival drug gangs fighting over turf. Lush Brandywine Park, across the street, with its 180 acres of woodlands, hiking trails, and a stream meandering through Wilmington a joy during the day, had become a place to avoid at night, with muggers lurking about and the homeless sleeping on benches. And two teenagers' bodies had been found, shot execution-style and wrapped in a tarp, in Rockford Park, a sprawling landmark that towered over Wilmington's fanciest mansions on the west side, little more than a mile from Annie's house. Much of the violence, in fact, was centered in the battered commercial and residential district just up the street from Annie's apartment.

Scanlan parked his tan Grand Cherokee under a towering

sycamore tree behind Annie's Jetta and emerged with Kathleen into the gloom of a dead quiet Wilmington night. Though it had its crime and danger, with only 72,000 residents Wilmington also retained many small-town qualities, including sidewalks that seemed to roll up after dark. Now, at ten, the only noise on Washington Street came from an occasional passing car. A weathered copper statue of an angel, a monument to Delawareans killed in World War I, stood silent sentinel in the park across the street.

Kathleen glanced up at Annie's darkened apartment, then hurried up the front steps of the turn-of-the-century house and onto its wide veranda. Landlord Olliver was waiting for them. He explained that another young woman and an older woman—probably Ginny and her mom, thought Kathleen—had just been by and that his wife had taken them up to the apartment. His wife had gone inside alone and had seen nothing unusual, said Olliver. But Kathleen was determined to see for herself. She especially wanted to know if any of Annie's clothes or suitcases were missing, probable signs that she was visiting friends at the shore for the weekend.

Kathleen and Mike trooped up the narrow staircase, not knowing what they might find. At the third-floor landing, Kathleen inserted the key in the double dead-bolt lock and slowly swung open the door. She had been in the large one-bedroom apartment many times in the two years her sister had lived here, but never without Annie, and not in the dark. A white glow from a streetlight bathed the room in shadow, and as she and Scanlan stepped in, a wretched smell engulfed them; it was the heavy, fetid air of a place undisturbed by human activity—and of something decaying. Scanlan gagged. Kathleen, who often worked with people injured in falls at her job, marched straight for the bathroom and flung the shower curtain aside. If Annie had fallen, she might have knocked herself out. But there was nothing.

Kathleen went next to Annie's bedroom, where the door was cracked and the hum of an air conditioner could be heard. "Oh, shit," she muttered after flipping on the light.

The bed, which Annie always kept meticulously made, often putting a mint by the pillow and powder on the sheets, was rumpled. The covers were pulled back and the sheet slightly caved in, as if two fists had hammered it. Shoe boxes, Annie's precious shoe boxes, littered the floor. Dry-cleaning bags, seemingly ripped off hanging clothes, lay on the closet floor. Annie's laundry basket still held the clothes she had neatly folded at Kathleen's house on Wednesday, including the outfit Annie had worn that night. This was not like Kathleen's little sister, the compulsively neat young woman whom friends and family called Anal Annie, the woman who folded dirty clothes before putting them in the hamper. Kathleen knew Annie wouldn't have left the apartment, even to run to the store, with her bedroom in such disarray.

Kathleen also spied an unmistakable red gift box from Talbots. The sisters had had a small quarrel in the upscale women's clothing store the previous Saturday, when Annie seemed intent on buying a $289 tan pantsuit Kathleen knew she couldn't afford on her $31,500 salary from the governor. This was the day Kathleen noticed that Annie was so thin her ribs showed.

Lifting the sticky seal on the thin tissue paper, Kathleen peeked in the box. It was the same pantsuit they had argued over. Annie must have bought it anyway.

As Kathleen continued to survey the room, she saw a bedside photo of Annie and Mike taken at Annie's thirtieth birthday party, five months earlier. They really were a perfect couple, both slim, tall, athletic, and fun. Annie, with long wavy dark hair and a boisterous laugh, was beautiful and, with Michael, seemed radiant. In a corner of the room Kathleen spied something she had been hoping she wouldn't see: Annie's suitcase, the one she likely would have taken away for the weekend—had she gone. So, if she didn't go to the beach, where was she? Becoming more unsettled by the moment, Kathleen walked into the kitchen. Scanlan was there looking ill because of the smell, but at least the source was now obvious.

Kathleen saw bananas, spinach, Rice-a-Roni, pretzels, and other groceries on the counter. In the trash—beneath a water bottle from Saul Ewing Remick & Saul, a law firm Kathleen and Mike knew did bond deals for the governor—rancid mushrooms emitted a foul aroma.

It was another bad sign. Had Annie left when she wanted to leave, surely she would have put the food in the cabinets and emptied the trash. On the kitchen countertop Kathleen found sample boxes of Xanax and Effexor, two drugs she knew were used to treat depression and anxiety.

"Something's not right," said Scanlan.

It was as if the occupant of the apartment, Annie, had been swooped up in midsentence.

Place mats on the kitchen table were arranged neatly, as usual, and Annie's pocketbook was even there, in plain view, as if she had just walked into the room and gone to hang up her coat. Inside the purse were her wallet, credit cards, driver's license, checkbook, passport, and forty dollars in cash. Oddly, perhaps ominously, Kathleen and Michael noted that Annie's house and car keys, which hung on a ring with a three-inch leather case of Mace, were missing. But why?

Nothing made much sense. The place was a mess, completely out-of-character for Annie, yet there was no sign of a struggle and, clearly, no robbery.

———

Kathleen picked up the phone to call the police and heard a fast bleep on the receiver, indicating messages in Annie's telephone company answering service. But Kathleen didn't know the code. She dialed Wilmington PD and begged them again to send police to 1718 Washington Street.

Kathleen and Mike then continued looking around the apartment, seeking clues to Annie's whereabouts.

In a drawer of Annie's living room hutch Kathleen discovered an unsigned and undated letter, with printed handwriting that didn't match Scanlan's penmanship. Kathleen had already come across cards from Mike, from Valentine's Day and Easter. This new find was definitely from a different man.

Making sure Mike was not in the room, Kathleen read the long missive with some uneasiness. She didn't know the author's identity, but the letter was clearly from a paramour with whom Annie had discussed intimate details of her life. Kathleen read:

Dearest Annie—

Please consider the enclosed an early—and only partial—
Christmas gift . . . Now you can afford to do what you
wanted to do. Also, since Robert has apparently changed
his dinner plans to Sunday, you can be part of the celebration. Should Robert decide to have you for dinner on Saturday instead, then please use this to buy dinner (no drinks!)
next week for Sherry and your hostess . . . All I want is to
make you happy and to be with you. I love you.

Kathleen recalled a weekend the previous December when
she had taken her husband to the Saloon, a swank Philadelphia
restaurant famous for its veal chops. Annie had been invited
but declined to attend. But who was the mystery writer?

Kathleen rifled through the desk drawers with more intensity, finding three more letters in the same handwriting. These,
however, did reveal the writer's identity.

Sent on the stationery of Saul Ewing, the notes were from
Thomas Capano, the millionaire lawyer from a well-known
construction family who was the firm's managing director, a
prominent Wilmingtonian, and a former prosecutor—and
Kathleen knew, a married man.

In fact, Kathleen knew Capano. Her ex-boyfriend Bud Freel
was one of Capano's buddies and political cronies, having
worked with him on various political campaigns. In 1984 Capano had been a strategist in the Wilmington mayoral campaign of the late Dan Frawley, a lawyer for DuPont, the
chemical conglomerate descendant of the gunpowder works
that put Wilmington on the worldwide map nearly two centuries earlier. After Frawley's victory, Capano had become city
solicitor, Wilmington's top lawyer, and later Frawley's top
assistant.

Kathleen only had to scan these "Dear Annie" letters to
know that Capano and her sister were more than friends. A
note dated May 2, 1996, seemed to suggest an already-
powerful relationship:

Annie—

This is not a gift; it is a loan to replace your windshield. You can repay half of it when you get a check from the insurance company.

There was more banter, Kathleen read, about the penalty for nonpayment—"you will have to scrub my toilets and iron my boxers"—and an offer to buy Annie an expensive car, a Lexus 300ES Coach Edition.

A similar note was dated June 25, 1996, just four days ago, in which Capano appeared to be sending more money, hoping, "You should not be penniless for several days, in case of an emergency (like an overwhelming yearn for a latte!)"

Kathleen tucked the notes in her pocket, saying nothing to Scanlan, who was poking around elsewhere in the apartment. The letters, revealing a deep secret about her little sister, stunned Kathleen. "Reading those letters," recalled Kathleen, "was like a kick in the stomach. This was not a part of Anne Marie's life we knew about."

Kathleen didn't mention Capano to Mike, who was still looking for clues to his girlfriend's whereabouts. Though feeling awkward about prying through her private affairs, Scanlan could see how much he meant to Annie. There was the picture of the two of them by her bed—they had never slept together—and on Annie's desk calendar every date and monthly anniversary through the end of the year was marked with the word *Miguel,* a pet name that Annie, who was fluent in Spanish, had given her new beau.

Their relationship had been on a steady trajectory toward marriage. She had helped him remodel his kitchen, even selecting the tile and wallpaper. The previous January, Mike had flown home from business in Bolivia for her surprise thirtieth birthday party. And four weeks ago, over Memorial Day weekend, he had driven her up to his boyhood home in the seaport of Bristol, Rhode Island, to meet his parents. Mike and Annie didn't speak every day, but she had never stood him up. On the contrary, she was always punctual and excited when they got together. Mike was mystified.

———————

Kathleen grabbed the phone, checked to make sure Scanlan was in another room, out of earshot, and called her brother Robert.

After filling him in on the condition of the apartment, the odd mess, the pills, and the purse still on the kitchen table, she whispered, "Was something going on with Annie and Tom Capano?"

"I don't think so," said Robert, who, like just about everyone in Wilmington, knew who Tom Capano was. And as a real estate broker Robert was well aware of the Capano family power in Wilmington. In fact, Annie had even introduced the two men, who had played golf together, feeling each other out in hopes of doing business together. Robert and Susan had been Capano's guests at Saul Ewing's dinner and reception at the Cézanne exhibit in the Philadelphia Art Museum a few weeks earlier. Though Capano was busy hosting other guests, he took great pains to make the Faheys feel comfortable and introduce them to others. Susan had such a nice time that she penned Capano a warm thank-you note the next morning. And just the previous Wednesday, three days ago, Capano had left Robert a message at his office, trying to set up a golf date.

"What was their relationship?" Kathleen now asked Robert about Annie and Capano.

"He's like a mentor for Annie," said Robert, "a friend."

"No, they are not," Kathleen countered. She then told him about the letters she had just found. "These are not letters a friend writes."

Not one to sit still during an unfolding crisis, Robert had been busy digging up information at home. He had left an urgent message with Michele Sullivan, the psychologist Annie had been seeing since February. Robert knew about Sullivan—and Annie's eating disorder—because his sister had asked for his help in paying her therapist bills. Hoping Sullivan might be able to provide insight into Annie's whereabouts, he had left an urgent message with her answering service. While he was waiting for Sullivan's call, Robert's wife, who worked for a pharmaceutical company, said she feared Annie may have overdosed on the type of pills found in her apartment.

Robert and Susan also tracked down Kim Horstmann, a Philadelphia stockbrokers' assistant who shared a summer beach house with Annie in Stone Harbor, New Jersey.

Susan had attended high school with Kim in suburban Philadelphia and found her old classmate at Kim's brother's house.

"Do you know where Annie is?" Susan asked. She told Kim that her friend had missed a dinner engagement and couldn't be found.

"No, I don't know," Kim told Susan, explaining that the lease for the house at the shore had expired the previous weekend. Susan thanked her former schoolmate and hung up.

Kim had not spoken with Annie since Wednesday and didn't know her friend's weekend plans. But she was one of a small number of Annie's friends who did know about the secret affair with Tom Capano. When Susan Fahey called, Kim had immediately suspected Annie was with Capano but wanted to protect her friend. Kim now called Delaware information and got two residential numbers for Thomas Capano. She didn't know Capano that well, but twice that spring Capano had taken her out to dinner at the Ritz Carlton hotel near her Philadelphia Smith Barney office. Though Kim, a tall unmarried blonde, liked Capano's company, she considered him a jealous older man. He didn't like the fact that Annie—seventeen years his junior—was spending time with guys her own age at the beach.

But during the two recent dinners Kim had with Capano, he had fretted about Annie's rapid weight loss and wondered whether he and Kim could force her to check into a treatment center. "You're going to be shocked at how skinny she is the next time you see her," Capano had cautioned.

Capano had also spoken of his depression at Annie's budding romance with Michael Scanlan. Capano had left his wife, Kay, the previous September in order to be with Annie, he told Kim, and instead of reciprocating, Annie had relegated him to mere friendship status. He asked Kim, who knew Annie was head over heels for Scanlan, for advice. She suggested that he give Annie space.

But Kim also knew Annie was having some difficulty separating completely from Capano and now wondered if indeed she was still spending time with him. This was the time to find out. Since the affair had always been a secret, it would explain why Annie seemed to have disappeared.

It was 10:30 at night when Kim dialed the first number for Capano. A young girl answered. Kim panicked and hung up without a word. *That must have been the wife's number*, she thought. She knew Capano had four daughters.

Kim dialed the second number, and this time a woman answered. *Oops*, Kim thought. *This must be Kay, Tom's wife.* She hung up again.

Seconds later, Kim's brother's phone rang. Kim answered. It was the same woman, who obviously had the Star 69 recall service, wondering why Kim had just called her house.

"No, you have the wrong number," Kim blurted, then hung up once more, figuring that it was Capano's wife.

Finally, Kim got her brother to call the first number back. When a young girl said hello this time, Michael Horstmann asked for her father.

Kim took the phone and heard Tom Capano say hello.

"It's Kim."

"Hi, Kim. How are you?" he replied in a calm, natural voice.

"Where's Annie?" Kim asked.

"What do you mean?"

"Where is Annie? She's missing. Do you know where she is?"

But Capano didn't answer the question. Instead he asked, "Where are you?" now sounding agitated.

"I'm at my brother Michael's house."

"I thought you were supposed to be at the shore this weekend," Tom said. "I thought Annie was with you at the shore."

"No," she replied. "The lease on the house expired today. I'm not supposed to be at the shore."

"Where are you?" Capano asked again.

"I'm at my brother's house. Where is Annie?"

"She was going to the shore with you this weekend."

"That was never the case," Kim replied.

"Well, you've blown my mind," said Capano. "I need some time to think." He asked for Kim's brother's phone number and told her he'd call back.

Robert Fahey jumped at his phone when it rang. It was Michele Sullivan, Annie's therapist, returning his call. Susan Fahey jumped on an extension to join the conversation.

But even after Robert explained that Annie seemed to have disappeared, the therapist, citing patient-client privacy privileges, was not overly forthcoming. She did offer that she didn't consider an overdose with Xanax and Effexor very likely; that wasn't in her patient's character.

Then the therapist asked, "Can you think of anybody who would abduct your sister?"

The words floored Robert. He asked what she meant, but Sullivan politely declined to elaborate, again citing her patient's privacy.

"Can you think of anybody who would abduct your sister?" the therapist asked once more.

Robert pressed again for information.

Sullivan resisted. "I can't tell you any more," she said, "but I'll talk to the police."

Where were the police?

By eleven o'clock, having found nothing but dead ends and mysteries, Kathleen was getting more frantic. With the police apparently taking their time, she decided to use her connections and called Ed Freel, Delaware's secretary of state, the brother of her former boyfriend Bud.

Ed Freel had been chief of staff to the governor, Tom Carper, Annie's boss. In fact, Freel had helped get Annie her first job with Carper, as a receptionist in his Capitol Hill office when Carper was lone representative in the House for Delaware, the nation's second smallest state and home to just 700,000 residents. All of the Faheys were close to the Freel family and, except for Annie, had worked at one time or another in O'Friel's Irish Pub, the popular downtown watering hole for politicos and office workers that the Freels owned.

And that's where Kathleen found Freel, having dinner and a beer with his wife, Maureen, and brother Bud on a warm summer Saturday night.

"There's a phone call for you," said the bartender.

Ed walked to the phone and picked up the receiver.

"Hi, Ed. It's Kathleen Fahey. I have a problem." Freel pushed the receiver close to his ear to hear above the noise of the Saturday-night crowd. "Annie's missing. No one's seen or heard from her for three days. I've called the police, but no one has responded."

"Let me get a quieter phone and I'll call you back."

Ed scribbled down the number, hurried downstairs to his brother Kevin's basement office, and called back.

Kathleen stuck to the basics, filling Ed in on Annie's failure to keep her date with Scanlan and the strange condition of her apartment.

"Things don't look right," she explained. "We called the police, but nobody's been here. Can you help?"

Freel said he would and hung up. Within moments the bedside phone of the governor's new chief of staff, Jeff Bullock, was ringing. "No one has seen or heard from Anne Marie for a couple of days," the secretary of state told Bullock, a long-time colleague. "She missed a date tonight."

Bullock, who had been Annie's boss and pal for five years in Carper's small, close-knit office, had developed a special fondness for the bright, vivacious young woman who he knew had survived a tough childhood. Bullock saw Annie as someone with a bright future. And he immediately dialed Karen Johnson, director of the state's Department of Public Safety, which oversaw the state police. After explaining the situation, he said, "Could you send a trooper to Annie's apartment?"

Johnson knew the difference between a question from the governor's chief of staff and an order. "Yes," she replied and quickly called the head of the state police, Alan Ellingsworth, who in turn dispatched Mark Daniels, a veteran detective, to Annie's apartment.

Bullock decided to wait until the morning before alerting Carper to Annie's disappearance, just in case she turned up.

But before going to bed, on what would be a restless night, he called Freel back to let him know where things stood. Freel called Kathleen.

"Someone will be there shortly," Freel told Annie's sister.

In the meantime, Ginny Columbus, Annie's friend and co-worker, had returned to Annie's apartment and called Sgt. Steve Montague, a state trooper on the governor's security detail. When she explained that Annie was missing, Montague, who lived fifteen miles away, threw on some clothes and raced to Annie's apartment.

2 A Jealous Maniac

At four minutes after midnight, Kim Horstmann answered her brother's phone.

"This is Tom," said the voice. "I've had some time to gather my thoughts."

During their nineteen-minute conversation, Capano continually reassured Horstmann that Annie would probably show up for work on Monday.

In a soothing baritone, the lawyer seemed to take pains to describe what he and Annie had done on Thursday night, telling Kim he had taken her friend to a Philadelphia restaurant and that they had stopped at his place on Grant Avenue on the way back. There, Capano said, he had given her a suit from Talbot's, as well as some groceries—a way of encouraging Annie to eat, he pointed out, since she was still having trouble with her eating—and returned some Spanish tapes. Capano said he then took Annie home, checked out her air conditioner, which was working fine, and returned to his house.

"She said she was going to Stone Harbor with you for the weekend, Kim," Capano said, repeating what he had told Horstmann during their brief talk earlier. "I haven't heard from her since, Kim."

As Capano talked, Horstmann sat on a couch, the phone cradled under her ear, growing more encouraged with his every word.

Annie, he said, had been through a tough week at work with the busy legislative session and fiscal year winding to a close. She'd also had a big fight with Kathleen at Talbot's. "Even though she lied to me about spending the weekend with you," said Capano, "she probably went away for the weekend with other friends."

Kim told Capano that Annie's family had filed a missing person report with the police. "I wonder if they'll be looking for me," Capano said matter-of-factly.

—————

Lt. Mark Daniels arrived at Annie's apartment at almost the same time as his old pal Sgt. Steve Montague and two Wilmington police detectives, Bob Donovan and Elmer Harris. Veteran cops, they all knew what kind of influence would bring four policemen from two different law enforcement agencies to an obscure apartment in this fringe neighborhood. This was not an ordinary missing person. Deferring instinctively to Wilmington's jurisdiction, however, Montague and Daniels immediately signaled their willingness to help, as eyes and ears, while Donovan and Harris began taking names and numbers.

The cops also immediately realized there was no sense in cordoning off the place as a possible crime scene—too many people had already contaminated it with fingerprints.

Kathleen Hosey, the missing woman's sister, and Michael Scanlan, the current boyfriend, who looked shell-shocked, told the police how strange all this was, completely unlike Annie.

Donovan also listened to the missing woman's coworkers Jill Morrison and Ginny Columbus, who had come to the apartment and now said that Annie had worked all day Thursday and had an appointment to see her psychiatrist at five o'clock that day. They said she had scheduled to take Friday off, which was why no one had missed her, and had plans for a pedicure and a stroll through Valley Garden Park, a lush, fragrant former du Pont estate in Greenville, the heart of Delaware's château country, the rolling countryside where fabulously wealthy du Pont heirs lived on magnificent estates. Neither woman had actually talked to Annie since Thursday. Hosey and Scanlan had not talked to Anne Marie since

Wednesday—though Scanlan had left a number of messages, all unreturned.

The investigators knew that people, especially young single ones, often took off for days unannounced, jeopardizing jobs and frightening families and friends in the process. But this seemed very different. From what they were hearing about Anne Marie Fahey, spontaneous and irresponsible behavior was not part of the profile.

Nor did Fahey's apartment, aside from the shoe boxes strewn around, unmade bed, and rotting groceries, appear to be the domicile of a flake. In fact, the cops quickly surmised that they were in the apartment of a neat freak. Her CDs, which featured a prominent number of James Taylor and Gipsy Kings selections, were in alphabetical order. In her bedroom closet, her clothes were hung by height and type—skirts, dresses, pants. The bathroom was spotless. And Detective Donovan was astounded to see dirty clothes in the laundry basket, all neatly folded.

Jill Morrison, Annie's freckle-faced pal from work, also told the police there were messages on Annie's answering service and gave them the password for accessing it.

Daniels dialed, punched in the code, then listened. "You have twelve messages," came the computer voice.

The state trooper listened to each message, one by one, taking notes, relaying parts of the messages to Annie's friends and her sister standing by.

The oldest message had been left by Mike Scanlan at 6:55 the previous Thursday evening. "Hey, Annie, remember me?" said the familiar voice. "It's around five of seven and I'm going to a little cookout thing for our interns. It starts at around six, I think, or six-thirty. I'll be home by around nine. Give me a holler; I'll talk to you when I get home. Thanks. Bye."

The next message was also from Scanlan, who had called back at 9:30 that same night, asking Annie if she wanted to join him at Kid Shelleen's, a yuppie bar and grill on Wilmington's trendy West Side, when he left the cookout. Fifteen minutes later Mike had called again, saying he was leaving the house and hoped to see Annie at the bar.

Daniels heard Scanlan's recorded voice again, this time Friday afternoon, evidently in no mood for chitchat after having been stood up the previous night. "Give me a call back," he said. "Let me know what you're up to."

That's how it went, through message twelve, from Annie's sister on Saturday afternoon, asking Annie to pick up her son's sneakers from Robert's house. "Love you," said Kathleen on the tape.

Nothing about the twelve messages seemed out of the ordinary to Daniels—except, of course, that none of them were answered. It suggested that Annie Fahey hadn't been home since Thursday—and none of her closest friends knew where she had gone. Even if Annie had listened to her messages from another phone, she didn't return any of them. Why not?

It was after midnight when Ginny Columbus handed Kathleen a hardcover rainbow-colored notebook that she had found in a drawer of the breakfront in Annie's dining room. The book had lined pages and was filled with the neat, tight script of the governor's appointments secretary.

Knowing, but not wanting to know, Kathleen handed the book to the police. It was Annie's diary.

"A lot has happened since my last entry," were the first words of the book. It was dated: "Wednesday, 3-2-94," more than two years before.

Over the next hour, the police, with the help of Annie's friends and sister, ruefully paged through the book.

On the first page Annie had written about the recent births of three nephews, her grandmother Nan's death, her therapist, Bob Conner, who had put her on Prozac, and her battle to stay thin. "I now think of food as poisonous," she wrote.

The reading was slow and painful—what if the missing woman were to walk in and find all these strangers pawing through her personal life?—but everyone knew what they were looking for. Would Annie tell them, through her diary, where she was?

"I have fallen in love with a very special person whose name I choose to leave anonymous," she had written in the fifth paragraph of that first entry. "We know who each other are. It happened the night of my 28th birthday. We have built an everlasting friendship."

Kathleen guessed who the diary's mystery man was. And Ginny and Jill now told her that they had known Annie was seeing Capano.

In the next entry, five days later, Annie identified her secret lover as "Tomas" and confessed: "I don't want to be in love, but I can't help it. By God, please don't judge me."

Police flipped through the forty pages, with Kathleen, Ginny, and Jill answering questions. It was suddenly and shockingly clear to Kathleen that her sister had been Tom Capano's lover for at least two years—and Kathleen hadn't known. Kathleen recalled the last time she had seen Annie, on Wednesday, and the conversation they had had about a friend's extramarital affair. "Annie thought it was wrong," Kathleen remembered. Now she realized that Annie might have been speaking from considerable experience, weighing her own acts on this moral scale.

There were references to "Tomas" everywhere in the diary. It was clear that Annie had fallen hopelessly in love—"I love you, T., please do not leave me hanging like this!" she wrote in February of 1995.

Interspersed in the diary were references to other boyfriends, sad ruminations about her alcoholic father, an upbeat account of her trip to Ireland with her brother Brian, and descriptions of her struggles with anorexia and bulimia. But the dominant topic seemed to be "Tomas." And they could track what had begun as a passionate love affair and ended, so it seemed, rather badly.

Oddly, the entries stopped with March 1, 1995, and did not pick up again for more than a year. Even then, there was just one more entry, on April 7, 1996, Easter Sunday. It was just three months ago and Annie wrote ominously: "I finally have brought closure to Tom Capano. What a controlling, manipulative, insecure, jealous maniac."

3 *Searching for Annie*

The four police officers knew the significance of the name Tom Capano. Jill Morrison explained—as she had earlier revealed to Kathleen, but not Mike—that she had known Annie and Capano had frequent out-of-town dinners in order to keep their relationship discreet.

The cops listened. Secret love affairs frequently ended badly; those involving prominent citizens were often messy. This was the Capano family, one of Delaware's most prominent—and most notorious, with several members previously involved in scandalous brushes with the law. And Tom Capano was its leading light, one of the most powerful and politically well-connected attorneys in Wilmington, if not all of Delaware. And a woman with whom he was having an illicit affair, who had described him as "a controlling, manipulative, insecure, jealous maniac," was missing.

Kathleen relayed the information about Michele Sullivan's abduction warning. Donovan acted immediately, calling Sullivan from Annie's apartment, even though it was past one o'clock in the morning.

But the therapist was still wary of betraying her patient. All that Sullivan would acknowledge was that Annie had a relationship with Capano and that it was, as Donovan recalled later, "hot and cold."

Then, in the dead of night, the cops began knocking on nearby doors in the row houses clustered around 1718 Washington Street. Only Bryon Short, wiping sleep from his eyes at 3:05 in the morning, was of any help. The young man lived in the building next door, but he also worked for the governor and knew Annie. Short told the police that a few times over the last six months he had seen Tom Capano sitting in a black "Bronco-type" vehicle outside the apartment building. The last time was two weeks ago, when Short said he saw the two leaving at lunchtime, carrying trash to the corner.

Short added that he was home Thursday night but neither saw nor heard anything unusual.

The cops conferred and agreed they should speak with Capano, right away. Clearly, as Short confirmed, the "maniac" was not out of Annie's life.

Maybe he knows something, Donovan thought.

Detective Bob Donovan, a stout Irishman with a crew cut, a hearty laugh, and a habit of chewing paper clips, was known on the force as a thorough, no-nonsense cop. At the time he got the call to come to Anne Marie Fahey's apartment, he was working the drug-related shootings plaguing the city, as well as carrying a heavy caseload of burglaries and robberies.

Donovan had been with the Wilmington Police Department long enough, nine years, to know who Tom Capano was. Insiders knew that the mayor's administrative assistant, called the "AA," which Capano was for nearly two years under Dan Frawley, ran the day-to-day operations of city government. Every city agency department head, including the police chief, had reported to Tom Capano. Street cops often bristled at orders from the big shots in the mayor's office, derisively known as the "Ninth Floor" for its location high above the madding crowd, but when Tom Capano spoke, the men and women in blue obeyed. Though he hadn't wielded such day-to-day clout since 1988, his power, even if mythical, remained.

The burly detective, who had grown up in Wilmington, had only come in contact with Capano once while performing his duties. As a rookie, he was working an undercover burglary sting in west Wilmington's Highlands, the elite neighborhood of stone mansions and manicured lawns where Capano lived. Among Donovan and the rest of the cops, even the police chief, who could only dream of living in such splendor, the Highlands were longingly referred to as the "high-rent district."

During that operation Donovan and another officer had found themselves in an alley behind a sprawling Spanish-style mansion once occupied by the Catholic bishop. Donovan had done his homework and knew that it was Tom Capano's home now. The detective had knocked on the door to alert the former solicitor and top mayoral aide that they might need to use his backyard for some surveillance.

Capano had answered the door and graciously thanked Donovan for trying to crack the case.

Now, at 3:30 A.M. on June 30, 1996, Donovan found himself about to knock on Tom Capano's door again. It was a different house and a very different occasion.

The ride from Fahey's apartment to Capano's rented house, a little less than a mile, took the cops—Donovan and Harris in the lead car, Daniels and Montague following—from a neighborhood of tiny brick row houses to one with majestic and palatial dream homes, some with price tags of more than a million dollars.

Donovan was entering vastly different terrain from the tough streets where he did most of his work. But the phrase "jealous maniac" kept ringing in his ears, like a mantra. And he also knew Capano could just as easily be the one to lead them to Fahey and solve the case right away. Maybe, Donovan thought, she was even at his house.

The police cars had the roads almost to themselves at this hour as they crossed over Brandywine Creek and hopped on Kentmere Parkway, an expansive grassy boulevard lined with towering oaks and sycamores. In a few moments they turned onto Grant Avenue, which gradually narrowed into a winding one-lane road through a hilly and secluded enclave of luxurious residences. Capano's house—given the diary entry he was privy to, Donovan guessed this was his bachelor pad—was a large but not ostentatious three-story brick colonial with a big backyard. Donovan knew it was only a few minutes' drive to Capano's own home, where, apparently, only his wife and four daughters now lived.

The policemen pulled up to the curb in front of the darkened house. It was a quiet, warm summer night as they walked up the brick pathway to the front door, well aware that they had not telephoned in advance. This was, in the parlance of the trade, a cold call, the kind of surprise that cops used with great frequency—and usually to good effect. You could tell a lot about a person at 3:30 in the morning. Donovan banged on the door with authority. The men waited. After a few minutes, Capano, wearing a dark housecoat and looking groggy, his short graying hair mussed, cracked open the door.

The cops, all in plainclothes, politely introduced themselves, by name and agency, to the man peering at them from the doorway.

Capano opened the door and ushered the men into the living room, where they took seats on couches. "Please be quiet," he whispered in a pleasant voice. "My girls are asleep."

Mark Daniels, a muscular, square-jawed man who had been a state trooper for eighteen years, spoke on behalf of the foursome. "Do you have any idea why we would want to speak with you, sir?" the detective asked.

"Yes," Capano said. And he told them about the call from Kim Horstmann. "Kim said Anne Marie has been missing since Thursday."

"When was the last time you saw her?"

"We went to dinner in Philadelphia on Wednesday or Thursday night," Capano said. Then he corrected himself. "I think it was Thursday."

Capano told police he had picked up Anne Marie about six-thirty on Thursday evening and driven her to the Ristorante Panorama in Philadelphia. He said they had eaten a fine meal and drunk some wine. Fahey, he remembered, wore a light-colored dress with a floral pattern. After dinner, he continued, Fahey had used his credit card to pay the bill, signing the check and calculating the tip because he wasn't good at such things, he said.

When they left the Panorama, he drove straight back here, to 2302 Grant Avenue, Capano said, to pick up a bag of groceries—rice, bananas, spinach, strawberries, and soup. He wasn't sure if an outfit from Talbot's he had bought for Fahey was already in his Jeep, but if the gift was in the house, he had picked that up, too.

Then he had zipped back to her place, where he walked Anne Marie upstairs and stayed a few minutes. Inside, he said, he had unpacked the groceries on the kitchen counter and put the spinach and strawberries in her refrigerator. Fahey had opened the gift, he said, but he wasn't sure if she had removed the outfit from the box. "Then I went into her bedroom, checked the air conditioner, and went to the bathroom."

It was about ten o'clock when he left, Capano told the cops.

Asked if he stopped anywhere before going home, Capano said yes, at the Getty station minimart on Lovering Avenue, on the route home, to buy a pack of cigarettes.

"I haven't seen or heard from her since that night," Capano said, adding that she had planned to take off Friday.

Daniels was disturbed by Capano's nonchalant demeanor, especially at this hour. "I just had a funny feeling from observing his body language," the detective later recalled. He pressed on, asking Capano how recently, if ever, he and Anne Marie had had sex.

The last time was about six months ago, Capano replied matter-of-factly.

Capano then surprised the police by offering his opinion about Fahey's mental stability.

"You know," he said, "she was kind of airheaded. And very unpredictable. She also said she was unhappy at work." Capano told the cops that Anne Marie had had a serious argument with her sister earlier in the week. "Kathleen puts her down," Capano said.

Capano seemed especially adept at the psychological profile, explaining that Anne Marie suffered from depression, anxiety, and anorexia. She took medication for her maladies, he said, and they often made her ill, causing her to wake up in the middle of the night. "A number of times in the past," he said flatly, "she had talked about committing suicide by taking an overdose of pills."

Was that what he thought might have happened to her now? Daniels asked. (They didn't tell Capano about the diary—and his prominent place in it.)

Capano said he doubted it.

Did he have any idea where she might be now? the police asked.

Capano told them what he had told Kim Horstmann. "I thought she was going to the Jersey shore with Kim Horstmann, but Kim called and told me Anne Marie couldn't be found."

"Do the circumstances seem suspicious to you?" Daniels asked.

"Anne Marie probably went off somewhere without telling anybody," Capano said. "I'm sure she'll show up for work on Monday morning."

As the police were preparing to leave—they had been in Capano's house for forty-five minutes—Daniels asked Capano whether if Annie was in the house and didn't want anybody to know she was, Capano would tell them.

"No, I'd probably honor her wishes," Capano said.

"Look," the detective said, in a voice that didn't disguise the urgency of the moment. "We've made it clear that her family is back at the apartment, worried to death, and it appears as if she's been missing for a number of days. If she's here, let us know so we can reassure the family she's not been harmed."

"She's not upstairs," Capano said in an even voice.

The policemen did not ask to search the house. The lawyer's answers had been responsive, and the police had no direct evidence linking him to Anne Marie's disappearance.

"Can we contact you in the morning if she has not turned up?" asked Daniels.

"OK," said Capano.

As the four cops walked to their cars, they agreed to meet later in the morning. Fahey's name was now entered into the "missing person" file of the Delaware Justice Information System as well as the National Crime Intelligence Center computer database.

Though Capano had been cooperative, answering every question, the four cops agreed on one thing: they needed more answers from Tom Capano.

After getting just three hours of sleep, Kathleen Hosey and Mike Scanlan were back at Anne Marie's apartment at eight that Sunday morning.

As they stood at the bottom of the stairs, Kathleen cradled Mike's arm in hers.

"Mike, there's something I need to tell you."

Looking sadly into his eyes, Kathleen told about the letters from Capano, the diaries, and the affair.

Mike listened, gazed softly back at her, and said three simple words.

"Let's go up."

In Newtown Square, Pennsylvania, Robert Fahey had tossed and turned all night. He thought about Capano. Damn, he had known Capano and Annie were friends but never thought it had gone beyond that. It bothered Fahey now to think that Annie had introduced him to Capano, believing the two men could do business together. Fahey's firm, Cushman & Wakefield, brokered multimillion-dollar deals for downtown Philadelphia skyscrapers and suburban malls. Capano, managing partner of Philadelphia-based Saul Ewing's Wilmington branch, was plugged into Wilmington's business community. It would be a feather in each man's cap to land the other's firm as a client.

To think that he and his wife had been wined and dined by Capano at the Cézanne exhibit just two weeks earlier also bothered Fahey. This was messy, much too messy.

Could Capano know where Annie was? Could he be responsible for her disappearance? It wasn't a serious suspicion, but a nagging one.

Waking at dawn, Robert and Susan woke their boys and went to 7:00 A.M. mass at St. John Neuman Catholic Church. Robert asked the priest, before the service began, if he could dedicate the mass to his missing sister.

After the service, Robert telephoned a fellow parishioner and neighbor, Tom Ostrander, a corporate attorney in Philadelphia.

"Something doesn't smell right," Robert said, after telling Ostrander about his sister's sudden disappearance and some of the clues found at the apartment. "This Capano family might have some involvement. They're powerful and pretty well connected. I think we're going to need some good advice from people outside of Delaware. Is there anything you can do to help us out?"

Ostrander suggested a name in his law firm's Wilmington branch, David Weiss, pointing out that Weiss was a former federal prosecutor. Ostrander promised to call Weiss first thing Monday.

Robert hung up and headed down to Annie's place, a half-hour drive. When he arrived, he saw four policemen, wearing slacks and T-shirts on this muggy Sunday morning. But his eyes fixated at the weapons on their hips.

Oh, my God, Robert thought. *This is a fucking nightmare.*

From the apartment Kathleen had put in a call to Ecuador, where her brother Brian was visiting his wife Rebeca's family.

Brian, the thirty-four-year-old family intellectual, was a fifth-grade teacher and basketball coach at Wilmington Friends School, a venerable Quaker institution favored by doctors, lawyers, and other wealthy Wilmingtonians.

He had told his family not to call him in Ecuador unless someone died. His in-laws didn't speak English, and any translations would have been impossible if he or Rebeca wasn't around to take the call.

But that morning, the phone rang. Rebeca picked up the receiver.

"Hi, Kathleen," Brian heard his wife say, and knew instantly it could only be bad news. Picking up the phone, he heard Kathleen say, "We have a problem. No one's seen Annie since Thursday night."

"What happened?" asked Brian, dumbstruck.

Kathleen explained the missed date, the disarray in Annie's apartment, the letters.

"That's really wrong," Brian said. "I'll catch the first flight back."

Brian packed within minutes and his father-in-law drove him to the airport. But there weren't any flights for at least four hours, so he returned to the house and waited, calling back to the apartment, desperate for more information.

Searching through the apartment that Sunday, Annie's family and friends noticed two more items missing: a red-and-white short-sleeved shirt she had nicknamed Waldo and a blue topaz ring, a gift years earlier from her first love.

———————

The police went full bore that Sunday.

Donovan, who played catcher in a local thirty-and-over baseball league, bagged his ball game, which started at nine and usually lasted until noon. He told his wife and two young children he'd be busy all day. The other officers on this make-shift interdepartmental force had also scuttled plans for their day off.

That morning the foursome—city cops Donovan and Harris, state troopers Daniels and Montague—fanned out for another door-to-door canvass of the homes near Annie's apartment. Montague, from the governor's security detail, got the Aviation Unit of the state police to send out a helicopter on an aerial search of Brandywine Park with a high-powered infrared scope. He also suggested that the chopper fly over Valley Garden Park, three miles west of the city, where Annie had told Ginny she was going on Friday.

Nothing.

The cops spoke again to the Faheys, to Scanlan and Morrison, and to landlord Carl Olliver and his wife, Theresa, seeking additional clues in the retelling of their stories.

Jill Morrison revealed some more information: Annie and Capano had often gone to Philadelphia for dates, keeping away from the prying eyes of their friends in Wilmington. Olliver, the landlord, told the cops Annie was close to Connie Blake, the second-floor resident, who had gone away Friday morning and would return later that night.

State trooper Daniels called Kim Horstmann. He was curious about why she would deny to Susan Fahey knowing anything about Annie and Tom and then call Capano on the phone to alert him to Anne Marie's disappearance.

"You know about Tom Capano and his relationship with Anne Marie," Daniels said, incredulous. "You called him and told him she was missing."

"You're right," Horstmann said, ashamed. "I didn't want to betray Annie. I'm so sorry. I was trying to protect her."

Daniels scheduled an interview with Horstmann for the next day.

Sullivan was contacted again. Informed that Annie still hadn't surfaced, the therapist now confessed that her patient feared Capano because he had harassed and stalked her. This piece of information, added to the fateful diary entry, was startling, especially given the fact that it appeared Capano was the last person to have seen Anne Marie.

The therapist told investigators she had advised Annie to report Capano's behavior to the Delaware attorney general's office, but that her patient resisted because an arrest would embarrass her and the governor.

Montague then drove to Jeff Bullock's house in Brandywine Hills, an old Jewish neighborhood of stately stone homes on the northern edge of Wilmington where several state and city government officials, including the governor, lived.

"We can't find her," Montague told the governor's chief of staff. The policeman also reported Annie's affair with Tom Capano and their interview with him earlier that morning.

Bullock had known Annie was friendly with Capano but hadn't suspected an affair. But the bigger problem, Bullock knew, was what he feared most. "My gut told me that Annie had come to harm," Bullock later said. "It was just so unlike her to go AWOL for three days, without any of her family or close friends knowing her whereabouts."

With a heavy heart, Bullock picked up the phone and called his boss. He told Governor Carper that his appointments secretary was missing and there was reason to believe that her disappearance was not voluntary. Bullock reviewed the facts for Carper, including the affair with Capano.

Carper was stunned. Mindful of where Annie lived and the chaos that reigned on nearby streets, the governor's first thought was that Annie had been abducted. The idea sickened him, because it could mean she was dead or being tortured. But even though he didn't really believe it, Carper had to hope Annie had just taken off for the weekend.

But Carper was also surprised to learn that his aide was having an affair with Tom Capano, a pillar of Wilmington society and one of Delaware's best-connected political strategists. Capano had served as a trusted adviser to Democratic mayor Frawley and had been chief legal counsel to Republican governor Mike Castle, who had preceded Carper. In fact, Capano had helped Carper's transition team in 1993. And the governor, a tall, wiry fitness buff and distance runner, also knew Capano's wife, Kay, a slender jogging fanatic, from their workouts at Wilmington's downtown YMCA. Carper knew the Capanos had four daughters. It wouldn't surprise the governor that Anne Marie knew Capano, since he was the managing partner of the law firm that handled Delaware's bond deals and was thus a frequent visitor to the governor's offices. But lovers? The notion had never crossed his mind.

Was this revelation only coincidental with Annie's disappearance? Carper hoped so. But now, as he and Bullock drove together toward Legislative Hall in Dover, they had more pressing concerns. How would they break the news about Annie to the governor's staff?

It was Sunday, but in state government terms, it was the last day of the General Assembly's legislative session, one of the busiest days of the year. Traditionally, it was a tense, mind-boggling day of lobbying, horse-trading, and power plays for the governor and his staff—the reason Jill Morrison had called Annie at eleven o'clock Friday night from work!—as they rammed bills into law and cut deals to move their agenda forward.

But the first thing Bullock did upon arriving in Dover early in the afternoon was call members of the governor's senior staff together and tell them about Annie. As the day wore on, Carper conferred by phone with Montague and Daniels, who said she still hadn't come home. *All we can do is wait,* the governor thought, knowing that the cops were doing everything they could, *to see if she shows up tomorrow morning.*

Back in Wilmington, working on limited sleep but knowing that every hour counted in a missing person case like this, police were covering every base they could.

Detective Donovan stopped at the Getty station where Capano said he'd bought cigarettes at ten o'clock on Thursday night. But the clerk, Steve Wright, told them Capano couldn't have stopped for cigarettes or anything else at 10:00 P.M. Wright was working that night, he said, and closed at 9:30, as scheduled. Wright also knew Capano, a regular customer, and said he hadn't stopped by at any time that evening.

Alarms went off in Donovan's head. A tiny, seemingly insignificant detail about Capano's story had a hole. Why?

Donovan called Capano, but there was no answer. He left messages on the lawyer's answering machine. The cops drove to his house several times; they knocked on the door, but nobody answered.

About two-thirty, Detectives Donovan and Harris drove to Capano's wife's residence at 17th and Greenhill. As they pulled in front of the big house, they saw a black Grand Cherokee backing out of the garage.

"There he is," Donovan told Harris, his voice rising with anticipation.

Donovan pulled his unmarked cruiser to a stop and approached Capano's car.

"We'd like to go back to the house and ask you some more questions," Donovan said through the driver's seat window.

Capano suddenly seemed agitated. He said, "OK," but quickly rolled up his window and sped off. Donovan and Harris followed. When they got to 2302 Grant Avenue, investigators noticed a marked change in Capano's demeanor. He was no longer the calm and cooperative man they had interviewed just twelve hours before.

In a terse, almost surly tone, Capano told the police he regretted telling them so much about his private relationship with Fahey. "I'm upset with myself," he said. "Some of the things I told you were personal, and I shouldn't have said them."

Police asked if he would escort them on a casual search through the house and the Jeep. "No drawers or closets," said Capano, frowning, reluctantly agreeing to the tour.

The four policemen walked through all four floors of the house, including a finished basement, with Capano moping along behind. "The house was spotless," Donovan later noted, "with nothing out of place."

The same was true of the Jeep, where investigators noticed nothing unusual.

At one point Daniels turned to Capano and asked, "Have there ever been any personal possessions belonging to Anne Marie in the house?"

"There were some clothes, but I got rid of them a long time ago."

"What's a long time ago?" Daniels asked.

"Months."

Daniels didn't respond but wondered why a man would discard personal effects of a former lover with whom he had remained friends.

"Listen, if she doesn't show up for work tomorrow, we want you to come in for a formal interview," Daniels said.

"OK," Capano replied.

He said he'd be at Saul Ewing early in the morning and left his number. The police said they'd call about ten.

This time, when the four officers left Capano's house, none believed Anne Marie Fahey would return the next morning. Too many years' experience told them that the diary entry, the Getty station miscue, and now the disturbed demeanor—it didn't feel right.

Next they visited the home of Ferris Wharton, chief prosecutor for New Castle County. Wharton, a lanky, athletic man, a former high school basketball and soccer star in Brandywine Hundred, was the prosecutor on call that weekend, carrying a beeper, available to help any police agency that needed him to go to court.

Donovan thought the Fahey case was moving quickly and that the Delaware attorney general's office should be briefed.

"Some things are not checking out with Capano's story," Donovan told Wharton, who, like everyone else involved with law enforcement, knew Capano, at least on a casual basis, and was aware he had been a prosecutor some twenty years earlier.

"Well, whatever you need, just let me know," said Wharton.

"We'll be back in touch tomorrow," promised Donovan.

Later that afternoon, state trooper Daniels drove to the *Wilmington News Journal,* six miles south of the city, to hand-deliver a color photograph of Fahey.

In the picture, provided by the family and taken several years earlier, Anne Marie wore a denim jacket and a serious, almost solemn expression. Daniels handed it to reporter Chris Donahue, who was working the police beat that night. The cop asked if the paper would run an article asking for the public's help in finding the missing woman. Daniels provided a few basic facts, such as Fahey's age and address, her job as scheduling secretary to the governor, and that she hadn't been seen since Thursday, and left. Donahue made a few more calls to some police sources, and the story was put to bed.

———

Delawareans woke July 1, 1996, to front-page headlines in the *Wilmington News Journal* about a small income tax cut for the state's residents and the arrest of a fourteen-year-old Wilmington boy who had claimed his mother shot herself to death the previous Thursday but later admitted pulling the trigger himself.

If it weren't for the fact that she was on the governor's staff, the missing secretary probably wouldn't even have gotten the twenty lines in the local section that Anne Marie Fahey's disappearance received that morning. Instead, under a modest headline on page B1, "Carper Staffer Is Sought," there was a spare article, written from obscure "staff reports."

"Authorities are looking for a 30-year-old member of Gov. Carper's staff who has been missing since Thursday night," it began. "Anne Marie Fahey, a scheduling secretary who lived alone in an apartment in the 1700 block of Washington St., was last seen about 10 P.M., Wilmington police said Sunday night."

The story continued, dutifully, noting that the woman was reported missing by family Saturday night, that she was "white, 5 feet, 10 inches tall, 128 pounds with dark hair," and that "a description of her clothing was unavailable." But the brief report managed to give the impression that the woman had wandered off on her own. Fahey "left," said the paper, "without her wallet or vehicle," and despite the fact that "police have checked hospitals," she hadn't turned up.

The story ended abruptly, without mentioning Annie's diary

or Thomas Capano, saying, oddly: "Fahey was taking unspecified medications."

Another sad story, not altogether different from that of other tragic lives seen in local news sections of papers all over the country. Even the picture—not a flattering one—depicting a plump-faced young woman wearing downscale denim, made Anne Marie appear more self-effacing casualty of interior demons than possible crime victim.

Behind the scenes, however, family, friends, and investigators were increasingly certain that "unspecified medications" had little to do with Annie's disappearance.

And one thing was abundantly clear as the Monday rush hour ebbed: Annie was still gone. At the governor's office that morning, staff members prayed for Annie to walk through the door. But she didn't show up and Steve Montague, the policeman from Carper's security detail summoned to Annie's apartment by Ginny Columbus, informed everyone that Annie hadn't returned home, either. The atmosphere in the warren of offices surrounding Delaware's chief executive was funereal that day as employees tried to go about the business of state. But the empty desk and chair, not twenty feet from the governor's private chambers, were a constant reminder that bubbly, bright, and beautiful Annie had vanished.

Sheri Woodruff, Carper's press secretary, told a reporter, "We're very concerned and certainly hoping for the best. It's not Anne Marie's nature to be out of contact with family and friends and her office for several days. When she left work Thursday, she seemed in very good spirits."

Jill Morrison and Ginny Columbus, meanwhile, told colleagues that a furtive dalliance with Thomas Capano may have spun out of control. Tom Capano? The sophisticated lawyer and counselor to governors and mayors? The millionaire son of one of the state's most respected developers? A husband, a father?

"This is very odd," Robert Fahey told a reporter who called. "It's so unlikely for her to be out of touch for more than an afternoon, let alone a whole weekend."

But now Capano, too, seemed to have disappeared. Detective Daniels called his office at ten that morning. A secretary said Capano was on the phone. Daniels left a message, waited a half hour, but Capano didn't call back.

Growing more perturbed by the minute, Daniels was contemplating his next move when his phone rang. It was Kathy Jennings, an attractive lawyer who happened to be a tough-as-nails former chief deputy attorney general. Daniels had worked with Jennings on a number of violent crime cases when she was a prosecutor, including the case of Glenn MacDonald, who had strangled his ex-girlfriend because he couldn't woo her back. Jennings had also gained acclaim for her successful prosecution in 1989 of serial killer Steven Brian Pennell, an electrician who had killed prostitutes along a seedy stretch of highway south of Wilmington. In 1992, thanks in large part to Jennings, Pennell became the first person Delaware executed in nearly half a century.

"How are you, Kathy?" Daniels asked.

"Charlie and I are attorneys for Tom Capano," she said, referring to former Delaware Attorney General Charlie Oberly. "He's very nervous and can't understand why the police need to talk to him again. Can you tell me whatever you're comfortable telling me and what you need from our client?"

Daniels had been around long enough to know where most successful prosecutors went: private practice and big bucks. In fact, Jennings had hooked up with Oberly, her former boss, who had lost a race for the U.S. Senate and was a formidable player in the close-knit world of Delaware power politics.

They were not enemies, but Daniels knew he and Jennings were no longer on the same side and he kept the discussion businesslike.

"We have a missing person and what we're learning doesn't fit her profile," Daniels said. "By all accounts she was very meticulous and would never have just up and left. We really don't know what we have, but we want to talk more with Tom because they had dinner Thursday night. The state police are on the case because the governor's office was involved."

"We'll confer with our client and get back to you," she said.

When Daniels told the other investigators on the case that

Capano had lawyers and probably wasn't coming in, they weren't surprised. The lie—at least, an oddly unnecessary misstatement—about stopping at the Getty station had raised serious red flags in the cops' minds; bringing in a SWAT team of lawyers, according to most cops, was simply more proof of guilt. "If you've got nothing to hide, you don't need an attorney to shield you from the police," Detective Donovan later recalled. "Something's being hidden here. You sure as hell don't need a lawyer if you want to be forthright."

When Daniels told Robert Fahey about Capano snubbing investigators, Anne Marie's brother was furious.

He fucking killed her, Robert said to himself.

A few hours after learning that Capano had surrounded himself with lawyers, three of Annie's siblings, frightened and teary, walked into the offices of attorney David Weiss in downtown Wilmington.

The Fahey kids were used to pulling together in crises. They had grown up in a working-class Wilmington suburb, surviving the premature death of their mother and their father's debilitating alcoholism. The family's subsequent poverty was so onerous at times that the electricity was shut off and Annie was sent to live with friends for weeks and months at a time.

"If I ever had to live through my childhood again," Annie once told Kim Horstmann, "I would slit my wrists."

Despite their background—or perhaps because of it—the children had emerged strong, proud, and dignified. By 1996 Kevin, then 42, sold insurance; Robert, 38, was making good money in real estate; Kathleen, 36, was a successful physical therapist; Brian, 34, was a teacher and coach; and Annie was a trusted aide to the governor. Mark, 40, the most friendly and outgoing of the Faheys, worked as a bartender.

With Annie suddenly missing, the siblings dug in as they never had before. Three of them—Brian, who had just finished a marathon airline trip from Ecuador, had joined Robert and Kathleen—were designated leaders of the search for Annie and now sat in David Weiss's office on the fifteenth floor of the Chase Manhattan building first thing Monday morning.

They bluntly told the attorney they suspected their sister might have disappeared as the result of foul play by Thomas Capano.

Weiss, the former federal prosecutor, had met Capano in 1989 after Capano's kid brother Louis, a flamboyant, gregarious, and wealthy Delaware developer, had admitted giving illegal campaign contributions to a New Castle County councilman. Known for his political connections, Tom, who was then working for the family business, helped arrange a deal with the feds on his brother's behalf.

"We're worried about Capano's political connections," Robert was now telling Weiss about Tom. "And we want to make sure the investigation is done aggressively. We need someone who can guide us through the process."

Weiss was instantly suspicious when he learned Capano had spoken twice to police but now seemed to be hiding behind prominent defense attorneys. He laid out for the family a possible scenario for the investigation, explaining that it could involve subpoenas for potential witnesses, search warrants, and other investigative techniques that would take time. But he agreed to help.

It was almost with a sense of relief that Kim Horstmann greeted troopers Daniels and Montague at the door to her apartment in Center City Philadelphia at six that Monday evening.

She had dashed home as soon as she finished work, knowing the investigators would be arriving. Horstmann had a major change of heart after realizing Annie was really gone and that, contrary to what she had thought and what Tom Capano had assured her, was not just away for the weekend. She wanted to clear the air and tell all she knew about Annie and Tom—do whatever would help to bring Annie back.

But when the Delaware troopers entered the apartment, they still considered Horstmann, who had lied to the Fahey family about Capano and then alerted him to the fact that police were looking for Annie, something less than an ally.

Before asking any questions, Daniels ducked into Horstmann's bedroom to make a phone call. His pager had gone off, and he recognized the calling number as that of Kathy Jennings. When he got her on the line, Daniels heard the lawyer ask him to submit a list of written questions to her client, who was then sitting in an adjoining conference room, she said.

"Kathy," Daniels said, "let's go back a few years when we worked together on the Glenn MacDonald case. Would we have accepted that kind of request from a defense attorney?"

"I see where you're coming from," Jennings told her former ally. "We'll get back to you."

Daniels hung up and returned to the living room of Horstmann's house, where she soon convinced the state troopers that her lies the previous Saturday had been an innocent attempt to protect Annie and the call to Capano an equally innocent attempt to find her. Horstmann wasn't going to hold anything back about her friendship with Fahey now. And she told the officers everything she knew about the clandestine affair, talking candidly about even her recent exchange of phone calls with Capano.

She said Capano had seemed nervous and evasive on the first call Saturday night but more composed and assuring an hour later. Capano had also called her early Sunday morning, she told the two Delaware troopers. During that eight o'clock conversation, she explained, Capano had told her he was annoyed because four cops had banged on his door at three that morning. He told Kim he had swallowed five or six Excedrin PM before bed, for his insomnia, and was so woozy it took him several minutes to answer the door.

During that Sunday-morning call, Horstmann continued, Capano also said he had thought some more and figured Annie was with Jackie Steinhoff, another friend, for the weekend and would surely return to work Monday.

Capano called again Sunday night, said Horstmann, from his wife's house.

"He said he couldn't really talk because he was dropping his daughters off," she explained, "and would call me later. But he never did."

Horstmann, five years older than Fahey, told police she'd

met Annie in 1988 while looking to rent a summer house in
Sea Isle City, a popular resort town on the New Jersey coast.
They'd become confidantes that summer, Horstmann recounted, and the younger woman felt comfortable sharing her
most private feelings with Kim because she wasn't judgmen-
tal.

The police listened intently as Horstmann told of Annie's
secret affair with Capano. Annie had often mentioned him,
telling Kim about the important lawyer's frequent visits to the
governor's office on bond work and his flirtations. But sometime in the summer of 1994, Annie confided to Horstmann
that she and Capano had been having sex since early that year
and that she was in love with him.

Horstmann also knew Annie had tried to end the relationship the following year, when she began dating Mike Scanlan.
But Capano was persistent, said Horstmann, almost obsessive,
about Annie, who seemed incapable of making a clean break
with the powerful attorney.

At one point, Horstmann recounted, Capano had stormed
into Annie's apartment to take back a television, clothes, and
other gifts he had given her. He later returned them, Horstmann said, and the two agreed to be just friends. But Capano
couldn't handle such an arrangement, said Horstmann, and
during the two dinners she had in May with Capano at the
Ritz he spent most of the evening professing his love for Annie
and complaining about her relationship with Scanlan.

From her observations and Fahey's remarks, Horstmann
told the police, she had come to believe that Capano was a
"control freak."

The cops looked at each other knowingly. Horstmann's
phrase "control freak" mirrored Annie's "controlling maniac"
observation in the diary.

"But Annie wasn't afraid of Tom," Horstmann concluded.
"And he wouldn't have anything to do with her disappearance.
Not Tommy."

———

With their heads spinning from Kim Horstmann's detailed
account of what was clearly an unconventional relationship—
or was it all too conventional, considering the players and the

stakes?—the two detectives drove to the Ristorante Panorama, the last place Anne Marie Fahey had been seen in public.

The Panorama was an ornate upscale eatery in Penn's View Inn, a restored brick building near the Penn's Landing entertainment and dining district along the Delaware River. It specialized in gourmet Italian dishes and was famous in Philadelphia and beyond for its extensive wine "cruvinet," a dispensing system that let patrons choose any of 120 different wines by the glass.

The cops first met Tim Kilcullen, the restaurant's wine steward, who said he was working the previous Thursday evening but didn't know Tom Capano or recall a couple fitting Capano and Fahey's description. The detectives showed Kilcullen the picture of Fahey that had run in the paper (they didn't have a picture of Capano), but the wine steward registered no recognition. He did, however, find a credit card receipt in Capano's name and the register check, which showed the first drinks being rung up at 7:10 P.M. and the bill, $154 including tip, paid at 9:12.

Two hours was about a half hour longer than most of the Panorama's customers stayed, Kilcullen said, but not unusual. He then pointed the detectives toward Jackie Dansak, the waitress whose number was on the receipt. A slim brunette who was waiting tables while attending college in Philadelphia, Dansak looked at the picture of Fahey.

"Sure, I recognize her," said the young woman. "Who could forget them?"

The couple had sat at her "deuce" table near the kitchen, Dansak told the two Delaware cops, and stood out like sore thumbs amid the cosmopolitan Main Liners, the upper crust of Philadelphia society who frequented the Panorama. The restaurant's male patrons usually wore tailored suits or outfits from the pages of *GQ*, Dansak explained; the women adorned themselves in fancy jewels and black jet-set outfits. This couple, Dansak told the investigators, was odd. The man wore an unfashionable dark suit; his date, much younger, was dressed in a floral print dress. He was domineering and she meek. The woman also looked a lot healthier in the picture than she did in person last week, Dansak pointed out. They also seemed to be not in a very good mood, Dansak offered. They barely spoke. They didn't look married, she said, but their mood was too glum for boyfriend and girlfriend. They weren't talking business.

Capano did all the ordering—from his predinner rum and tonic and her vodka and cranberry (called a Sea Breeze) to a bottle of white wine, two appetizers, her swordfish, his chicken, and, after dinner, his Sambuca and her "very cold" white wine.

The man never consulted the woman, who mostly wore a solemn expression. Whenever Dansak approached the table, Capano gave her the impression he didn't want her around. After she opened the bottle of wine and poured their first glasses, he did the rest of the pouring.

They only picked at their food, barely eating any of their main courses. Dansak said she felt bad for the woman and had asked if there was something wrong with the swordfish, the entrée the waitress had promoted before they ordered. The woman, whose flyaway hair looked almost moppish, had "forced a smile" but said nothing. Finally, the man asked Dansak to package the dinners to take home. So she wrapped them in foil and returned them to the table in paper bags.

That was all she could recall, Dansak said. The policemen thanked her, knowing that the waitress had painted quite a vivid picture of what was looking more and more like a last supper for Anne Marie Fahey.

Early the next morning, Tuesday, Tom Capano called Keith Brady, an old friend who was Delaware's chief deputy attorney general, to inform his fellow lawyer that he had had dinner with Anne Marie Fahey on Thursday, before she disappeared. Brady, who knew of the affair and realized the ramifications of the case, took notes of the meeting.

"I'm blown away by what's happening," Capano said, "and I'm spooked by the way the cops are treating me. Anne Marie and I have become good friends. That night we had dinner and went back to my house and took some things back to her apartment."

Brady kept scribbling.

"She told me she was going to be taking Friday off and didn't want to be dragged down to Dover for the end of the legislative session. I left, but then on Saturday night I got a call from her friend Kim, asking where she was."

Capano went on to tell his friend police had visited him twice and thought he might be hiding her out. "I was sure she would stroll into work Monday, but when she didn't, I died."

Daniels was fast losing hope of finding Anne Marie alive— and lingering doubts about a primary suspect were dispelled the next afternoon, when he picked up another ringing phone.

The caller identified herself as Lisa D'Amico and said she worked at Michael Christopher Hair Designs, a chic salon. She quickly added that she had been Anne Marie Fahey's hairdresser for the last several years and thought police should know about some of the things her client had shared with her in the months preceding her disappearance.

D'Amico knew about Michael Scanlan, whom, she said, Anne Marie was in love with. But Annie Marie had also confided to D'Amico that Tom Capano, her previous boyfriend, was "crazy" and scared her. Since Capano's name had still not surfaced publicly in connection with Fahey's disappearance, Daniels was paying close attention to this unsolicited story. And it was amazingly similar to Horstmann's. D'Amico explained that Annie Marie had tried to break up with Capano and he took it badly; he was argumentative and possessive and had begun waiting outside her apartment in his car.

"Anne Marie," D'Amico said, "was scared to death that Capano might hurt her."

Detective Donovan was talking to Al Frankey that same afternoon. Frankey knew Annie from their days working at TGI Friday's on Route 202, a few miles northwest of Wilmington. Frankey was then the restaurant manager; Annie, a waitress. They had stayed in touch, and Frankey was now telling the policeman that Annie had told him Tom Capano was an extremely possessive lover.

"About six to eight weeks ago," Frankey said, "she told me that Capano climbed up her fire escape, forced his way into her apartment, began hollering and screaming, and started taking back various gifts."

"Are you guys going to print Tommy's name?"

It was about four o'clock on Tuesday, July 2, 1996, and the caller, one of my best sources, sounded distraught.

"Tommy who?" I asked, wondering what in the world the source was talking about.

"Tommy Capano. He was the last one seen with the woman who's missing."

I knew who Tom Capano was—I also knew that Anne Marie Fahey, one of the governor's secretaries, had been reported missing three days earlier, after failing to show up for dinner with her brother.

My paper, the Wilmington News Journal, *had run a brief police item about Fahey's disappearance on Monday morning. The story had piqued everybody's curiosity at the paper and around town because Fahey worked for the governor. On the day that first, short item was published, I asked my editor, Al Mascitti, what he thought. He said police had indicated to our cop reporter that the case might be a suicide.*

At the time, I was working on a series of investigative stories about a rash of shootings, some of them gangland-style murders, by crack dealers warring over turf in Wilmington's ghettos. Although the cop reporters were handling the secretary's disappearance, I made sure I had read that morning's paper, which said Fahey was last seen having dinner in a Philadelphia restaurant.

Now, by Tuesday afternoon, word had apparently spread that Fahey's dinner companion had been Tom Capano, who I knew as a suave attorney with serious political connections. A big-time Democratic contributor, he had been a top mayoral aide and legal counsel to the governor and had even considered a run for attorney general in 1994. Capano's family, one of the richest in New Castle County, had made a fortune in the construction business. Tom, the oldest of four brothers, had become a lawyer and political consultant, getting involved in the family business only to rescue his scandal-prone brothers. He had a sterling reputation, a wife who was a respected nurse-practitioner, and four pretty young daughters.

I told my source to hold on for a second.

Looking around the newsroom, I spotted Ted Caddell, a veteran police and court reporter, who had written that day's story. "Do you know about Capano?" I hollered.

"Sure do," Caddell said. "Got it off the record, but we'll probably be running it tomorrow."

"So what's the deal?" I asked my source.

My caller sighed and began.

"Tommy's been seeing Anne Marie for a long time and he left his wife in the fall. Then Anne Marie started going out with some other guy, and Tommy's been bugging the shit out of her to go back out again. Obviously she went out with him last Thursday."

"Do you think he killed her?" I asked.

"It doesn't look good."

When reporter Caddell heard the name Capano, he immediately perked up—he had been around long enough to know who the man was and that a Capano connection to the missing secretary story would be very big news. Caddell immediately began contacting his extensive list of police and legal sources to find out what they knew. It didn't take him long to confirm the Capano connection and to get permission from the paper's editors to use Capano's name in the next day's story.

Caddell also called Brian Fahey, who taught the reporter's son and daughter at Friends School. Brian clued Caddell in on much of what the family had discovered, including the broken dinner date with Scanlan on Saturday night.

Caddell then tried several times to reach Capano at home and at Saul Ewing, but his messages were not returned.

At the same time, reporters from all over the region were beginning to get interested in the story of the governor's missing secretary. At a bill signing that afternoon, Carper was peppered with questions about his absent aide. "She was beloved," said the governor, already sounding a mournful tone. "We're hoping against all hope she will be found. There was nothing at all to indicate something was wrong. We are just baffled."

Other reporters were also starting to hear about a prominent person Fahey had been with on the night she disappeared. And even though cops were not confirming names or suggesting that they considered anyone a suspect, even the slimmest Capano connection was enough to bump the story to page 1, which is where editors at the *News Journal* put it on Wednesday.

Though the editors chose to downplay the Capano connection—"No Trace of Carper Aide" was the front-page headline—Caddell didn't. He began his story by writing that Fahey "was last seen by Wilmington attorney and political insider Thomas J. Capano when the two had dinner Thursday night in Philadelphia."

That bombshell ensured that Anne Marie Fahey was no average missing secretary.

Besides reading of Tom Capano's link with Fahey, the 125,000 Delawareans who regularly read the paper also learned that Fahey's purse was found in her apartment, along with all her credit cards, her license, and some cash, all her luggage had been accounted for, there was no sign of a struggle, and her car was parked out front.

And trying to counter speculation that Fahey had committed suicide, her brother Brian told Caddell that his sister had not seemed distressed about anything when he last spoke to her eleven days earlier.

But Caddell also quoted Ferris Wharton, the New Castle County prosecutor, being vague. "The last person to see her saw her Thursday," Wharton told Caddell. "Between then and now, we don't have a clue what went on. She's just missing, and there's no way of knowing what happened."

The Faheys, well known in the city's Irish community and its Democratic political circles for their intense political and cultural activism, couldn't sit still while lawyers and police worked. They knew that if Annie was still alive, time was not on her side. Whether she was lost and hurt or being held against her will, every hour counted.

Led by Robert, Kathleen, and Brian, the Faheys offered themselves to reporters as interview subjects and immediately decided to post a $10,000 reward for information leading to

Annie's return. On the same day that Tom Capano's name was beginning to circulate among reporters covering the case, the Faheys, with the help of a phalanx of friends, began distributing a reward flyer, with Annie's photo. They fanned out everywhere, nailing and taping copies to poles, putting them on countertops in businesses, dropping them on doorsteps. Within days of Annie's disappearance, there were few places one could go in the county without seeing Annie's face. Flyers also found their way to beach resorts in Delaware, New Jersey, and Maryland; someone had even attached one to a post outside Thomas Capano's home on Grant Avenue.

At Annie's apartment, friends and family kept a round-the-clock vigil in the hopes that someone or something would show up there. One of the Faheys—usually Brian, who was off for the summer, or Mark, who was between jobs—would spend the night. They tied yellow ribbons to the wooden beams on the porch, reminiscent of the simple symbols that had kept Americans focused on the hostages held by Iranians for 444 days, from 1979 to 1981. During the day, even the sweltering, sticky afternoons of July, various Faheys could always be seen sitting on lawn chairs on the wide circular porch outside the Ollivers' first-floor apartment, consoling each other, plotting strategy, conferring with police, praying, taking turns calling every number in Annie's telephone book.

They kept waiting for someone to call back, someone who would tell them where their little sister was, or hoping that a car would pull up to the curb and Annie would bounce out with a perfectly plausible explanation.

That same Wednesday morning that the Fahey story was splashed across the front page of the *News Journal,* Bud Freel, candidate for Wilmington's City Council, wolfed down a ham omelet, hopped into his blue Plymouth Voyager, and drove to Annie's apartment. He wanted to get there before a crowd gathered so he could talk to Kathleen in private.

The brother of Delaware's secretary of state, Bud, now a spokesman for the state's Department of Transportation, had dated Kathleen for almost six years—a romance that ended in 1988—and had remained close to the Fahey family. Having seen the paper that morning, he was not going to remind Kathleen that he had told her earlier that year about the rumor of an affair between Annie and Capano.

Instead, he was going to offer to talk to Capano, a good friend of his. The two were longtime political cronies and had worked nearly hand-in-hand managing Dan Frawley's successful campaign for mayor. They were also rugby buddies. Freel was a hulking man who looked like he could stop a truck; Capano was slim, known not for his physical prowess as much as his combative style.

On the drive to Annie's apartment, Freel wrestled with his conflicting feelings about the terrible situation. Worried deeply about Annie's safety, having seen the morning's paper, he was also concerned that Capano might get railroaded by the media. Freel had considered the affair, which he had heard about months earlier, an unwise liaison. But the Thursday dinner, which his brother Ed had told him about, was a terribly unlucky coincidence for Tommy. In fact, Bud had called Capano on Monday but only got his answering machine. "I feel bad about what is happening," Freel had said in the message. "If there's anything I can do, let me know."

Capano had called back later that day. But their conversation had been brief.

"You're going to be hearing a lot of shit about me," Capano told Freel. "Don't believe any of it."

At Annie's apartment on Wednesday morning, Freel was relieved to find the porch empty. He pushed the buzzer in the small entryway and was immediately clicked in. Upstairs, in the apartment, Freel found Robert, Kathleen, and her husband, Patrick, looking, as Freel later recalled, "upset and frantic for information."

"What did you know about the relationship?" Kathleen immediately demanded.

"Don't you remember?" Bud replied. "I called you several months ago and asked you because I had heard about it. You called me back and told me they were just friends."

Kathleen did remember and quickly relented.

Robert explained that Capano had blown off the cops the day before and then taken off for Stone Harbor, the Jersey shore resort town where his mother, Marguerite; sister, Marian; and brother Gerry all owned houses.

"Do you want me to go talk to him?" asked Bud.

"Yeah, that might be helpful," Robert said.

Kathleen wasn't so sure. "I don't know if that's a good idea."

Bud said good-bye and left. As he was on the way to his car, Brian pulled up, and the two began commiserating.

Brian agreed with Robert. "If you could go talk to him, we would appreciate it," Brian said. "We're looking for any help we can get."

Bud said he would take the ride.

First, Freel drove to the home of Peggy and Al Carter, who lived down the block from Governor Carper in Brandywine Hills, less than two miles up Washington Street from Annie's apartment. Peggy Carter had worked under Capano in the city solicitor's office. And her husband was the city's personnel director at the time. They were close friends of both Tom and Kay Capano and were heartbroken over the separation.

"I'm going down to see Tommy," Freel told Peggy. "Can you tell me how to get to his place at the shore?"

Peggy gave Bud the directions, saying she was certain Tom had done nothing wrong.

That is exactly how Bud Freel felt as he pulled up to Marguerite Capano's sprawling Stone Harbor oceanfront house two hours later. He was coming to help his rugby partner out of a jam, to clear up a misunderstanding about something that was turning out to be a terrible tragedy.

Freel knocked at the front door of the million-dollar house, set like a jewel near the sandy shoals of the Atlantic, a perfect symbol of the wealth of the Capano family. When no one answered, Freel followed a weathered wooden walkway to the rear of the house, which faced the ocean. He peered into a glass picture window and spied Capano's oldest daughter, sixteen-year-old Christy.

"Is Tom here?" Bud asked, tapping on the screen.

"Yeah," Christy replied, barely looking up. "He's in the back room."

Freel let himself in, walked down a hallway, and heard Capano talking on the phone. He looked in a bedroom and saw his friend with the close-cropped beard sitting on the couch, puffing a cigarette. Capano, who was wearing a pair of light khaki slacks and a polo shirt, looked up. Seeing Freel, his eyes bugged out as if to say, "What are you doing here?" He hung the phone up.

Freel got right to the point.

"Do you know or have any information about where Anne Marie could be?"

"No, I really don't," Capano responded calmly.

Capano stood up, let his bigger friend have the couch, and took a chair.

"Well, where do you think she is, Tom?"

"She might have gone to the beach with friends," said Capano. "Maybe she just decided to leave town for some time alone. She might even have checked into a clinic for her anorexia. I really don't know, Bud."

The old pals spoke for more than two hours. Freel, an emotional, ruddy-faced man, begged for Capano to return to Wilmington to talk to the police.

But Capano said he had told them everything and, anyway, the cops were just interested in lurid details.

"All they wanted to know was how often we had sex and where we had sex," Capano complained. "I don't trust them. Besides, there's other reasons. Anne Marie was very trusting of me. She opened up and told me things in confidence, and I don't want to break that trust. So I'm not talking to the police again."

Bud pleaded, cajoled, begged his friend to change his mind. "Just go back and answer the questions you want to answer and tell them the other stuff is none of their business," Freel suggested. "You might know something that could help find her."

But Capano, argumentative as ever, was not to be swayed. He sat cross-legged, chain-smoking, yet oddly serene in demeanor. "You have to understand," he said. "I'm pretty upset about this also."

At one point, Capano, no stranger to the media from his

political days, surprised his friend by wondering aloud if he should hold a press conference.

"What are you going to have a press conference for?" Bud asked, incredulous. "The first thing they are going to ask is, 'Why aren't you cooperating with the police?' Don't you understand, Tom? If you don't go back and cooperate, there's going to be a cloud over your head, and before you know it *Hard Copy* is going to be in Wilmington."

But Freel couldn't change Capano's mind and drove home a confused man. Still certain his friend couldn't be wrapped up in a murder or abduction, neither could Freel understand why Tom seemed so unconcerned that his ex-lover was missing.

If it were me, Bud thought as he traveled the tree-lined country roads back to Wilmington, *I would be a wreck, even if the relationship was over. Why is Tom so calm? Why isn't he cooperating with the police?*

Freel drove straight to Annie's apartment. Sitting on the porch, in sentinel repose, were Brian and Kevin Fahey and their uncle, James McGettigan, their mother's brother, a Catholic priest.

"Was he any help?" Brian immediately asked.

"He doesn't know anything," said Freel morosely. Freel didn't reveal his own ambivalence about Tom's demeanor, saying only that Capano had nothing to add to what he had already told police and didn't feel it was in his interest to speak to them further. The bottom line, Freel said, was that he didn't know where Annie was. Later that evening Daniels and Montague knocked on Bud Freel's door. He told the detectives the same thing he had told the Faheys. His meeting with Capano had left him exhausted and confused. "I just don't have anything more to tell you," he said, shrugging.

By Wednesday, July 3, nearly a week since anyone had seen her, my editors at the News Journal *had decided that the Anne Marie Fahey case was Hot Topic No. 1—and they decided to run a story every day, if at all possible.*

When they asked me to write a story about the case, the first thing I did was try to track down Tom Capano, whom I had first met six years earlier, as he strutted with Wilmington mayor Dan Frawley and some of his top aides through City Hall. I had just taken over the city beat at the News Journal.

The six-foot-seven Frawley, a gregarious and earthy Irish-American who spent more than his fair share of time in Wilmington's bars, instantly realized that Capano—who had left the administration two years earlier—hadn't met me.

"Tom, this is Cris Barrish, our new reporter!" Frawley bellowed. Capano and I shook hands.

"Call me anytime," Capano said. "Normally, I don't talk to reporters, but you played sports, so I'll talk to you."

Obviously, the mayor had already told Capano about me; they had done their homework. And Capano made an instant, positive impression on me. Smart and articulate, well-dressed and self-assured, he seemed a man in command of himself. I made a mental note to call on him down the road.

But I never used Capano for a source. My editor, who was the previous city hall reporter, told me that Capano would be too protective of the administration, so I went elsewhere. Occasionally, however, I'd see him at city bond meetings—his law firm did the city's bond work—and he did nothing to change my first impression. In the summer of 1994, I even spent a couple of delightful hours drinking beer and eating roast beef sandwiches with Capano at a baseball game fundraiser for Dan Frawley's kids—the mayor, who had lost his 1992 re-election bid, had dropped dead of a heart attack while playing pickup basketball the previous February. Tom Curley, a fellow reporter, and I sat with Capano and a few of his pretty, suntanned daughters in the box seat behind home plate. In fact, the stadium had been named for Frawley.

We chatted easily throughout the game, about Frawley, his untimely death, and our own families. Capano bragged about his wife and kids. And I told him I had just gotten married a year earlier and that my wife was a nurse who might someday be a nurse-practitioner, as his wife was. He showed a genuine interest in my future, which was flattering coming from someone so well regarded. He was congenial, interesting, and sincere, a pleasure to be around.

Later that night, I thought to myself, Goddamn, that guy

has it all. Great family. Beautiful kids. Super job. Tons of money. And he's not an asshole.

The next time we spoke at any length was in April of 1996, just two months before Fahey disappeared. A well-known barber in the city had been injured when a pipe bomb exploded in his car. The barber, Vinny Monardo, had told police the bomb had just flown in the window while he was driving. Because of Monardo's high-profile clientele—including the former Wilmington bishop, U.S. Sen. Joe Biden, and Capano—I was assigned to do a longer story about him. Capano granted me an interview. Again he was congenial and said the pipe bomb explosion surprised the hell out of him. He described Vinny as an earthy cutup who abused everybody who sat in his chair. "You always get busted on," was Capano's quote for the story.

Some digging had also revealed that Monardo sold jewelry from his hole-in-the wall shop and was in financial trouble. A bank had foreclosed on his shop and was letting him stay only until he could come up with tens of thousands of dollars to pay off his debt. I learned that Capano was bailing Monardo out financially, and I asked him about his help. He didn't deny it but said he would rather not discuss it.

Still, he was polite and friendly, as always. When we hung up, we wished each other well. Like almost everybody who had ever come under Tom Capano's spell, in the first days and hours following Anne Marie Fahey's disappearance I believed the police when they said Capano was not a suspect.

But why had he suddenly disappeared? After calling various possible places where he might be that Saturday, July 5, I finally dialed his mother's beach house in Stone Harbor. A man with an imperious voice answered. It sounded like Capano.

"Is Tom Capano there?" I asked, realizing as the words were leaving my mouth that it was him.

"Who's calling?" he asked in a suspicious voice.

"Cris Barrish."

Click.

That's the last time I spoke to Tom Capano.

———————

Connie Blake had met Anne Marie Fahey in 1993, after Dan Frawley lost his bid for a third term and Blake, Frawley's secretary, landed a job with one of his Democratic political allies, the governor. The older woman took an immediate liking to Annie, the governor's pretty, outgoing, and efficient scheduler. And in 1994 Blake told Fahey that she was moving into a larger apartment in the house she lived in on Washington Street and her old apartment, on the third floor, would be available. Blake knew Annie was looking for a place because her roommate was getting married. Fahey jumped at the offer.

"We had a real nice relationship, but we never imposed on each other," Blake told a reporter, speaking reverently but already slipping into the past tense. "I can't believe this is happening. But any scenario you work out there's a dead end. I'm just devastated. I wake up at night and think I'm going to see her upstairs, getting ready to go to work. None of it makes any sense. I just really feel for her family. I can't imagine what they are going through, waiting twenty-four hours a day."

Did Blake know who Tom Capano was?

Yes, she said. She knew him from his days as a top Frawley aide but didn't know what to make of his connection to Annie. Blake said she had seen Capano stopping by Annie's apartment and knew he was married but had never asked any questions.

And though she had heard footsteps in Annie's apartment on Thursday night, "I never heard any arguing or loud noises or anything."

Just as Connie Blake was unconsciously speaking about her friend in the past tense, law enforcement authorities began speculating that Fahey would never return.

"Each day, you become more pessimistic about the outcome," Ferris Wharton told Valerie Helmbreck, who was helping prepare the *News Journal*'s Fourth of July article on the case.

Wharton also allowed himself to express serious doubts that Fahey had taken her own life. "If she committed suicide, where is she?" the prosecutor said bluntly.

Fourth of July dawned hot and muggy and, at Baynard Stadium, melancholy. The parking lot of the 5,000-seat football, soccer, and track arena began to fill with cars at 7:30 that morning, as friends of Anne Marie Fahey started to gather for a solemn, even grisly event: a search party. Police investigators had told the Fahey family that missing persons often were found, tragically, near their homes. If Annie had been accosted while walking in the neighborhood or even getting out of her car, it was probable that the perpetrator would take her to a secluded spot. That was why state police investigator Montague had ordered an infrared-equipped helicopter to Brandywine Park, just across the street from Annie's apartment, the morning after she was reported missing. Even though the chopper would more than likely have spotted a human body, it just as likely could have missed it had Annie been shoved under a rocky outcropping or into a drainage pipe. Or buried. The Faheys knew that, at this stage, a successful search would be a hideous success indeed. But with no other leads, after four days of round-the-clock investigating, the family was determined to leave, literally, no stone unturned, especially in Brandywine Park.

With an increasingly interested local media, the family had no problem getting attention for their grim Fourth of July rally. In three days the mystery of the missing gubernatorial secretary had become the dominant topic at beauty salons, softball games, and office watercoolers throughout the state. Even the governor had appealed to residents to come to Baynard Stadium's parking lot, adjacent to Brandywine Park, to help with the search. He himself was there at 7:30 that morning when the Faheys arrived. Dozens of cars were pouring into the lot— of politicos, old friends, perfect strangers, all engrossed by the same sad story of the pretty woman, friend, sister, stranger, who had simply vanished.

Such a turnout wasn't unusual in a small, parochial state like Delaware. Al Mascitti, assistant city editor at the *News Journal,* was fond of calling Delaware the prototypical locale for playing out "Six Degrees of Separation." Only in Delaware, went Mascitti's theory, there were two degrees of separation. Everybody, it seemed, was connected, if not actually related, through family, school, work, or play.

This familiarity seemed to lead to a strange phenomenon in Delaware: when something happened, the word almost always got out.

But the phenomenon was a double-edged sword for the newspaper. With such close ties among people, reporters often ran into brick walls trying to verify rumors. People talked about one another, but they also protected one another and didn't want news of scurrilous activities to appear in print. They liked to keep things "in-house."

Delaware's insular nature was perhaps best attributed to its small size—just 100 miles long and 35 miles wide—and its longtime dominance by a single employer, DuPont, a chemical empire formed in 1802 when Frenchman Eleuthère du Pont built a powder mill on the banks of the Brandywine. As the company grew and flourished, so did the little town—midway between New York and Washington along the busy Delaware River shipping lane—that was already known as a center of commerce, where factories churning out products such as vulcanized fiber, leather, dyed cotton, rubber hose, and autos would spring up.

Over the next two centuries, as DuPont prospered, so did Wilmington, New Castle County, and all of Delaware. The company made vast sums of money, and its owners built opulent estates in the countryside surrounding the city. Thousands of chemists, engineers, and other professionals settled in the suburbs, creating bedroom communities like Brandywine Hundred and Hockessin. By the late twentieth century the region had become so prosperous and its history so noteworthy that tourists from all over the world came to visit two former du Pont family estates—Winterthur Museum, located in what had become known as "château country," and Longwood Gardens, just over the state line in Pennsylvania.

Though DuPont's influence had waned in recent decades as the company had cut jobs and the credit card and financial services industry had gained a foothold (thanks to Delaware's favorable banking laws), such was the company's grip on upstate Delaware that when people said the words *Uncle Dupie,* no one questioned whom they were talking about.

The southern part of the state, Kent and Sussex Counties, known derisively to upstaters as "slower Delaware," had retained its agrarian heritage, dominated by huge farms that grew corn, potatoes, soybeans. At the bottom tip of the state was Delaware's playground: Rehoboth Beach and other small resort towns that were packed over the summer with hundreds of thousands of visitors, principally from the Washington–Baltimore corridor.

The Faheys greeted well-wishers with hugs and kisses that Fourth of July morning. Before the search, the group, now numbering several hundred, gathered on a gravel road behind the bleachers and said a prayer. Police who had volunteered to help kept a map to monitor the search and record any discoveries.

Delawareans had clearly rallied around Fahey's family. Silvio Garbati, manager of Cafe Verdi in west Wilmington's trendy Trolley Square shopping district, came to the rally because Fahey was one of his customers.

"Maybe one day I'll need the help," Garbati explained.

The searchers, trailed by reporters with notebooks and television camera crews, fanned out on both sides of the Brandywine Creek to canvass the park, which stretched for nearly a mile, in a rectangular bowl, north of Annie's apartment. The goal was to cover every square inch of the park before the hordes of Fourth of July revelers descended that afternoon for barbecues.

Over the next several hours the search party combed through the hilly woods, peered under brush, checked the river's bank, rummaged through garbage cans, stared into viaducts, and rooted around the edges of the small city zoo located near the park's center.

One woman thought she discovered a clue when she found pieces of women's clothing, but they weren't Fahey's size. Another group uncovered freshly turned dirt. That discovery brought police rushing to the scene with shovels. But their hurried digging turned up nothing.

By 10:00 A.M., many of the searchers were feeling the strain of fruitless efforts. Nick Halladay, a college friend of Annie, seemed to speak for everyone as he poked through some brush. "It's a horrible, empty feeling," he told a reporter.

By noon, it was all over. The searchers had covered nearly every inch of the 180-acre park—and had found no trace of Anne Marie Fahey.

During the hot and ugly search, Bud Freel was home. He had planned to be at Brandywine Park but had such a difficult night, unable to sleep because of his dismay over Annie's disappearance and Tom's odd reaction to it, that he couldn't pull himself out of bed until ten.

And when he did finally get up, he almost wished he hadn't. At least, he might have wished he hadn't answered the phone.

"What's going on?" said the caller, whom Freel recognized as Tom Capano.

"There's a search in the park today," Freel said.

Capano didn't respond. Freel then told him he had read in the morning's paper that Connie Blake, Frawley's old secretary, had heard footsteps in Annie's apartment that fateful Thursday night.

But Capano didn't respond to that, either. Instead, he said, "Charlie told me I shouldn't have talked to you yesterday." Bud knew he was talking about Charlie Oberly, former attorney general and Capano's recently hired lawyer.

"Why shouldn't you talk to me?" asked Freel.

"He just doesn't think I should be talking to people," said Capano. "He also thinks I should ask you whether you were wired with a hidden tape recorder or a microphone."

"Fuck you!" barked Freel, shaken by his old friend's comment. But he quickly regained enough of his composure to say the same thing in longer sentences. "That's a ridiculous thing to say. Why don't you cut out all this crap and get your fucking ass back home and cooperate!"

Freel cursed plenty more before calming down. After a sleepless night of worry about his friend, he was in no mood to be accused of deceit by him.

"Look, why don't you just do everybody a favor and come

back," Freel finally said. "Talk to the police to clear this up. If you don't want to answer questions about your and Anne Marie's private life, don't fucking answer them. But tell them everything about that night."

There was a brief pause at the other end of the line before Capano said, "I'll think about it."

Freel calmed down. They talked some more, and Freel asked if Capano wanted him to do anything.

"Would you talk to the Faheys?"

"Any particular one?" Freel asked.

"Robert."

"I'll try, but maybe not today. It's Fourth of July and all these people are around. What do you want me to say?"

"Tell him I'd like to meet with him and that I was very good to Anne Marie, that I bought her gifts, clothes and other things, that I gave her money when she was broke, bought her groceries the other night because I was so concerned about her not eating."

"I'll try to arrange a meeting," Freel said.

The next day, July 5, Freel called Robert at home and left a message. Robert soon returned the call.

"I talked to Tom again. He'd like to talk to you," Freel said.

"Well, I'm not going to call him, Bud. But if he wants to call me I'll listen."

Freel relayed the message to Capano, who called Freel back about nine that night.

"Listen, I'm not going to call Robert, but I am going to come home on Monday and meet with the police. But I'm going to meet first with my attorneys and I'm not going to answer every question."

"Great," Freel said. "It's the best thing you can do."

Tom Carper wondered why the president of the United States would be calling this July 5. Yes, Carper knew Bill Clinton—they had worked together on the National Governors' Association when Clinton, then governor of Arkansas, was the group's chairman and Carper was an active member of the group. And the two men still spoke, about policy and political matters, every couple of months. But Delaware's governor couldn't think of any subject that was of such national interest to merit a presidential call on the day after Fourth of July.

Could Clinton be coming to town? Carper wondered as he picked up the phone on his large mahogany desk in the governor's office, twelve floors above the streets of Wilmington.

"Tom," said Clinton, "I'm calling about Anne Marie Fahey."

The governor was shocked. But Clinton explained that though he had never met Annie, members of his staff had often dealt with her when scheduling appointments or phone calls with Carper and they had told him about her disappearance. Clinton expressed sympathy for Fahey's family but was still hoping, he said, for her safe return.

"If there's anything I can do," Clinton told Carper, "let me know."

Shocked that Clinton's aides would know about the matter, much less inform their boss, Carper nevertheless took advantage of the offer. "The Wilmington city police and the Delaware State Police are working on this," he told the president. "Might it be possible for the FBI or other federal investigative agencies to lend a hand?"

"Federal assistance can probably be made available if it's necessary and appropriate," said Clinton. "I can't give you any assurances, but I'll look into it."

"Thank you, Mr. President," said Carper. "On behalf of my office and Miss Fahey's family, thank you."

Later that day, Carper's press secretary, Sheri Woodruff, issued a brief press release about Clinton's call. The significance of the call was not lost on the local media. The *News Journal* slapped the news on its front page the next morning, July 6, under the headline "Clinton Offers Federal Aid for Fahey Search."

That Saturday afternoon, nearly a week after Anne Marie was first reported missing, Greg Sleet, Delaware's U.S. Attorney, ran into one of his top young prosecutors, Colm Connolly, in the Acme supermarket in Brandywine Hundred. Sleet was picking up sodas for a family outing; Connolly, some chips.

Both men, who, like nearly everybody in town, were following the case, had been startled and slightly amused to read in the paper that the president and the governor had discussed the involvement of their office—but hadn't told them. Up to that point, both men had assumed it was a local case. The U.S. Attorney's Office automatically prosecuted federal crimes committed in Delaware, coordinating efforts by the Federal Bureau of Investigation, the Bureau of Alcohol, Tobacco, and Firearms, the Internal Revenue Service, and any other federal agencies in the state. The president's authorization wasn't really needed, they remarked. The FBI routinely contacted local police to see if they needed help in criminal investigations; they just hadn't done it in this case yet.

"Nobody called me," Sleet told Connolly. "But I'll check with the state to say that if they need our assistance, we're there."

I paid a visit to Anne Marie Fahey's apartment building that holiday weekend. Her family was there, holding what had become a round-the-clock vigil. It was a hot, muggy day, and the first thing I noticed as I approached the wooden porch was Kathleen, Bob, Kevin, Brian, and a few in-laws sitting on chairs, rocking slowly back and forth, their eyes reddened, faces solemn masks.

The Faheys eyed me suspiciously as I walked up the stairs to the porch.

I introduced myself and told them I was from the Wilmington News Journal. *They answered my questions politely, but it was obvious they were wiped out. They said they suspected Capano had done harm to their sister and asked if I had any inside info. I didn't but told them I'd probably be working the story and I'd share anything I learned. I also told them I knew how they were feeling. My wife's older sister, I explained, had been shot to death the previous Fourth of July by a young man who had been renting a room from her in an old stone home she had bought and was renovating in Wilmington. They had heard of the case, they said, and expressed genuine sympathy for my family's plight.*

We commiserated for a while and exchanged numbers. I told them to call me anytime.

Bud Freel kept in touch with Capano that weekend and was able to report to police that the unofficial primary suspect was still planning on coming in on Monday.

So certain of the arrangement was Freel that he spent that Monday at his Department of Transportation job, not bothering to find out how it had gone. As he walked through the door of his house that evening, however, his phone was ringing.

"They're trying to make me a scapegoat!" Tom Capano was yelling at the other end of the line. "But I am not going to answer all their questions."

Freel knew that Capano had ditched the promise to talk to the police. Rather than lash out at his friend for raising the same tired objections, this time Freel remained calm.

"Tom," he said, "you just don't get it. Nobody cares about how much sex you had with her or anything else. She's been missing for more than a week. All they want to do is talk to you to see if you know anything about her or where she can be. If you're not willing to do that, to help out that family, I have nothing else to say to you."

Capano said nothing and Freel hung up.

As Tom Capano was thwarting police efforts to find his former mistress, some fifty thousand commuters driving northbound on Interstate 95, into and through Wilmington, were passing a huge roadside billboard that pleaded, in five-foot-high letters: HELP US FIND ANNE MARIE FAHEY. There was a phone number—1-(800)-847-3333—but no picture. Creating the picture for the billboard would have held up the placement of the billboard by two weeks. The family couldn't wait—Annie, they knew, couldn't wait.

"It's a one-in-a-million shot," said Jim Lloyd, general manager of Revere Outdoor Advertising, which had donated the billboard space. "But it's the least we can do."

"It can't hurt," Mark Fahey added, trying to sound optimistic. "It is not a last gasp."

It was day twelve and, despite hundreds of hours of investigating and daily accounts in the press, not even a hint of Annie had been uncovered. Robert Fahey drove home from his missing sister's apartment this hot July 9 as if commuting from work. The daily vigil had taken on a life of its own, with routines that now went unremarked. Still, every day that passed without a shred of new evidence being turned up convinced Robert that Thomas Capano was involved. Bud Freel had raised expectations with Capano's promised cooperation, but his canceling of the deal seemed only to confirm Robert's instincts.

Driving through Wilmington in his silver Audi sedan, Robert punched in the code on his cell phone to pick up messages from his Philadelphia office. He listened to the familiar female voice saying he had a message and, keeping an eye on the midafternoon traffic, punched the button to play.

"Robert, this is Tom Capano."

Fahey almost drove off the road as he heard the voice of the man he believed knew what had happened to his sister. Pressing the phone hard against his ear, Robert listened to the familiar intonations. "It's Tuesday; it's a little bit after twelve. I think you know from Bud that I really want to speak to you and anybody else in your family who cares to."

What was this all about? As Robert drove, he listened. It was not the usually smooth and articulate lawyer talking; Capano stammered, hesitated, and rambled.

"Bud tells me you're maybe not really interested in speaking to me and I guess I can understand, Robert, I don't know what to say. I really do want to talk to you. If you would consider that, please call me. My number is 421-6849. I'm in and out a lot, so you'll get my voice mail. I'd like to see you face-to-face if you're willing to do that. I have some things I want to show you. I have some things I want to tell you. I care for Anne Marie a great deal, Robert. I don't know—I guess apparently from what Buddy's telling me that that hasn't come through and I don't understand that. And I know I'm babbling because I'm out of my freaking mind with everything, but if you'll consider it, I'd really like to do it—anytime, anyplace, anywhere. And there's one thing, if you decide you don't want to talk to me, there's one thing I want you to know."

Maybe he was out of his "freaking mind." But praying that Capano might divulge some crucial detail, any detail, Robert drove slowly as he listened to the conciliatory man suddenly become defiant.

"I have talked to the police twice. I have told the police I will talk to them as many times as they want. But I am not going to talk about ancient history. Anne Marie has a right to privacy and I have a right to privacy and I am not going to tell them details of things we did a year ago or eight months ago or all this incredible personal stuff they want to know from me, OK? Stuff they've already tried to ask me that I am not going to answer. It's got nothing to do with anything. I'll tell you, if you want to know, but I am not going to have all those details on the front page of the newspaper and I will talk to them about anything else in the world. I will talk to them about last Thursday night. I will talk to them about anything, but I am not going to talk about ancient history and I just am not budging from that. Maybe you can't understand that, but I'm sorry, but it's irrelevant. It can do nothing. I mean, do you and Kathleen want to read stuff in the newspaper? 'Cause you know it's going to leak. It's personal. So. Well, I said I'd stop. I know I'm rambling, but I desperately would like to talk to you, have you hear from me everything and let you ask me anything you want to ask me. OK, my number is 421-6849. I wanted to come see you all at that apartment, but I know that Kathleen would just frankly gouge my eyes out. I'll stop. Please call me, Robert."

Robert slammed on the brakes and raced back to Annie's apartment. He parked, ran inside, and found Detective Daniels.

"I have something," he told the state trooper, "you'll want to hear."

4 *Falling Too Hard*

Tom Capano strolled into the lobby of the Holiday Inn in downtown Wilmington to catch a smoke during a break in the speeches at a Delaware Democratic Party fund-raiser in the spring of 1993. Considered a party bigwig, the lean forty-four-year-old corporate lawyer and former adviser to both the mayor and the governor actually couldn't stand these functions. But as a financial backer of Delaware's new chief executive, Tom Carper, he felt obligated to attend. Besides, his law firm, Saul Ewing, handled the state's bond financing business, and Capano coordinated the deals.

As he lit up, Capano spotted two young women he recognized as aides to the governor, crossing the lobby toward him. Ginny Columbus was a striking dark-haired Italian-American, and Anne Marie Fahey, of Irish descent, was the long-legged and beautiful youngest sibling in a family of Democratic campaign volunteers. Capano recalled Fahey, the governor's appointments secretary, as fun and forward. "So when am I going to get a lunch out of you?" she had joked several weeks earlier, when Capano had stopped by the governor's office for a bond business meeting.

"Soon, Anne Marie," he had chuckled.

Now, seeking an excuse not to return to the speeches, the two women began flirting innocently with the older man. Capano also relished the opportunity to avoid the ballroom speeches—as well as the attentions of two gorgeous women. The three truants joked with one another as speakers droned in the background. At one point Capano allowed his eyes to wander to Fahey's trim, sexy friend and found himself staring.

"Hey!" Fahey teased, jabbing Capano on the arm. "What are you doing flirting with her? You know, I'm the one you owe a lunch to."

"OK." Capano smiled, shaken out of his momentary reverie.

A few days later, Tom Capano called the governor's office and asked the assertive young secretary to lunch.

As different as Anne Marie Fahey and Tom Capano were in age and background, their attraction seemed inevitable.

Capano, tall, dark, and handsome, was a man of power and influence, at the top of his game, an attorney who had already been deputy attorney general, the mayor's right-hand man, and the governor's legal adviser and now was managing partner of one of Wilmington's most prestigious law firms. Always in command of himself, Capano was engaging, articulate, funny, and a sympathetic listener. And, at forty-four, in a bit of a midlife crisis.

Anne Marie Fahey was only twenty-seven, almost seventeen years Capano's junior, and, as she approached a different kind of midlife, vulnerable to the charms of a man of means and security. Though bubbling with effervescence, the outgoing nature masked the scars of an impoverished and chaotic childhood. Everything she lacked Capano, eldest son of a millionaire contractor, had in abundance.

Their first lunch, in the spring of 1993, set the tone for their relationship—going in style. The setting was the Green Room of the Hotel du Pont, the finest restaurant in Wilmington's only four-star hotel. Gabbing over a gourmet meal beneath crystal chandeliers and towering wood-paneled walls, they became instant pals.

The friendship developed slowly, almost awkwardly, over the next six months. From time to time Annie invited Tom to visit her after work, in the small house she shared with two friends near Wilmington's Little Italy.

Annie liked to challenge Capano, who was a trivia buff, at Jeopardy. Laughing like high school kids, the two enjoyed getting acquainted. On occasion Annie invited Capano to her house for lunch. And the high-powered attorney, used to expense-account meals at three-star restaurants, would pick up a salad and dash over to his young friend's small apartment, just a mile west of downtown. Capano loved Annie's sassiness and sense of humor. Having grown up with four brothers, Annie also knew her share of dirty jokes, which she was happy to share with her new friend. They also talked about relationships. Despite having a model family and devoted wife, Ca-

pano told of his unhappiness in his marriage. Fahey confided
her worries about ever meeting the right guy.

Both felt sexual yearnings but held back. They kissed a few
times, clutched each other in romantic embraces, but nothing
more—until January 27, 1994, Annie's twenty-eighth birthday.

Capano had asked Annie out to dinner that night and made
reservations at Ristorante Panorama in Philadelphia, an intimate bistro with a vast selection of wines by the glass—and
far away from the prying eyes of friends from Wilmington.
Delaware's largest city was just thirty miles from Pennsylvania's largest, but Wilmington was as small and parochial as
Philly was big and cosmopolitan. Wilmington gossip, a beloved pastime, traveled fast to all corners of the city. Lunch
between a married man and single woman was business, unnoticed; the same couple going to dinner could whip up a
brushfire of whispers. But a snow-and-ice storm hit the Delaware Valley that night. The roads were a slippery, dangerous
mess, and even in his four-wheel-drive Jeep Capano decided
against trying to navigate the narrow streets leading to the
Panorama. Instead, he steered off Interstate 95 at Penn's Landing and headed for the Chart House, a fine restaurant, if lack-
ing the Panorama's elegance.

The couple toasted each other with several glasses of wine,
acclaiming Annie's birthday and quietly celebrating a romance
that was in full bloom on this nasty, wintry evening. After
dinner they drove back to Annie's house. She ushered him
into her second-floor bedroom, and they made love.

Fahey fell hard for the debonair man with the lean build
and close-cropped gray-flecked beard. After Annie's birthday,
they communicated almost daily, by phone or E-mail, and he
visited for sexual liaisons when Annie's housemates weren't
likely to be home—when he could give his wife, Kay, an
excuse about business or political obligations. His wife? Annie
knew about the wife but, in full enthrallment, tried to ignore
it.

By March Annie was so taken with Capano that she
couldn't keep the secret of their affair any longer. And on the
first Wednesday of the month she sat down with a new friend,

one with lined paper, and began writing. She eased into the big secret, first telling her diary about family, then about therapy. "I am back in therapy," she confessed, writing in a tidy scrawl. And she loved her therapist, Bob Conner. "Bob is great and I am able to trust him 100%. He is one of the few whom I know beyond a shadow of a doubt that will never judge me. That is a pretty great feeling."

Trust loomed large as a personal, if unconscious, issue for Annie. Her two traumatic abandonments—her mother dying when Annie was nine and her father, unable to cope, falling into alcoholism—seemed to prism her life, conveying new experiences and new people through their intricate emotional geometry. Even tonight, writing in her new diary, Annie felt compelled to recall the death of her grandmother almost two years earlier. "The most tragic part of my life!" she wrote. "I always believed Nan's life would be eternal. She was the most reliable, stable, sober adult person in my life." But just as quickly as she imbued her grandmother's death with tragedy— "a part of me died with Katie"—Annie bounced back, with the protective optimism that must have helped her survive in childhood. "The world is a less fortunate place," she said of her grandmother, "but Heaven is dancing with her arrival."

Annie then complained that the Prozac she had been taking for three weeks was having no effect—except "it's giving me horrific headaches!"—and noted that her family and some friends had begun to worry about her weight loss. Almost defiantly, however, Annie wrote that she was "quite pleased!" with having dropped five more pounds and seemed unbothered by her weight loss methods. "I am starving myself as well as avoiding situations where food is involved. I now think of food as poisonous. I cannot ever imagine eating a sandwich! (too much food). I'll be okay, I will stop before it gets out of control." Abruptly, as if to fend off her fear of being "out of control," and with no transition, Annie wrote: "I have fallen in love with a very special person." It was a fall, as if in a dream, over which she had no control. A free fall—no penalties—through billowy, sensual clouds. "It happened," she told her diary, "the night of my 28th birthday." Since then, she said, in just one month, "we have built an everlasting friendship. I feel free around him. He makes my heart smile." But even then, as if still unsure of her diary confidante, Annie would not reveal Capano's name. "We know who each other are," she wrote in the manner of a spy. But apparently there were some strings—small ones, filaments, really. "He deserves some happiness in his life," she concluded, without explanation, other than to say: "It makes me feel good to know that I can provide him with such happiness."

Five days later, on March 7, Annie wrote again. This time she put the name of her lover in parentheses—and, as if still needing some deflective code, in Spanish—and allowed herself to wonder, ever so briefly, about the wisdom of hooking up with a married man. "We (Tomas and I) had lunch on Friday at the Shipley Grill. It was very good. I hope that tonight he will visit me before working in Philadelphia. I am alone in my house tonight drinking a beer and listening to music ('When Harry Met Sally')." She was in love but lonely. And in his absence, a whisper of doubt crept in. "We have problems because he has a wife and children also." Annie saved the best and worst thoughts until the beer was sipped and the CD had spun. The not-so-free fall made her suddenly protest: "I don't want to be in love, but I can't help it. By God, please don't judge me!"

No transition: "No news on the weight loss. I am stuck at 135 pounds, and it's pissing me off!" Tom Capano came with baggage, and she was starving herself. "I can't starve myself any more than I already am," she now wrote. "I suppose I should be thankful that I have not gained any weight either." She was gorgeous and outgoing and yet, she wrote, "I still avoid situations where there is food involved." She declined a dinner invitation because of it, she wrote, then pined: "Where is my friend?"

Her friend? Just three weeks later, Annie revealed a new twist to the love affair.

"My boyfriend (Tomas) asked me today if I wanted to be a girlfriend and live alone and he would pay rent for my room," she confessed on March 24. "I need to think. I love him, but he has four children (girls) and a wife. I will be a silent girlfriend. Oh my God."

Tomas (Annie often used her Spanish to translate boyfriend names) was evidently feeling the need to have Annie to himself. But it was not to be resolved tonight. In the next sentence, she was reliving her past: "Today is the day my father died! How sad. My dad was a bad father, but he was the only father I ever had, so therefore I loved him. I do not think that he consciously meant to be a bad father—he just had no clue. He really made my life very sad & lonely. I will never forget the pain he caused me. He forced me to lie to protect my identity."

For the first eight years of Annie's life, she lived a normal middle-class existence in a large Irish-American family.

Her father, Robert Fahey Sr., a lanky, convivial insurance salesman with wavy red hair who had played baseball at the University of North Carolina, and her mother, Kathleen, a slim, attractive DuPont secretary nine years his junior, had been introduced by fellow Irish-American Bill McLaughlin, a congenial DuPonter who became Wilmington's mayor in 1977.

Kathleen, who spoke with an Irish brogue, quit work after the marriage to become a full-time mother. She had six children in twelve years. The oldest three, Kevin, Mark, and Robert, were known as "the three boys." Kathleen, Brian, and Annie were "the little ones."

Annie, freckle-faced with dazzling blue eyes, was the youngest, doted on by the rest of the brood and its enormous circle of friends.

The Faheys weren't affluent, and both parents enjoyed their booze a little too heartily. But Dad made a decent living and even opened up his own insurance office. They lived in a modest two-story brick home in McDaniel Crest, a post–World War II development off Route 202, the commercial artery through Brandywine Hundred, just north of Wilmington. The refrigerator was stocked; the children wore nice clothes.

Little Annie was a mimic. Sheila Albanese recalled how they would put on cowboy hats and strum wildly on guitars. "One time, when her dad poked his head in the room, Annie looked up and said in a deep voice, 'Hi. My name is Johnny Cash'!"

Devout Roman Catholics, the family went to Sunday mass at St. Mary Magdalen Church. The children—tall, wiry, and tough—were good students and athletes and attended a mix of parochial and public schools. Robert and Mark excelled in baseball, Brian in football, and Kathleen—whom everybody called Cass—played field hockey. Annie, too, would excel in field hockey. And in basketball.

But before that, in August 1974, tragedy struck. Her mother was diagnosed with lung cancer. Kathleen McGettigan Fahey spent the next eight months moving between home and hospital, finally dying on March 16, 1975. She was only forty-five. Annie, her youngest, was nine. The older children sheltered Annie—brother Brian later recalled that the day after their mother's death Annie played outside with her friends, "just like it was a normal day"—but couldn't do anything for their dad.

Robert Fahey Sr. fell apart. His drinking, heavy before the illness, now consumed his nights, then his days, then his life. He stopped working, and the family subsisted, first, on money he had saved, then on insurance policies, then on Social Security payments and pension money. Finally, his mother-in-law, Katherine McGettigan, Annie's beloved Nan, drove once a week from her home in Media, Pennsylvania—thirty miles away—to help out while other relatives and friends of the family began chipping in with support, for the kids' sake. Some of the older children took jobs, mostly at restaurants, busing tables and washing dishes. Bob, seventeen when his mom died and the third eldest child, loved tinkering with cars and took a part-time job at a gas station. But the kids' efforts could not prevent the household from collapsing, and the older ones went off to college or moved out, leaving Kathleen, Brian, and Annie, "the little ones," to cope with their father's failures. Bills went unpaid. Electricity and water were frequently shut off. And in 1978, when Brian was a senior in high school and Annie just twelve years old, there was no phone. The next year, after Brian had gone off to college, the electricity was shut off for the winter, leaving the house without hot water. Annie, then a freshman at Brandywine High School and the only one still at home, often showered in the school locker room. Although her siblings tried their best to provide surrogate parenting, Annie raised herself those teenage years.

And the worst part of it was not the poverty, but her father's emotional and psychological ruin. Though he was usually a harmless—though embarrassing—drunk, on bad days he'd sit at the kitchen table, pounding down one glass of vodka or gin after another, and erupt. Sometimes he'd just scream at Annie. Other times he hit her. To protect herself from beatings, she learned to hide under furniture. Once she beat him with a hockey stick. Another time she punched him because he had stolen some of her money. At night, after he passed out, she'd pour out the booze and hide the liquor bottles.

Ashamed of her father, Annie never invited friends to the house. But everyone knew what was happening, and her friends' parents often took Annie in for days, weeks, even months at a time. She'd often sneak out her window and spend the night at the home of her best friend, Beth Noetzel, who lived in Sharpley, an affluent neighborhood across Concord Pike.

Finally, Annie's father stopped paying the mortgage. The county sold the house at a sheriff's sale, and Robert Fahey was forced to move in with his youngest son, Brian, then a student at the University of Delaware. Annie, just a sophomore at Brandywine High, moved in with Carol Creighton, a cousin of Beth Noetzel. Creighton, a single mom, appreciated the fact that Annie would baby-sit her daughter and became very fond of the engaging teenager.

For some of her junior year Annie lived with Brian and her dad in Newark, but the commute, twenty miles, was difficult and when her brothers Robert and Kevin bought a semidetached brick home on 21st Street in Wilmington she moved into one of the spare bedrooms.

Somehow, Annie turned her adversity on its head and became practiced at showing a cheery face to the world. She told jokes and had a hearty laugh that could be heard across a room and was popular with classmates. One of her favorite pastimes was packing into someone's car and heading to the Charcoal Pit, a 1950s-style burger joint, where everyone grabbed spoons and stuffed their faces with an ice-cream creation called the Kitchen Sink.

She also became a neat freak, more compensation, perhaps, for the dysfunction and turmoil at home.

Her friends knew about the problems at home but never brought them up in conversations, to spare her from embarrassment and even more pain.

"Annie had the shittiest life," Beth (Noetzel) Barnes recalled. "A lot of people who had what she had would fold, but she was strong."

Annie's next stop was Wesley College, a small private two-year school in Dover, the state capital. She paid her way at Wesley with a partial field hockey scholarship and pickup jobs—receptionist for a dentist, clerk at the Limited women's apparel store, and waitress at J. T. Smithers.

In the meantime, her father kicked the bottle and the two patched up their fragile, painful relationship. But the reconciliation was short-lived. In March of 1986, when Annie was a sophomore at Wesley, Robert Fahey Sr. died of leukemia at age sixty-four. Annie took it the hardest.

That fall, having graduated from Wesley, Annie enrolled at the University of Delaware. But she felt isolated at the larger campus, stopped going to class, stopped even leaving her dorm room, and dropped out by Thanksgiving. Her brother Brian, who by then was teaching at the Quaker Friends School just outside Wilmington and owned a modest home, let her come stay with him.

But Annie climbed back, returning to Wesley, which had become a four-year school, spending a semester in Spain, majoring in international relations, and, in 1989, graduating with a degree in political science. Her world, as she entered adulthood, seemed full of promise. A native resilience combined with some deep genetic drive. She applied for an internship, translating documents from Spanish to English, at the prestigious Organization of American States in Washington and was accepted. Though uncertain of her future as the internship ended, Annie, then twenty-five, stopped in the office of her congressman, Tom Carper, to ask Ed Freel, Carper's chief of staff and a Fahey family friend, if he knew of any job prospects. Freel was in Wilmington with Carper, but Annie began entertaining the rest of the office.

Jeff Bullock, another top Carper aide, called Freel, with Annie sitting nearby, and used the speakerphone to tell him about a lady who had wandered in off the street looking for a job. "She said she knows you," Bullock told Freel.

Annie yelled at the phone, "Fast Eddie, it's me! Anne Marie! These people want you to hire me!" In fact, Annie had walked into the office that afternoon not knowing that Carper was looking for a receptionist. And within minutes of stepping through the door she had so engaged the office staff that they were begging Carper to hire her.

Freel laughed. Annie was hired. And in 1992, when Carper launched his bid for governor, Annie returned to Wilmington and a job on the campaign staff. By this time the young woman's fastidiousness was well known in the office, and after the victory she joined the governor's staff as Carper's scheduler. Annie moved in with childhood friend Jackie Binnersley, who had bought a house on Clayton Street, a block of tidy two-story brick row houses on the edge of Little Italy, west of downtown Wilmington.

Annie blossomed in her new job, one that demanded extraordinary organizational skills. An endless stream of political suitors, from powerful lobbyists to lowly grassroots groups, made constant pleas for the governor's precious time. Annie, whose desk was next to that of the governor's personal secretary, on the twelfth floor of the Carvel State Office Building in downtown Wilmington, fielded calls with grace, efficiency, and, perhaps most important, good humor. Orderly and meticulous, she was among the first to arrive every morning and did the coffee runs to Brew-HaHa on nearby Market Street Mall every day, usually picking up for herself a double latte.

Annie also brought her fanatical neatness to the office. She arranged sticky yellow Post-it notes neatly across her computer. And in the top drawer of her desk she lined up rows of pennies, each with Abraham Lincoln's face up. Her smile and boisterous laugh lit up the office. She was known for defusing tense situations with just the right light comment—a skill learned as a child, at the table of an angry alcoholic father.

Over the years Tom Carper came to value Annie as a critical cog in his staff but also considered her a member of his extended family. "Often, when I was on the road or in my Dover office, she would drop off my schedule at my house and always spend a little time with my two boys," Carper recalled. "She'd kid them, tease them, and just fuss over them, being her vibrant, bubbly self."

"I had a great day on Friday," Annie wrote. It was Sunday afternoon, April 24, 1994, three months since she had begun her affair with Tom Capano, and she still couldn't overcome her ambivalence about carrying on with a married man. "My friend and I," she continued, "went to his house to eat. What a house! He enchants me. During the weekend, my thoughts were devoted to Tomas. I am afraid because I am in love with a man who has a family. I need to realize that our relationship will never be anything other than a secret. I fantasize my life with him all the time. He is very gentle, intelligent, handsome and very interesting. Why does he have to be married??? More information later."

Annie's alliance with Capano coincided with her resumption of intense therapy for the psychiatric problems that had begun dominating her life.

Despite some treatment in 1986 and 1987, following her father's death, Annie's anxieties kept resurfacing. In 1988, her last year at Wesley, becoming obsessed with losing weight, she had begun taking laxatives and exercising up to three hours each day.

In 1991, she sought the help of Bob Conner, a Wilmington psychologist, whom she would see off and on for the next several years. She established a strong rapport with the therapist, admiring his patience, radiant smile, and soothing voice, and reported to him a long list of problems, including claustrophobia, panic attacks, lack of appetite, feelings of doom and powerlessness, overwhelming fatigue, and the inability to assert herself. Her mood, she told him, could "snap" suddenly.

On Conner's advice, Annie also saw a psychiatrist, who prescribed the antianxiety drug Ativan.

By the spring of 1994, as her romance with Capano was blooming, Annie told Conner about her fear of abandonment and rejection. And she reported becoming more obsessed with her weight, admitting she was taking laxatives again. At work, she told Connor, she had finally gotten up enough nerve to ask for a raise, only to be shot down. Another source of angst, she said, was the impending marriage of her housemate and landlady, Jackie Binnersley; she would have to move to an apartment of her own. She didn't tell Connor, however, about the man who was, at the same time, encouraging her to get her own apartment so that he could have her all to himself.

Her symptoms persisted. Her doctors took Annie off Ativan and prescribed Prozac, the popular antidepressant. And despite feeling comfortable with Conner, she couldn't bring herself to confide her Capano secret, saying only that she was in a relationship with a "lawyer" whose name she would not divulge.

Everyone could have used more information about Tom Capano, the eldest son of a charming, respected Wilmington home builder who had moved to America when he was seven years old and created a real estate development fortune. Becoming a lawyer instead of going into the family business, as his younger brothers would do, Tom combined charm, wealth, and brains in such a neat package that he was considered a nobleman around Wilmington. And it was this prince who wooed—and quickly won—Anne Marie Fahey.

Though Tom's dad started as a poor man, Louis Capano Sr. had already become well established when his first boy was born, in 1949. And Tom was not only born with a silver spoon in his mouth; he was also blessed with dark good looks, an athletic build, and a keen intellect. Tommy knew his immigrant roots but grew up wealthy, living most of his life in a sprawling stone colonial house, built by Dad, in an exclusive section of Brandywine Hundred.

"I come from a blue-collar background," Tom would say. "My father was a carpenter. All my uncles were in the building trades." His two grandfathers were immigrants. One was a stonemason and the other a bricklayer. "My father believed in putting the boys to work as early as possible." He and his brothers did "pick-and-shovel work" as teenagers. "I dug a lot of ditches. I pushed a lot of concrete, moved a lot of lumber."

But while he may have spent summers cultivating calluses, during the school year Tom cracked books, first at the expensive St. Edmond's Academy for Boys elementary school and then at the equally elite, equally Catholic, Archmere Academy high school. "Half the time I didn't know he was around," recalled his mother, Marguerite Capano. "All he did was want to read. He was not a problem at all. Never. Never. Never. Never. He studied all the time."

Tom played tackle on the Archmere football team, ran track, and served as student council president, establishing early his reputation as a quintessential Renaissance man.

"He associated very well with the jocks, but he was also in the top academic section of the school," recalled Tom Shopa, a classmate from Philadelphia and one of the few boarders at Archmere. "In sports, he was rugged, no-nonsense, very focused. But when he was off the field, he was a fun-loving guy, very easy to talk to, laid back."

Tom's mother recalled that if any of his friends found themselves in trouble, "they knew they could come to Tom."

On weekends, Capano, Shopa, and other Archmere buddies attended parties in suburban Wilmington, made out with girls, hung out at the Charcoal Pit restaurant just as Annie would do nearly two decades later, and cruised the rolling hills of the Valley, the name teenagers gave the château country populated by du Pont bluebloods. Capano and his buddies drank beer and smoked cigarettes, but though it was the mid-1960s, they avoided the drugs other kids were beginning to experiment with.

Joseph Smagala, who played center on the Archmere football squad and thought the world of Tom Capano and his family, recalled that "Tom's father, Lou, was the leader of the family and kept everybody in line. Mrs. Capano was a strong mom, but the father was the chief."

And Tom, though second child, was the first boy, a respected position in Italian families. His three younger brothers, who followed him to St. Edmond's and Archmere, also looked up to Tom, who blazed a trail that was difficult to follow. "Tom was the smartest and most dynamic of the brothers," recalled Smagala, "the diplomat in the family."

Tom provided the same fixer services to friends. "At parties, when guys would start getting too drunk," said Smagala, "Tommy would keep them from getting in trouble."

High school friend Blair Mahoney said Capano "was always a leader. No one ever saw Tommy lose his temper. He was a stabilizing force in our group." At the same time, his father was making money by the bushel—building homes, shopping centers, and apartment complexes in the mushrooming Wilmington suburbs—and spreading it around.

"They were just an outstanding Catholic family," recalled the Reverend Thomas Hagendorf, a teacher at Archmere who often joined other school priests for dinner at the Capano home and was among those clergy who frequented their Jersey shore getaway.

Quiet, conservative, disciplined young Tom Capano, Father Hagendorf observed, was his parents' favorite, "a shining star."

Tom went to Boston College and married his college sweetheart, Kay Ryan, in 1972—"on the day of the Watergate break-in," Tom would recall. Kay was a pretty nursing school student from Connecticut. The newlyweds stayed in Boston for another two years, while Tom finished law school and Kay worked as a public-health nurse. Tom's parents paid his tuition.

Louis Sr., who could remember his own youth of struggle and hardship, broke down in tears of joy the day his Tommy graduated from Boston College Law School.

The young couple returned to Wilmington in 1974, and Tom, after passing his bar exam, become a public defender. Two years later he became a prosecutor, spending about a year putting criminals like Robert "Squeaky" Saunders, who shot a man to death and dumped his body in a creek, in the slammer.

By 1977 Capano was ready for meal ticket law—a more appropriate position for the son of a widely respected and wealthy father—and went to work for one of Wilmington's largest homegrown legal firms, Morris James Hitchens & Williams. The following year, Tom, still not yet thirty years old, moved with his wife into an appropriately upper-crust house, the former Catholic bishop's residence on the corner of 17th and Greenhill, in the prestigious Highlands of west Wilmington.

The kids arrived—Christy in 1980, Katie in '82, Jenny in '83—as Capano spread his legal wings in Wilmington. And by the time Alexandra was born, in 1985, he had become a political strategist. He helped get his rugby buddy Dan Frawley, the hard-drinking Irishman with a bone-rattling handshake, elected mayor in 1984. In return for his expert campaign counsel, Capano was offered the job of city solicitor. He took it, quitting his law firm and taking a significant pay cut in order to oversee a staff of twenty-two, mostly defending claims against the city and prosecuting a multitude of misdemeanors, from public drunkenness to assault. Like a kid in a candy store, Capano himself would prosecute one of these petty cases every couple of weeks, he would later say, "just to have fun." But he did not take his eye off the big picture, and within two years Frawley had given Capano the job of administrative assistant, overseeing all department heads. Capano charged into the job with zeal, and as friend Brian Murphy, Frawley's press spokesman, recalled, "Tommy ran the city." With Frawley safely re-elected in November of 1988, just days after a drunk-driving accident for hizzoner, Capano went to work in the family business. His three younger brothers, who ran the business, paid a good deal more than a city job did, but they were operating with a kind of abandon that concerned Marguerite Capano; Tom took the job as a favor to her. "I promised my mother I'd try it for a year," he recalled, "and I stayed exactly 365 days."

After straightening out some legal problems for his brother Louis, Tom, proving his continued prowess as a power broker, took a job as chief legal counsel to the governor of Delaware. Even more remarkable, in a state that takes its party affiliations seriously, Michael Castle was a Republican. Capano served on two blue-ribbon panels, one investigating Wilmington's overcrowded Gander Hill prison, another looking at political donations by Delaware law firms.

By 1992, with Castle's two terms nearing an end, Capano went back to the private sector, now as managing partner of Saul Ewing's Wilmington office. Capano briefly pondered a run for attorney general that same year, when his friend Charlie Oberly decided, after twelve years on the job, to run for the U.S. Senate. But Capano decided against jumping into the volatile and public political arena and so settled, at age forty-three, into a comfortable life as a rich middle-aged attorney with a loyal wife and four beautiful daughters. He continued to dabble in politics, as a backroom negotiator, and was active in community service projects. He served on the board of his parish church as well as three of the local Catholic schools: his alma mater, Archmere; Ursuline Academy, which his girls attended; and St. Mark's. Some of his friends, amazed by his dedication to St. Anthony's and other church-oriented projects, called him "the monk."

Suave and personable, he strutted around Wilmington like a man who was a pillar of the community—and knew it. And when he strode into the governor's office, Anne Marie Fahey found him irresistible.

Tom Capano, worldly and wise, introduced Annie to the world of opulence. He took her to the finest restaurants in Philadelphia—Le Bec-Fin, Pamplona, the Saloon, the Panorama—and did all the ordering. He bought her expensive clothes from Talbot's, gave her a new twenty-seven-inch television, bought her art prints for her apartment, and gave her cash when she was broke. He listened calmly and compassionately as she told the story of her tortured life.

He was like no other boyfriend in her life. Annie's most serious relationship prior to Capano had been with Paul Columbus, a military pilot and brother of her friend Ginny. Annie first got to know Paul, known as P. J., when she lived with Ginny's family during one of her forced evacuations from her dysfunctional household. She reconnected with him when she was in her early twenties and emerging from the tailspin of guilty grieving for her dead father. She was finishing up at Wesley, and he was an aeronautical engineering student at Delaware State, also in Dover. They dated for three years— and Annie loved him. But it didn't last. The couple argued frequently and finally broke up in the summer of 1991. "I always thought my life would be with P. J.," she confessed to her diary. "But not anymore. I wish him well, and there's a part of me that will always love him."

With her good looks, sparkling blue eyes, effervescent personality, and an eye-catching figure she maintained by jogging and biking, Annie was never short of boyfriends. Even during the time when she was first seeing Tom Capano, she dated various young men and kept in touch, platonically, with a former professor from Wesley, who visited her in Wilmington for periodic dinners.

Annie also found plenty of time for her family. She was close to her five nephews, especially Kevin, her sister's oldest son. When he was sickly as a baby, kept in the hospital for days, Annie visited him religiously in the intensive care unit. She called him Buster Brown and when she visited Kathleen's house would yell that name. "Kevin would just run up," Kathleen later recalled, "and she'd scoop him up and he would just hold onto her so tight." Annie also volunteered, devoting time to Creative Grandparenting, where she mentored a young Wilmington girl. She also read to poor inner-city kids at lunchtime for the Ministry of Caring.

"Wow. What a day!" Annie wrote in her diary on April 26, 1994, two days after she had recorded her devotion to Capano. "I talked with Tomas last night," she said. "Our relationship is finished." Love's roller coaster. Did it have something to do with her coming to his house and boldly treading on territory occupied by another woman? "He told me I need to find a man without children who has a lot of time for me, because I am very special and deserve much more." This kind of letdown only made things worse for Annie. "After what he said, I was very sad and I cried all night," she wrote. "I know it is my problem and my fault because from the beginning I knew what I was getting myself into." He didn't? Why was it just her problem and not also his? Was it Annie's instinct that she needed him more than he needed her?

"Sometimes," she continued, "it is very easy to write, but very difficult to cope. I have dreams about him and me making love and living together—but it will never happen. After he left, I was so empty, sad, lonely. I told him things that were hidden inside me. I feel so comfortable with him—I can say anything. I watched him get in his car and drive away. I went to bed and cried myself to sleep. Ciao, T., I love you. AMF."

All next morning Annie sweated, wondering if he would call. "I prayed he would," she later recounted, "but vowed to myself that I would not call him." And he did call. He told her he wasn't breaking up after all. "We decided that we will still see each other," she said. She melted into tears that afternoon, during a therapy session, and that night lost herself in her diary. "I feel that my world is so out of control, the only thing I can control is my food intake."

Capano then told Annie he couldn't see her for several days since he was going to Canada for a law school conference. "Poor thing!" Annie cried. "Ciao, Tomas, I love you!"

BOOK TWO

I want to hurt this bitch. I want her hurt very bad.
—TOM CAPANO,
asking a favor of a friend in the late seventies

5 *Crazy for You*

Montreal was a safe city. Tom Capano knew very few people at the legal conference—and few knew him. Nevertheless, he didn't flaunt the pixie-haired blonde on his arm. In fact, it was the first time Deborah MacIntyre had joined him on a trip—and she spent most of the weekend in the hotel room or sightseeing and shopping by herself. The couple was always discreet. Tom Capano would not embarrass his wife and children with an affair, even if, in today's world, it would not be so terribly scandalous. Nor would he tell his newest girlfriend, Annie Fahey, that she was not his only mistress. There was a lot about Tom Capano that Annie didn't know about, including Debby MacIntyre, his secret lover of more than thirteen years.

It began on a Memorial Day weekend in 1981. Pushing a mower over his large lawn, working up a sweat, Tom Capano looked up to see the pretty blond woman coming down the street on her moped. He stopped and watched. The thirty-two-year-old attorney, a partner in one of Wilmington's top law firms, might have been thinking about his good life, his flourishing law career, the trust fund from his wealthy father, who had died the previous year, and his pretty young wife and new daughter, who were visiting his wife's sister in San Francisco.

Instead, Capano turned the mower off and watched the blond woman turn into his driveway. He knew who she was—Debby Williams, wife of one of his law firm colleagues. He helped her hide the moped behind some bushes and escorted her in a side door of the large house.

The seduction had evolved just the way Capano had hoped it would. He'd had his eye on the athletic woman with the twinkle in her eye for a couple of years. She and her husband, Dave, were one of a group of couples the Capanos socialized with from Morris James Hitchens & Williams—founded by Dave's family. Life for the young, affluent professionals, whose homes were concentrated in the Highlands, Wilmington's most prestigious neighborhood, was a succession of cocktail and dinner parties, golf outings, and social teas. In Wilmington, a town settled by ancestors of the du Ponts and whose outskirts were still home to 8 of the 400 richest Americans, the high life tended to be very high indeed.

Debby Williams, born a MacIntyre, herself the daughter of a textile executive, had good bloodlines and a country club childhood. Like Tom Capano, she and her siblings spent summers in Stone Harbor, the New Jersey beach resort that attracted many of Wilmington's well-to-do. Her great-uncle was one of Notre Dame's legendary Four Horsemen, and Debby, a former swimmer and field hockey player, kept a lithe figure by jogging around the Highlands and golfing at the Wilmington Country Club.

The previous summer, she and her one-year-old daughter, Abigail, were regular visitors to the Capanos' beach house in Stone Harbor. Debby and Abby would sit on the beach with Kay, then eight months pregnant, and Tom when he could take time off from work. Tom's wandering eye fell on Debby's trim and taut body immediately, and by summer's end he was pleased that Debby finally seemed to be paying attention to him.

That's when, as he would later describe it, he "began desiring her," and he made his first serious pass at a New Year's Eve party. During an evening of drinking, he managed to maneuver Debby away from her spouse and pull her into a bathroom. "I'm in love with you," he said, and he kissed her passionately on the lips.

"You're crazy, Tom," she told him. "I'm married. I'm flattered, but I'm married. I can't believe you could be in love with me. And you're married."

But Debby instantly became entranced by the prospect of an illicit encounter with the confident, handsome young lawyer. Over the next few months, the two began talking on the phone. Capano asked Debby to help him plan Kay's surprise thirty-first birthday party in April. And one day that month, while Debby was visiting her husband, she stopped by Capano's office on the other side of the floor. He invited her in, and she shut the door behind her. Before long, Tom and Debby were kissing ardently and fondling each other. Again Debby pulled away. "We've got to stop this," she told Tom, aroused but suddenly afraid at the prospect of getting caught. "Somebody is going to walk in. There are no locks on this door."

They stopped but left for a downtown restaurant, where they resumed their mutual seduction and planned for an intimate rendezvous.

Memorial Day weekend was the perfect time. With Kay away, they had the big house to themselves. Capano lived on a prominent corner, 17th and Greenhill, with plenty of friends of his and Debby's for neighbors, so she parked her moped behind the hedges. Capano, dirty from the yard work, and Debby, perspiring from the ride, entered the house.

It wasn't long before they were naked on the floor of his den, having sex. Their couplings soon became a weekly event, meeting mostly at Motel 6, a lowbrow establishment located on a seedy highway at the foot of the Delaware Memorial Bridge. Capano, busy with his legal work and a budding interest in politics, both of which kept him away from home after hours, never had trouble finding an excuse when he wanted to see his new mistress.

In fact, Tom Capano's affair with Debby Williams was far from the first time he failed to control his sexual impulses. In 1977, when he was twenty-eight and married for only five years, Capano began pursuing twenty-three-year-old Linda Marandola, a legal secretary of a friend of his. Marandola had accompanied the two men to lunch on several occasions, and Capano soon asked the secretary to lunch alone.

Several months after their lunch liaisons began, Marandola bumped into Capano at a Wilmington bar. The lawyer bought her drinks and they later made love. Engaged to be married, however, Marandola immediately felt guilty about the dalliance. When Capano called to arrange another tryst, she declined. Capano, though polite, was persistent. He continued to call the young secretary, who, after an evening of heavy drinking at her bachelorette party, which Capano attended, accepted his offer to go to his home in the Highlands. His wife, Capano explained, was away.

By then, Capano had developed a fascination with Marandola, who again regretted having sex with Capano and again rebuffed his further sexual advances. But Capano was a charming pursuer and remained friendly enough with Marandola to be invited to her wedding. There, during a brief conversation with the new bride, he told Marandola that he loved her.

Capano began calling the newlywed frequently, wrote long love letters to her, and complained all the while how upset he was that Marandola had gone through with her marriage. He told her he wanted to divorce his wife, wished Marandola would leave her new husband, and offered her a job. In August of 1980, when Christine Capano was born, he wrote Marandola a letter saying he wished she had given birth to his first child.

Finally realizing that he was disturbed, Marandola attempted to cut off all contact with Capano, telling him not to call her anymore. But her repudiation seemed only to incite Capano.

"This is my town. This is my state," he boasted during one call. "You should leave or you'll be sorry. If you don't, I'll do everything in my power to make sure you go." He said he knew where she parked her car.

Within days, Marandola noticed Capano standing at the window in his office, watching her walk to her car. She began getting hang-up calls at work.

When Marandola received an eviction notice from her flat in the Cavalier Apartments, a complex owned by the Capano family, she went to her boss, Capano's friend, and told him of the harassment. He figured Capano had gotten carried away but he knew he was not a man to be denied and advised his secretary to move. But he also gave her tape-recording equipment and told her to tape the calls.

Capano, meanwhile, contacted Joseph Riley, an older man whom Capano had befriended. The lawyer knew that Riley had once been convicted of threatening bodily harm and disorderly conduct and, even though he was not a real criminal, a tough-talking Riley had encouraged Capano to think of him as a "wise guy."

Capano asked Riley to give Marandola a message.

"I'm crazy about her and I can't live without her," the married thirty-year-old lawyer told Riley. "She blew me off and I can't eat or sleep."

Capano's next words gave Riley a chill.

"I want to hurt this bitch. I want her hurt very bad. Could you get someone to knock her over the head or have her run over by a car?"

Riley was surprised by Capano's request. "The bar association would kill you if they ever learned about this," Riley told him.

"Don't worry. I can take care of that."

As the short meeting wrapped up, Capano wondered aloud, "Why did I tell you all of this? I've never told anybody else."

Riley hoped Capano was having second thoughts. But a couple of weeks later, the lawyer brought it up again.

"You've got a nice wife and home," said Riley, trying to dissuade Capano. "Are you sure you want to do this thing?"

"Yes. I want to get even with this woman."

Riley now decided Capano was out of control and contacted Dean Wedge, a private investigator retired from the FBI.

"This guy's not thinking straight," Riley told Wedge. "I want to do something to scare him and get him back on the right track so he doesn't do anything stupid."

Wedge, who did work for the Delaware Supreme Court's Censure Committee, which reviewed alleged misconduct by attorneys, advised Riley to tape his and Capano's subsequent conversations.

During one of the next calls, Riley asked Capano what he wanted him to do.

"I want you to hurt that bitch," Capano said again.

Capano eventually changed his mind and told Riley not to hurt Marandola—only to harass her and her family with phone calls. He even gave Riley equipment to tape the calls, to ensure that the work he was paying for was being done.

Riley called Marandola several times, but she hung up on him. Capano then suggested beginning "phase two" of the plan and directed Riley to begin bothering Marandola's husband.

"Well, you think it's at the point that you would want me to do that now?" Riley asked.

"Absolutely."

"You want to do that now?"

"Unless I should just forget about it," Capano said.

"You want to forget about it."

"I can't."

"You can't forget about it."

"That's right," Capano said.

In a subsequent call, Riley told Capano he was having difficulty getting through to Marandola's husband.

"You getting bored?" Capano asked.

Riley asked if Capano wanted him to keep trying.

"Yeah," said Capano, "because the pressure's got to be strong."

Early in 1981, with Capano now pursuing Debby Williams, Riley took the tapes to Wedge, the former FBI agent turned investigator, who took them to Capano's boss, Henry Herndon. The managing partner at Morris James, Herndon had resigned from the Censure Committee in March 1980. Wedge played the tapes of Capano and Riley for Herndon, then hid them away.

A few weeks later, Capano called Riley. "You set me up," he said.

"I don't want to hurt you," Riley retorted. "But I was trying to put some sense in that fucking head of yours."

Capano's dangerous pursuit of Marandola never became public, nor did his wife ever find out about her husband's secret life. What did become public, however, were the problems Capano's brothers seemed prone to. In fact, their troubles burnished Tom's own reputation as the family's white knight— and a fixer of considerable skill.

The Capano family troubles seemed to begin almost as soon as Tom got out of law school. In 1973 one cousin, a builder, paid $10,000 to a seventeen-year-old girl for agreeing to drop a morals charge against him. Three years later, another cousin was charged with obstructing a federal investigation.

Tom's brothers' troubles seemed to begin after their father

died, suddenly, in the winter of 1980, from a heart attack. Louis Jr., then twenty-nine, a chatty, flamboyant man-about-town who zipped around in a white Mercedes convertible, pleaded no contest to second-degree reckless endangerment in 1982 for throwing a chair through a sliding glass door of his brother-in-law's house and attacking the smaller, older man.

Then there was Gerry, the baby of the family, almost fourteen years younger than Tom. Gerry's parents and siblings fussed over the sweet, cute boy who loved riding through the woods on his minibike. But as an adolescent, after his father died, Gerry, a student at Archmere, began using drugs. Marijuana, speed, Quaaludes, LSD, cocaine—Gerry swallowed, smoked, or snorted just about everything available in the early 1980s.

Priests at Archmere, Capano family friends and grateful recipients of Capano family financial largesse, were finally forced to ask Gerry to leave after his sophomore year. At Brandywine High, the same public school Anne Marie Fahey was attending, Gerry was soon arrested on drug charges. A judge threatened to send the young Capano to Ferris School for Boys, the county's jail for juvenile criminals, known simply as the Hole, but Tom, as usual, intervened. He used his connections to keep Gerry out of jail, but as a reward Tom had to leave work to drive Gerry to his court-ordered therapy sessions.

Tom consulted with his mother and siblings about what to do with Gerry. When they told him that he would be going to a New England boarding school, Gerry was defiant and said he would run away. Instead, after receiving his diploma from a night school, Gerry was sent to Boca Raton, Florida, where his family owned a condominium and he enrolled in the local college. But he bombed again. He became a heavy drinker and got arrested for drunk driving. Once more Tom played the fixer, hiring former law school buddy Jack O'Donnell to handle the case.

But proving that blood was thicker than water, Louis and Joe brought Gerry back to Wilmington and put him on the payroll. They tried him at all sorts of jobs, even drafting plans for their building projects. But nothing worked. Gerry would show up late or not at all. He'd scream at customers and sub-contractors. And after a few years of putting up with his intolerable behavior, Louis and Joe told Gerry he was on his own.

Gerry didn't seem to mind—and didn't have to. The trust fund and his mother's sympathies allowed him a carefree life, and he acted the spoiled rich kid that he was. He spent the monthly stipend his father had left him on cars, boats, hunting trips, women, drugs, and booze. And while his problems were never chronicled in the press, to his family Gerry was a source of embarrassment.

But Gerry only seemed to be the most innocuous of the Capano troublemakers. In 1989, even as the family's construction and development business fortunes were growing—sons Joe and Louis, Jr. had transformed their dad's prosperous yet midsize company into a real estate empire—Louis was in legal hot water again. This time he had become embroiled in a political corruption scandal and admitted to the FBI that he had given illegal campaign contributions to New Castle County councilman Ron Aiello—$10,000 in 1987 and another $9,900 in 1988—in exchange for a favorable rezoning vote.

Marguerite Capano, the family matriarch, begged Tommy to help. And the eldest son once again came to the rescue, agreeing to drop his law practice and budding political career and join the family business. But only for a year, he told his mother. It was Tom who got federal authorities to drop the charges in exchange for Louis's help in getting Aiello.

But the problems didn't end there. In 1991 police charged Joe Capano, age thirty-nine, the middle son who ran the family's home-building business, with kidnapping and repeatedly raping a twenty-seven-year-old woman in his home on Halloween night. Tom, who had resumed his legal and political career and had become an adviser to the governor, was immediately called.

Joe claimed he had been having an affair with the woman, a former baby-sitter for his kids, and denied the rape charge. Tom helped convince the woman to ask the police to drop the charges and helped get Attorney General Charles Oberly to let Joe plead guilty to misdemeanor charges of assault, unlawful sexual contact, and criminal mischief. Joe was also spared jail time.

The sweetheart deal, everyone assumed, was orchestrated by Tom. He seemed to be a master at keeping everyone happy while getting his way.

———

As he came from such a notorious family, it was no wonder that Tom Capano was considered "the good Capano."

But Tom had his own Achilles' heel—a friend would later describe him as a "serial adulterer." As this was considered a victimless activity by those who knew about it—and kept it to themselves—Capano was able to contain his bimbo eruptions by being discreet or, as he had been with Linda Marandola, ruthless.

———

By 1983 Debby Williams had became such a dependable sex partner that she and Tom Capano had moved beyond the secret sessions at fleabag motels and risked having sexual romps in their own homes, almost under the noses of their spouses. Debby had fallen deeply in love with Capano. She considered Tom her soul mate. He listened to her more than any other man, even her own husband. She could share everything with Tom. Her husband, meanwhile, knew the marriage was in tatters and filed for divorce. Debby didn't contest it. In fact, Debby, who quickly retook her maiden name, bought a $255,000 three-story farmhouse at the edge of Rockford Park, just four blocks from Tom and his growing family, and began begging Tom to leave Kay. He refused.

Debby took a part-time job at her alma mater, the Tatnall School, an expensive private institution in the rolling hills of Greenville, where she eventually became head of extended care, running before- and after- school programs and summer camp. Her own children, good-looking, bright-eyed kids named Abigail and Michael, became friendly with the Capano girls. Debby remained close to Kay, who still had no clue what was going on behind her back.

To people who knew her, Debby seemed an athletic divorcée who dated a little and was content with her life. She kept her blond hair, once long and flowing, in a boyish cut and looked like a high school gym teacher. And when she and Capano found time together, they indulged their mutual athleticism with sex. They watched pornographic films together and engaged in sexual voyeurism as well as group sex.

Once, when a former high school boyfriend who lived in Boston was visiting Wilmington for a Tatnall reunion, Debby alerted Tom that she planned to have sex with the man. Instead of reacting jealously, Capano asked if he could watch the lovemaking. That night, after getting a call from Debby, Capano drove to her house, hid in the bushes outside her living room window, and watched her and the man have sex. After the man left, Tom went inside and also had sex with his mistress.

On another occasion, while he was counselor to the governor, Capano invited his deputy, Keith Brady, over to Debby's house after a morning golf outing. The three shared a few drinks, then turned on a pornographic video. Tom and Debby retired to the bedroom, inviting Brady to follow.

Capano seemed to have a good thing going, especially with a mistress who allowed him to call the shots. Unlike the younger women he pursued, Debby didn't need to be wined and dined for sex. She hoped for a life together, but Capano treated her as a plaything—and worse. One night in the late 1980s, she and Capano had a spat and he stormed out of her bedroom. "I blew it off, took his car keys," recalled Debby, who said Capano did not take it as a joke. "He grabbed me and pushed my head on the bed and pushed hard on the other side of my head with his hand. Frightened, I escaped, apologized, and gave up the keys."

Capano decided not to leave, and the two were soon making love. In bed, Debby would later say, "Tom was never rough. He was very gentle and loving."

Bob Weir saw his teammate go down, with the ball, at the edge of the scrum. But he couldn't believe his eyes when he saw Tom Capano step in and kick the downed player repeatedly. Rugby was a rough game, but this was an alumni match for the Wilmington Rugby Club, an annual event in which older players, in their thirties and forties, played a casual, semicompetitive match with the current crop of muscled hard-chargers.

Tom Capano was one of the old-timers—all the more reason that Weir, captain of the team, was shocked to see him pummeling the player on the ground. The muscular, blondhaired Weir acted quickly, grabbing the lighter Capano and slamming him to the turf.

After the game, when the teams gathered for beers and sandwiches at Oscar's, a downtown watering hole, Weir was sitting at the bar when Capano, with his arm in a sling, approached.

"You must think you're a real motherfucker, eh?" Capano sniffed, and stomped off.

Anne Marie Fahey, in love with the successful and seemingly sensitive lawyer, was not so submissive—or stable—as Debby MacIntyre. And by the beginning of 1995 Annie was fielding some nasty emotional curves from many directions.

In January, her beloved therapist, Bob Conner, was killed in a car accident. Annie had been scheduled for a session that evening, January 24, but Conner had called her shortly before she left her office, asking to postpone their meeting because he had a patient in crisis.

Driving home that night, after staying at a bar well past closing time, a drunk driver plowed into Conner's car.

The phone call from Conner's secretary at 7:45 the next morning, Annie would write in her diary, "was one of the most lonely, difficult times in my life! I loved Bob, and he has helped me grow so much." She also felt partly responsible. If she had insisted on keeping her appointment, perhaps Bob would have made it home safely that night.

Now what? "We had a lot more to do until I got to where I need to be at this point in my life," she lamented. "He was the only person who knew everything (even a little bit about Tommy) about me, and it felt great to get all this shit inside of me—out."

As another therapist would remark, Conner's death was a "tremendous loss" for Annie.

"Bob was funny, intelligent, had a great voice and sense of humor. He believed in me, and actually liked me for me. Not many people know the real Annie. Bob was, and probably will be, the only person who really knew me and understood my insecurities. I love you, Bob, thanks," Annie wrote.

The tragedy of Conner's sudden death was soon exacerbated by Tom Capano.

It was several weeks after Conner died, a Saturday afternoon, when Capano called Annie to say he was having a birthday party for Bud Freel, his former rugby buddy and political ally, at Al and Peg Carter's house. After the party broke up, the gang was heading to O'Friel's.

Annie took it as an invitation. And that night, close to midnight, she took her girlfriends Jill Morrison and Jackie Binnersley, now Steinhoff marriage, to the pub for drinks. As soon as Annie entered the place, she saw Tom. He was at the bar—and with his wife—and glared at her, as if furious that she had come. Annie stayed away. But watching him and his wife hold court with their friends still cut deep.

"I was sad and very sick in my stomach," she wrote in her diary two days later. Annie had gone back to her diary, the friend she had all but abandoned after writing page after page of happy accounts of her journeys through Ireland with her brother Brian the previous August. "Where to begin?" she now wrote, seven months later. She poured out her feelings about Bob Conner, the only one who knew everything about her, and about Tom Capano, her secret love. "I am madly in love with him and did not truly realize just how deeply I felt until that night when I could not be near him, and I then realized the fact that he is not and never will be mine!"

She was so bummed by Capano's reaction to her at the bar that "Sunday, the day after, I thought about Tomas every minute of the day. I had a feeling that he did not want me at the bar so I stayed clear across the room from him. I am sorry, Tomas, I never wanted to hurt you or make you feel uncomfortable."

But that was just the beginning. The following Monday she waited all day to hear from him. Finally, at five o'clock, she called him. "He was cold and seemed very disinterested in talking with me," Annie had recalled.

"What's up?" Annie had asked.

"Nothing, Ana Maria," he said, using one of his favorite terms of endearment. "My life sucks."

"Are you mad at me?" Annie asked.

"No. Just that everything in my life is wrong and sucks," he said, sounding eager to get off the phone. "I had a very busy week." He hung up.

This was a new Tom. And on Tuesday Annie called his office and left a message. He didn't call back. "What the fuck is going on?" Annie asked her diary. "Why won't he talk to me? What did I do? God, please tell me what the fuck is going on!!! I spent Tuesday night lying on my couch and falling asleep. By 9:00 I woke up only to take 2 laxatives and climb into my bed. Tomas, please talk to me! I love you."

She woke up the next morning feeling sad and depressed. "I need to talk to Tommy," she cried. "If it's over between us, I need to have some closure. Tomas, why won't you talk to me? Jesus, how and why did I allow myself to fall in love w/ a married man??? I know exactly why: Tomas is kind, caring, responsive, loving, has a beautiful heart, extremely handsome, and was kind and gentle to me. If he loves me like he used to say (which I still believe he does) then why is he treating me like this??? God, please help me!"

She got an answer, of sorts.

"He called and was nasty," she recounted. "It was the first time that T. raised his voice at me."

"What is it?" Annie pleaded. "You are furious with me. Why? Why aren't you talking to me?"

"Drop it, Annie," he sneered. "And quit fucking talking like this in the office. We'll talk later."

"Will I ever hear from you again?" she asked.

"Do you want to?"

"Of course!"

"All right!" he barked. "I will call later." Capano hesitated, then asked, "How would you like to spend your last day on earth?"

Annie, anxious to do anything to keep Tom on the phone, answered forthrightly, "Play hooky from work, make marinara sauce together, make love while it was cooking, drink red wine, eat bread, and watch all the movies we have talked about watching together."

"I don't believe any of it!" Capano barked and hung up.

Annie cried and cried. "I am losing T.," she moaned, "and I do not know why." She racked her brain trying to think of something that would explain this sudden turn by her lover. "Did somebody say something to him?" she wrote. "What has he heard? I wish I knew because I also would like you to know you are breaking my heart, T. Please communicate with me what the fuck is going on in your mind!"

It was possible that Capano didn't know what was going on in his mind, that he was simply experiencing the same intense emotional upheaval that had sent him reeling madly after Linda Marandola, out of control, as his friend Riley had seen, caught up in an unyielding all-consuming indignation.

Why had he asked Annie about her last day on earth?

"I often fantasize about T. and me, and how I would love to spend the remaining years of my life with him," Annie wrote, herself blind to the malevolent meaning of his passion. "There is so much I want to do with him. Wake up in his arms in my bed, lay next to him and read books together, travel with him. Will any of this ever happen? I am madly in love with T.!"

There was a voice that told Annie to be careful. "There were so many things I wanted to say to him," she confided to her diary on Thursday, "but I was afraid that he would fly off the handle again, like he did on Wednesday." More tears. "I wanted to tell him that he was breaking my heart and ask him to please STOP!"

But Annie saw Capano's behavior as a reflection of her own. She went home and cried herself to sleep.

The next day, Friday, February 24, Capano walked into the governor's offices and said hello. "Your high beams are on," he added, indicating that her nipples were showing through her blouse, then walked into the governor's office.

"Again, I wanted to ask him to please, please, please talk to me, but I felt I would be nagging, bothering, annoying him so I left it alone." Annie saw Capano as if in a mirror. "Again, feeling like total shit, and sacrificing my feelings in order not to hurt someone else. I love you, T. Please do not leave me hanging like this! God, I love you, sweetheart, please stop breaking my heart!"

But in the absence of Tom talking to her, of Bob Conner listening to her, Annie cried on her diary's shoulder:

> I have shared my soul with T. I gave him my whole world, body and love. What I have not shared with T. is my fear of abandonment. I will withhold thoughts, info., etc. about myself if I think that it may steer one away from me. If I ever have the opportunity to speak to T. again—I will share everything (even my soul) and let him know exactly the way I feel. If I'm rejected—at least I know that I told him about me, and let him into my world.
>
> I love you, T.

This was a major step forward for Annie, resolving to tell him everything and take the consequences. But she wasn't prepared for his next mood swing. He called her Saturday afternoon, sounding depressed, instead of angry and mean.

"His voice was sad, like suicidal," Annie noted, and she lost her nerve, didn't tell him everything. Instead, she told her diary. "T., talk to me, please."

She thought about Capano "every minute" that weekend. She had a dream that she and Tom took "Alex and her friends to the movies. Will that dream ever come true?" Annie asked forlornly. "I think not. I hope yes."

She even prayed for Tom that Sunday, went to church and asked God to "provide T. the strength that he needs."

Annie called in sick on Monday. "I said I was sick," she rebuked herself. "What a liar! I was sad." She dragged herself to work at 2:00 that afternoon and was rewarded with a phone call from Capano at 5:30.

"Hello, Tom," she said.

"I needed to call you," he said.

Annie was bursting with joy. But her lover only confused her.

"I feel very strongly about you, Annie," he said, "and feel jealous when other men say something about you." He asked her to think about her future.

"Future? My future is with you, Tommy!" she wanted to shout but didn't. *I can't think of my life without him,* she thought, but she didn't say so. She cried; then she said, "Tommy, you have to go. Your child has a basketball game. We'll talk later."

She hung up and drove home. And, like some hallucination, as she pulled up in front of the old brick-and-clapboard house, she saw his Jeep. He was waiting. "We were talking and kissing and crying," she recounted, giddy like a schoolgirl.

"Tommy, please don't leave me," she sobbed. She begged him to stay and make love. She told him, finally, that she fantasized about spending the rest of her life with him.

"Ana Maria, no," he said sternly. "I need to go."

Capano left and Annie fell to her bed, sobbing for what seemed like hours. Nevertheless, she felt some pride in having confessed her fantasy. And she thought of Bob Conner's constant admonition: "There are no thought crimes!"

The next day, buoyed by the brief embraces she and Tom had shared the day before, Annie told her diary that she would try to make the relationship work:

> I am not letting go. Love is so infrequent (true love) and I am not giving up. I love to make him smile, laugh, hug him, make love, etc.
>
> He deserves happiness—he does not deserve to be miserable. I'll wait 4-ever. He's a wonderful, kind, caring, generous, sensitive man who deserves to be showered with the same kind of generosity he gives. I want to be that person!

Two days later, the couple ran into each other in the morning as Annie was leaving the Hotel du Pont with coffee. They walked together to her office building but couldn't talk.

She called him from her office, but he didn't call back.

Annie would not write another word in her diary for thirteen months.

Perhaps worried that Annie might be talking about him behind his back, sharing stories of his bizarre behavior, Capano sought out her friends. He took them to dinner and did them favors. He helped Jackie Steinhoff set up her business, filing incorporation papers for her new Java Jack's Cafe, a gourmet coffee and sandwich shop in downtown Wilmington. He didn't send her a bill, and when she opened Capano made it a point to be her first customer. He also arranged for much of Saul Ewing's catering to be provided by Java Jack's.

Capano knew that Annie's friend Jill Morrison had a dispute with her landlord and offered his assistance. Capano made some calls and drafted some letters that helped her straighten out the mess. Once again, he did the work for free.

Even Kathleen Hosey, Annie's sister, was surprised that spring, after giving birth to her son Brendan, by a hand-delivered basket of fruit. The note said it was from Tom Capano. She knew who Capano was, worked with him at various political events, and had seen him at the closing of Bud Freel's tavern in March, when she was seven months pregnant. But he hadn't sent her anything two years earlier, when Kevin was born. What was going on now? *Gee, that's strange,* Kathleen mused, *but thoughtful.*

She considered that it might have something to do with Annie, who she knew saw Capano at the governor's office. And even when Bud Freel told Kathleen about the rumors of an affair between Annie and Capano, she laughed, dismissing them as idle gossip in a nosy town. "They're just friends," she told her ex-boyfriend.

Her brother Brian had sensed that something might be up with Annie and Capano when he asked his sister out to lunch one day that same spring.

"Sorry, I can't do it today," Annie said. "I'm having lunch with Tom Capano."

"What's on his mind?" her brother asked, curious about why the governor's appointments secretary would need to have lunch with one of the state's most influential attorneys.

"Nothing. We're just friends," she said.

"Well, be careful," said Brian.

"Why?"

"Because these things sometimes start out as being friends and end up as other things."

"Don't worry. We're just friends."

As if he were paving the road back to Annie through her friends and relatives, Capano slowly reconciled with his young paramour. But there now seemed to be a price—and it stumped Annie.

The gifts that he now gave her had a different meaning. Presents of clothes became demands about how to dress. When Annie wore a red skirt, he accused her of looking like "a whore." Dinners, once romantic, were now clouded with orders about what to eat. It was a subtle but smothering takeover. And by the time Annie realized what was happening, Tom Capano possessed her.

Capano also tried to lure her away from the governor's office with the promise of a cushy job with his brother Louis, as his personal assistant. She'd get a free apartment out of the deal, Tom said.

But Annie balked.

"I think he's trying to control me," she told a friend. "Why does he want to control me like that?"

Capano offered to pay off several thousand dollars that Annie owed on her credit cards. But she gathered her strength and refused that offer as well.

They continued to have sex, but Annie was now realizing, by virtue of his controlled intimacy, that Tom would never give up his wife, that he and Annie would not be the couple she had fantasized about, that she would never have him—but that he still wanted to have her, superficially, sexually, and silently. And slowly, she rebelled.

Capano, increasingly insecure because of Annie's rejection of the job offer and the financial help, began exhibiting a more biting jealousy. When he found out she was making plans to rent a summerhouse at the shore with friends—and that the fellow tenants included men—Capano hit the roof. He told her not to go.

Annie put up her money anyway, taking yet another stand against Capano. But she only made it to the house for a few weekends, as her covetous lover found ways to disrupt her life. On one Saturday, Annie stood up Kim Horstmann and another woman, who were waiting for her to drive to the shore house. When Annie finally called, several hours after the appointment had passed, she told Kim it was Capano.

"He just left," Annie explained. "We had a huge fight because he didn't want me to go to the shore." Annie said he showed up, unexpectedly, bringing wine, shrimp, salmon, and gifts for the apartment. Knowing his intent was to keep her from going to the shore, Annie had balked. "We got into an argument," she told Kim. "I'm sorry, but now I'm drained from the fight and just too exhausted to go."

Capano, so sure of his hold over Annie just a few months earlier, now recognized that he was losing her. And as the summer of 1995 progressed, he began talking of leaving his wife so he and Annie could be together.

"I can give you anything you want," he told Annie. "You won't have to worry about money anymore."

Annie, still confused by the moral dilemma of an illicit affair, now found herself, despite all the earlier fantasies, telling Capano she didn't want to be responsible for his leaving Kay.

"If you're going to do it," Annie told him, "I don't want it to have anything to do with me."

Late that August Capano summoned his wife and the four girls to a midweek dinner, an unusual event, especially in the summer. He had told them that he had a special announcement. And he did.

"I've been very unhappy for a long time," he began, looking at his wife of twenty-three years. "I'm going to move out of the house for a while."

"What's wrong?" his wife and girls inquired, stupefied. They hadn't seen it coming. They knew he was moody but couldn't imagine something could be bothering him that much.

"It's nothing against you guys," he insisted.

"Was there another woman?" Kay asked.

"Nobody else is involved," he lied.

A few days later, Capano packed up his clothes and went to stay in his brother Louis's stone mansion, situated on a thirty-two-acre former du Pont family estate. Capano also began scouting around the Highlands for his own house. Eventually, he settled on a $2,000-a-month three-story brick colonial at 2302 Grant Avenue, recently renovated, located on a sizable lot in a secluded, treed enclave of hills and culs-de-sac that sloped to lush woods and the Brandywine. Plenty of room to entertain and big enough for each of his girls to have a bedroom for their weekend visits.

Gerry helped Tom move in. Brian Murphy, his political and rugby pal, and Keith Brady, his fellow attorney, helped him lay a new beige rug, nearly wall-to-wall, in the upstairs den, where Capano would be doing most of his entertaining.

And now, free of his family after twenty-three years of marriage, Capano began pursuing Annie as a permanent partner.

———————

The first thing he did was convince Annie to spend a few days with him at the Homestead, a luxury resort in the Allegheny Mountains of Virginia. It would be a chance, he explained, to see how they got along away from home.

Annie took golf lessons from the pro at the Homestead. She and Capano went horseback riding, received massages, read books, and ate exquisite meals.

Though Capano later called the getaway a wonderful, relaxing, loving weekend, Annie described the few days to Kim as horrible. "We fought the whole time," she told her confidante.

To kill time on the five-hour drive home, they compiled a list of their likes and dislikes. As Capano drove, Annie jotted down the categories and their choices. They dubbed the inventory the Coke-Pepsi list. Capano was Coke. Fahey was Pepsi.

The inventory laid bare stark differences, perhaps revealing to both of them that they actually had little in common. One might even call them polar opposites.

The list:

Coke	Pepsi
food	anorexic
Mex food	Loves Mex
Red M.	No meat
N. Sleeps	Sleeps
Analytical	Non-analytical
History	Hates history
B(and)wagon sports fan	Sports fan
Non-stubborn	Stubborn
Italian	Me
No beach	Beach
Cars (no)	Piston head
Conservative	liberal
$ (?)	$ conscience
baby boomer	Gen X
Impatient driver	More patient
Non-smart	Smart-ass
dislikes old p.	old people
judgmental	non-j
n-snob	snob
academic	Non-academic
Observant	Spacey
Double stand	N-2 stand
Night owl	Morning
Home body	Travel
Control freak	??
Smoker	hates cigs
dumper	non
serious	goofy
room temp.	cold
Pr. Ed.	Public Ed
Married w/kids	Non-M
Sane	Clinically dep
W. known	Not well known
Bud Freel	Non-buddy

Perhaps seeking some solace in the relationship, underneath the Coke-Pepsi list Annie wrote down things they had in common.

Likes

Bread
Sinatra, music, etc.
NPRNews
Politics
Pasta, Itl. food
Generous
Movies
Read
Rest, Finer things
Kids
Wines
People
Body ornamentation
(No) Camping

It wasn't much to go on. Or was it?

―――――――――

What was most significant about the list was what Tom
Capano left off: his dishonesty. Returning from the Homestead, professing his love, Capano was also thinking about
Debby MacIntyre. He had told his longtime lover, whom Annie still didn't know about, that they could now get married.
He would just need some time to quash suspicions that he was
leaving his wife for another woman; then they could finally
come out as a couple.

And somehow Capano also managed a liaison with a fun-
loving, sexy blond secretary from his law firm. Though the
relationship was casual, Susan Louth took a liking to Capano
and loved being taken to fancy restaurants or just lying around
watching movies. Films with mobster themes were his favorite, Louth noted, especially *GoodFellas* and the *Godfather* tril-
ogy.

―――――――――

That June, Governor Carper sent a routine business letter to
Michael Scanlan, an executive at the MBNA bank, one of the
huge financial institutions with headquarters in Wilmington.
At the end of the letter, the governor put in a personal note

to Scanlan, whom he had come to know as a smart humanitarian and savvy banker—and single. "Someone you should call," the governor wrote on the letter, and scribbled Annie Fahey's name and number in the margin. Bemused, Michael Scanlan stared at the name. It didn't ring a bell. He had never met her during his frequent visits to Carper's office.

In fact, Scanlan, thirty-one, was just two years older than Annie and wasn't seeing anybody at the time. But as community affairs director of his bank (responsible for the institution's charitable donations), he was traveling extensively that summer, throughout the country and overseas, and wasn't able to act on the governor's suggestion. Back in town for a night in August, Scanlan was sitting in O'Friel's Irish Pub sipping a beer with Bill McLaughlin, Wilmington's white-haired former mayor, and a few other men when he asked if any of them knew an Anne Marie Fahey.

McLaughlin, a Democratic ally of Carper, laughed. He then told the story of how he had introduced Fahey's parents nearly fifty years earlier.

"She's quite a gal," McLaughlin assured the young banker.

A few nights later, Scanlan picked up the phone and dialed Annie's number. She agreed to meet him at O'Friel's that Friday, September 15, for happy hour. Knowing it would be crowded in the pub, they described themselves over the phone.

The date wasn't romantic by any means; as nine-to-fivers slugged down beers at the noisy bar, Annie and Mike, who each had brought along a friend, had drinks in the dining area, still having to almost shout to hear one another. A few hours later, they went their separate ways.

Annie told her brother Brian the date had been a flop, no sparks between her and Scanlan. "The guy basically brushed me off," she complained.

Scanlan, however, had a different opinion, telling his friends that the slim, tall brunette from the governor's office was beautiful, smart, and fun.

And the following week, Scanlan asked Annie out again— and the week after that and after that.

By the end of October, the relationship had blossomed in such a straitlaced, almost sappy way that Annie was actually excited about Scanlan's invitation to see the pope celebrate mass at Camden Yards in Baltimore. Scanlan, a Georgetown graduate, was a practicing Catholic, and Annie, Irish to her roots, was a Catholic despite herself. Even more amazing for Annie was that Scanlan shared her love for music, especially jazz and rhythm and blues, and, after seeing the pope, took her to a concert by R and B sensation Boyz II Men.

Annie soon found herself fascinated by the earnest, socially conscious young man from Rhode Island who also possessed many of the traits that had attracted her to Capano, including good looks, affluence, and seeming sensitivity. It wasn't long before she was telling her friends and family that Mike Scanlan was "the guy."

———————

The son of an executive for Monet Jewelers, a division of General Mills, Scanlan had grown up in Bristol, Rhode Island, the fifth of seven children, in a devout Roman Catholic family. His mother was the librarian at Portsmouth Abbey, an expensive all-boy Catholic school that Mike had attended.

Scanlan had followed his father to Georgetown University, where he majored in history, receiving average grades, and swam on the Hoyas' swim team, setting the school record in the 100-yard and 200-yard backstroke.

MBNA, the credit card company that grew out of Maryland Bank, recruited Scanlan into its executive training program, but after a few years he left for a nonprofit agency that attempted to rehabilitate teenage criminals, working in Baltimore and later Florida.

"He really stood out as a wonderful kids' advocate and had a genuine love for the work," recalled a woman who worked with him. "He was such an ethical person. He always did the right thing."

But in 1992, MBNA persuaded Scanlan to return as director of community relations. His job was doling out MBNA's grants to nonprofit agencies, monitoring how the money was spent, and overseeing volunteer efforts of MBNA's 14,000 employees. The post, paying well over $100,000 a year, put Scanlan among the top sixty officials in the bank before he had turned thirty.

Scanlan was soon driving a Jeep Grand Cherokee and a red Mercedes convertible and living in a $200,000 brick ranch home in Sharpley, an upper-middle-class neighborhood north of Wilmington, next to the DuPont Country Club, on the edge of the Brandywine Valley and château country. Though the area was favored by older DuPont engineers and chemists, young Scanlan enjoyed the sedate surroundings. And, as Annie pointed out, he was near her childhood home, just across Concord Pike.

Every Sunday Scanlan went to mass at St. Mary Magdalen Church—the same church Annie had attended as a girl. He became a Big Brother, mentoring a young fatherless boy from a rough section of Wilmington. Scanlan also swam a few mornings a week at the downtown YMCA and competed regularly in long-distance ocean and bay swims.

And Scanlan pursued Annie with the relaxed yet purposeful pace of a long-distance swimmer. They spoke or saw each other only a few times a week. They spent evenings talking and listening to music at his house or her apartment, attended a Luther Vandross concert, went to the ballet, saw an opera, and spent Thanksgiving and Christmas together—which meant, since Scanlan was from New England, with the Fahey family. And while the romance was budding, there was no sexual intimacy.

They had talked about sex before marriage. Annie said she thought it was wrong, and Scanlan, who didn't have a lot of experience in the dating scene, assumed she was a virgin. Annie shared some of her troubled past with Mike, who listened with compassion, but she never breathed a word about Capano. She thought it would doom the relationship if she confessed an illicit affair to this religious young man, whom she didn't want to lose.

But as the good-looking young couple went out together more often, they began to be noticed, especially by Tom Capano.

In fact, Capano had been wondering why Annie was often busy when he wanted to get together, but now he knew why. Capano confronted Annie about her new boyfriend. She admitted dating Scanlan but insisted it wasn't serious. Of course, she lied. Her affair with Capano was sputtering—she just didn't know how to stop it.

Since childhood, Annie had learned how to avoid confrontation at all costs. In junior high, her pal Jackie Binnersley used to call Annie's boyfriends to break up for her. Nothing had changed. But her indecision gave Capano what he saw as the opening he needed. He asked, then begged, her to break off the relationship with Scanlan. Capano reminded her that he had left his wife for her. He sent imploring E-mails, called Annie at all hours. Some days, including hang-ups and haranguing messages, he logged as many as twenty-five calls to Annie.

A year after her own pleading entreaties to Capano—"T., talk to me, please"—T. was now begging Annie: "I have to see you. I'm going to kill myself. I swear I can't live without you. Please see me. Please see me."

He proffered new and better gifts, including a brand-new Lexus, her favorite automobile. He said they could live together in a mansion. Annie, rejecting the individual offers as they were made, was giving Tom—and herself—the larger message: she no longer wanted a life with him.

When this type of persuasion failed, Capano resorted to starker appeals. He told Annie he had driven by Scanlan's house one night and seen her Jetta outside. He started parking in front of her apartment, waiting for her to arrive, then would beseech her to get back together with him. Once he climbed up her fire escape and banged on the door until she let him in.

He knew when Annie attended St. Anthony's and began taking his daughters to the same mass, making sure that Annie saw him. When she changed her time, he changed, too. Finally, Capano informed her that he'd told one of the parish priests about the affair and threatened to expose her to others. Humiliated, Annie switched churches.

"He would attack her insecurities and refer to her as white trash," recalled Horstmann, in whom Annie confided. "He said she should be lucky that he's even going out with her because of who he is and what he could buy for her and where she came from."

One day, he coaxed Fahey into taking a ride with him. But once she got in the car, he locked the doors and drove to his Grant Avenue house. Pulling into the garage, he locked the garage door as well. Refusing to let her leave, Capano ranted about all he had done for her and why she should choose him over Scanlan. The shouting seemed to calm him; eventually, he drove Annie home.

As Christmas approached, Capano brought Annie a round-trip ticket to Spain, a country she loved and had been hoping to return to someday. He told her he would make all the arrangements for her hotels.

When she refused, Capano became incensed, grabbed her arm, and pushed her against the wall.

"OK. I'll take back everything I've ever given you!" he yelled.

"Fine! I don't want any of this stuff!" she yelled back.

Capano marched to the twenty-seven-inch color television he had bought her, unplugged the set, and lifted it off its stand to the floor. He then went around the apartment gathering up outfits and other gifts he had given Annie.

"No man is going to watch the TV I gave you or see you in the dresses I gave you!" he screamed. He even marched into the kitchen and removed a bottle of salad dressing from the refrigerator.

The rage that possessed Capano was so intense that Annie had all but frozen in place. She thought about calling 911, but she was too afraid to move.

Capano stormed out of the apartment with the gifts, leaving Annie shaken, only to return them fifteen minutes later.

On another occasion, as Capano was dropping Annie off at her house after an unpleasant date he again locked the doors of his car. Lashing out, he called her a "slut" and a "bitch." Terrified, Annie reached for the door, but Capano grabbed her and pulled her back. He was still yelling when he wrapped his arm around her neck. She screamed. Finally breaking loose, Annie bolted from the car and ran into her apartment, sobbing.

"Sometimes I feel," she told Horstmann, "that I have to move out of state to get away from him."

6 *Eye of the Storm*

Tom Capano's wrath toward Anne Marie Fahey, inexplicably, turned to soft, sobering depression as Christmas of 1995 approached. And one day in December, not long after the blowup over the tickets to Spain, Capano went to Jackie Steinhoff's café and slumped at a table, looking skinny, pale, and morose.

Despite Capano's help getting Java Jack's off the ground, Steinhoff had initially been distrustful of the suave lawyer. And she was extremely uncomfortable with the fact that every time he came into the shop in those early days, he walked to the counter, wrapped his arms around her, and kissed her on the lips. Eventually, she got used to him and came to appreciate the fact that he sent her business, took her and Annie to sumptuous lunches at the Hotel du Pont or the Shipley Grill, and never asked for anything in return.

"This guy is nice," Steinhoff would later say.

So that December afternoon, Steinhoff approached him with genuine concern.

"Is something bothering you, Tommy?" she asked gently.

"I'm not doing well. Actually, I'm doing horribly. It's my first Christmas without my children. I want to kill myself."

Steinhoff tried to cheer him up, to no avail. Finally, he asked if she and Annie would like to go out to dinner some night.

"I'll talk to Annie," Steinhoff said.

Capano also called Siobhan Sullivan, a state trooper on Carper's security detail who he knew was a friend of Annie's. He asked Sullivan, a former Delaware All-State basketball player, if she wouldn't mind working with his daughters on their hoops. Then he changed the subject.

"Have you spoken to Anne Marie today? She's really mad at me."

Sullivan, an attractive woman with short blond hair, knew

Capano had bought Annie tickets to expensive political functions and suspected they were more than friends. But she offered Capano some advice.

"You have to let her be, Tom," said Sullivan.

"You know, I just left my wife and I'm just really lonely now."

Sullivan told Annie about the conversation and was surprised at her friend's response.

"He is a possessive, controlling maniac," said the normally cool and controlled secretary. "I'm just getting tired of him." She then stormed out of her office.

Capano, master of manipulation, managed to turn even his personal problems into opportunities for gain. At a holiday party for Democratic stalwarts that year, friends and acquaintances remarked on Capano's subdued demeanor. Usually one to waltz through a crowd of politicos like a conquering hero, on this night Capano stood alone, seemingly uninterested in talking.

A woman whose husband was friendly with Capano noticed him standing alone in the foyer and asked other guests what was wrong. "He split up with his wife," everyone said. "Kay probably found out he was running around," one person added.

Nonetheless, the woman felt empathy for the gloomy man.

"I'm sorry about the breakup," she said, trying to engage him in conversation.

"It's really hard, especially this time of year," Capano replied.

"I understand. It's hard on men because they often don't have the kids."

"That's why I have a big house, so they have enough room and can stay with me overnight."

"That's good."

"God," he said, abruptly shifting topics, "I wouldn't even know how to go on a date. I haven't asked anybody out for so long I wouldn't know what to do or say."

Taken aback by the philanderer's words, the woman nonetheless tried to soothe him.

"Don't worry about it, Tom. Don't worry about it. It's a man's world."

In January, Steinhoff asked Annie to let Capano buy them dinner. Annie initially declined the dinner offer, but Jackie urged her to be nice.

"Come on," Steinhoff exhorted. "He's real depressed; he's losing all this weight; he needs a friend. Let's just go out to dinner."

Annie relented but said she was agreeing only so Capano would leave her alone. She warned her friend not to mention Scanlan to Capano because the two men didn't get along.

Jackie picked Annie up and they drove to Capano's Grant Avenue home, where Jackie presented Capano with a house-warming gift—a pasta maker. They each drank a glass of wine, and Capano, the proud bachelor, showed off his new place.

He then drove the pair to La Famiglia, a ritzy Italian restaurant in Philadelphia. Despite several more glasses of wine, Jackie noted that Annie was unusually quiet. When she excused herself to use the bathroom, Capano turned to Steinhoff.

"Why does she hate me?" he asked.

"What do you mean?" Steinhoff replied, jolted by his use of such a strong word as hate and wondering if he was thinking about Scanlan.

"She hates me," he repeated. "She hates me."

"No, she doesn't," Jackie protested, instinctively trying to promote peace. "She doesn't hate you. Why would she be here if she did?"

The fevered pitch of Capano's pursuits went unnoticed because of his prowess at compartmentalizing his obsessions. Simultaneously grieving for his failed marriage and pursuing Annie, Debby, and Susan Louth—none of whom knew about the others—he now opened yet another front, tracking down his former obsession, and affliction, Linda Marandola.

They had last spoken in 1987, when Capano had called her out of the blue, "acting like we were long-lost friends," Marandola later recalled. By then divorced and thinking, *He de-*

serves a second chance, Marandola agreed to let Capano take her to Atlantic City for her thirty-third birthday. They had checked into a beachfront hotel, where Capano presented her with a birthday gift, a gold watch with both of their initials engraved on the back, then asked if she was dating anybody else. When Marandola said she was, Capano had become indignant, calling her a "slut" and a "whore." He had stormed out of the room and spent the night in the casino.

Now, in January of 1996, nearly nine years later, Marandola answered her phone and heard the still-familiar voice of Tom Capano. "I was just looking through the phone book and saw your number listed," Capano explained.

He asked if she was dating and said he had had a rough time over the holidays because of his recent separation. He asked Marandola out to dinner, but she declined. Over the next few weeks, Capano called Marandola several more times, only to be snubbed. The calls stopped around Valentine's Day.

Not long after their odd threesome dinner in Philadelphia with Capano, Annie confided to Jackie Steinhoff that she and Scanlan were getting serious.

"I'm so happy and excited to be with Michael," she told her old friend, bragging that she was losing weight to make herself more attractive to the slender young executive.

Annie also learned that her sister was planning a surprise birthday party for her—on January 26, the day before she turned thirty—and worried that Capano would arrange to get himself invited. She called Kim Horstmann and asked if he was on the guest list. "I'm scared to death he might be coming," Annie told Kim.

Horstmann called Ginny Columbus, who had prepared the list, and found out Capano was not on it.

The party, at her sister and brother-in-law's house the night before her birthday, was an especially happy event for Annie. Michael Scanlan, who had been in Bolivia on business, flew home early for the party. Surrounded by her siblings, girlfriends, nieces, and nephews, and her special man, Annie basked in her good fortune. Photos taken that night show a beautiful young woman flashing a perpetual smile.

The next night, her actual birthday, she attended Wilmington's Grand Gala with Scanlan. It was the city's premier charity and social event of the year. Held at the Grand Opera House, the black-tie ball drew a virtual Who's Who list of Delaware's elite—bluebloods from the du Pont dynasty, top chemical and bank executives, lawyers, and politicians. And Anne Marie Fahey and her handsome young star. With MBNA one of the ball's chief patrons and Scanlan head of its charities, he was sure to be well known.

Annie thought of the ball as a kind of coming-out party. After nearly two years skulking around in a secret relationship, she felt especially free, legitimate, with Scanlan. She bought a $400 floor-length gown at Morgan's, one of Wilmington's finest women's apparel shops. Black, with a high neck, sequins along the back, and cut away at the shoulders, the dress bathed the slender Fahey with a royal patina. The afternoon of the gala Annie went to Michael Christopher's salon, where Lisa D'Amico did her hair.

Jill Morrison, excited for her friend, stopped by Annie's apartment to help her get ready. But when Jill arrived, she found Annie in tears. "He called," she sobbed. Morrison didn't know who she was talking about. "He's always calling. He's psychotic."

As Jill tried to calm her friend, Annie confessed that she had been seeing Capano all this time, that he had become unstable when she tried to break up the previous fall. She tried to placate Capano by saying she and Scanlan didn't have sex, but, Annie cried, nothing seemed to stop him. Now, she said, Capano was threatening to use his law firm's tickets to the gala, show up with his own date, and make Fahey miserable, perhaps even telling Scanlan about their affair.

"He won't leave me alone," Annie told Morrison. "He's stalking me."

Jill, now alarmed at what she was hearing, continued trying to console her friend. The phone rang and Annie picked it up.

"Hello," she said, then put the receiver down. "He hung up. I know it's him."

The phone rang four more times as Annie finished dressing;

each time the caller hung up without saying a word. Annie
looked out the window, frantic.

"He could be outside, waiting for Mike to pick me up, and
make a scene," Annie said.

But Capano never showed up, at either her house or the
ball. Annie and Mike had a splendid evening. They enjoyed a
gourmet meal and a concert by the Velvet Fog, silver-tongued
singer Mel Tormé, who walked around the floor and chatted
with the well-heeled guests.

Scanlan ran into a few friends, who asked if his new date
was a model.

The couple joined the other partygoers in a procession up
the brick-paved Market Street Mall to the Hotel du Pont,
where classical, jazz, and other music played in five ballrooms
and tuxedoed waiters served desserts, coffee, and fine cham-
pagne.

When those gathered in the Gold Ballroom formed a conga
line that snaked around the dance floor, Annie and Mike joined
in the revelry. "My wife Linda and I were right next to them,"
former mayor Tom Maloney later recalled. "They both looked
so happy and excited."

The next day, Annie told Kathleen the gala had been "the
best night of my life."

The following Monday morning, Annie arrived at her office
early and composed an E-mail for Capano.

"Tom:" she began, formally, as if hoping the colon would
help her compose the Dear John letter she knew she should
write. Instead, she immediately pulled on victims' robes and
took responsibility for Capano's suffering.

"First let me start off by saying that I'm sorry for the pain
I have caused you over the weekend. I am afraid and I do not
where to begin. I spent a good part of yesterday morning/
afternoon at Valley Garden Park thinking about a lot of stuff:
Us, Girls, Eating disorder, my family, etc. I desperately want
to talk to you, but I'm too afraid to place the call."

She didn't explain the fear—or give expression to the reason she wanted to talk to Capano. But it was the voice of

psychic health beginning to whisper to her: she was desperate to tell Capano to leave her alone but was terribly afraid she couldn't pull it off successfully. She didn't want to hurt him.

"I do love you, Tommy," she concluded, "and no matter what happens, I will always love you. Annie."

Capano didn't get the message until the following day, because Saul Ewing's E-mail system was down. But upon receiving Annie's message, he dashed off a fevered reply.

"I desperately want to talk to you, too," he wrote, "and I'll go out of my mind if I don't soon. Please don't be afraid to place the call. I need to hear your voice. I'm leaving now for a meeting and will be back this afternoon. Please call me. Not hearing from you since Saturday afternoon is making me crazy. And you know how much I love you and need you. I'll wait for your call. Te amo."

These two E-mail messages gave proof to the powerlessness of words to express meaning—and to their power to hide the truth. Annie, trying to break up, said: "I love you." Tom, trying to hold on, said: "I love you." Their notes were the proverbial ships passing in the night.

They exchanged several more E-mail messages over the next few days, chatting about work and friends and families, even planning to see each other.

But on Wednesday, February 7, Annie again said, though ambiguously as usual, that the affair was over.

"I know we were supposed to get together the last two weekends, and things have come up," she wrote. "Tommy, I meant what I said on Sunday night about right now only being able to offer you my friendship, and if you cannot deal with that then I understand. I'm still very much confused, and I am trying to work out a lot of personal things on my own. Annie."

Two hours later, Capano responded, asking her to dinner the next weekend while expressing mixed feelings about the current status of their relationship and concern about her weight loss:

I understand that you're confused and want to limit our relationship now to friendship. I love you enough to accept that and ask only that we treat each other kindly and hon-

estly. I don't want to lose you. I also think we shouldn't
lose the closeness we've developed . . . You cannot do all
of this [battle an eating disorder] on your own, Annie—no
one can. Let me help. Please call me when it's convenient
or send me an E-mail. I'd like to know about Saturday. You
look like you could use a good meal! And you have to admit
I've always fed you well. Te amo.

As Annie tried to break free from Capano and solidify
her bond with Scanlan, she was sharing details of her struggle
with Gary Johnson, a Wilmington therapist.

Her brother Brian, who taught Johnson's children at Friends
School, had referred her to the psychologist in July of 1995.
After canceling several appointments, Annie finally began seeing Johnson that fall. And she immediately confessed her
problem of trying to extricate herself from a relationship with
a "prominent" man in Wilmington. The former lover, she said,
was a possessive man who tried to dominate her and couldn't
get the message that they were through. He'd appear out of
nowhere at places or events, apparently having waited for her.

Annie was aware that Johnson lived two blocks from Tom
and Kay Capano in the Highlands—and didn't dare reveal his
identity. "You might know him," she told the therapist.

Near the end of 1995 she had told Johnson the man's behavior was starting to frighten her. Without mentioning his
name, she told Johnson about the night Capano had angrily
taken the television and other gifts. "She was quite terrified,"
Johnson later recalled.

Then on January 30—three days after the Grand Gala—she
told Johnson, "I haven't been telling you the full story."

Most of the secret spilled out. "The guy I've been telling
you about is married and he has children," she revealed,
though still not telling Johnson who the man was. "And I'm
so ashamed." She also told Johnson she lived in terror that she
would ruin her chances with Scanlan, the first healthy relationship of her life, by exposing the illicit affair. She told him
how the man had threatened to blow her cover and she now
knew that he was desperate.

Johnson counseled her on ways to assert herself and cut the

ties. But at the same time, he became just as concerned by her weight loss and avoidance of food. Although Annie wasn't bone-thin or emaciated, she was taking up to fifteen laxatives a night.

It was clear to the psychologist that Annie suffered from some form of anorexia nervosa and bulimia and was in danger of getting worse. He suggested a few specialists in eating disorders, and Annie chose Michele Sullivan, who also had expertise in treating adult children of alcoholics.

On the same day that Tom Capano wrote Annie that: "You can tell me your fears and hopes and rely on me to support you," he went to his younger brother Gerry with an odd request.

"I need to borrow $8,000," Tom said. "A man and a woman are extorting money from me, threatening the kids. They say they're going to ruin my career. The girl is crazy."

Gerry, startled by his brother's words, asked why anybody would want to blackmail him.

Tom wouldn't tell him.

"How much money are they after?"

"A lot. I've been paying them for a while."

"Why don't you call the police?"

"I don't need to, and I don't want to."

Gerry realized Tom had told all he was willing to reveal. So, as a dutiful brother, Gerry agreed to get Tom the cash. That was the Capano way. When one of the fold needed help, the others did whatever they could. They had their battles, but when push came to shove, they circled the wagons. *Besides,* Gerry thought, *Tom must really be having some kind of problem.*

The next day, Gerry wrote a check for $8,300—might as well get some spending money for himself—cashed it at Wilmington Trust, his bank, and took $8,000 in big bills to his older brother.

On February 9, Tom repaid Gerry with a check for $8,000 and swore him to silence. "If anybody ever asks you what the check was for," Tom told his little brother, "tell him it was for landscaping you did at my house."

That Friday and Saturday, while Annie wasn't home, Capano kept trying to arrange the dinner date, leaving a dozen messages on her answering service.

She didn't call him back, but on Monday, February 12, at 7:34 A.M., she E-mailed him from Carper's office. After some chitchat, she got to the point.

"Anyway, enough of that BS. Tommy, you scared me this weekend. Starting with Friday, and all the calls you placed. It really freaks me out when you call every half hour. I truly understand how fragile you are these days, and I feel the same way. But, when you keep calling that way, it makes me turn the other way, and quite frankly shut down."

Though Scanlan had contributed to Annie's break with Capano—and was ostensibly the immediate cause of the lawyer's wrath—he had also given Annie the strength to confront, if only by E-mail, her former lover. Her emotional health was returning, along with instincts appropriate to it. But it was a hard job—and she slipped up, kept trying to ameliorate Capano's obsessions by taking responsibility for them. She didn't realize she was fanning the flames.

"I'm sorry that I am nothing but a constant disappointment to you these days," she continued. "It is not fair to you. I have an idea of what I need to do, I just cannot bring myself to start the process. I apologize for being such a horrible person to you. You are the last person on this earth I want to hurt."

On Valentine's Day, just forty-eight hours later, a dozen long-stemmed roses arrived at the governor's offices. Ginny Columbus, at the receptionist's desk when they arrived, buzzed Fahey that there was a package for her. Annie emerged, saw that Scanlan had sent them, and beamed. She put the roses in a vase and displayed the blooms on her desk.

The next afternoon, another dozen long-stemmed roses arrived. Annie read the accompanying note, from Tom Capano.

"He's interested in a romantic relationship and I've told him no," Annie told Ginny.

Ginny walked past Annie's desk later that day and noticed that the new bouquet had been thrown in the trash can.

A few weeks later, while visiting Gerry's, Tom asked for another favor.

"Look," Tom said. "I need a gun for protection. I'm afraid this guy is going to break into my house and hurt me if I don't keep paying him money."

"Why don't you call the police?" Gerry suggested for the second time.

Again Tom dismissed his brother's advice.

Gerry reluctantly agreed to show him a gun and led Tom upstairs to his spare bedroom, where a gray steel safe held nearly two dozen pistols, rifles, and shotguns he had collected and used for hunting.

Tom asked for a handgun.

But Gerry opened the safe and told Tom a shotgun would suit his purposes best.

While his older brother might be a hotshot lawyer and leader of the family, Gerry knew he didn't know anything about firearms. Their father had collected antique guns, but Tom had never shown the slightest interest in weaponry.

"Shotguns are better for home protection," Gerry insisted, trying to persuade his brother to take one. "If you don't know how to use a handgun, somebody can take it from you."

But Tom persisted, and his little brother eventually knuckled under, retrieving a shiny nickel-plated pistol from his collection. A 10mm Colt revolver.

"All you have to do," said Gerry, holding the gun out, "is shove the clip in."

He handed Tom the pistol and its ammunition clip and showed him how to put the clip in the gun and operate the safety latch.

Tom asked Gerry if he knew anybody who could break somebody's legs. Gerry said he might and would get back to him, hoping Tom would come to his senses.

The brothers had several discussions about the extortionists. And during one, Gerry recalled, Tom made another request.

"If this guy or girl hurts my kids and I kill them, can I use the boat?"

Gerry was thunderstruck. "Absolutely not," he said. Tom was asking if he could use his twenty-five-foot Hydra Sport to dispose of bodies. The request went beyond the pale of anything Gerry had ever been involved in—and these kinds of conversations with Tom were brand-new. Sure, Gerry snorted cocaine and drank and got in fights, but now Tom was acting like they were a Mafia family and Gerry was one of his henchmen. But then Gerry figured Tom was overwhelmed by stress and fear for his children and just blowing off steam.

Gerry never followed up on the leg-breaking request—and Tom never brought up the topic again. And in April, Tom returned the Colt to Gerry.

"He had never fired it," Gerry recalled. "It was in the exact condition that I gave it to him."

Perhaps the extortionists had given up.

Anne Marie Fahey, the patient, and Michele Sullivan, the therapist, connected so well during their first visit, on February 28, that Annie could tell Sullivan about her secret affair with the married man on that visit. Annie also told the petite, wiry woman with a comforting voice about her impoverished childhood, her father's drinking, and the anxiety it caused her as an adult. She felt unattractive, unworthy of a healthy life.

Annie also detailed her eating habits, saying she'd try to get through each day with only a bagel or a pretzel. And she discussed her budding relationship with "Michael from MBNA" and her attempts to break off with the forty-six-year-old married man with four kids who was separated from his wife.

Sullivan's notes for that session indicated that Annie told her the man was "incredibly controlling, possessive," but that there had been "no violence." She noted that he manipulated Annie with gifts and she was unable to be firm about calling it quits.

Sullivan ended her notes about that session with the words "very ashamed," drawing three lines under the word "very."

After that first visit Sullivan thought her new patient's anorexia, while not severe, was troubling and potentially dangerous. Annie's disease, Sullivan believed, probably stemmed from her deep-seated fear of not being in control and her inferior self-image. Limiting food intake to two or three hundred calories a day, the therapist knew, was a way of exerting control—and a method of punishing oneself for perceived faults.

Helping Annie improve her self-esteem and learn how to assert herself in relationships—in essence controlling the real source of her anxiety—could be the key to freeing her from anorexia, Sullivan concluded.

On Annie's next visit, March 8, she revealed that the man's name was "Tom" and disclosed that she was afraid of anyone knowing about her affair with him—even though she was trying to end it. Sullivan noted that Annie had "difficulty hanging on to her own reality" and was "easily intimidated." She didn't believe Annie suffered from delusions, but rather was malleable and susceptible to somebody who might try to convince her that some fact she was certain about was wrong.

"Acknowledge yourself as a child of God," Sullivan encouraged her patient, who she knew was a churchgoing Catholic. "Ask for God's forgiveness for things you feel ashamed about." The therapist also referred Annie to a dietitian so she could resume normal eating habits.

Annie next mentioned "Tom" on April 3 and this time uttered his last name. She said his unending calls and E-mails, which she called "his haunting," were her punishment by God for the affair. Sullivan urged Annie to cut off communication completely, but Annie said no, she couldn't. Tom had been good to her, almost like a father, and she simply wanted to transform the relationship into a platonic one.

But Annie was gaining perspective, and three days later, on Easter evening, she sat down with her diary, the first time in over a year that she felt like writing.

Sunday. 4-7-96.

Happy Easter! Well, another year has passed since my last entry and man o' man has a lot happened. I've been through a lot of emotional battles. I finally have brought closure to Tom Capano. What a controlling, manipulative, insecure, jealous maniac. Now that I look back on that aspect of my life I realize just how vulnerable I had become. It hurts me when I think about that year. For one whole year I allowed someone to take control of every decision in my life. Bob Conner's death hurt me / affected me more than anything. I lost my best friend, mentor, the man with the greatest smile. My being after Bob's death became the little girl growing up in a chaotic world. I lost all sense of trust. I thought it would be easier that way.

I have been fortunate enough to find another therapist, Michele Sullivan. No one will ever take the place of Bob, but she's pretty damn close. Five weeks ago, I was diagnosed with bulimia. My weight is currently 125 pounds. Pretty skinny, but I want more. My brother Robert is the only sibling that knows anything. Most likely that will remain the case. At this point, I'm afraid to share this news with Michael. I don't want him to run. I truly love him. I'm afraid of what he might think of me. Michael is the most wonderful person. This is the first "normal" relationship I've ever had and I can't screw it up!

During their April 10 session, Annie revealed something that chilled the therapist.

A friend had suggested Annie could "get kidnapped," she told Sullivan. "What do you think, Michele?"

"What is this about?"

"Well, my friend thinks somebody could kidnap me."

"Talk to me more about what this is about."

"Oh, I don't know. Somebody could just take me away or something."

"Who would do this?"

"Well, probably a third party."

"What do you mean, that someone would hire a third party?"

"Yeah."

"Who would do that?"

"Tom Capano."

Sullivan, now worried about her patient's safety, urged her to report her fears to the attorney general's office or police, if for nothing else at least to have them documented. She also advised Annie to keep a record of Capano's harassment and to write him ordering him to cease contact.

But Annie dropped the subject. During their next session, a

week later, Annie said she had called a friend from the attorney general's office and said a constituent wanted advice on how to protect herself from an intimidating ex-boyfriend—but she couldn't bring herself to report Capano to police or prosecutors, she said. Perhaps more than Capano's harassment, she feared that if he was arrested, someone from the newspaper would find out, and because of Capano's prominence and her job with the governor, the clandestine affair would be exposed.

Annie also wondered if perhaps she had been overreacting to Capano's jealousy. In recent weeks, his mania had subsided, she reported. The phone calls had dwindled to a trickle, and he no longer seemed so desperate.

Perhaps not desperate, but busy. Capano had renewed his fixation on Linda Marandola. He called her, assuring her he wasn't calling for sex or romance, but to offer her a job as his secretary at Saul Ewing. Out of work and desperate for money, Marandola agreed to discuss the job over dinner, which, in typical Capano manner, was a $175 affair at Philadelphia's Ristorante La Veranda.

By the end of the meal Marandola had agreed to interview for the job, and several days later she agreed to take it, starting May 29, the Tuesday after Memorial Day weekend.

During this same period Capano also made an odd request of Debby MacIntyre, with whom he continued an active sex life. Would she buy a handgun for him?

"What? Why?" Debby inquired, shocked by the notion.

"Somebody is trying to extort me," he told her. "I'm not going to shoot it. I just want to use it to threaten this person. Besides, I'll give it back to you and you can use it for self-defense. It would be good for you to have a weapon in the house, crime rates the way they are and a single mother living at home, sometimes alone a lot; it would be good to have one in your home."

"No, Tom, I can't do that," Debby protested.

"I really want you to do this for me," Capano pressed.

"Why don't you just get it yourself?"

"I'd rather not," he said. "And I really want you to do this for me. It's very important. It would mean a lot to me."

Anxious to please the man she still hoped to marry, Debby finally agreed. Capano instructed her to visit the Sports Authority and go to the hunting section, located on the left after entering the store.

He knew exactly where the firearms were located because he had just been there. On April 20, in fact, Capano had gone to the store on Concord Pike and asked where he could find a large cooler. His brother was a deep-sea fisherman, he told the clerk, and he wanted to buy him a nice birthday present. The clerk showed Capano the biggest ice chest the store carried, a 162-quart Igloo marine model. Forty-four inches long and almost two feet wide and deep, it was the granddaddy of coolers. The cost: $198.84. He hauled the bulky chest home and stashed it in a crawl space in his basement.

Several days later Debby MacIntyre found herself at the same store, standing at the hunting counter.

"I'd like to buy a gun for a friend," she said nervously.

"I can't sell you a gun for anybody else. It's against the law," the man said, explaining the ban on straw purchases. "I would get in trouble if I sold you a gun and you gave it to somebody else."

Mortified, Debby said, "Thank you," turned away, and exited the store. She told Capano what had happened, and he shrugged it off.

"Fine. Don't worry about it," Capano told his mistress.

The topic came up again, however, on May 12, Mother's Day. Capano had taken Debby to a lawyers' conference in Washington, D.C., the previous week—just their second trip in fifteen years—and she was more in love than ever. And while they spoke on the phone that holiday Sunday, Capano said, "I really would like you to buy this gun for me. Don't worry; I'll help you."

"I'm afraid, Tom. It's illegal to transfer firearms."

"That's ridiculous. People do it all the time. It's nothing that you should worry about. It's nothing."

"OK," Debby said. "I'll do it."

The next day Capano picked Debby up at Tatnall and drove her to Miller's Gun Center on U.S. 13, a commercial strip south of Wilmington. It would, he assured Debby, be a snap. Capano parked under the white-and-red sign, and Debby hopped out. A salesman walked out from behind a counter, and Debby told him she wanted a small weapon for self-defense.

The man showed her a few pistols.

"Which one do you want?" the salesman asked.

"Whatever you think is best."

He picked the black .22-caliber Beretta revolver, and Debby said that would be fine. She also asked for a box of bullets. The guns and ammunition cost $181.99. The man then handed her three federal forms that gun buyers had to fill out. One allowed the store to request her criminal history from authorities. Another was from the Bureau of Alcohol, Tobacco, and Firearms, making her vow under penalty of perjury that the gun was for her personal use only and she wouldn't give it to another person. The third asked if she was a felon or a drug addict.

Debby signed the forms, worrying that she was lying about the straw purchase but just as concerned that Capano would leave her if she let him down. "Don't worry about it," Capano told her when she thrust the forms at him in the car. "It's a formality. People transfer guns and borrow guns all the time."

Two days later, Capano loaned $3,000 to Linda Marandola. She was hurting for money, she said, and wasn't due to start work for another two weeks. She promised to repay the money from her salary.

But a week later, Capano called her and complained about the message she had on her home answering machine— "Leave a message and maybe I'll call you back"—charging that it sounded childish and unprofessional and should be changed.

Marandola thought he was joking. But Capano called back several times, repeating his demand. One day he called five times, leaving messages, saying on one, in a disgusted voice, "Hope you check your goddamn messages."

Enough was enough, Marandola decided. On May 29, the

day she was supposed to report to work, she called Saul Ewing
and told a receptionist she would not be taking the job.

While Annie tried to distance herself from Capano, he continued to scheme up ways to remain in contact with her and
ingratiate himself with her close friends.

In early May, Capano appeared unexpectedly at Kim Horstmann's desk in her Philadelphia office. He explained that he
was working on a project with a broker in Horstmann's office
and wanted to say hello. "Let's get together sometime," he
suggested, and called later to make a dinner date.

Over their meal at the Ritz Carlton, Capano made Annie
and her anorexia the main topic of the evening.

"You're going to be shocked the next time you see her,"
Capano said. "She's gotten very skinny and I'm concerned that
she's in serious danger."

Seeing Kim's immediate concern, he suggested they collaborate on an intervention, such as forcing Annie to check into
an inpatient treatment center.

Kim suggested they bring Robert Fahey into the loop.

"No, don't call Robert," Capano protested. "Let's think
about it some more before we do anything."

Then he explained that he had talked to a friend who was
a psychologist and recommended that Annie see Michele Sullivan. He had given her money to pay Sullivan. He bought her
Gatorade and bananas to restore her electrolytes and regularly
bought her a bag of groceries. Annie had recently given him
a book on anorexia, and he'd read the entire book that very
night.

But Robert, Capano said, hadn't even looked at the same
book.

(Robert had, in fact, read the book and had paid Sullivan
$2,500 for his sister's treatment. Capano had given Annie
$500, but she never turned that cash over to the therapist.)

Eventually, Capano complained to Horstmann about his reduced role in Annie's life.

"I'm in love with her," Capano told Horstmann, "and I can't
understand why she won't see me again. I can have anybody

I want. Look where she comes from. I can offer her the world. I have more money than I can spend in a lifetime. I can give Annie anything she ever wanted. A Lexus. A ten-bedroom house. Anything."

Horstmann listened to the curious litany of complaints, including gripes against Michael Scanlan. "He's just a geek," said the lawyer, arguing that Annie didn't even take Scanlan seriously but just wanted to look good in front of her family.

"Am I crazy? Should I back away from her?" Capano wondered aloud.

"Yes, Tommy," said Kim, who knew Capano was wrong about Annie's feelings for Scanlan. "I think you should back away from her. I think you should definitely back away and leave her alone."

A week later Capano asked Horstmann to dinner again, explaining that he'd enjoyed himself the week before and was back in town for another meeting.

Again they went to the Ritz Carlton.

While they ate, Capano bragged that his immigrant father had made all of his children millionaires and how the company had diversified and thrived. He raved about his daughters, saying they were going to Europe for the summer.

But his enthusiasm was tempered with concern. One of his daughters, he said, had been ill and had undergone brain surgery. In fact, Capano was lying. While Katie, then fourteen, had been experiencing some dizzy spells and received neurological testing, she had undergone no operation.

Capano again changed the subject to Annie and again expressed concern about her health and his hopes they could be lovers once more. He also remarked that when he had recently dated a woman from Smith Barney in Wilmington, Annie had become jealous.

But the tenor of the dinner was generally upbeat, and Kim left thinking Capano would be just fine.

Capano used his daughter's health problems to tug at Annie's heartstrings as well. He lied about Katie, saying she had had surgery, and even encouraged Annie to visit her in the hospital. He assumed Annie wouldn't go visit a child she'd never met but decided the maneuver might curry more sympathy from Annie.

The tactic failed.

"She came in one time very angry because Mr. Capano had once again invited her to be with him," Michele Sullivan reported. "And the way to do that would be to have her go to the hospital where he reported that a daughter was ill. This tore Anne Marie a great deal. She has a tremendous amount of compassion for children. She is an incredibly generous and warm and giving person and would not want to say no to somebody in need. Even at the same time she felt that Mr. Capano was manipulating her and she said as much in our meeting."

Curiously, however, Capano's intimidating and jealous behavior had ceased. And with Scanlan on the road for days at a time, Annie told Sullivan, she felt she could manage a platonic relationship with Capano. She even saw her resistance to his offers, especially refusing to go with him to see his daughter, as signs of health.

"She said, 'I'm simply not going to do it. I'm mad enough. I feel manipulated. I'm not doing it,' " Sullivan recalled about Annie's decision not to go to the hospital. "And in some ways it represented a sign of making more progress."

It was refreshing to have the new "old Tommy" back—especially as a reminder of one's emotional progress. The former lovers resumed regular E-mail contact and even started going to lunch and dinner again. Occasionally Capano pressed for more time together, but now he seemed to accept her refusals. If he offered help with her anorexia, she thanked him but said she'd prefer to cure the problem herself. When she mentioned that a rock had dinged the front windshield of her prized Jetta, it became a source of concern for Capano and he urged her to replace the windshield.

Hi [Capano wrote on April 29 in one of their now joking, casual E-mails]. The guys from Smith Barney just left. I gave them a note to hand deliver to Kimmie. Anyway, here's the trivia question: Who owns Coach Leather? You probably know but if not you can have some fun guessing.

What more did you find out about the price of windshields? I enjoyed our phone call this morning. Thanks for the time. Please call if you can. Oh, almost forgot, if you answer the trivia question correctly, you win a prize. Hope your day is okay.

Eighteen minutes later, Annie responded. "Well look here, Mr. Smartie Pants," she typed. "The owner of Coach Leather is SARA LEE! How do you like them apples? What do I get for this discovery? As for the windshield, 3 separate places quoted me $460.55. Exactly. I will call you later this afternoon. I enjoyed our chats this morning, thanks for making me laugh, and getting my mind off my financial problemas! Call you later, Annie. P.S.—Nobody does it like Sara Lee!!!"

Capano fired back an answer at 3:04: "Okay, okay. You win fair and square and get the prize (which I will describe later), but tell me, did you already know or did you do some research this afternoon? Maybe a phone call to a friend? Can't believe the news about the windshield. I'm going to find out what the windshield in Kay's Suburban cost? We should talk about it—the crack is going to get bigger and could be dangerous. Look forward to your call."

At 3:18, Annie dashed off a jocular retort: "Well, I cannot lie, soooooooooooo, I did some quick research. I called the Coach Outlet in Rehoboth Outlets, and told them a song and dance about how I needed to know ASAP so it did not look like I did not already know the answer. Who'da thunk it, Sara Lee? I thought they were into food and shit. I can be quite resourceful when put to the test! I'll call ya later. amf."

A little later a courier arrived at Annie's desk, delivering Annie an envelope with nearly five hundred dollars in cash in it. There was a note enclosed that said, "This is not a gift; it is a loan to replace your windshield." Capano suggested repaying him when she received insurance money but exacted a penalty. "You will have to scrub my toilets and iron my boxers."

Annie didn't call him that night, so the next afternoon he E-mailed her:

Hey. It's 2:30 and I ain't heard from ya so I was wondering what was up.

Please give me a call or E-mail me when you get a chance. Is there a good time for me to call you? Hope you're having a good day but my guess is that you're not. Think mussels . . . in a white sauce.

A half hour later, Annie wrote back.

First she mentioned that she had told Robert and her Uncle James, the priest, about her eating disorder: "Well, the cat is outta da bag on this one. I felt a sense of relief and one of sadness."

Then she expressed gratitude for the money: "Tommy, thanks for your kind note/offer last night. You know what I thought when I first opened the letter and saw the Monopoly money fall onto the floor. (I cannot accept such a gracious gift!! But we will talk about that in person.)"

A few days later, Annie sent Capano a short, amiable letter:

Hola, Amigo? I wanted to drop you a wee note to let you know how much I appreciate all you've done and continue to do for me. You're a very genuine person. [Here Annie drew one of her characteristic smiley faces.]

We've been through a lot the past couple of years, and have managed (through hard work, determination and perhaps a bit of stubborn Irishness and Italian tempers?) to prevail. You'll always own a special piece of my heart.

Love you
Annie (Me)

On May 20, the Monday before Memorial Day weekend, the two got their signals crossed.

Capano, who had shared a picnic lunch in Valley Garden Park with Annie the previous Friday, thought the two were going to Victor's, a highbrow Philly eatery, on the coming Thursday.

But Annie had other plans. Scanlan had asked her to accompany him to Rhode Island, to spend the holiday with his parents, and also to Cape Cod, to see his college roommate. The trip meant much to Scanlan and to Annie. He hadn't taken a girlfriend to visit his parents since high school. She saw it as another significant event in their courtship.

"I'm confused about Victor's," Annie wrote on the morning of May 20. "We never talked about it. I am leaving on Thursday after work to go to Cape Cod for Memorial Day."

Capano, surprised Annie was going to New England, responded that afternoon: "I thought we had talked about doing dinner again on Thursday, but obviously misunderstood. What's up with the Cape? How about dinner on Wednesday."

He also expressed more concern that Annie was starving herself. "Annie, I'm trying to be light but it ain't working," he wrote. He had been trying mightily to keep the lid on and now seemed to be alerting Annie to the fact that he was losing it, even as he was telling her to take care of herself: "I'm real worried about the bad couple of days you've had, the weight loss and nearly fainting in Church. Maybe you should call Michele [Sullivan] today. Please call me this afternoon or E-mail to let me know we can talk tonight."

Annie wrote back: "Brian is coming over after dinner tonight to help me with my air conditioner and chat about some things. I'll try and call you after he leaves. I am leaving today by 4:30 to go home and get some sleep before I tackle [nephew] Brian Michael. Keep you fingers crossed. amf."

He dashed off an answer: "My fingers are crossed. And my toes. I'll wait for your call tonight. Did you get the fax? Check it before you leave."

That same week, which was unusually muggy for May, she messaged Capano first thing Tuesday morning, May 21, that it was so hot "I am not sleeping well." Her air conditioner still wasn't working properly.

"Your apartment must be unbearable," he wrote back. "I'd be glad to put it in for you today; just let me know when."

Again he tried to get her to go for dinner that night, not Wednesday: "It would be good for me and, at the risk of sounding pompous, I think you might get something out of it too under the circumstances."

Still trying to keep Capano at a reasonable arm's length, Annie said she had plans with Kathleen and Patrick, Kathleen's husband. She also told Capano she wanted to battle the anorexia without having to lean too heavily on him and had almost checked herself into the hospital the day before. She E-mailed Capano:

> Please don't worry about me. Hey, I'm scared to death that I am killing myself, but that's a positive thing, because I am forced to do something to make myself better. It's kind of a bittersweet device if you know what I mean. Tommy, I know you want to feed me, but believe it or not, it's not the right answer. I have learned through Michele and a lot of reading that the more someone tries to get you to eat, the less interested and more determined you become to do the opposite. I almost sent myself to St. Francis [Hospital] yesterday morning, because of how weak I felt. Believe me, Tommy, when I tell you that all of this is good for me, because for the first time, I am afraid that I am killing myself. As for tonight, I am going over to talk to Cass and Patrick, and tomorrow night I am spending it with Robert up in Newtown Square. Susan is out of town on business. I'm ready to tackle this problem I have—whereas before I did not see it that way. I know all you want to do is help, and believe me it's greatly appreciated, but I also need some time alone to work out a lot of stuff. I hope you understand all this mumbo. Anne Marie.

That Thursday, as she and Scanlan prepared to leave, Capano reminded Annie they had a definite date for the Thursday after she returned. But before saying good-bye for a few days, Capano made one last effort to keep her in Wilmington: "I miss you already. You know, if you really don't want to go, don't."

That weekend, while Annie was away, Siobhan Sullivan got a telephone page from Capano.

"Have you talked to Anne Marie?" Capano asked the state trooper.

Sullivan, who knew Annie was with Scanlan in New England, said no.

"Do you know where she is?"

"No, I don't, Tom."

Capano then asked how Sullivan was, briefly inquired about her plans for the weekend, and said good-bye.

Annie and Mike had a splendid weekend. She hit it off with his parents, and his mother even put pictures of Michael as a child in the spare room where Annie slept.

When Annie returned home that Monday night, she called Capano to say hello. He E-mailed her the next morning, thanking her for checking in and letting her know he had made a reservation for Thursday at La Famiglia.

Sometime that day, trooper Sullivan approached Annie in the office and said Capano had called over the weekend, asking about her whereabouts.

Annie blew up. "He's fucking stalking me!" she shouted. All her hard work at winning him over to a friendly relationship now seemed for naught. "I'm afraid he's going to be waiting outside my apartment one night and he and Mike are going to have a confrontation," she told Sullivan.

Sullivan told Annie to file a criminal complaint.

"Annie, that's a crime. We can give you protection. We're here for the governor but also for the staff."

"No, I can handle it myself. But I have to end it."

7 A Dangerous Dance

How was Annie to know that she was in the becalmed center of an enormous storm?

"She knew the sky was blue," Michele Sullivan would say. "But she could easily be persuaded to believe something different. If somebody was very persuasive and said to her, 'You know, the sky is really purple,' she would give that serious thought about whether she was simply wrong. And with any more kind of pressure, she might just shrug and say, 'OK, it's purple.'"

Tommy had come back saying that everything was all right. The sky was purple. He was stalking her, but in much the same way as her past stalked her. And he was persuasive, as a good lawyer is. Fifteen, twenty, twenty-five phone calls a day? Annie saw it as a way of gauging her own health—not his problem. Fighting her past, she forgot that he had one, too, one that tossed him to a phone over and over and over. Struggling to understand the destructiveness of her eating disorder— "I'm scared to death that I am killing myself, but that's a positive thing"—she couldn't see that Tom Capano was slavishly reenacting his own disorder.

"She was the kind of person who believed that you could move from a romantic relationship to one of friendship," Michele Sullivan would recall. But what about Tom Capano? Where was he going?

Sullivan, too, was in the eye of the hurricane. "One of the difficult things you have to choose, when you're a therapist," she would say, "is what do *you* do and what do you need to teach your patient to do."

She heard the stories, Sullivan did. Every week, Annie visited and recounted, in fifty-minute sessions, what was happening in her life. The therapist heard about Capano making scenes, stalking Annie, phoning her dozens of times in a day, "haunting" her. But she also heard Annie describe the good times, and Sullivan, too, could be persuaded. Did she have a choice? She knew only the Tom Capano Annie described. "She described him as a man who had in the past been extremely supportive of her," Sullivan later recounted. "He was somebody she could turn to to talk about problems."

And that he was.

"Anne Marie was a person who was excruciatingly aware of the feelings of other people," Sullivan recalled, "and never ever, ever wanted to hurt anybody. If she perceived she was hurting somebody, she would be incredibly remorseful and probably end up with a tremendous amount of shame."

Where did Tom Capano fit into this rubric of remorse? Where did Michele Sullivan fit?

"Even though she reported to me that she did not want a romantic relationship and she wanted to see Mr. Capano less and less, she did not want to hurt him and hoped that, somehow, their relationship could be a platonic friendship."

She played a somewhat dangerous game with her eating— "Believe me, Tommy, when I tell you that all of this is good for me, because for the first time, I am afraid that I am killing myself"—but, in fact, was playing Russian roulette with Capano.

She needed to feel the pain, she had convinced herself, in order to heal herself. And saving Tommy, however painful at times, was part of her own salvation.

Annie told Sullivan how happy she was that she had confronted Capano at an affair she attended with Scanlan. The event had been preceded by a flurry of phone calls from Capano, warning her he would be there and suggesting that he might make a scene.

In fact, "Mr. Capano did approach her and guide her into a different room to talk to her," Sullivan later recounted, and Annie "expressed a great deal of pleasure in being able to say pretty clearly, 'I don't want to be here. I want to go back to the party.' And I believe that she found her own way to escort herself back."

That experience, Sullivan reported, gave Annie confidence that she was "more and more capable of saying no."

Throughout June, Annie and Tom continued their steady stream of E-mails, phone calls, and Thursday dinners—nights when Scanlan was often with coworkers or out of town. Capano kept pushing her to eat—her weight had plummeted to 117 pounds—and she kept dancing with the danger of it.

On June 4, she wrote him a check for $112.50, partial payment on the windshield. She wrote: "Thanks," and drew a smiley face on the memo line.

The next day, Capano took Ginny Columbus to lunch at the Hotel du Pont. They didn't discuss Annie at all, not once. Tom was effusive about everything else: Ginny's life, politics, the weather, his new life as a bachelor, his pain and sorrow over the separation. But no Annie. Then, on the way out of the hotel, Capano stopped at the gift shop and bought a bag of macaroons, a trademark treat at the hotel.

Out in the car, Capano handed Ginny the macaroons and another bag with pretzels and fruit.

"Could you give these to Annie, please?" he asked.

Columbus delivered them to her officemate, saying, "Tom told me you liked the macaroons."

"I don't want any cookies," Annie retorted abruptly. "I don't want anything. Throw them away."

"I'll just put it in the refrigerator," said Ginny, wondering why her friend was so snippy about a little bag of cookies. "If you want them later you can get them."

Annie said nothing.

But when Capano called later that afternoon, Ginny, at the receptionist's desk, confided in her lunch companion that Annie wouldn't touch the food, making up an excuse for Annie. Also thinking she was helping her friend, Ginny told Capano, when he asked to speak to Annie, that she had stepped away from her desk.

Fifteen minutes later an E-mail zoomed into Annie's message box. "Ginny said you wouldn't eat the fruit or pretzels because of cramps," Capano wrote. "I hope you try the macaroons and bring the fruit home. Lunch was interesting. Please give me a call when you can."

This was Tom trying to help. It upset her, but endearingly so. She had spent enough time with Sullivan to know that Tom's gifts were not so much signs of affection as manipulations to gain it, but that very understanding had given her hope that she was on the mend, that she could tell the difference. Her resistance to the gifts, she believed, was proof of her improving emotional health; thus Tom Capano had become, not part of her problem, but a key element in her search for a solution. In such circumstances, she could allow herself to enjoy the good that first drew her to Tom Capano, the caring, listening man she had once loved so dearly. And she now had the firmness of spirit, she believed, the perspective, to dance with him. "Hey, I'm scared to death that I am killing myself, but that's a positive thing."

And so Annie stepped back into Tom Capano's orbit, determined, the good Catholic girl that she was, to find his goodness and save herself in the process. They ate out, as they had in the past—though Annie usually only nibbled at her food. He wined and dined her, talked, and listened, as he had in the past. On June 7, he ordered tickets to an August 5 Jackson Browne concert and E-mailed Annie to reserve that night for "a very special event." Annie went to a wedding, and he loaned her his credit card to buy a gift. Five days later, Capano showed up at Annie's apartment with a new air conditioner.

On June 12, Annie fainted at work. Not willing to let Scanlan see her in such condition—he didn't even know she was anorexic—Annie called Capano, who rushed to the office and took her home and pumped her with beverages. Later that afternoon, she felt better and returned to work, where she E-mailed her rescuer with an ever-so-brief word of gratitude: "Thanks! I will get better. Annie." She did know, after all, that she was playing with fire, accepting his gifts.

But Capano knew better. "You're welcome," he wrote, responding to her brevity with his own cryptic note. "Sleep well, now, and for the rest of the summer," he continued. "I know you'll get better. I just wish you'd let me help you. Kind of like a coach, know what I mean?"

And Capano benefited from Annie's need to keep him a secret. When she spotted him at a street festival while walking with Scanlan, Annie hustled her boyfriend away. She confessed to Kim Horstmann that she couldn't tell Scanlan about her continuing relationship with Capano: "It would make me weak in Mike's eyes."

Mike was an unwitting partner in the dance. Quiet, unassuming—and constantly on the road—he was the perfect foil for Capano, the brash, manipulative, constant presence. Capano E-mailed Annie on Monday, June 17, knowing perhaps that Scanlan was at the MBNA offices in Maine all week, asking Annie if she wanted to hit some golf balls with him and his oldest daughter, Christy, who, he pointed out, had finished the semester with a 3.86 grade point average.

"I'd love to go hit some golf balls this week," Annie E-mailed back. "You should be very proud of Christy! I am and

I don't even know her! Nor does she know me. Hope you have fun today. Annie."

But even before the golf date, Annie was confessing to Capano that she didn't have enough money to take an old professor of hers out to dinner. Not surprisingly, a $100 bill arrived in an envelope, followed by an E-mail message.

"I meant what I said about the brief loan," wrote Capano, fully aware of Annie's sensitivity to gifts. "Do it. It will make you smile to see him." And he couldn't resist taking a shot at her missing boyfriend, who, he knew, was now winning the war for Annie's true heart, the one found between the beats. "Besides, I'll make money on the interest you'll pay me. I'll pretend I'm a credit card company and charge you 19%."

The next Tuesday, June 25, Annie was again out of money, four days from payday, because she had treated her friends to beer and nachos the night before. When she shared her problem with her new best friend, Capano had a courier sent to the governor's office with an envelope containing $30—willing to give her a $30,000 car, he now realized that $30 worked better—along with a cheery note:

Annie.

Just add this to the balance. Consider it a consolidation loan. (That's a joke.) Kidding aside, you should not be penniless for several days, in case of an emergency (like an overpowering yearning for a latte!). I'd have sent more but I know you'll have a hard time even accepting this. Please accept it in the spirit in which it's given. And don't spend it on Jill. Tom.

In what spirit was it given?

Annie was hooked again. And so was he. She had allowed Capano back into her life, but now as both confessor and banker, a man who expected to be repaid.

Annie then let Capano buy her the pantsuit she had drooled over in Talbot's when she was there with her sister the previous Saturday. At least, she told Capano about the outfit and about her fight with Kathleen over whether to spend that much money on it. That was enough for him. He called the Talbot's in Greenville, where the saleswoman knew him—a good customer, Mr. Capano was, buying clothes as he did, for his wife and other women. The saleswoman had to have the outfit sent over from the Christiana Mall store, but it was ready when Capano stopped by later that day to pick up the $289 outfit.

Annie saw Sullivan, her therapist, on Wednesday, June 26. They talked about Kathleen and how she and Annie had progressed from a contentious mother-daughter relationship to a loving and sisterly, if not perfect, one. Annie was still much too skinny and told Sullivan her sister had been horrified days earlier at Talbot's to see Annie's ribs poking out of her torso.

The psychologist thought Annie was significantly more upbeat than in recent visits, which hadn't been so reassuring. The fainting spell had concerned Sullivan, and she was annoyed that Capano had tried to manipulate Annie into visiting his daughter in the hospital. On May 29, when Annie reported that she was having disturbing repetitive thoughts and panic attacks, Sullivan decided she needed some medicine.

Seeing Annie in a good mood on June 26, Sullivan assumed the antidepressants were helping. Annie had even completed her "letter to her legs," part of the process of getting in touch with herself, part of winning the ability to say no, to speak up for herself. Saying no to Capano was too big a deal for her, so they had been practicing what Sullivan called "lower level kinds of assertions," like not answering every phone call and not responding to every E-mail. This "stair-step" approach was how Annie would build up her assertiveness abilities. And writing a letter to her legs, though Sullivan knew it sounded "weird," was a beginning, a way to first start coming to terms with one's own body. "I knew that Anne Marie loathed her thighs," recalled Sullivan. "So I encouraged her to write a letter to her legs as though they were something separate from her."

Annie showed her the letter, which she wrote in the form of a memo:

Subject: Legs

I must admit I feel somewhat silly writing a letter to my legs.

I have many insecurities surrounding my life, but the one most prevalent to me is the size of my legs. Below is a list of what goes through my mind on a daily basis:

1. I cannot wear a skirt because people will see just how big my calves really are.
2. I struggle through the summer because we wear less which means more of my body is being exposed.
3. Every morning I wake up, I talk myself out of wearing a short or dress.
4. I have complete anxiety every time Michael sees me in shorts, because I think this just might be the last time. I get embarrassed for Michael if we are out in public and I wear shorts.
5. I often look in the mirror when I get out of the shower and yell at my legs.
6. If I had thin legs, then perhaps people would classify me as "thin."
7. I will look at other women and say, "God, if I only had their legs, then maybe I would not be so ashamed of myself."
8. A day does not go by that I don't spend some part obsessing over the size of my legs.
9. Blah, Blah, Blah

Seeing her patient's buoyant mood and willingness to address one of her phobias, Sullivan thought they were finally making progress. "She felt really wonderful," Sullivan recalled.

Capano's name never came up. Was that good? Or bad? Annie had once again gotten so used to Capano's entreaties and offerings—and, most important, her ability to manage them—that she now took them for granted. He had become a good friend again.

After returning from her session with Sullivan, Annie shared her melancholy with Capano in an E-mail, apologizing for being morose during a phone call earlier in the day: "I feel that some days I can handle my anorexia and other days I feel overwhelmed by the whole thing. Today has obviously been an overwhelming day. My appointment with Michele was hard and in-depth today, and quite frankly it drained all my energy. I really do appreciate you offering me the Phillies tickets, but right now I am going to focus on trying to get better. Sorry for being such a Doggy Downer today. Take Care, Annie."

Knowing she wouldn't read it until the next morning, Capano wrote at 6:19: "I appreciate the apology, but you don't need to worry about it. I just hope you know that all I want to do is help in any way I can. I promise to make you laugh tonight at Panorama, to order calamari and to surprise you with something that will make you smile. Please call when you get a chance."

That same afternoon, Annie talked to Kim Horstmann on the phone. "I felt very good when I hung up the phone from her because it was just kind of a checking call to see how she was feeling with this eating disorder," Horstmann said later. "She said that she had actually gained a couple of pounds and that she had cut the amount of laxatives down in half and she was feeling really good and she was happy about her relationship with Michael. And there was a certain peace with her relationship with Tom. She felt everything in her life was going in the right direction."

That evening she went to her sister's house, as she did every Wednesday. "She would do her laundry at my house on Wednesday evening and play with the kids and have dinner," Kathleen recalled about the routine. "This day she didn't do her laundry. My husband's car was being serviced and he was out of town, and Anne Marie helped me—we all drove up in my car to pick up Pat's car and then she drove my car home. She stayed and had dinner and then she went to the gym." Kathleen recalled how much in love Annie was with Michael Scanlan and how she was ready to move on with her life. "We talked about her plans to leave the governor's office," said Kathleen, "about going back to graduate school to obtain a degree in education and teach." Kathleen's son Kevin came in, and Annie hugged the little three-year-old. "She had a very special bond with Kevin," said Kathleen. "She was his godmother. She had a bond with all of her nephews, but Kevin was ill as a child and Anne Marie really helped in nurturing him."

He called her Aunt Annie.

———

Thursday, June 27, dawned a perfect summer day, sunny and warm with just the slightest caress of a breeze. Capano E-mailed Annie at 11:50, after he tried unsuccessfully to reach her by phone. He had a busy day planned, the closing of a bond deal with the city of Wilmington.

"Good morning," he typed. "Called you at 11:45. Hope your day is better than yesterday. I'm crazy again today but winding down. I left a message for you so hope to talk to you soon. Please call if you can."

At work Anne Marie went about clearing her desk of duties in anticipation of taking the next day off. She prepared the governor's schedule for the busy weekend that capped the legislative session and E-mailed the rest of the governor's staff to remind them she would be out of the office Friday.

Annie told Ginny she planned to primp the next day, with a pedicure, and go for a relaxing walk through Valley Garden Park.

"She was going to take a long weekend because the week ahead was going to be a little hectic for her," Columbus later said. After the legislature adjourned Sunday night, the governor had an overflowing slate of bill signings and public appearances scheduled.

Annie left work at five and stopped off at the Allied Mental Health offices on Concord Pike to check in with Dr. Neil Kaye, the psychiatrist who was prescribing her antidepressants, before going home.

Was she looking forward to her date with Tom Capano that night? No one will ever know. She parked at the curb across the street from her house, checked her mail, then climbed the stairs to her small apartment. She changed into a floral-patterned Laura Ashley dress and waited for the buzzer to ring.

About 10:00 P.M. that night, Connie Blake sat in her living room watching television, excited about her trip to the shore that weekend. The former mayoral secretary, now a divorced grandmother who lived alone, heard footsteps from the apartment upstairs, where Annie Fahey lived. Blake loved Annie, such a sweet girl, but hadn't seen much of her lately. The divorcée bustled about, still packing, half-following *The American President* on the TV, then climbed into bed. She didn't pay particular attention to the footsteps.

"I just assumed it was Annie upstairs," Blake recalled. "And I went to sleep about 11:00 P.M. with the windows open."

8 *A Cold Summer Wind*

The sky had barely turned from black to grayish-blue when Gerry Capano opened the door of his Emma Court house on Friday morning, June 28, heading for his white Ford pickup truck.

Woozy from a night of partying, Gerry had managed to pull himself out of bed. Though he was part-owner of Commercial Ground Care and rarely performed any actual work, mostly serving as a financial backer for his old buddy Terry Hannig, Gerry did have some duties. One of those duties was picking up Tommy Pitts and driving him to the job. But on this summer morning, as Gerry clicked his garage door opener and exited the house, he was startled by the sight of a black Jeep, engine idling, in his driveway at the end of a small cul-de-sac of grand brick colonials.

What the hell is he doing here at quarter of six in the morning? Gerry wondered to himself, meeting his brother's glance. Tom Capano sat in the driver's seat reading Gerry's morning newspaper. The passenger-side window whizzed down as

Gerry approached the car. He felt a blast of cold air from the air conditioner as he put his head in the window. His brother looked pale and haggard, like he hadn't slept all night.

"What are you doing here, Tom?" Gerry asked.

Tom smelled booze on his brother's breath. "Are you hung over?" he asked.

"Yeah. I had a rough night. What are you here for?"

"Can we go for a boat ride?" Tom asked, his voice calm yet determined. "I need to dispose of something far out in the ocean."

Gerry's stomach jumped. He suddenly recalled the strange series of conversations with Tom the previous winter. Extortionists. Guns. Breaking legs. And the boat request, to dispose of a body. He had forgotten about it. Tom hadn't said anything about his troubles for months.

"Did you do it?" Gerry hadn't taken his older brother's ranting seriously back then.

"Yeah," said Tom, nodding. "Can you help me?"

Gerry was stunned. "No way, man," he blurted. "I don't want to be involved in this. I have a beautiful house, a good life, great kids. I don't want to ruin my life."

"You have to!" Tom shouted. "I've got nowhere else to go, nobody else to turn to. Don't leave me flat. Don't leave me hanging. Come on; I need you, Bro'."

Gerry resisted, trying to press Tom for more details.

"The less you know, the better," said his brother. "Look, why don't you just give me the keys to the boat?"

"No," Gerry said. "You don't know how to operate the boat."

Tom's voice hardened in anger. "Just give me the keys to the goddamn boat! I can drive it. If I mess it up, I'll pay for it. Just give me the keys."

Gerry's dilemma overwhelmed him. Tom had always been there for him, *through everything*. Now, when the brother he idolized needed him, Gerry was turning his back.

"OK," he finally said. "If you're going to use the boat, I have to be part of it."

Tom told Gerry to meet him at Grant Avenue, begged him

to hurry, then sped off. When he got to his house, even though it was still not yet seven in the morning, the phone was ringing. It was Debby.

"Do you still need my help?" she asked.

The previous evening, during a testy phone call with his longtime mistress, Tom had browbeaten Debby into agreeing to help him "with something" early the next morning.

"No," Capano now said and hung up. He drove to his estranged wife's house, arriving as she was cooling down from her morning jog, moving about in the backyard, hosing down her running companion, her black Lab, Nicky.

Tom startled Kay when he appeared. He was wearing shorts and a T-shirt and looked as if he hadn't slept in days.

"Can I use the Suburban, Kay?" he asked. He often used the big indigo blue Chevrolet when he needed extra space, often just to haul the four girls around. The couple simply switched vehicles. Kay would take Tom's Grand Cherokee.

They spoke for a few minutes; then Tom went inside to make some phone calls. One was to the home of Henry Supinski, the Wilmington city treasurer, with whom he walked most mornings on the quarter-mile track at nearby Tower Hill School.

"Hi, Henry. I'm busy this morning and I won't be able to make it," Capano told his walking partner.

Supinski, a jocular, heavyset man who was more prone to canceling than his lean buddy, said OK and blew off the session himself.

Tom was being his efficient, responsible self, tying up all loose ends.

His other call went to the law office of David McBride, a close friend and fellow attorney. The two were supposed to play golf at two that afternoon. But Capano left a message on McBride's machine, saying he had to take his daughters somewhere at two but could play at four if McBride wanted.

"I won't be in the office," Capano said. "So leave a message on my voice mail at home telling me what you decide."

He was guessing that McBride wouldn't be able to play golf at four, but the offer would confirm his play for an alibi—that he was only delayed a couple of hours.

Before driving off, Tom gave Kay a peck on the cheek and said he'd talk to her later that night, when he came to visit the girls. Then he headed to the track at Tower Hill School, a few blocks away, and took a few laps. As he was leaving, Debby drove up and the couple chatted for a few moments. He said he'd see her that night, and they parted.

When he got back to Grant Avenue, Tom made yet another call, to the office of Keith Brady, Delaware's chief deputy attorney general, the state's number-two law enforcement official. Capano recognized the voice of Brady's secretary, Laura Kobosko.

"Hello, Laura," Tom said. "What are you doing in so early? Is Keith in?"

"No," Kobosko said.

"Do you know what he's doing tonight?" Capano asked.

"No," she said again.

"Could you tell him that I'd like to meet him later tonight and to call me at home and leave a message?" Capano said in a congenial voice.

They chatted for a few more minutes, Capano saying he was off on the lovely summer day and planned to play golf.

But as she typed up a note for her boss, Kobosko thought it odd that Capano would call so early—he never had before.

Gerry pulled his white truck up to the two-car garage of Tom's house with some trepidation. He had been trying to imagine what kind of horror show he might be entering.

Kay's Suburban was backed up to the open bay, and Gerry pulled in beside it. He saw Tom walking down the steps from inside the house. The brothers exchanged somber greetings.

In the middle of the garage floor Gerry saw a long rolled-up carpet and a group of green Hefty trash bags, all stuffed.

Next to them was a giant white Igloo cooler, familiar to Gerry as a container for storing large fish caught in the ocean, bait, or beer. Wrapped around the chest was a thick chain, secured by an industrial-size padlock. Nearly four feet long, two feet high, and two feet wide, the cooler, Gerry knew, could hold a body.

Gerry locked his eyes on Tom.

"Can we put this stuff in your truck?" the older brother asked.

"It won't fit," Gerry said, looking toward the pickup, which had a cover over its bed. Besides, he didn't want to haul a body and other evidence in his vehicle. In fact, he didn't want to have anything to do with the whole deal.

Tom had expected as much—which was why he got the Suburban from Kay. In fact, he was thinking quite clearly this morning and was proud of himself for being able to make all these arrangements, including the phone calls setting up and canceling appointments. He had found an old horsehair rug in the garage and laid it in the back of Kay's truck, to make sure there would be no evidence there. Gerry removed the chain and padlock, pointing out that the cooler would sit flat on the floor that way. The brothers—one short, muscular, and clean-shaven; the other, tall, slim, and bearded—each grabbed a thick handle on either side of the cooler.

They slowly lifted the big white container. It was heavy and unbalanced. Gerry could hear the jostling of melting ice cubes inside as they slid the load into the back of the sport utility vehicle.

Tom started to put the rolled-up rug in the car. "We can't take the rug," said Gerry. "It'll float." He also knew that a rug on a fishing boat, unlike a cooler, would arouse instant suspicion.

Tom next directed Gerry to park his truck at the Acme supermarket parking lot in Trolley Square. "I'll meet you there," he said.

It was a Friday rush hour as Gerry drove through the ritzy, bustling commercial district of restaurants, yuppie bars, hair salons, boutiques, and cappuccino shops just a mile west of downtown Wilmington. He prayed nobody he knew would see him.

Tom stopped at a bank machine, careful not to withdraw too much money—just $200—then picked up his brother. Tom at the wheel, they drove I-95 north to New Jersey and then traveled east over a succession of one-lane country roads that the brothers could have driven blindfolded. They didn't talk much during the drive. The younger brother used his cell phone to call two friends he planned on seeing that day, saying something important had come up.

"Hey, I'm scared," Gerry finally said.

"Don't worry," Tom said. "I'll never let anything happen to you. Everything is going to be fine."

They pulled up to Gerry's big bayfront home a little after ten-thirty that morning. Unbeknownst to the Capano brothers, the town police had been inside the house just a half hour earlier, after a landscaper, who had come to work on the sprinkler system, unintentionally set off the security alarm.

The brothers—who would have been stunned to see a police cruiser in front of the house—exited the Suburban, stretched in the blinding sun, and went inside.

Gerry used the bathroom.

Tom called Debby at Tatnall. "I'm still trying to get a golf game together," he said, not mentioning his whereabouts. "I'd really like to come see you tonight and stay with you."

"That would be wonderful," said MacIntyre, always delighted to spend the evening with Capano.

Tom also called his wife's house and asked the baby-sitter how the girls were doing. Still asleep, she said.

As Tom worked the phone, Gerry gathered up some fishing gear and loaded it on the *Summer Wind,* the twenty-five-foot Hydra Sport that was moored conveniently in the private slip behind his house. Named after the Johnny Mercer song—"The summer wind came blowing in across the sea, It lingered there to touch your hair and walk with me"—the sleek boat had cost Gerry $30,000 when he bought it, in Florida, five years earlier. And he had it up for sale. Ever since being eaten alive by bugs during a shark-fishing contest several weeks before, Gerry had determined he needed a boat with a bigger hold. In fact, he had already made a down payment on another boat the week before and had a potential buyer for the *Summer Wind* coming by over the weekend.

Tom finally emerged from the house, summoning Gerry to the Suburban. The men lugged the cooler to the boat and heaved it—carefully—on the bobbing deck. They went back to the Suburban, Gerry throwing the chain and padlock into a plastic bag and taking it to the boat while Tom parked the

Suburban down the block. He didn't want anyone to think someone was home.

Gerry started the *Summer Wind* engines, stared up at the azure cloudless sky, and felt a soft, warm breeze on his deeply tanned face. An experienced marlin and shark fisherman, Gerry was a well-known angler in the area and hoped that if anybody saw him today, they would think he was just on another fishing expedition. At the same time, he shook his head and cursed his fate.

Once Tom was on board, Gerry motored the boat under the Stone Harbor Bridge to a waterside Texaco gas station he normally didn't use. Gerry didn't dare go to his normal fuel and bait store, at Smuggler's Cove, where gregarious owner Lou Bachman was sure to chat him up about his fishing trip.

At the Texaco a young female attendant waited on the Capano brothers, who almost choked when they saw a marine police boat pull up behind them. Gerry and Tom tried desperately to look casual as their boat's two tanks were filled. Finally, the pump stopped: 100.7 gallons. Tom gave his cash to Gerry, who hurriedly shelled out $138.86 and pushed away.

Idling slowly out into the bay, Gerry glanced back to make sure the police boat was not following, then guided the twin-engine vessel under the bridge, into Hereford Inlet. Turning off his navigational and electronic equipment—radar, short-wave radio, and loran system—he threw the throttle open and followed the sun, due east.

Gerry was familiar enough with these waters that he normally didn't need any navigational tools or maps; on this trip, especially, he didn't them. His destination today was, simply, far away, deep water. Sullen and dazed, Gerry stood behind the wheel as the engines droned on. Tom, who often became seasick on the water, leaned against a nearby post, trying to stay steady. They chopped through the shallow swells of the Atlantic for nearly three hours, plying the waves far into international waters, well beyond the continental shelf, until the coastline had dipped below the horizon.

The prolonged silence was finally broken by Gerry's shrill

voice. "This is crazy. This is wrong!" he yelled at Tom as the
boat raced out to sea.

"I won't let anything happen to you!" Tom yelled back.
"You'll be OK. Everything will be fine."

Tom asked why they were going so far out to sea; he had
hoped for a quick trip, so he could get back to Wilmington,
dump the rug, and still make, if McBride had called, the four
o'clock tee time. Gerry flipped on his depth gauge and said
they would stop when he was certain the water was very, very
deep.

In fact, he had already decided they would go to Mako
Alley, some sixty miles offshore. Gerry hunted shark there and
knew the chances of seeing other craft, except for an occasional shark- or clam-hunting party, were slim. The depth
would be 200 feet, enough, he hoped, for a sea burial.

When the depth finder showed 198 feet, Gerry knew they
had arrived in Mako Alley and cut the engines. The only sound
was that of the lapping green water against the gunwales. But
bobbing in the gentle waves several hundred yards away was
another boat, about the same size as *Summer Wind*. Gerry
couldn't see anybody on board but did notice a "dive flag," a
sign that the boat's occupants were probably scuba-diving and
wouldn't see them.

Under a cloudless sky, the brothers dragged the big white
cooler to the rear starboard side of the boat, lifted it off the
edge, and tipped it into the water. There was a gulping splash
as the heavy cooler started to submerge, then a whoosh as it
popped back to the surface.

The brothers groaned as the cooler floated away from the
Summer Wind. Gerry panicked and ran to a cabinet in the
foredeck, returning to the back of the boat with a big 12-gauge
Mossberg shotgun. He carried it for shark hunting. Tom
watched as Gerry loaded a single slug into the chamber,
pressed the butt of the gun to his chin, looked down the long
barrel, and fired. The cooler, now almost fifty yards away,
jumped slightly.

The slug caught a corner of the cooler, near the bottom of
one of the larger panels. The impact was enough to turn it a

few degrees, but it didn't sink. Worse, as the cooler wobbled even farther away from the boat, Gerry could see blood dribbling out of the bullet hole.

Though he was already sure what was inside the cooler, the red liquid on the green sea erased any lingering doubt.

Stunned that the slug didn't work, Gerry turned the boat around and maneuvered alongside the cooler. Tom reached for it as Gerry shut off the engines again. Gerry grabbed an anchor from a front cabinet and hauled it back to Tom. He picked up a second anchor and thrust both toward his brother, glaring with bitterness and disgust.

"You're on your own, Tommy. I don't want anything else to do with this," Gerry said, turning his back and marching to the helm.

Tom, hanging onto the bobbing cooler, didn't say a word.

As he stared forward off the bow, Gerry heard the rustling of chains and anchors, the banging of the cooler, and the sound of Tom retching.

"I can't fucking believe you did this. Why did you get me involved?" Gerry screamed, refusing to look at his brother. "This is wrong! This is wrong!"

Tom had tethered the cooler to the boat and was now leaning over its edge, vomiting into the ocean. When he had recovered, he opened the lid. Gerry could hear the rattling of chains, the banging of plastic against fiberglass, and the grunts from his brother. He guessed what was happening, Tom wrapping the anchors around a body, tilting the cooler over, *splash.*

"Are you done yet?" Gerry screamed. "Are you done?"

"Yeah!" Tom yelled.

Gerry turned around. He saw the open cooler bobbing on its side in the water, and next to it, just disappearing below the surface of the ocean, a human foot and part of a calf.

It was 3:30 in the afternoon when the *Summer Wind* pulled into Stone Harbor, five hours since they had left. Tom rushed inside and called his voice mail. As hoped, Dave McBride had declined the four o'clock golf offer. Gerry called his wife, but she wasn't home.

Both men were anxious to resume their normal lives, and

Tom now raced home, hitting speeds up to 80 mph, seeing passing hordes of Friday traffic heading in the opposite direction, to the shore.

Finally, Tom blurted out an explanation. "The person in the cooler was threatening my children," he told Gerry, refusing to say more. Gerry asked what he should say if he was ever questioned by the police or anybody else.

Tom provided him with an alibi. "He told me to say that he and I drove to the beach," recalled Gerry, "and we were with each other in the morning, that he was talking—I think that he was talking to my brother Louis about some properties that we owned—and that we went down and I went to the beach with him to show him my beach property and we just turned around and we had lunch down there and we turned around and went home."

They arrived in Wilmington at five, Tom convincing Gerry—now a reluctant but fully involved collaborator in some kind of killing he didn't want to know much about—to help dispose of a love seat from the Grant Avenue house.

Gerry still didn't know who the dead person was, but when Tom pointed to a maroon sofa the younger Capano knew that the end couldn't have been pretty.

"I tried to clean it off with Clorox, but it didn't work," Tom told Gerry, adding that he also had scrubbed the hardwood floor beneath the sofa with bleach. Gerry stared at the love seat, which he had helped haul into the house the previous October. It had a red basketball-size stain on the right back cushion, shoulder height. Blood.

"We've got to get rid of it," Tom said.

To get the soiled piece of furniture to the car, the Capano brothers had to carry it out the front door and around the side of the house, walking in plain view of the few houses that faced Tom's. Once in the garage, Gerry told Tom, "You better cut that stain out."

Gerry cut the bloodied piece of fabric out of the cushion with his knife, then tried to break the legs off the couch, kicking at them with his sneakers. If anybody saw the sofa, Gerry wanted it to look old, worthy of dumping. Gerry also instructed Tom to throw the bloody chunks of foam from the cushion into Hefty bags and to cut the rug into pieces and put them in plastic bags as well. They then lifted the love seat onto the Suburban and drove to a Capano construction site, where four Dumpsters sat, side by side, waiting for demolition debris. Gerry climbed into one of the containers and moved trash around. Then they heaved the love seat in, upside down, and Gerry hopped back in and used old office rugs and other debris to camouflage the evidence.

Gerry went home, but Tom had more work to do. He hustled back to Grant Avenue, where he threw the Hefty bags into the Suburban. He started cutting the rug into pieces but eventually gave up. He took the rest of the detritus of the dead to another Capano Dumpster site and returned home. He took a shower, then called Debby MacIntyre, telling his lover he was going to visit his daughters before coming to her house.

He was rushing. He had been rushing for almost twenty-four hours. He made yet another trip to yet another Capano property, a Holiday Inn his family owned in Penns Grove, New Jersey, near the Delaware Memorial Bridge. He jumped out, dragged the ripped and shredded rug pieces from the vehicle, and tossed them into yet another Dumpster.

His grisly deed finally finished, Capano drove to his wife's home and greeted each of his girls in a warm embrace.

Drained, but determined to hang on for a few more hours, Tom asked his kids if they felt like going to a restaurant. But they said no, opting instead to order a pizza and watch a video they had rented. While the movie played, Tom finally dozed off, not waking until eleven. Saying good night, he drove to Debby's house, let himself in—he knew the code for the alarm system and had the key—and tramped upstairs, where Debby was watching television.

"I'm sorry I'm late," he said. "Can I still stay?"

"Sure, honey," Debby said.

Capano climbed in bed next to her. But there was no sex tonight. Within seconds, Tom Capano fell fast asleep.

9 *Business as Usual*

Tom Capano seemed to resume a normal life Saturday morning. He and Debby slept late, had sex when they awoke, ate breakfast. He bought a new Oriental rug at Air Base Carpet Mart—to replace the one splattered with Anne Marie's blood—and joked with the salesclerk, who recognized the Capano name and asked if he was one of the builders. "They're relatives of mine," Tom laughed. "I'm the black sheep of the family."

Kay Capano thought Tom seemed agitated when he picked up the girls that evening, for their regularly scheduled overnight visit, but didn't give it much thought. Tom had always been moody. He drove the girls to Grant Avenue, where they played in the backyard, ate takeout, and watched videos. The house was now clean, not a sign of what had happened just forty-eight hours before. He had done a good job cleaning up.

The girls were just getting to sleep in their upstairs bedrooms when Kim Horstmann called to say Annie was missing. Capano thought he handled Kim quite well, telling her he had believed Annie was at the shore, with her. But he worried that he hadn't sounded concerned enough and called Kimmie back.

Now he told her all about his meal with Annie Thursday night and went on, in great detail, about what he and Annie had done that night. Detail was the key. As a lawyer, he knew the importance of being specific as a way of establishing credibility; as a practiced manipulator, he understood that the power of narrative, even if fictional, came from detail. He told Kim he had given Annie a gift from Talbots, bought her groceries, returned some Spanish tapes, and checked her air conditioner. He reassured Kim again that Annie would probably be home by Monday.

Tom Capano, of course, knew Annie wasn't coming home. But he trusted in his powers of persuasion. He had grown up getting what he wanted and in adulthood found that he had a prodigious ability to get anything he desired. He could handle this. Annie was dead, but no one else knew that. And if they never found her body or any clues, they would declare her missing and that would be the end of it. Sure, there would be questions and probably a brief investigation, even suspicions thrown his way because he'd had dinner with her that night, but he could talk his way around that, as he had just done with Kimmie. Within a couple of weeks, Annie would be in the inactive missing persons file and everyone could get on with their lives.

Capano had expected to be interviewed by police—just not in the dead of night. The knock on the door at 3:30 that Sunday morning startled him, threw him off balance. And it bothered him to see state troopers among the group; he was counting on Wilmington police to handle the case, a police force he once oversaw. He knew mostly everyone in City Hall who counted, and they knew him. A few well-placed calls and persuasive conversations with the right people and Tom would be moving the investigation toward a theory he knew he could make stick: Annie had run off and killed herself.

"Do you have any idea why we would want to speak with you, sir?" one of the men asked.

Of course he did, Capano said immediately. It was perfect, in a way, that Kimmie had called him, giving him an opportunity to show his concern and prove he was part of Annie's circle of friends. The fact that so few people knew about his affair with Annie would only prove his discretion about such matters, that he was a stand-up guy who didn't want his wife hurt. And he had made sure, these last several months, that he was on friendly terms with Annie's closest friends and that they knew of her severe eating disorder.

Capano ushered the four cops into the foyer of his house. They seemed deferential enough, though extremely curious about the house. He asked them to keep their voices down because his kids were sleeping upstairs. That had a nice ring of truth—it *was* true. He didn't want anyone messing with his girls. They had nothing to do with this. Otherwise, he was an exemplar of cool, calm innocence. The police didn't even ask to look around. At the end, he even planted the suicide notion. He knew Anne Marie well, Capano said, and knew she was having lots of psychological problems and often spoke of taking her own life.

He couldn't tell whether the cops bought that story or not. But they would. Once they started talking to people who knew Annie—especially her therapists—they would understand what had happened. He thanked them for their interest and said good night.

The cops did not tell Tom Capano about the diaries and the letters that had been found in Annie's apartment—or how many times his name came up in them. Nor did they mention that they already had spoken with Annie's therapist and that she had suggested kidnapping was a more probable explanation than suicide.

There were some things, Capano was to learn, that he couldn't control.

Capano took his first break from routine on Sunday morning, June 30, a day he normally would have taken his daughters to mass at St. Anthony of Padua Church on North Dupont Street. The towering stone landmark was in Wilmington's old Little Italy, a modest and well-kept neighborhood just west of downtown. For nearly two decades Tom Capano had been a leading benefactor of the church, a member of the parish board, a friend of the priests.

It was a place, at Sunday-morning mass, where Anne Marie and Tom often had seen each other.

But on this bright summer Sunday morning, Tom Capano skipped mass. He told his girls he wanted to let them sleep in, but he really needed to work the phone, the closest thing to an extension of his mind that he had. And his mind was working hard this morning.

He called Kim Horstmann and told her the cops had banged on his door at three in the morning and treated him rudely. But he said he'd been thinking and suggested that Annie had probably gone away with Jackie Steinhoff.

Another call went to his brother Louis, who was home at his Greenville estate.

"Could you come over here?" Tom asked. "I need to talk to you about something right away."

Louis, in fact, had never been to Tom's Grant Avenue house in the eight months his brother had lived there. But when Tom called, Louis acted. He got directions and rushed over. Tom greeted his brother at the door and ushered him into an enclosed porch.

"I've been seeing this woman, Anne Marie Fahey, for a couple of years," he began, in a calm, matter-of-fact voice. "She's the governor's scheduling secretary and she's apparently disappeared. The cops were here in the middle of the night, asking me questions while the kids were upstairs. They think I'm somehow involved."

Louis paced around the den of his oldest brother's five-bedroom bachelor pad, puzzled by the words he was hearing.

Tom continued his perplexing tale.

"This girl's anorexic and bulimic and she's got a lot of problems, so I stopped seeing her several months ago."

Tom rattled on. In fact, he *had* probably stopped "seeing" Annie months ago. But these slips were not anything that Louis noticed right now. In fact, he didn't know who Tom was talking about or why he was telling this story.

"I've been sending her to a psychologist and trying to convince her to go away for treatment. But we're still good friends. We go out to dinner once in a while, and I took her to a restaurant in Philadelphia Thursday night.

"So we came back here after dinner and I went upstairs to use the bathroom. When I came down, she had slit her wrists and some blood got on the sofa."

Louis now understood what was going on. "Did you take her to the hospital?" he asked, suddenly stunned by Tom's words.

"No, they were just superficial wounds and we bandaged them. Then I took her home. I gave her some cash. She probably took off for the weekend and she'll show up for work Monday."

Tom was trying out a variation of his disturbed-woman-runs-away story, adding the wrist slitting for Louis in order to explain why he and Gerry had to throw stuff away at Louis's construction sites.

"Can you have the Dumpsters emptied?" Tom asked.

Louis said he would.

Always trying to manage the story—now more than ever— Tom also told Louis that he and Kay were seeing a therapist in the hopes of reconciling and asked his brother not to mention any of this to Kay.

Louis, who had his own girlfriend on the side, didn't question his brother about his love life and was more than sympathetic to the need for secrecy on that score.

But Louis was curious enough about Tom's tale to drive to Concord Pike, location of the First USA construction site, and peer into the Dumpsters. He did see the legs of an overturned couch under some broken-up drywall, but that was it. Louis shrugged and went home, still a little mystified about his big brother, white-knight Tom, being mixed up in a caper about a missing girl with slit wrists.

After stopping at Happy Harry's drugstore in Trolley Square to buy some stain remover—just in case, he thought—Tom drove to Debby's house.

She was in her living room when Tom stormed in, muttering and pacing.

"I feel like I've been set up!" he barked. "Somebody has set me up."

"What's going on, honey?" Debby asked. She had never seen Tom so upset.

"I can't tell you now," he said. "Not now."

He sat down in a chair, and she knelt in front of him, pressing for more information. Tom told her about the police coming to his house in the middle of the night but wouldn't tell her why. He then rose and left, as abruptly as he had entered.

But a few minutes later, Debby's phone rang. "I'm in the driveway!" she heard Tom bark. "Come on out."

Debby hurried to the Suburban, and Tom handed her a plastic bag.

"Hang onto these," he told Debby. "It would be embarrassing if somebody found them."

Inside were three pornographic videotapes. Tom was beginning to realize that he had to clean up more than just the blood in order to cover his tracks. But how much more was there? And could he cover all his tracks?

Congressman Mike Castle and his wife, Jane, were walking down Grant Avenue to a neighbor's party that Sunday afternoon and saw Tom Capano vacuuming his wife's big sport utility vehicle. Like every well-connected political person in Delaware, the Castles knew Tom Capano, who was also an aide to Castle when he was governor, but they had never been good friends and didn't socialize. Today, however, Capano greeted the Castles and seemed in an extremely voluble and chatty mood. He was "overly friendly," recalled Castle.

When he finished cleaning the Suburban, Capano gathered up his four daughters and drove them back to their house. But he seemed in a hurry, saying he was returning for dinner that night, and quickly switched cars, jumping into his Jeep. As he pulled out of the driveway, however, he saw two cars pulling slowly up to the curb in front of the house. Capano immediately recognized Detective Donovan behind the wheel of the lead car and guessed that the other vehicle had cops inside as well. Capano was angry. How dare they come to his wife's house; this was not her business. A *stunt*, Capano thought as he motioned them to follow him to Grant Avenue.

Overhead, as the small convoy drove the leafy roads to Grant Avenue, a helicopter could be seen whooshing back and forth just above the treetops of Brandywine Park.

Capano didn't know the chopper was searching for Anne Marie Fahey. But there was a lot he would begin to learn about Annie—and, most poignantly, about the power of love, an emotion that quietly drove the search for the missing woman but which had not figured in Capano's calculus of deceit.

Uncomfortable with surprises, Capano was no longer an accommodating man as Donovan and his colleagues entered his Grant Avenue house again. In fact, he told them flat out that he regretted revealing so much the night before about his and Annie's relationship. Showing up at his wife's house, Sunday afternoon, they clearly weren't playing by the rules, and Capano obviously couldn't trust them.

Reluctantly, he allowed them to look through the house and poke through his car.

"Don't worry; we won't toss your drawers or anything like that," one of them said.

Capano forced a smile. He did know the game. If he really wanted to, he could throw them out, tell them to get a search warrant. But that, he knew, would only arouse suspicion. He had nothing to hide—he had taken too many precautions, even getting rid of the telltale porn flicks, which, even he knew, would be thought of as dirt associated with crime—and so could be calm as the four men wandered through his house. He followed, however, just in case, watching closely as they scanned every room, attic to basement, poked their heads in every closet, and looked inside the Jeep.

They discovered neither Annie nor any sign of a struggle or foul play. Nothing was even out of place. The house was immaculate. The officers thanked Capano for his time and said they'd want to conduct a formal interview the following morning if Fahey didn't show up for work.

Capano said that would be fine.

After the police left, Capano drove to Debby's house, still seething over the inspection.

"The police came back to my house," he told Debby, spinning the tale slightly to help make the case for harassment but again without revealing what they were bothering him about. "I had to pack up the kids and take them back to 17th Street and then meet the police back at Grant Avenue. They searched the place."

Debby begged him to tell her what was happening, but Tom still refused. Instead, he asked to use the phone and went into another room. He knew he had to stay clear of all but normal phone calls from his house, knowing how easy it was to track phone records. Making sure Debby was out of earshot, he called the general manager of the family's Penn's Grove Holiday Inn and asked the man to make sure the hotel's trash containers were emptied as soon as possible.

He hung up, then stormed out of the house, keeping Debby in the dark.

From Kay's house that evening, where he went for his regular Sunday dinner with the kids, he called Louis and told his brother the cops had come by again and were treating him like a suspect. Tom also reminded Louis to empty the Dumpster, then said good-bye.

Charles Oberly picked up the phone that Sunday afternoon and heard the caller identify himself as Tom Carper.

"Can I come over and talk to you?" he asked Oberly.

"Sure," Oberly replied, wondering why the governor, a political ally and casual friend, would want to meet with him on a Sunday afternoon. *Must be some political or personal issue,* Oberly thought to himself.

"Hey, Tia, guess what?" he called to his wife. "The governor is coming over in an hour or so." Tia, who had multiple sclerosis and spent her days in a wheelchair, wasn't happy that the state's chief executive was just stopping by their house. She didn't have nice clothes on, and the house needed tidying. Charlie quickly began straightening up, keeping an eye out the window.

A car soon pulled in to the driveway, but he didn't think Carper drove a black Jeep. Oberly then saw Tom Capano get out and come to his door.

"What are you doing here?" Oberly asked.

"I just called you," Capano said, startled.

Oberly realized his mistake and welcomed his visitor. Although he and Capano didn't travel in the same social circles, Capano had supported Oberly's three campaigns for attorney general and his unsuccessful 1994 bid for U.S. Senate. Over the years, Oberly had developed a habit of dropping in at Tom and Kay's after work, unannounced, inquiring, "What's for dinner?" and leaving with a full belly.

Oberly now offered Capano a Coke, and the two moved into the living room. Oberly knew this wasn't a social call.

Capano spelled out his dilemma—that cops had been to his house twice, asking about the governor's secretary, with whom he'd had an affair. He said that Gerry, with whom he had spent several hours the morning after her disappearance, could vouch for his whereabouts.

This was how it was supposed to work. A Sunday afternoon, sitting in a living room, sipping Coke, telling the state's former attorney general, a buddy, to take care of things. Oberly, who had been doing defense and corporate work since his Senate loss twenty months earlier, agreed to act as Tom's attorney.

Tom then suggested they go to Gerry's house and apprise him of the situation.

Gerry had just gotten back from Richmond, finishing off a two-day road trip to the drag races. After the freaky Friday trip with Tom, Gerry had gone home and spent the night bar-hopping with buddy Ed DelCollo until well past last call and then returned home, to snort cocaine and drink beer alone. The next morning he drove to Richmond—five hours south—with three buddies.

The last person Gerry wanted to see at his door was his brother Tom, source of his problems. And seeing that Tom was with Charlie Oberly only made Gerry feel worse.

"They said that a woman was missing and the police may come asking me questions about it," recalled Gerry about what Tom and Charlie told him. "It was somebody that Tommy knew, that Tommy had dinner with last or something."

Standing in his driveway, listening to his brother, hearing the name Anne Marie Fahey, Gerry now knew who was in the cooler. But he said nothing. He assumed Tom knew what he was doing and was content to listen. Oberly now weighed in, advising Gerry to hire an attorney and not speak to any investigators before seeing a lawyer. They gave him the number of Dan Lyons, a Wilmington native and former federal prosecutor in San Francisco, who now worked as a criminal attorney.

"One more thing," Oberly said. "If the press come nosing around, don't lose your cool."

Louis Capano had arrived early Monday morning at his company's offices, a four-building brick complex next to the First USA site in Brandywine Hundred, to get some work done without interruption. But the phone rang anyway. As it was only seven-thirty, he couldn't imagine who would be calling his office at this hour.

"It's Tom," said the familiar voice. "Anne Marie, the missing woman I told you about, didn't show up for work," he blurted. "Did you have the Dumpsters dumped?"

"No, Tom," Louis said. "I forgot all about it."

"Could you have them dumped?" Tom pushed. "Right away. I'm afraid the police might start looking around and check them."

Louis asked more questions, but Tom cut him off. "Just dump the damn Dumpsters!" he ordered.

Louis passed the order to Chris Nowland, his property manager at the First USA site, who left a message on the answering machine of Shaw Taylor, the man overseeing the renovation project. Taylor, a slight man with sandy-blond hair, listened to the message when he arrived at work that morning and shook his head. He knew that none of the four Dumpsters at the site needed emptying.

Worried that there might be something illegal in the bins, Taylor went to look for himself, taking Louis Capano III with him; the boss's twenty-year-old son, a college student, was learning the family business that summer by being a company gofer. The men looked in all four bins but saw only scrap metal, drywall, tile, studs, and other construction debris—nothing out of the ordinary.

Taylor asked Louis III to call his dad and tell him the trash bins were only half-full and weren't scheduled to be emptied for days. But when Louis III asked, his dad barked, "Get off the phone right away and don't talk about this assignment!"

Taylor got the Dumpsters dumped.

That same Monday morning, readers of the *Wilmington News Journal* learned about the governor's missing secretary—and Tom Capano canceled his interview with the police. The next day, his name was leaked to the press as that of "the man who had dinner with Anne Marie Fahey the night she vanished."

Leaving a dental appointment that Tuesday morning, Tom Capano turned on his car radio and heard his name on a local station as Fahey's last dinner companion. After lunch he stormed over to the Delaware Avenue office of Oberly and Jennings.

Capano had planned to leave Wilmington for Stone Harbor the next day, July 3, for the holiday weekend. But, he told his attorney, he was heading immediately to the shore.

"I can't take this anymore," Capano told Oberly. "I'm out of here."

Tom called Debby MacIntyre at Tatnall.

"I have something very shocking to tell you," he said to his mistress of fifteen years. "You better sit down."

Debby sat down.

"Do you recall reading about a woman who is missing who had gone to dinner with a prominent Wilmington attorney?" he asked.

Debby had seen the story. "I got a terrible feeling," she recalled.

"That was me," Capano continued.

"Oh, no!" Debbie said, aghast at what she was hearing.

"I'm a suspect in her disappearance and I've hired Charlie Oberly as my attorney. He's going to want to speak with you."

"Who is this woman?" asked Debby, who thought Capano was in Philadelphia the previous Thursday for a Saul Ewing partners' meeting.

"Look, I'm heading to the beach in a few minutes. I'll call you later tonight and we'll talk about it then. Can you speak with Charlie today?"

Debby said she would, then hung up the phone. Devastated, she stood up, gripping her desk so hard it hurt her hand, and walked to the office of Joan Brady, her assistant, where she repeated the story Capano had told her.

Debby left work early and at five-thirty that afternoon spoke with Oberly on the phone, reviewing all her contacts with Tom, but leaving out many details.

Tom called her at nine-thirty that night, from his mother's Stone Harbor house.

"Who is this Anne Marie Fahey?" Debby asked again.

Capano explained that he'd been seeing the woman for about three years and had briefly fallen in love with her. "But it's over," he said.

The revelation sent Debby's mind spinning. While the relationship with Capano was not exclusive, she always told him when she had a date. Though she was the same woman who was having an affair behind her friend Kay's back, Debby still felt betrayed that Capano had hidden his relationship with Fahey.

And now, Debby thought in disbelief, the woman Capano once loved was missing, and he was a suspect.

Over that holiday weekend, Capano was joined by his mother and his daughters. But it was not a festive holiday for Tom, who spent much of his time on the phone. He called Kim Horstmann, other friends, law colleagues, and his own attorneys—assuring them all, as he had told his family, that he had no involvement in Anne Marie Fahey's disappearance.

When Bud Freel drove down, on behalf of Annie's family, Capano resisted, as pleasantly as he could, Freel's pleas to go home and assist investigators.

On the Fourth of July—as nearly three hundred people up in Wilmington scoured Brandywine Park for Anne Marie Fahey—the Capanos had a barbecue, their traditional summer kickoff party. But with the cloud over Tom, the shining star of the family, it was a somber holiday.

Gerry Capano had brought his wife and children to the barbecue but spent much of the time huddled with Tom, trying to straighten out their story. Gerry had already messed things up, telling Rob Hafele, a Stone Harbor real estate agent who had seen the Suburban on the twenty-eighth, that Tom had been there. "I told him you were using the boat with your girlfriend," Gerry said to Tom.

"Just hang in there," Tom told his brother, who kept asking him for more details, without success. "Don't worry. I told you I won't let anything happen to you."

Sometime that weekend, Tom strolled over to the nearby summer home of his sister, Marian, and her husband, Lee Ramunno.

"If you're innocent, you should talk to the detectives," Ramunno, a veteran attorney and former prosecutor, told his brother-in-law, whom he considered one of the most honest, ethical men on earth.

"I can't talk to police," Tom Capano explained, "without involving somebody else."

Already, Tom was hatching a new cover story.

BOOK THREE

By the way, Mr. Capano, I sleep very well at night.
—COLM CONNOLLY,
November 12, 1998

10 *Chasing the Spin*

Poring over Tom Capano's credit card bill at the polished oval mahogany table in the U.S. Attorney's Office conference room on July 25, Colm Connolly's eyes were drawn to a $308.99 purchase on June 29—two days after Anne Marie Fahey vanished. The charge had been made at Wallpaper Warehouse.

Connolly, a federal prosecutor with a Notre Dame education and a steel-trap mind, was now overseeing the investigation into the disappearance of Fahey, already nearly a month old. The case had moved quickly from the jurisdiction of local police to the hands of state authorities, then, with a call from the president of the United States, to the arms of the federal government, amassing more investigative firepower as it moved. Finding Fahey and catching the person responsible for her disappearance was now almost a round-the-clock effort, with few budgetary constraints. But no one understood better than Connolly, who wielded the resources, that snaring Tom Capano would require the intelligence and precision of a surgeon.

"What the hell is a guy like Capano, who lives in a rental house, doing buying three hundred dollars' worth of wallpaper?" Connolly asked, turning to Bob Donovan, the burly crew-cutted Wilmington police detective who had been working the case full-time for four weeks and was just getting his second wind.

"It makes no sense," Donovan said, agreeing with the young prosecutor with jet-black hair.

The thirty-two-year-old cop was as big and easygoing as the thirty-one-year-old prosecutor was lean and coiled. They often laughed about how they first met, four years earlier.

Fresh out of Duke Law School, Connolly had just joined the U.S. Attorney's Office in Wilmington when he was pulled over near the downtown Amtrak train station by a city police cruiser. After Connolly had exchanged some harsh words with two cops, who said Connolly's well-dressed wife and a male friend fit the profile of drug runners they were seeking, the men went on their ways.

But the following Monday, Connolly was called in to interrogate a Jamaican drug dealer picked up at the same train station carrying a semiautomatic pistol, cash, and a load of crack cocaine. Waiting in a conference room, Connolly looked up to see the same two Wilmington cops march into the room—the same two who had shined their flashlights into Connolly's combative face two days before. The rookie prosecutor and the cops immediately broke into wide grins.

Four years later, Greg Sleet, the U.S. Attorney for Delaware, handpicked Connolly, still the youngest prosecutor on the twelve-attorney staff, to run the Fahey show. Sleet, Delaware's first black U.S. Attorney and the son of a Pulitzer Prize–winning photojournalist for *Ebony* magazine, had been mildly amused to read about Bill Clinton's offer of help on the case. A presidential hand in the pot would not affect investigative procedure per se—the feds were used to helping local authorities—but it was a clear sign that this would be a high-profile case. And no one blinked when Sleet turned to the prosecutor called Pug—for pugnacious—by his Duke classmates. During four years as an assistant U.S. Attorney, Connolly, the homegrown son of a DuPont engineer, despite his altar-boy looks, combined the wrath of an avenging angel, pit bull tenacity, and prodigious courtroom skills to rack up a string of successful convictions against gun runners, drug dealers, tax cheats, and mob soldiers.

He would need all the skills he could muster for this case, one with a suspect but no victim. Plenty of psychological threads—friends who described a secret affair that had gone sour, a shrink who said her patient was afraid of the man, and a diary entry that all but predicted the end for Fahey—but nothing tangible, nothing a judge could even use as probable cause for a search warrant, let alone to arrest Capano.

"Let's check it out," Connolly said about the Wallpaper Warehouse receipt, already halfway to a phone at the other end of the room. The prosecutor did not do anything slowly

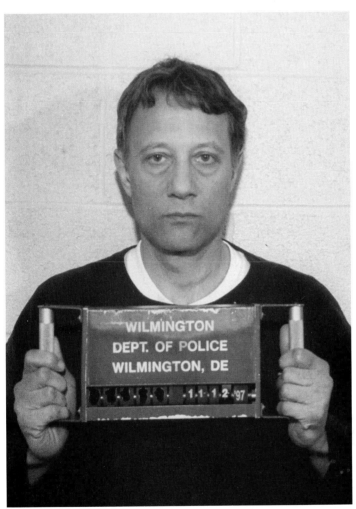

Under arrest: Wealthy Wilmington lawyer Tom Capano is charged with murder, more than a year after Anne Marie Fahey disappeared. (Wilmington Police Department)

(above) Governor's scheduling secretary: beautiful, outgoing, friendly and terrifically organized, Anne Marie Fahey not long before she died. (Fahey family)

(left) Discovering her roots: Annie took a trip to Ireland with her brother Brian two summers before she was killed. (Fahey family)

Finally happy: "She loved the guy," Kathleen Fahey-Hosey said of her sister's feelings toward Michael Scanlan, here helping Annie open presents at her surprise thirtieth birthday party, five months before her murder. (Fahey family)

Michael Scanlan entering Wilmington Courthouse: two weeks before her death, Anne Marie Fahey told her sister that the MBNA executive was the man she wanted to marry. (Robert Craig)

Kathleen Fahey-Hosey, Annie's sister, on the porch of Annie's apartment house, helped organize the search of Brandywine Park a week after she vanished. (Ginger Wall)

(above) Telling evidence: This speck of blood on a baseboard in Capano's house helped seal the defendant's fate. (Federal Bureau of Investigation)

(right) Early withdrawal: Disheveled and unshaven, Tom Capano visits a cash machine several hours after murdering Fahey.

Number-one mistress: Debby MacIntyre, outside the courthouse after the verdict was announced, had been Tom Capano's steady – and secret – girlfriend for fifteen years. (William Bretzger)

Two of Tom Capano's teenaged daughters, Alex and Jenny, leave the courthouse with their uncle, Lee Ramunno, during a break in their dad's murder trial. (Brian Branch-Price)

Mom: Marguerite Capano is helped into the courthouse by niece Loretta Farkas (left) and daughter Marian Ramunno. (Brian Branch-Price)

Defense team (left to right): Gene Maurer, Joseph Oteri, Jack O'Donnell, Charles Oberly. (Robert Craig)

Second sibling: Tom Capano's brother, Louis, Jr., with his attorney Katherine Recker, after testifying before a federal Grand Jury. (Chuck McGowen)

Filial agony: Gerry Capano, the baby of the family, would provide the key testimony that resulted in a death sentence for his brother. (Brian Branch-Price)

Plastic coffin: The cooler, found floating in the sea by a fisherman, into which Capano stuffed Fahey's body. (Cris Barrish)

Prosecution team (left to right): FBI agent Eric Alpert, IRS investigator Ron Poplos, federal attorney and lead prosecutor Colm Connolly, state police lieutenant Mark Daniels, state prosecutor Ferris Wharton, and Wilmington police detective Bob Donovan. (Robert Craig)

The Judge: William Swain Lee, a former Marine, presided over an often raucous courtroom with a firm hand. (Jennifer Corbett)

Sunday morning: A crowd gathers outside the Daniel L. Herrmann Courthouse in Wilmington on January 17, 1999, after the verdict is announced. (Fred Comegys)

(left) The case had been front-page news for nearly three years. (Cris Barrish)
(right) The price for murder: Tom Capano leaves the courthouse on March 16, 1999, after being sentenced to die by lethal injection. (Brian Branch-Price)

or ambiguously; his mind and body, as if created by a crafty metaphysician, at times seemed one. At his phone he punched out 555-1212.

"Operator, may I have the number for Wallpaper Warehouse?" Connolly listened, then dialed another number. He listened again, a smile crossing his face, then hung up, pumping his fist in the air.

"Unbelievable!" he shouted to Donovan. "Wallpaper Warehouse is Air Base Carpets. He rolled her up in a rug."

"Oh, my God," Donovan said.

After twenty-nine days without a sign of Fahey—no ransom note, no sighting—Connolly and his team considered themselves homicide investigators. Their only suspect: Thomas Capano. Every psychological crumb Annie had dropped led to Capano. But he was an elusive target.

During a phone interview three days earlier, Ruth Boylan, Capano's elderly housekeeper, said she had just been in the Grant Avenue house—her first visit since June 24, three days before Fahey disappeared—and hadn't noticed anything different about the home. Now, with the Air Base Carpet Mart receipt in hand, Connolly instructed Donovan to talk to Boylan in person.

Connolly also called Eric Alpert, the FBI agent who had been assigned to the case, and directed him to get over to Air Base.

———

The forty-one-year-old Alpert, a bushy-haired New York native with a gravelly voice, had joined the FBI in 1982 after receiving a law degree. He had planned to stay just a few years, to get some field experience before becoming a prosecutor, but found he enjoyed the chase more than the courtroom. He had been with the FBI's Wilmington bureau since 1990 and with his boss, Tim Munson, out of town for several weeks, was running the office when the Fahey case broke.

Realizing it might involve multiple jurisdictions, Alpert had called Donovan on July 9.

"Do you need any help on this thing?" Alpert asked the detective. Donovan said he was getting ready to request a "pen register" on Capano's phone, to track the numbers of all incoming and outgoing calls, including local ones.

"If you want, we can get it running today," Alpert offered.
That was what it meant to have the feds helping. Donovan
was happy to have their assistance.

The detective also brought Alpert up-to-date on details of
the case that hadn't been made public, most of them about
Thomas Capano. Donovan told Alpert about the diary entry
referring to Capano as a "controlling, manipulative, insecure,
jealous maniac" and the attorney's refusal to come in for additional interviews. Alpert figured Capano was guilty of something; innocent people don't surround themselves with
attorneys and stop cooperating.

Alpert got Greg Sleet's authorization to seek the pen register, and with that the feds were involved. That same day,
Colm Connolly, who ran into Sleet and discussed the pen register with him, said about the Fahey case, "You know, we can
do our own investigation here." Connolly argued that because
Capano might have taken Fahey from Ristorante Panorama in
Philadelphia to his house in Wilmington against her will,
crossing state lines in the process, there were good grounds to
launch a federal kidnapping investigation.

The call from President Clinton to Carper didn't hurt Connolly's argument. Sleet said yes.

After his name started appearing in the newspaper, linked
to Fahey, Capano's friends rallied to his side. Though investigators were careful not to call Capano a suspect—they
weren't divulging what they had—Brian Murphy urged his
buddy to take the initiative and proclaim his innocence publicly. Murphy, an easygoing, baby-faced man who had served
as Mayor Frawley's spokesman and later commerce chief, believed a public pronouncement would help clear Capano's rapidly deteriorating reputation in the public eye. Murphy was
indebted to Capano for loaning him $15,000 for his daughters'
tuition at Ursuline Academy. Murphy had never paid back his
wealthy friend.

So on July 9—the same day investigators were getting permission for the pen register and the same day Capano left
Robert Fahey a message saying he wanted to meet with him—

Murphy invited Capano to his Wilmington office, where he worked for a developer. Together they prepared a press release.

Statement by Thomas J. Capano in the disappearance of Anne Marie Fahey: July 9, 1996.

The disappearance of Anne Marie Fahey remains as much a mystery to me as it does to her family and friends. I can only say I share the gut-wrenching emotions of Anne Marie's family and pray for her safe return. While I can do nothing to end the speculation of the public and press, I can state for the record the pertinent facts of my last meeting with Anne Marie. I did have dinner with Anne Marie in Philadelphia on the evening of Thursday, June 27th. We returned to Wilmington. We drove to her apartment at approximately 10 P.M. I walked Anne Marie into her apartment, stayed a few moments, said good night and left. I noticed nothing unusual as I left. That was the last time I saw or spoke to Anne Marie. I then drove home, where I remained until I left for the office the next morning.

While Anne Marie had some problems, there was nothing out of the ordinary in either her conversation or behavior that would lead me to believe anything was amiss. I am at a complete loss to explain what caused her disappearance.

It is difficult to respond as to how others may characterize our relationship. Frankly, the nature of our relationship is and will remain a matter between Anne Marie and myself. What is relevant and important is that Anne Marie and I are good friends and parted company good friends that evening.

I was informed of Anne Marie's potential disappearance by phone late on the evening of Saturday, June 29th, by a mutual friend. While I was concerned, I was also aware that Anne Marie had taken Friday off from work and concluded she had probably gone off with friends for the weekend. At that time, there was nothing to lead me to believe she would not be at work on Monday morning, July 1st. At approximately 3 A.M. on the morning of Sunday, June 30th, I was awakened by four police officers at my home. Since then,

I have and will continue to fully cooperate with investigators. As much as anyone else, I want to know Anne Marie's whereabouts.

I will not be granting interviews or making further statements. I want to thank my friends who have offered their many kind words of support and encouragement and ask all concerned to pray for Anne Marie's safe return.

When they showed the statement to Charles Oberly, however, the lawyer nixed it, saying the timing wasn't right.

Other friends of Capano agreed with Murphy and urged Capano to step up and publicly fight.

By mid-July—with Capano's name and face splashed across the newspaper and television screens on a daily basis—Mike Harkins, one of Delaware's most influential Republicans, called Oberly with advice for a friend he presumed was a victim of circumstances.

"Hey, you guys are getting killed in the press," Harkins, a portly, jovial man who was a former Delaware secretary of state, told Oberly. "I know you're a lawyer and you are supposed to tell your client not to say anything, but you've got to take the other side on this."

After more stories appeared, Oberly called back and asked if Harkins would join Capano and some others for a meeting to discuss public relations strategy. Oberly still didn't want Capano talking to the media or issuing a statement but was willing to listen.

Meeting in defense attorney Bart Dalton's office in downtown Wilmington with Tom and Louis Capano were Harkins, Murphy, and Bob Perkins, former chief of staff under Governor Castle. Harkins, who had played golf with Capano in the past and believed in his innocence, addressed the group.

"Look, I don't know any of the facts, but the way it's being reported in the paper, you guys are getting killed. You're guilty even if you are innocent."

Murphy and others expressed similar sentiments, but the meeting broke up without any decision being made.

———

Early results from the pen register indicated that Capano spoke frequently with his girlfriends Debby MacIntyre and Susan Louth and his children—on the assumption that he wasn't talking to his wife when he called his old house.

Connolly and Alpert then subpoenaed Capano's earlier phone records and some of his financial records, including bank and credit card statements. Other men Fahey had dated were also investigated, but only Capano kept bringing up hits.

By the middle of July, Connolly had assumed leadership of the probe and, with Donovan and Alpert as leaders, had assembled an impressive team of city, state, and federal investigators. They set up a "war room" in the U.S. Attorney's Office, on the eleventh floor of the Chase Manhattan building, a glass-and-steel skyscraper at 12th and Market Streets, outfitting it with blackboard, file cabinets, chairs, maps, and electronic listening equipment. Their initial goal, Connolly told them, was to get enough information about Tom Capano to make a search warrant stick.

Interviews with Annie's friends, if not conclusive proof, were surely indicative of a stormy relationship. Jill Morrison told Trooper Daniels and Detective Donovan that Capano was "psychotic" and recounted an incident when Capano picked Annie up, drove her to his garage, locked the car doors, and wouldn't let her out until she heard him out. Morrison also told the police about a barrage of harassing calls from Capano before the Grand Gala in January.

Phone records showed that on June 27, at 11:52 P.M, the night Annie had dinner with Capano, someone had dialed Star 69, a phone service that automatically dialed the phone of the last incoming caller, from Fahey's apartment. At 12:05 A.M on June 28 someone had also dialed Star 69 from Capano's house. The thirteen-minute gap, investigators suspected, gave Capano ample time to drive from Annie's apartment to his own house. And from studying Capano's phone records they knew he was a frequent user of Star 69.

Connolly asked IRS agent Ron Poplos to help analyze Capano's financial records and offer suggestions about what various transactions could mean. If nothing else, investigators got a good idea of the man's wealth and spending habits. For the six-week period ending July 18, Capano had deposited $90,200 into his Wilmington Trust bank account. They knew he often spent several hundred dollars on weeknight dinners—that kind of extravagance made the purchase of an inexpensive rug at Air Base Carpet Mart seem odd indeed.

———————

With a call to Air Base manager Mike Longwill on July 25, Agent Alpert quickly confirmed that Capano had purchased an eight-by-eleven carpet on June 29. Longwill said it was green-blue with an Oriental pattern.

The significance of the rug purchase now depended on Ruth Boylan. If she couldn't recall a new rug in the house, there was no reason to ask for a search warrant. Capano could easily say he had bought the Air Base rug as a gift; no law against that.

That evening Detective Donovan drove through a summer thunderstorm to Ruth Boylan's home in a modest Wilmington neighborhood, wondering if this were just another dead end. The detective knew that witnesses often had to be asked the right question to kindle a memory, but Boylan, a pleasant white-haired woman, had seemed sure of herself when she said that nothing in Capano's house had changed. Now, Donovan hoped, he had the right question. "Did you notice if any rugs or furniture had been replaced?" he asked.

"Yes," said Boylan without hesitation.

Click. The ball dropped.

The housekeeper now told the cop that in Capano's den, which he called the great room, a rose-colored sofa with a pineapple motif had been replaced with two chairs. And the beige carpet that had covered most of the floor had been taken up. In its place was a blue-green multicolored carpet with an Oriental design.

Bingo.

Donovan asked if the old rug or sofa had been damaged.

No, the housekeeper replied. They were in fine condition. No rips, tears, or stains.

As soon as he was in his car, gliding over the rain-slicked

roads, Donovan called Connolly, who pumped his fist upon hearing the good news.

―――――――

Connolly continued to push his men to get more information. They re-interviewed Lisa D'Amico, Annie's hairdresser, who added more detailed information about Annie's fear of Capano. The stylist said her client had mentioned in May an incident in which Capano had become outraged when Annie told him she wanted to break up. He started yelling, said D'Amico, calling Annie a "slut" and a "whore," grabbing her by the neck, and forcing her to flee.

Michele Sullivan seemed to provide the ribbon to wrap the package with. Alpert met with Annie's therapist on July 29 and explained that the waitress at the Panorama had described the dinner as somber. Sullivan, who wasn't aware Annie and Capano had almost weekly dinners, theorized that Annie would only have gone out with Capano that night to break up for good.

The therapist also reiterated Annie's kidnapping fears and expressed doubt that Annie would have "gone willingly" to Capano's home that night. Sullivan's words clinched the search warrant application, Connolly decided.

The next day, Connolly and his boss, Richard Andrews, summoned state prosecutor Ferris Wharton to the U.S. Attorney's Office. Wharton assumed the topic was the Fahey investigation, but he wasn't told that until after he arrived.

"Here's the deal," Connolly said. "We've put together enough evidence to go forward with a search warrant. We could continue our investigation. We believe it's been productive and would continue to be productive."

Connolly also offered to give the state all the information his team had gathered. And he warned that if the state decided to let the U.S. Attorney's Office run the show, "we will not be able to share information with you."

Wharton didn't even blink. "If you've got it," the laid-back prosecutor said, "why don't you just go for it?"

Connolly, Alpert, Donovan, and Daniels worked feverishly on the affidavit, with Connolly typing it himself, finishing late in the afternoon on Tuesday, July 30. FBI agents from Wilmington, Baltimore, and Washington, D.C., along with a team of city and state police officers, were ordered to report to the Wilmington FBI office the next morning, on the supposition that the court would order a search of Capano's home, his Jeep, and his wife's Suburban.

Mary Pat Trostle, a federal magistrate, opened the door to her Brandywine Hundred home a little after eight that night, greeting Connolly, Alpert, and Donovan. The prosecutor handed her the lengthy document—"Search Warrant" form for case number 96-93M—which Trostle read carefully before giving her written consent for the search. She also granted Connolly's request that the warrants be sealed to prevent public disclosure of their contents.

———————

Back at Grant Avenue, Tom Capano was relaxing with Debby MacIntyre, who was sleeping over that Tuesday night. Capano wasn't in a good mood. The Wilmington paper had printed that day that Capano was officially a suspect in Fahey's disappearance. Being branded in the paper was just the latest blow to Capano's rapidly diminishing reputation.

All month he had worked overtime trying to cover his tracks, assuring lawyers, friends, and family he had nothing to do with the troubled young woman's disappearance.

He had told MacIntyre he had given Fahey a great deal of money and that she had probably run off to some Spanish-speaking country—likely Mexico or Spain—to get away from Delaware.

"She'll be able to survive for quite some time," Capano told his faithful lover, who believed him.

Earlier in the month Charles Oberly had asked Capano to prepare a "time line" of his whereabouts on June 28, an accounting of his recent contacts with Fahey, and a list of gifts he'd given her. Capano stalled his attorney and, though it was a self-serving document that made him out to be a good sugar daddy and repeated the alibi he and Gerry had cooked up, instead of turning the document over to Oberly—a move that Capano knew would have locked him and his lawyers into a story—Capano stashed it on a shelf in the office of his law partner, Tim Frey, without telling Frey.

Capano also continued to work the phones, placing several calls to Kim Horstmann. He called on Saturday, July 13, from his mother's beach home, the first time since their late-night June 30 conversation. On Robert Fahey's advice, Horstmann took notes of the conversation and later typed them into her computer at work.

"I'm feeling horrible," Capano told Kim. "The press in Delaware is crucifying me."

The previous day, the *Wilmington News Journal* had revealed that Capano had refused persistent efforts by police for follow-up interviews.

Calm and collected—Horstmann recalled that he sounded "scripted"—Capano told of his shock when Annie hadn't arrived for work and of the visit by Bud Freel over the holiday weekend. Then Capano again recounted the events of June 27, adding more exacting and pointed detail to the story he had earlier told Horstmann and the police. While dropping Annie off that night, Capano said, he had hugged her, told her she was getting too thin, and remarked, "Have a good time at the shore with Kim or shopping at the outlets, if that's what you are going to do tomorrow."

He also told Horstmann that Annie had two phone messages from Scanlan the night of the twenty-seventh and suggested Scanlan might have been waiting outside Annie's apartment, spying on his girlfriend, and become jealous upon seeing Capano leave—an interesting piece of projection by the man who had done exactly that.

Similarly, Capano smeared the governor, telling Horstmann that Annie and Carper had had an affair when they worked together in Washington.

Horstmann listened—and Capano was content to talk. He wanted his story out. And two days later, he called again.

"My mind is playing games on me concerning the conversation we had Saturday," he said.

Then he changed the subject. "The Wilmington paper is writing a lot about me. I haven't read much of it, but it's upsetting my wife very much, what they're printing about me. But I think that eventually this nightmare is going to end. Annie will come home and it will all be over."

Capano suggested that he and Horstmann put their heads together and try to figure out where Annie was, because they knew her best. Horstmann asked Capano how often he spoke with Annie.

"Every day," he replied.

"Did you speak to her that Friday?" Horstmann asked, referring to the day after their dinner.

"No, I was planning to call, but I went out for my morning walk and never got around to it."

And Saturday? He had forgotten, Capano said, to call her on Saturday as well.

Suddenly another thread was unraveling in Capano's well-crafted story. He hadn't figured on the negative—that his *not* calling Annie was a sign that he knew she wasn't around. There were two days, Horstmann was suggesting, when Capano didn't try to reach Annie, two days when no one knew she was missing, when other friends were calling, as usual. Two days when Tom Capano, who said he spoke with Annie every day, suddenly didn't call. Why not? But Capano seemed to ignore the implication and pressed on with his theory. Annie was deep in debt, he told Horstmann, and owed a small fortune to the office of her former therapist, Bob Conner. He'd offered to pay all of her debt, including credit cards, but she'd rejected the offer.

And again, he fingered other possible suspects, among them a state trooper who worked in Carper's office and, Capano charged, had been harassing Annie; a neighbor who had offered to show her nude pictures of himself; and a man who had met Annie working out at the YMCA. Conveniently, Capano didn't know the names of any of these people. Horstmann, who had never heard Annie talk about any of them, much less an affair with the governor, figured Capano was just trying to be helpful. Finally, on Friday afternoon, July 19, Capano called Horstmann just as she was leaving her office.

"Where are you going to be for the weekend?" he asked.

"At the shore," she replied.

"I'll be there, too. I was thinking of inviting you down. But if you stayed down on Monday, maybe we could get together and put our heads together and come up with where she is. I'm convinced she is alive."

Capano told Horstmann he was afraid he would lose her friendship because of this mess. "You don't think I would hurt a hair on her head, do you?"

Horstmann said she didn't.

11 *Tom Turned Inside Out*

Once the warrant to search 2302 Grant Avenue was signed, Tim Munson, the FBI's top man in Wilmington, ordered a couple of agents to stake out Capano's house without being seen, starting at daybreak the next morning, July 31.

Meanwhile, Connolly and some two dozen agents and police had assembled at the FBI's downtown office to await word that Debby MacIntyre had left Capano's house. That word was squawked over police radio at seven. The time had come.

The caravan of police cruisers, a forensic van, and unmarked sedans and sport utility vehicles snaked up Kentmere Parkway to Grant Avenue as Capano's well-heeled neighbors left for work in their Jaguars, Porsches, and BMWs. While other officers began unpacking their evidence detection gear at the curb and in the driveway, five men—Munson was flanked by Connolly, Alpert, Donovan, and Daniels—walked up the brick pathway and banged on Capano's front door. There had been no notice of this search given to Capano or any of his lawyers.

The suspect, perhaps thinking MacIntyre had returned, opened the door still wearing his bathrobe. In recent days, he had shaved his thick, graying beard, and his clean-cut, more youthful-looking face now showed shock.

Munson stared him in the eye, announced in a booming voice that he was with the FBI, and presented Capano with the federal search warrant. "His face turned ashen," Munson recalled. "You could actually see the blood drain from his face. He never, ever expected the FBI to come knocking."

Capano, who couldn't slam the door on the interlopers with badges, let the men in, asking immediately for permission to call his lawyers. Munson nodded but directed one of his agents to go with Capano.

All pretense of politesse was now over. Tom Capano was an official suspect in what authorities now believed was the murder of Anne Marie Fahey.

There was "reason to believe," read the search warrant, that "there is now concealed a certain person or property," which included:

(a) hairs, fibers, blood, semen and any bodily fluids and parts of Anne Marie Fahey and Thomas Capano;

(b) any weapons or objects which could be used to inflict blunt force injury or strangulation;

(c) tools, mops, brooms, vacuums, cloths, other instruments, devices, containers, blankets, rugs, carpets, boxes, papers and other objects which could be used to dismember or conceal body parts, hairs and fluids;

(d) letters, notes, diaries, journals, calendars, files, memoranda, receipts and records which would provide proof of an affair between Capano and Fahey and establish that Fahey had been attempting to end their relationship and that Capano had attempted to prolong their relationship by blackmail, threats, gifts and harassment;

(e) cleansers, soaps, detergents, solvents and chemicals that could be used to conceal, dissolve or dismember body fluids or parts;

(f) the Oriental rug he bought at Air Base Carpet on June 29, 1996;

(g) new furniture which replaced the sofa removed from Capano's residence.

Capano's house was no longer his castle; it belonged, for today at least, to a small army of men and women, some in uniform, some in plainclothes, who swarmed over it like ants, carrying metal detectors, ultraviolet light projectors, vacuum cleaners, cameras, cotton swabs, walkie-talkies, and notebooks. They picked and peeked, crawled, swabbed and dusted, looking for evidence of what they clearly believed was a grisly crime.

The first things they noticed in the den were the two chairs and Oriental rug—just as housekeeper Ruth Boylan had described them—that had replaced a love seat and a wall-to-wall carpet after Fahey disappeared.

A mile away, agents intercepted Kay Capano on Greenhill Avenue, the wide boulevard through the Highlands, as she drove to work. They showed her the search warrant, explaining that they would have to take possession of the Suburban. While a policeman took her to work in an unmarked car, other agents drove the sport utility vehicle back to her house and searched it there, vacuuming up fibers, dirt, and hair that would be sent to the FBI lab for analysis.

Agents also pulled over and questioned Debby MacIntyre, making sure she hadn't smuggled any evidence out of the house. She hadn't and they let her go.

Back at Grant Avenue, Connolly paced around his prey's house in a starched white shirt and tie, monitoring the activity of his search team, while, upstairs, Munson, Alpert, and another agent shadowed the shaken Capano as he got dressed. It was a humiliating scene for the powerful attorney. Agent Alpert checked each article of clothing before Capano put it on. They inspected his bathrobe as he removed it, finding a Xanax pill, the antidepressant Capano had been on for several weeks. Capano seemed so distracted and disoriented that Alpert helped him pick out a suit to wear. "It's hot out there," said the agent, suggesting a suit in a light fabric instead of the heavy wool one Capano had taken out of the closet. As Capano dressed, he stepped into the adjoining bathroom. Alpert heard the toilet flush and jumped up.

"Did you just flush the toilet?" he screamed.

"Yeah, I threw in a cigarette," Capano replied, surprised at Alpert's strenuous rebuke.

"Get the supervisor!" Alpert called to the other agent.

Munson, who had left the bedroom, ran back in and, after being briefed by Alpert, ordered agents to dismantle the toilet and inspect the drainpipes. They suspected Capano might have tried to discard the blue topaz ring, a gift from Annie's former boyfriend Paul Columbus, that was missing from Annie's apartment. Experts in the bureau's Behavior Sciences Unit had said that killers often kept a souvenir of their victim.

By the time agents carted the toilet out of the house, television vans, their twenty-foot satellite antenna telescoped skyward, were at the curb, camera crews were set up in the street, and reporters were shouting questions at investigators.

Kathy Jennings and Bart Dalton, two of Capano's attorneys who had rushed over to his house, escorted the suspect to Dalton's shiny silver Mercedes sedan and drove off.

Investigators kept poring over every nook and cranny of the house. Since all they had up to now was a missing person, and a good deal of circumstantial evidence against Capano, they needed some evidence of a crime. And it wasn't long before FBI agent Linda Harrison, an evidence detection specialist, shouted, "I think we found blood!" On her hands and knees in the great room, Harrison was peering at a minuscule black-purplish spot on the bottom of one of the radiators.

Alpert rushed over.

Harrison immediately conducted a Hemostix test, applying a chemical solution that revealed that the speck was probably blood. She used a cotton tip to remove a swatch for DNA testing.

Minutes later, Harrison noticed another speck, this one on the baseboard in the same room. The Hemostix test produced the same positive result. Another agent found a spot on the laundry room door; the test, again positive.

For the investigators who had been working the case for dozens of hours and who had come to believe that Fahey was murdered in Capano's house, the spots of blood, however small, were cause for rejoicing.

Thank God, Alpert thought to himself, recalling that Harrison's discovery of the two spots "was like finding gold."

The search team gave each room the same intense scrutiny. Anything that looked suspicious was put in a plastic bag and cataloged as potential evidence. Box after box was carted to the waiting vans, a staggering inventory that included two mops and one broom from the laundry room, a wet/dry vacuum cleaner from the garage, a Black & Decker Dustbuster, carpet samples, two Shout stain sticks, a bottle of Carbona blood and milk remover, duct tape, two hairs from the laundry closet, lint from the dryer, a blue rubber glove, a small hatchet with fibers, and a broken fireplace poker—all possible keys to solving a murder, each treated as if it were a precious gem.

By one o'clock that afternoon, as word of the search spread, nearly two dozen reporters, including all the major network affiliates from Philadelphia, had arrived at the ritzy leafy enclave. A news helicopter hovered in the sky. Neighbors opened their doors or walked up Grant Avenue to join reporters craning their necks for glimpses of the scene, unimpeded by trees or fences, that was unfolding on the muggy summer day at Tom Capano's rental house and in his backyard.

Tim Munson, a tall, rugged man who played a mean game of tennis, finally emerged, at two o'clock, to face reporters who were desperate for some official comment. A Vietnam vet and former Philadelphia police officer who had investigated organized crime during the reign of mob boss Angelo Bruno, Munson stood in his shirt and tie, sweat glistening on his forehead, as the press crowded around him. "The FBI, Wilmington Police Department, and Delaware State Police have a joint kidnapping investigation," Munson said. Reporters fired questions at the stone-faced agent, but he simply referred all questions to the U.S. Attorney, pivoted, and disappeared behind Capano's front door. If anybody harbored any doubts that the feds were in charge of the investigation, Munson had erased them with two terse sentences.

This was not a good development for Tom Capano, who could no longer rely on the power of his local network of friends.

Charles Oberly arrived minutes later. The short, balding attorney planted himself on Capano's lush front lawn and complained to reporters about the FBI's tactics. His client would have been happy to consent to another search of the house, if only they had requested it, Oberly declared.

Asked why his client would allow a search of his house when he wouldn't even answer questions, Oberly said Capano wouldn't agree to answer questions about personal matters unrelated to Anne Marie Fahey's disappearance, questions authorities insisted on asking.

"I think it's one more effort to show how confused they are. But let them go and do their job," the former attorney general said, arguing that investigators were "totally stymied" and acting in an outrageous manner.

Oberly then said the search had traumatized his client. "He can't believe all this has happened. If he knew anything, he would tell you. He took her home and that's the only thing I can tell you."

Behind him, agents continued their work. And they were not dainty about it. When they discovered that a stairwell wall had been repaired recently, Munson ordered a section of the wall removed. When preliminary tests showed that a spot on the backseat of Capano's Jeep was blood, Munson ordered the piece cut out and inventoried.

Outside, near a swing set and playhouse with discarded toys—a football and a Tweety Bird stuffed animal—police found a clump of earth and thought they detected signs of recent digging. Investigators rushed over with shovels and a metal detector and, with a clutch of reporters and photographers leaning over a neighbor's wooden stockade fence, dug nine circular holes, each a foot in diameter. Nothing.

Capano's brother Joe, hearing news of the digging, called Tom, who had gone to his law office. "Tommy, they're digging up your backyard. Are they going to find anything?" Joe asked.

"Of course not," Tom scoffed.

At five o'clock, an unmarked white cruiser pulled into the driveway. Two frisky black Labrador retrievers bounded out, with police officers in tow. Trained to sniff out cadavers, Casey and Hunter romped around the lawn, pawed the ground, and jumped up on the fence, before being led into the house. The dogs left about five-forty-five, having found no body.

By then, investigators had begun parading the boxes into two vans parked in Capano's driveway. They finished packing and pulled slowly out of the driveway, taking their haul to the FBI laboratory in Washington.

Later that day, Capano broke his self-imposed silence long enough to call the *News Journal* and tell Valerie Helmbreck, "I've personally been devastated by this." He refused to say more.

The following day's paper featured pictures of blue-jacketed FBI agents trooping around Capano's yard. An accompanying story revealed, for the first time, that in Fahey's final diary entry she had called the former prosecutor and gubernatorial adviser a "maniac."

Shaw Taylor, the construction manager for Louis Capano, would wrestle with his conscience throughout the month of July. About a week after Louis ordered the Dumpsters emptied, ahead of schedule, Taylor had paid a visit to the office of Chris Nowland, Louis's right-hand man, and closed the door behind him.

"What do you think was in those Dumpsters the other day?" Taylor asked Nowland.

Nowland looked at Taylor with surprise, saying Louis hadn't told him.

"Well, what do you think about the whole thing about Anne Marie Fahey and Tom Capano? There might be a connection."

Nowland dismissed Taylor's suggestion as ridiculous.

On the day of the raid on Tom's house, Louis sent word to employees that they were not to say anything if the FBI or police came asking questions. But Taylor let it be known that he was going to talk if anyone asked questions. Later that day, Taylor was sitting with Louis Capano's son, looking at pictures the college kid had snapped at the Olympics in Atlanta, when the boss came into the room.

"I hear you are not comfortable with this Dumpster issue," Louis said.

"No, I'm not comfortable with this. What's the deal with it?"

"I can't tell you," Louis said, trying to put a quick end to the conversation.

Days later, Taylor went to Louis's office and pressed him again. Taylor had always thought Louis was a little slippery but now suspected he might be covering up a murder.

Louis told Taylor in a pleasant but firm voice that he just couldn't say what was inside the bins. "Look," Louis said. "This could be very damaging to me and my company."

Taylor left but mentioned to a coworker that Louis should give him some explanation. "At least he could tell me somebody put asbestos in the Dumpster," Taylor complained.

A few days later, that's exactly what Louis did. "A friend called me up," Louis explained to Taylor in a phone call. "He asked if he could get rid of asbestos in my Dumpster and I said it was OK."

Taylor thanked Louis, knowing in his heart Louis was just making a desperate attempt to placate him and keep him quiet.

And now worried for his safety—the only others who knew what Taylor knew were loyal longtime employees and Louis's son—he contacted a friend who knew an FBI agent in Philadelphia.

The intermediary arranged a meeting between Taylor and two agents at the northbound Interstate 95 rest stop in Pennsylvania, a half-mile north of the Delaware line. Taylor told the agents his story, adding, "I don't know what to do. I don't want to come forward if it's going to jeopardize my family's safety."

The agents, who knew about Louis from his previous assistance in the sting operation against former New Castle County councilman Ron Aiello, told the petrified witness that the Capanos weren't a Mafia family. They also convinced Taylor to meet with the investigators in the Fahey case.

A few nights later, several days after Tom's house was searched, Taylor drove from his Chadds Ford, Pennsylvania, home to the Wilmington Hilton off I-95 at the state line. Waiting were Alpert and Donovan, who drove Taylor straight to Tim Munson's house, where the FBI boss was sitting with Connolly.

Sipping a soda to calm his nerves, Taylor told his story. The investigators listened intently. Connolly explained that he was convening a grand jury and would need the names of all employees who might be able to corroborate Taylor's story.

Taylor provided a list of about ten names, hoping that with so many employees subpoenaed, no one would know for certain he was the whistle-blower.

Armed with this new information and knowing that Capano had replaced a rug and sofa, Connolly subpoenaed the records for Harvey & Harvey, the hauling company that had emptied the Dumpsters, and decided to search through the two local landfills where the bins' contents had been deposited.

During five steamy days, from August 12 to 16, Connolly supervised as FBI agents and police wearing white protective suits and headgear, aided by a backhoe, picked over the stink and stench at the moonscape of Cherry Island, a massive household garbage dump near the port of Wilmington. Buzzards and turkey vultures circled the rotting garbage, which gave off a suffocating stench under the oppressive sun. A police evidence detection van stood by to assist.

Three miles away, at the Delaware Recyclable Products construction landfill off U.S. 13, Munson, wearing a white protective mask, oversaw nearly a dozen agents and three backhoe operators sifting through forty-foot-high mounds of dirt and splintered wood, rugs, and other construction refuse.

The investigators didn't find a sofa in the dump but gathered up three tan carpets, green carpet padding, some carpet strips, and a stained brown carpet. All were stuffed into boxes and shipped to the FBI laboratory, to be tested along with the other potential evidence.

While the landfills were being searched, Tom Capano—who had gone to live with Louis immediately after the raid—confided to his brother that he had tossed a gun into the Dumpsters with Annie's belongings, as well as thrown rug pieces into the Dumpster at the Holiday Inn in New Jersey. Louis, becoming more bewildered each day by Tom's behavior, but still convinced he was innocent of any crime, didn't ask any questions.

"I hope they find the gun," Tom told his younger brother, "because it would prove that it wasn't shot."

On August 15, while the landfills were being combed, Alpert got a call from fellow agent Chris Allen, who worked at the FBI lab in Washington. Allen confirmed that all four samples of the red spots from Capano's house—from the baseboard, radiator, laundry closet door, and Jeep seat—were blood. Now it was a question of determining whose blood.

Investigators were already striking out trying to get a good DNA sample—a single strand of hair was all they needed—for Anne Marie. After examining dresses, underwear, pillowcases, even a baseball cap, they found nothing. Annie, the neat freak, had not even left a hair on her hairbrush or in the drain trap of her sink for FBI forensic scientists to analyze.

Amazed—and frustrated—investigators turned to Capano. But the attorney, now all but hiding out at Louis's mansion, refused to provide a sample of his blood.

In the past, Capano might have been able to make a few phone calls and take care of the annoying proffer. But with the feds involved, he was denied use of his most precious weapons, his political connections. His defiance of the request for blood simply sent Connolly and Alpert back to Magistrate Trostle for another search warrant, this time demanding that Capano "produce in the presence of the FBI, two vials of blood, 25 head hair samples and 25 pubic hair samples." Again, Trostle signed and sealed the document. And Capano, on the morning of Friday, August 23, presented himself at the Wilmington police station to have pubic and head hairs clipped from his body and sealed in plastic bags. He then went to Riverside Hospital, where two vials of his blood were drawn from his outstretched arm.

Both the drawing of blood and the landfill search drew prominent next-day coverage in the Wilmington newspaper. Capano's life was now completely turned inside out—which was exactly how Connolly and his team wanted it. And they were also gratified when the blood test results showed that Capano's blood didn't match the spots found in his home.

Getting a sample of Anne Marie's DNA was now more essential than ever.

One of Annie's siblings recalled that she had just given

blood. And a check of her office E-mails confirmed that she had provided a sample on April 24 to the Blood Bank of Delaware. Trooper Daniels called the blood bank and learned that Annie had indeed given blood two months before she vanished, but because blood has a short shelf life, the plasma had already been sold to a distributor, who had shipped it to Europe. Daniels ordered the blood bank to find it.

A few days later, Chris Hancock, a donor advocate for the blood bank, reported that he had found Annie's donation in Switzerland, with the Red Cross there. Alpert authorized a bureau check for $600 to cover the costs of shipping a sample back to the United States, and it was delivered to the FBI lab. Alpert knew that this was probably their best, and only, shot.

While investigators kept poking for clues, Capano dug in, refusing all cooperation. Connolly offered him the chance to meet with investigators and only answer the questions he wanted to, but Capano turned him down.

Police knew that this posture, on the part of the man who had admitted to having dinner with Annie just hours before she disappeared, did not bode well for the possibility that she was still alive. Connolly, up against a suspect who was both wily and willful, planned for a lengthy siege.

On August 5, he sent Capano's attorneys a "target letter," informing them that their client would be the subject of a grand jury investigation into the suspected kidnapping of Anne Marie Fahey. He also prepared dozens of subpoenas for people he planned to interrogate under oath, with the considerable weight of perjury charges for lying to a grand jury.

The prosecutor had a hunch that Louis Capano's wife, Lauri Merten, the former Ladies Professional Golf Association U.S. Open champion, might hold the key that could break the case wide open. An informant had revealed that Merten, suspicious that Louis was philandering while she traveled on the LPGA tour, had installed recording devices on the phone in their Greenville mansion. The tapes, according to the informant, contained the voices not only of Louis but also of Tom, who had been staying with Louis and, Connolly hoped, may have inadvertently confessed to something on Louis's phone.

Connolly subpoenaed the tapes and also demanded that Merten testify before the grand jury. The golfer appeared on August 20 to testify but was sent home because a quorum of sixteen grand jurors hadn't shown up. Merten also refused to surrender the tapes, arguing that the government had no right to private recordings, and set up a legal battle that would last for months.

"Please don't tell them that I got rid of the sofa." Tom Capano, standing in the master bathroom of his brother's house, was half-shouting, half-begging, half-demanding that Louis, who was stepping out of the shower, not sell him down the river this morning, August 29. "You can admit that you had the Dumpsters emptied," Tom continued.

Louis, standing with a towel draped around him, was getting ready to drive to the federal courthouse in downtown Wilmington to testify before a grand jury investigating the disappearance of Anne Marie Fahey. He agreed to lie for his brother, who had helped him out of some legal jams of his own.

"Tell them that I had put some of Fahey's personal belongings in there so that my wife wouldn't learn about the affair," Tom added.

"I'll tell them that it was my idea to have the bins taken away that Monday morning," Louis volunteered.

Tom suddenly had another, more important request. "I also need an alibi for Friday morning," he said, a sense of urgency in his voice about the morning that he and Gerry had loaded the cooler into the Suburban. "Can you tell them I came here about eight on Friday morning to discuss Capano Investments business?"

Again Louis said yes. And a few hours later, sporting a deep tan, wearing a gray tailored suit and wire-rim glasses, and flanked by two Philadelphia attorneys, Louis ducked through a small crowd of reporters outside the J. Caleb Boggs Federal Building, rode the elevator to the third floor, sidestepped another crowd of reporters, and disappeared into the grand jury room. He emerged ninety minutes later and left without comment.

One of Louis's attorneys, Katie Recker, a slim, pretty brunette, told a reporter later that day that her client had "answered all the questions they asked of him."

Colm Connolly, who had asked all the questions, doubted Louis's candor. Connolly had heard Shaw Taylor's description of the odd, off-schedule dumping and figured Louis was lying through his teeth. And since Taylor, Louis's son, and some other Capano employees had testified before Louis, Connolly guessed that the twenty-three members of the grand jury would also have serious doubts about Louis's story.

For the next session of the grand jury, which met for only one day every two weeks, Connolly enraged Capano by subpoenaing his sixteen-year-old daughter, Christine, to testify. The prosecutor had asked to interview the girl, an introspective, scholarly Archmere junior, informally, promising that her mother and a family attorney could sit with her during questioning. But Kay and Tom Capano would not allow it, forcing Connolly to take the formal route. The Capanos then filed court papers to squelch the subpoena, claiming that child–parent communications were as privileged as those between priest and penitent, lawyer and client. But federal judge Sue Robinson denied the claim.

Holding her parents' hands, Christine arrived at the federal courthouse, cleared of reporters by federal marshals, at eight o'clock in the evening on September 9. Prosecutor Connolly, who had never met Capano or even been face-to-face with the suspect, stood in the hallway outside the courtroom as Christine and her parents approached. Kay and the girl looked down, almost sheepish, as they passed within inches of Connolly. But Tom Capano looked directly at the young prosecutor, a fellow Archmere Academy alumnus, and hissed contemptuously, "I hope you can sleep at night."

Connolly turned and walked away.

Inside the grand jury room, Christine refused to answer any questions and was later held in contempt of court.

Over the next several months, every two weeks, the Boggs courthouse would be the scene of media camp-outs as a parade of witnesses shuffled through the revolving doors to answer more questions about what had happened to Anne Marie Fahey.

But all of the grand jury testimony was secret. Reporters jockeyed for scraps of information, rumors of what was said, and an occasional comment—most often, however, "No comment"—by one of the participants. The public watched a parade of people being ushered in and out of the Boggs courthouse but was denied news of what they said. "Snacks," said one reporter. "That's all we could serve them."

But it made the ground fertile for rumors. The public, fixated on the bizarre mystery involving the governor's pretty secretary, was more than happy to pass their inside information around. Psychics routinely contacted police and the Fahey family with their theories. The press, shut out of the investigation, were swamped with rumors, which only got more bizarre the more they were shut out.

There was talk about one of the city's drug thugs abducting Fahey off the street and of other men who might be involved—a state trooper, a man from the YMCA. Others spoke with certainty of how Annie had simply checked herself into a psychiatric clinic under an assumed name and panicked after learning how much hubbub her disappearance had caused, and was now too afraid to return home. Capano even instructed his attorney, at one point, to tell Connolly that a friend had told him that he had seen a woman resembling Fahey at Newark International Airport in New Jersey.

The rumor mill had Fahey's body hidden in a refrigeration unit inside the former Wanamaker's department store, a building not so coincidentally owned by the Capanos. The Wanamaker's rumor made it into the paper, but not many others.

Hundreds of people believed that the Christiana Hospital, a sprawling medical complex south of Wilmington, was storing Fahey's corpse in a vault in its morgue until authorities decided the time was right to pronounce her dead.

Variations on the cement-boots theme—that Fahey was buried in the foundation of a Home Depot or other building the

Capanos were erecting—were common. Once it had been reported that Capano had purchased a new carpet for his house just after Fahey disappeared, the police hot line seemed to ring every time someone spotted an old rug on the side of a road. "All sorts of dead ends were called in," recalled Connolly, who had investigators check out most of the tips. He also made certain Annie's passport hadn't been used.

One preposterous rumor—fanned by Capano—that did not make it into print was that the governor himself had gotten Fahey pregnant and bumped her off because she was going to expose the affair. The word on the street, where the rumor gained legs, was that Carper had instead framed Capano for his own crime.

I thought the Carper theory was ridiculous but nonetheless decided I'd better check it out, as I was trying to do with every rumor I fielded. Feeling foolish, I called Governor Carper's office and asked press secretary Sheri Woodruff if Carper had ever been romantically involved with his missing secretary. Woodruff didn't know whether to laugh or cry but categorically denied any affair.

Behind the scenes, not just behind the grand jury's closed doors, information kept piling up. Tim Munson received a call one day from a man who worked at the General Motors assembly plant in Newport, a small town six miles south of Wilmington. The man said he had been reading about the Fahey case and thought he might have some information that could help. A coworker, said the tipster, had recently bought a fishing boat from Gerry Capano. The boat didn't have an anchor, the man speculated, suggesting to Munson that it could have been wrapped around Fahey's body.

Munson thanked the caller and said agents would follow up the lead. Though agents had been fielding dozens of calls from well-intentioned anonymous citizens, this one, Munson thought, was worth passing on to Connolly. It made sense that Tom would have involved Gerry, the loose cannon in the family, and when investigators inspected phone records from Gerry's beach house, they showed someone had indeed called

Debby MacIntyre and Kay Capano on the morning of June 28. MacIntyre was queried and confirmed that she had spoken with Tom that morning.

Alpert, meanwhile, had been checking up on the youngest Capano. "Several people called us and said we should look at Gerry," Alpert recalled. "After we learned that he sold the boat without an anchor so soon after Fahey was missing, we figured maybe there's a reason for it."

Agents went to the home of the man who had bought Gerry's boat, Mike Caputo, who confirmed that he first met Gerry at the Avalon Marina on July 6. Gerry had walked Caputo around the *Summer Wind* showing off the twin motors and bragging about its fine condition, but said that the usual Coast Guard package—life jackets, flares, anchors, fire extinguisher—would not come with the boat because he needed it for his new vessel. Caputo signed a contract with Gerry that afternoon, agreeing to buy the *Summer Wind* for $27,000. He didn't ask any more questions about the missing anchor.

When Gerry heard that the FBI was nosing around his old boat and knew about the missing anchor, he rushed to Tom.

"What are we going to do?" he asked his big brother.

But Tom urged Gerry to remain calm, stick to the cover story, and see Dan Lyons, the lawyer who was a friend of Tom's. The brothers reviewed their alibi again, and this time Gerry wrote it down, on yellow Post-it notes, which he slipped in his checkbook for quick reference.

You were at my house at 5:45, wanted to talk about Capano Investments. I went to work, then met you at your house about 7:30, 8:00. We talked, I left for the beach, did my thing, saw you around 11ish. We talked again because you saw Louie. Then I left. You stayed, I met at your house around 5:00 to help you move a love seat. It looked old, that's all. Helped you throw it in a Dumpster and then I left. That's what I'm telling Dan Lyons on Friday.

In fact, the alibi was an intelligent deception: it was an accurate representation of when the two brothers met and where they went—it was wrong only in what it left out, which was why Gerry needed to write it down. It was as hard knowing what to leave out of a real story as knowing what to add to a deceptive one.

That Friday, August 30, the youngest Capano met Lyons, known around Delaware for his vehement opposition to the death penalty and his appeals on behalf of men facing execution. The handsome attorney with light brown hair was well aware of the supercharged nature of the Fahey case and was, from a distance, like most other observers, beginning to wonder about Capano's profession of innocence. The first thing Lyons told Gerry was that if the police ever interviewed him or he testified under oath, he had to tell the truth or invoke his Fifth Amendment right against self-incrimination. Lyons also told Gerry to tell him the truth or, if he couldn't, say he didn't wish to discuss a particular matter.

Gerry listened, then promptly lied to Lyons, telling the lawyer he had met Tom at Stone Harbor on June 28, talked about a land deal there, walked around a property Gerry wanted to buy, then grabbed a pizza and returned to Wilmington. Yes, they threw away an old sofa, but that was it. Lyons's notes from the meeting reflect that Gerry insisted he knew nothing about Fahey's disappearance. "Gerry is adamant that he has no knowledge of where Anne Marie Fahey is at present or whether any foul play was involved," Lyons wrote of the meeting.

By the end of 1996 Connolly and his men were convinced that Gerry had helped Tom dump Fahey's body at sea, using the *Summer Wind* as the vehicle. Everything was pointing, without contradiction, in that direction, including Capano's own time line, which came to light that fall.

When Connolly heard of the time line, he immediately ordered it seized. Studying the scrawl, written on a page of yellow legal paper, the prosecutor was amazed. Of course it had been written as a convenient cover-up and most likely was filled with lies. But it locked Capano into a story and confirmed the prosecution's theory of the case; it put Capano in Stone Harbor, with Gerry and access to a boat, a boat later sold without an anchor. This from Capano's own hand.

The paper also gave prosecutors what they loved to have, more leads for corroborating—or tripping up—their suspect, as he mentioned his brother Louis, mistress Debby MacIntyre (DM), and sister, Marian Ramunno, as well as Gerry himself. There was no heading or introduction, just:

    6:30—Gerry
    7:00—Kay
    7:15—track
    7:45—DM—8:00
    8:00—Louis?
    8:30—calls
    8:45—Louis
    ?—MAC machine
    9:15–10:30—track
    11:00–12:00—Marian's
    12:00–12:30—Mom's
    12:30 +/− —Gerry
    12:30–1:30—Lunch w/Gerry
    1:30–3:00—view property; discuss price and Capano In-
             vestments sale
    3:00—Gerry leaves
    3:30—Tom leaves
    5:00—dump love seat
    5:30—17th St.—dinner
    11:00—leave kids

Though he intended it to be a breezy account of a fairly typical day, Capano knew that he had given the prosecution a sheath of arrows and ordered his attorneys to get the document back.

At the same time, members of Connolly's team studied another curious document from Tim Frey's shelf: a list of Capano's recent contacts with Annie, including gifts he'd given her. And though they knew that this, too, was intended to be self-serving, investigators also knew that a suspect's worst en-

emy was his own mouth. If Capano revealed himself as a
selfish and mean friend when trying to protect his interests,
what was he like in an unguarded moment?

*Thursday, 5/23, came to deliver book re: anorexia; re-
trieved from Robert previous evening; disappointed that he
had apparently not read it since retrieved it from laundry
room; cried in my arms, shoulders so thin; "high maintenance?" "materialistic?"; showed me freckle on belly needing attention—pulled up jumper; no modesty;
*called me 6/6 to ask for credit card for Noreen's wedding
gift;
*AMF came to my house for dinner on Tuesday, June 18,
got salmon from Toscana; irrational; fear of pregnancy;
sexual contact;
*dinner at Dilworthtown Inn on 6/20; lobster tail; Freixenet;
upbeat; discussed second job (waitress at fine dining establishment); showed me check register (writes on every
line); take home pay of $844; complaints about finances;
returned to Grant Ave.;
*6/25—depressed because broke—not a cent; I send $30
via messenger and say to add to bill (joke);
*6/27—appointment with Dr. Kaye; don't like him; expen-
sive ($55 for 20 minutes); offer ticket to [a fund-raising
event by City Council candidate Mike] Hare; I had 12; she
chooses Panorama instead; reservation for 7:00; call at
6:25 from office to advise on way; very depressed.

Capano had done the best he could to explain his close
relationship with a woman who had vanished after having dinner with him. But the explanation, investigators believed, revealed a man fumbling desperately for an alibi.

As pieces of the puzzle fell—not into place but onto the
board—Gerry Capano's name kept emerging as a key. The
first entry on Tom's time line, at 6:30 in the morning, the day
after Anne Marie Fahey disappeared, was "Gerry." If some-

thing happened to Annie after dinner on Thursday night, Friday would be a day when things happened. And they did. But in Tom's lawyerly mania for detail, he missed the larger meaning of his time line; it was not an ordinary day. How often did he call—or see—Gerry at the crack of dawn? How often did he have lunch with Gerry? And why would he be discussing a Capano Investments deal with Gerry, who everyone knew was the family screwup?

Gerry was their man.

But instead of hauling the youngest Capano in for questioning, Connolly devised a strategy designed to reel Gerry in slowly, forcing the young Capano to beg for mercy as he gave up his brother.

Ironically, Connolly had been a sophomore at Archmere while Gerry was a freshman. They had played soccer on the same junior varsity team, but Connolly didn't remember they were teammates until several months into the investigation, when a reporter scanning Archmere's yearbook pointed it out to the prosecutor.

Connolly's strategy for Gerry Capano included launching a full-scale investigation, putting him under surveillance, infiltrating his circle of friends with undercover detectives, doing background checks, finding out where he bought his drugs and guns, tapping his phone, and investigating his finances. FBI agents from New Jersey visited Stone Harbor, talked to his neighbors, asked questions in the bars and marinas where Gerry was known. Connolly wanted Gerry to know that the feds were investigating him. He wanted Gerry to sweat.

"We made the decision not to interview Gerry until everything was over," Connolly recalled.

Connolly also figured he could get to Tom through his and Louis's girlfriends.

Detective Donovan interviewed Debby MacIntyre in July and September, and Connolly subpoenaed her to the grand jury on September 10. MacIntyre proved a loyal mistress. Though telling the truth about not knowing of Fahey's relationship to Capano, she said she hadn't gotten romantically involved with him herself until after he separated from his wife the previous

September. And she did not reveal the fact that she had bought a gun for Capano.

Donovan's notes of his first interview with MacIntyre stated that "she is very supportive of Tom Capano, and does not believe that he has anything to do with the Anne Marie Fahey disappearance."

After a rocky start, Louis's girlfriend proved much more helpful. Kristi Pepper, a friendly young blond woman, came to the U.S. Attorney's Office with her own attorney, Tom Foley, in October. Connolly, joined by Alpert and Donovan, wasted no time asking Pepper for intimate details about her relationship with Louis, who, she said, she had been dating since March of 1996.

Pepper, a divorced real estate agent with two young boys and more than willing to cooperate, was astonished by the line of questioning. "Why is that relevant?" she huffed, and stormed out of the room. In the hallway, Foley explained to his angry client that the investigators needed to know how close she was with Louis to evaluate whether information she provided was credible.

Pepper calmed down and reentered the room. Eventually she told her interrogators that she accompanied Louis to dinner at the Columbus Inn in Wilmington and other fancy restaurants and that she was a frequent guest at his mansions in Greenville and Rehoboth Beach when his wife, Lauri Merten, was out of town.

The night Fahey disappeared, June 27, Pepper said, Louis spent the night, for the first time, at her modest brick house in Arden, a bohemian village north of Wilmington. He left in the morning. But she also told Connolly that Louis did something strange in the middle of the night, getting up to check phone messages and going out to his white BMW convertible to make a phone call of his own.

Then, in the intervening weeks, Louis became unhinged, according to Pepper. He called her incessantly, came to her house and pounded on her doors and yelled in her windows, and followed her around in his car. One day, tired of his harassment, she rammed into his car in a parking lot where he had confronted her, just to get away. Pepper also received an angry call from Merten and other hang-up calls. Windows in her house were broken.

So Pepper, frightened for herself and her boys, called Foley back and asked him to arrange another meeting with prosecutors. Connolly called her on a Sunday in November and said he wanted to come to Arden to talk. She agreed, and the prosecutor showed up with Donovan and Alpert.

Pepper told them about Louis's strange behavior and repeated the story they already knew—and thought was a lie—about Tom visiting Louis's mansion early on June 28.

The investigators asked Pepper for permission to install a wiretap on her phone. She agreed. Alpert asked if she would call Louis, who was in Arizona, where Merten's family lived, trying to patch up his tattered marriage.

The investigators gave Pepper a script to use, with questions about the meeting with Tom on June 28 and the Dumpsters. Louis sensed something was up and became angry. But in subsequent conversations, the tapes, compiled over several weeks, revealed a desperate, haranguing Louis Capano trying to influence Pepper's upcoming grand jury testimony.

Also that fall Alpert received a call from a man who said he had helped Tom Capano harass a legal secretary sixteen years earlier.

When he met Joseph Riley and heard the story of Linda Marandola, Alpert couldn't believe his luck. This was the kind of information that drops into an investigation as if delivered by a messenger from God. Riley was now nearly blind and walked with a cane, but he recalled that his buddy Tom Capano had once ordered him to "hurt that bitch" Marandola for rebuffing his advances. Most miraculous about Riley's story was that he told Alpert he had made secret recordings of his conversations with Capano and Marandola and turned them over at the time to Dean Wedge, a retired FBI agent.

Alpert, who had suspected Capano's harassment of Fahey probably had a precedent, finally had what appeared to be proof. He tracked down Marandola, who confirmed Capano's bizarre reaction to being rejected and gave the agent the gold watch Capano had inscribed with his and her initials in 1987. Alpert then found Wedge, who still had the tapes.

Alpert received more welcome news around Thanksgiving. Alan Giusti, a DNA analyst for the FBI, informed Alpert that the blood specks found on the radiator and woodwork, dubbed Q36 and Q37 by the lab, were a positive match for K24, the sample of Fahey's blood.

The results, explained Giusti, showed there was only a 1-in-11,000 chance that another white American besides Fahey had bled on the radiator or woodwork.

A delighted Alpert told Munson, who rushed to the U.S. Attorney's Office to tell Connolly. Connolly, who had expected the match, smiled with satisfaction.

"It was another step in confirming our theory," Connolly later explained, "that he killed her in his den and took the body to Stone Harbor."

But Capano was ready with a response. In fact, he had already been telling friends that even if the blood turned out to be Fahey's, it could have occurred during her menstrual cycle, because she was a heavy bleeder.

He also offered another theory—that his two oldest girls, Christy and Katie, had bled while roughhousing in the den.

It didn't take long for Gerry Capano to feel the heat. Reporters were now sniffing around the story of the missing anchor. And the fact that people seemed to know about it frightened the hell out of Gerry. He talked to Tom, who advised him to hang tough and offered the same vague reassurance as before, that nothing would happen to him. But Gerry, unaware that the authorities were tapping his phones and tracking his drug use, doubled his consumption of cocaine from about two grams a week to four. He stopped going to work and spent most of his free time, when he wasn't with his wife and kids, drinking and taking drugs.

Louis, who was called before the grand jury a second time—while Connolly made Gerry even more nervous by *not* confronting him directly—had come to the conclusion that Tom might be lying to him. He went to Gerry, thinking his youngest brother either was involved or knew what had happened to the Fahey woman, and in an emotional scene in Gerry's Emma Court driveway Gerry spilled his guts.

"I can't take it anymore. I've been having nightmares," Gerry said, his face flooding with tears. He then blurted out about the extortion story, the boat ride, the cooler, the sinking foot, the bloody love seat.

Louis rushed home to confront Tom, who was still living at his house.

"Are you happy now that you found out?" Tom asked Louis, his voice haughty with contempt. "You're stressing Gerry out. Leave him alone."

12 *Be a Man*

While Tom Capano hardened his resolve—pressing his two brothers to keep theirs—the Fahey family agonized. Annie's brothers and sister were certain that Capano had killed their little sister. And it sickened them to know that he was walking around town instead of pacing a ten-by-ten prison cell. They tried to get on with their lives, working, raising children, even playing, but Annie's mysterious fate intruded at every juncture, distracted every thought. They finally had to carry her belongings out of her apartment and give up the vigil on her porch. They donated most of her things, including the air conditioner Capano had bought her, to charity. They sold her car and used the funds to help defray the costs of searching for her. Annie's clothes and personal effects were neatly, lovingly placed in boxes, carefully marked in case the police needed them, and stored in the basement of Kathleen's home. Kathleen, who in the first weeks of July spoke about her sister in the present tense, by Thanksgiving openly talked about "Annie's death."

The family's bitterness was made more acute by having to

watch Annie's private life picked over in public. The Faheys nevertheless continued to cooperate with newspapers, magazines, and television shows in order to keep the case in the public eye and, they hoped, the pressure on Capano. *People* magazine was the first of a long line of national media outlets to become interested in the case of the governor's missing secretary, running a story in September of 1996. *Vanity Fair, George, Time,* and *Newsweek* would all follow. As would the *Today* show, *Good Morning America,* and *PrimeTime Live.*

People quoted Kevin Fahey saying that "Annie got in over her head." But the magazine, not privy to the information investigators had, compared Capano to Richard Jewell, the suspect in the Atlanta bombing case who had been quickly named by police but was never charged for lack of evidence. Capano, through his attorneys, denied "any involvement," the magazine said, then quoted Capano friend Brian Murphy saying that the suspect was "devastated" by Annie's disappearance.

This was the kind of judicious journalism, the Faheys knew, that could not be justified by the facts. But the family also knew how difficult it was getting the facts. The U.S. Attorney's Office simply wasn't talking.

"It's like being in a black hole," Robert complained to reporters. But as much as Connolly wanted to fill the family in, federal grand jury secrecy rules prevented any disclosure of facts, even to a victim's family. He tried to soften the pain by having Susan Baldwin, a victim-witness counselor for the U.S. Attorney's Office, alert the Faheys to any upcoming news stories. And about once a month he met with Annie's siblings and their attorney, David Weiss, to listen to their concerns and let them vent their frustrations. The siblings would repeat rumors they had heard and information that Butch Hyden, a former FBI agent they had hired as a private investigator, had tracked down.

Connolly gladly accepted their tips and leads but couldn't reciprocate. He pleaded with them to keep the faith, tried to assure the Faheys his team was working on a strategy designed to bring Tom Capano to justice, and assured them his team was making progress.

"It was very hard for me," Connolly said later, "because you could see the suffering on their faces. But that also motivated me."

As Christmas approached, the Fahey family, accustomed to drawing strength from adversity, decided to lift their spirits—and those of Annie's friends—with a party. And if they had any doubt about how much Delawareans cared about their sister, it was erased when more than one thousand people, including U.S. Sen. Joe Biden, U.S. Rep. Mike Castle, and Gov. Tom Carper, crowded into O'Friel's Irish Pub on a rainy December night to remember Anne Marie Fahey and contribute to charities she had volunteered for while she was alive. Guests wore "Friends of Anne Marie" buttons, nibbled on hors d'oeuvres, sipped pints of Guinness and Harp, exchanged hugs, and told stories about a woman whose boisterous laugh could light up a room. Bill McLaughlin, the former Wilmington mayor who had introduced the Faheys' parents, told a reporter about the last time he had seen Annie, two weeks before she disappeared.

"She looked up at me and said, 'Bill, if it hadn't been for you, I wouldn't be here.' "

But the light tales masked the sorrowful reason that had brought them together. Governor Carper, addressing hundreds on the bar's jammed second floor, said simply, "We all know we've lost Anne Marie and she's not coming back." The guests signed yellow ribbons that became a wreath, which was hung inside the Carvel State Office Building, where Annie had worked. The Friends of Anne Marie Fahey raised $21,000 for her charities that night.

By that same Christmas, Tom Capano had become a pariah in Wilmington. Like O. J. Simpson, who had inexplicably been found innocent of murder the previous year, Capano was free to walk the streets but shunned almost everywhere he went. He continued seeing Debby MacIntyre, whom he promised to marry after his legal troubles were over, spent time with Susan Louth, and had dates with other women around town. He kept going to work but was all but an outcast after

Connolly seized the time line from Tim Frey's office in November.

Tom's brother Louis, when he learned the truth about the sea burial and the Dumpsters, told him to get out of his house. Tom Capano, forty-seven years old, moved in with his mother. He became increasingly dependent on Xanax and other antidepressant medications and watched his once-expansive social circle shrink to nothing. Except for his girlfriends and a couple of old pals from the Frawley administration, everyone kept their distance. He was a virtual recluse, in the same sedate white colonial house where he grew up.

When he did venture out, taking his kids to Pala's, a Little Italy pizza and sandwich joint, or attending one of Katie's volleyball or basketball games, people would say hello to Capano but then whisper to each other when he was out of earshot.

Capano's battered public image took another nosedive on January 3, 1997, when Magistrate Trostle unsealed the probable cause affidavits that had been used to support the requests for search warrants of Capano's home, vehicles, and body. The release concluded a six-month struggle by the *News Journal, Philadelphia Inquirer,* and *Philadelphia Daily News* to unseal the search warrants. The government, in fact, had dropped its opposition to release two months earlier, after Capano sought permission to look at the documents. Trumping Capano in this high-stakes legal game, Connolly argued that since Capano reclaimed that he already knew so much about the probe, there was no longer any reason to keep the papers sealed. This forced Capano to stand alone in opposing the release of the documents, and he quickly gave in, setting up the dramatic unsealing. And on a cold winter afternoon the government finally laid bare for the public the guts of its rationale for suspecting Capano. And it was immediately clear that he was no Richard Jewell.

The documents traced Capano's stalking of Fahey, his jealous outbursts, her attempts to break off the relationship, her fear of him, and, finally, a description of a somber Fahey at dinner on June 27. The documents also described how Capano had replaced a rug and sofa after Fahey disappeared, but they did not reveal the results of the blood tests. FBI agent Alpert chillingly, if clinically, summarized the case for a public that had up to this time heard only rumor: "There is probable cause to believe that Thomas Capano took Anne Marie Fahey without her consent from the Panorama Restaurant in Philadelphia to his home at 2302 Grant Avenue in Wilmington, Delaware, that he killed her at his residence and then attempted to clean evidence relating to the cause of her death in his laundry room and then removed at least some of that evidence from the residence in his black Jeep Grand Cherokee."

The damaging release of documents led the Philadelphia television news shows that night—but Capano's response was right behind. Celebrated local defense attorney Joseph Hurley announced he was joining the Capano team.

Known for his polka-dot ties and an endless stream of off-color one-liners, the silver-haired fifty-three-year-old Hurley was on the best run of his legal life. He was also defending another high-profile client—Brian Peterson, a New Jersey teen and University of Delaware freshman who, with his high school sweetheart, Amy Grossberg, was charged with killing their newborn son and tossing the corpse in a trash bin.

With Capano, Hurley now had the two hottest cases to hit Delaware in more than a decade, since the trial of serial killer Steven Pennell, and trumpeted his entry with a news release, faxed to media outlets:

> History teaches that MacArthur proclaimed: "I shall return." Without fanfare and without further explanation either needed or required, his three words said it all. In a media atmosphere rife with speculation of "when, why and for what reason," I now declare "I have arrived." Without fanfare and without further explanation either needed or required, my three words say it all.
>
> Over the course of the past six months, I have watched, from afar, as Tom Capano, a kind, decent, caring, gentle and loving father, has been savaged, I repeat, savaged by the combined news media—disgraced in the eyes of the

public and, most importantly, in the eyes of his children. In what is required by the Law of the Land to be a most secret investigation, to date, the federally-based investigation has sprung more media leaks than the Titanic.

To offer any explanation other than "I have arrived" is to play into the hands of those who would not only further tarnish, but utterly destroy the reputation of Tom Capano. That will not be done.

Enough said!

The pompous testimonial left the reserved Oberly, Hurley's new partner, cringing. But it did distract attention from the fact that Bart Dalton and Kathy Jennings had quietly quit the case.

The next day Oberly issued a news release of his own—his first public comments since the July 31 searches—excoriating investigators for smearing his client with "one-sided presentations" and "unsubstantiated hearsay." And to counter the government's portrayal of Capano as a jealous murderer, Oberly also released a few of the tender notes Fahey had written Capano in May and June of 1996.

But despite the friendly "Hola, Amigo?" tone, one of the notes released by Oberly seemed to confirm his client's anger. "We've been through a lot the past couple of years," Annie wrote, "and have managed (through hard work, determination and perhaps a bit of stubborn Irishness and Italian tempers?) to prevail." Oberly then borrowed a page from *People* magazine and compared Capano to Olympic security guard Richard Jewell, who had been cleared of bomb charges in October. And paraphrasing Brian Murphy's news release that he had mothballed months earlier, Oberly declared that his client was "devastated by Anne Marie's disappearance and like everyone else hopes she will be found safe."

Reading Oberly's statement, David Weiss was stunned by the Capano team's arrogance and issued an immediate statement on behalf of the Fahey family. "I assume [Oberly] says this because he believes he knows something that neither my clients nor anyone else seems to know," Weiss wrote. "If he has no particular information, we ask him to recognize that these comments are extremely insensitive and offensive. Anne Marie Fahey is never coming back."

While the public relations battle was being waged, Tom Capano's stalled legal career came to whimpering end. In anticipation of the search warrants release, Capano had taken a three-month leave of absence from Saul Ewing on December 31. And on April 30, 1997—ten months after Anne Marie Fahey vanished—the prime suspect resigned from Saul Ewing.

Oberly tried to blame the government for his client's job loss.

"I think he felt it was real difficult," Oberly told the *News Journal,* "to give his employer a fair day's work in light of continually receiving adverse publicity, incessant publicity, all of the leaks."

Early in February of 1997 Louis Capano summoned Shaw Taylor to his office. They were discussing family business when Louis suddenly changed gears and shoved a copy of *Philadelphia* magazine toward Taylor.

"Here, take a look at this," Louis said.

Taylor skimmed the article, stopping at two long paragraphs that detailed his boss's order to empty the Dumpsters and his refusal to tell Taylor what was inside them.

"Look, Louis, you've got to understand," Taylor said. "This has to come out."

"You went to the feds, didn't you?" Louis said calmly.

"They would have figured it on their own," said Taylor, who had also informed the Faheys through a mutual friend.

Louis just sat at the table, showing no emotion. Taylor got up and walked out of the room.

The pressure on Gerry also kept building. In mid-February 1997, *George* magazine published "Diary of a Lost Woman," by Lisa DePaulo, which revealed, for the first time, that the FBI was investigating "another Capano brother" who had "sold a boat . . . without an anchor." And on February 20 the *News Journal* published a story with more details about Gerry's anchorless boat.

Oberly tried to downplay the significance of the sale, telling the paper that the boat was only sold without an anchor because Gerry kept it for his new boat. "It never disappeared," the defense lawyer claimed.

Spooked, Gerry visited his lawyer, Dan Lyons, wondering if he should issue some sort of press statement. They both agreed to keep mum.

But the pressure kept building on Gerry, especially from Louis, to tell the authorities about the sea burial. And Gerry continued to implore Tom to surrender. But Gerry's older brother scolded him for being weak.

"Act like a man. Act like a man," Tom said. "Just relax and everything is going to be fine."

Finally, on Monday, April 7, Gerry marched into Dan Lyons's office. "I didn't tell you the whole truth before," he said.

And, as he had done with Louis, Gerry told his lawyer about the extortion story, the $8,000 loan, Tom's 5:45 A.M. arrival at his house, the trip to Stone Harbor, and the gruesome details of the boat ride.

Gerry confessed that Tom had concocted the story he told Lyons during their first interview eight months earlier.

Lyons advised Gerry that he could go to authorities or wait for the subpoena that would surely come. Gerry said he and Louis both wanted to secure immunity and testify.

"Both of us can't sleep," Gerry said. "We're falling apart."

But in the end Gerry still couldn't muster the courage to come forward.

On April 25, a federal appeals court handed Colm Connolly his first real defeat in his pursuit of Tom Capano; it ruled that Lauri Merten did not have to give up the tapes she had made to find out if her husband, Louis, was running around with another woman.

"We do not believe Congress intended the grand jury and the courts to use their respective powers to compel violations" of the federal wiretap law, wrote Circuit Judge Walter K. Stapleton, who once had employed Connolly as a clerk.

"If Lauri Merten had any idea of the whereabouts of Anne Marie Fahey," her attorney declared, "she would say so."

A month later Charles Oberly and Joseph Hurley were on national television proclaiming their client's innocence. "He's a destroyed person," Hurley told Sam Donaldson on his ABC news magazine show *PrimeTime Live.* "They've won." Capano allowed the camera crew to photograph him, but he wouldn't submit to an interview. "I mean, whoever it is that's behind the whole thing," Hurley continued, promoting a modified conspiracy theory, "it's been push, push, push. 'We've got to have Tom scapegoat in here.' They've won. They've drained him of everything that he was."

Oberly dismissed the relevance of finding Annie's blood in Capano's house. "I'll bet you couldn't search a house in America that you're not going to find blood of various people who've been in and out of that house," said the attorney.

Donaldson was incredulous. "You mean people bleed all the time in other people's houses?"

"You're talking traces of blood," Oberly protested. "Somebody could cut a finger on a piece of paper."

The camera then cut to a Philadelphia television studio, where Robert, Kevin, Kathleen, and Mark Fahey faced Donaldson. The veteran newscaster, famous for shouting questions at presidents, now asked Annie's siblings what they would say to Capano if they could talk to him.

"I'd ask him, 'How do you take a body, just dump it somewhere, and go on with your life?' " Kevin responded. " 'How do you face yourself in the mirror every morning?' "

Robert jumped in. "I would ask him what he would tell his children."

" 'Stand up and be a man,' " Kathleen said she would tell him.

Then Mark, the ruddy-faced bartender with angelic blue eyes, said, "I would ask him why he killed my sister."

One of the segments of the *PrimeTime* show left on the editing room floor showed Hurley and Oberly brandishing an anchor, claiming it was proof that the prosecution was trying to frame their client. Gerry simply had taken the anchor with him when he bought a new boat, the laywers argued; it was preposterous to say that it was used to weight a body.

Oberly and Hurley were perhaps lucky that *PrimeTime* producers decided to cut the segment. What no one knew, including the defense attorneys, was the chain of events that had put the anchor in front of the television cameras. As Gerry would later tell the story, after the February *News Journal* article about his boat sale to Michael Caputo, he and Tom agreed they needed an anchor. So Gerry went to their brother Joe, who was also a boater, and asked him to find one. He did. Gerry stashed the new used anchor in his garage at Stone Harbor and that spring, despite Lyons's imprecations not to move it, gave it to Tom, who turned it over to Hurley and Oberly for the dramatic stage prop performance that turned into a malapropism of tragic proportions.

As the one-year anniversary of Annie's disappearance came and passed, Tom Capano resigned himself to the fact that he would be arrested. But he was just as determined to make the authorities come get him, if they thought they had a case.

Knowing the keys to any prosecution would be Gerry and Louis, Tom continued bucking his brothers' efforts to browbeat him into surrendering and tried to twist their arms, preying on their brotherly loyalty, to keep them from becoming government witnesses.

Early that summer, Louis met Tom at the Imperial Deli, a gourmet shop in the Fairfax Shopping Center on Concord Pike. The brothers sat outside at a table, eating lunch. Louis fixed his eyes on his brother.

"Gerry and I want to go in and talk to the police," Louis said. "This isn't fair to the family."

"Don't go in," said Tom. "They don't have enough evidence. I don't want to ruin my life or my daughters' lives."

Later in the summer—after he had learned he was the subject of an investigation for racketeering, wire fraud, perjury, obstruction of justice, and tampering with a witness—Louis demanded a meeting among himself, Gerry, and Tom at Oberly's office. The brothers met in a conference room, without Oberly. "Gerry and I are going in," Louis said in a stern voice.

Tom again played the family card, telling his brothers how

much their testimony against him would hurt his four girls, their nieces. "If the situation was reversed," he said, "I would do the same for both of you. Look, if either of you guys get in trouble, I'll protect you and tell them everything."

Gerry, emotional and angry, yelled at Tom for putting him in such a dilemma. "Grow up," Tom scolded. "Be tough. Be a man."

Gerry and Louis looked away. They would tough it out. Tom was their brother.

On September 28, sixty of Annie's friends and relatives gathered under rainy skies at the base of a wooded slope in Brandywine Park. Their eyes were fixed on a polished wooden bench. Attached to it were two metal plaques—one in Braille—with the same inscription: "Anne Marie Sinead Fahey, In Our Hearts Forever, Te Queremos, God Bless."

Fahey's friends had suggested to her siblings that they dedicate a bench to her memory because they didn't have a grave where they could pay their respects. As the waters of the Brandywine whispered in the distance, Fahey's uncle, Msgr. James McGettigan, blessed the bench. Tears flowed as the guests, one by one, walked up, said a prayer, and placed flowers on the bench.

13 *One Hell of a Burden*

On October 8, 1996, as darkness fell in the autumn sky, Gerry Capano was hanging out in the garage of his Emma Court home, working on his 1963 red Corvette and drinking Coors Light with friends Terry Hannig and Rudy Dryden.

In the dusk outside, five unmarked police cars pulled slowly to a stop in Pierson Farm, the neighborhood off Shipley Road bordering Marianne, the one-block subdivision where Gerry lived. About fifteen men and women, all wearing dark blue nylon jackets and carrying pistols and rifles, crept through the backyards leading to Gerry's house and took positions at his windows and doors. They could see through the open garage door, where Gerry and his pals were working and talking and drinking.

"Police! This is a raid! Put your hands up!" Detective Bob Donovan shouted, rushing toward the open garage door, as fellow investigators, most of them members of an Alcohol, Tobacco, and Firearms task force, stormed into the garage and slapped handcuffs on Capano, Hannig, and Dryden.

Michelle Capano, Gerry's wife, who was also in the garage, dashed into the house where her children, Danielle, four, and little Gerry, three, were watching television before bedtime. An agent caught up to Michelle in the house, searched her, then allowed her to leave with the kids. She raced off to her brother-in-law Joe Capano's house, but no one was home, so she drove to Marguerite Capano's, a half-mile away, where Tom was now living.

At Gerry's house, officers were rifling through drawers, overturning beds, and emptying clothes pockets, while, in the garage, Donovan had Gerry on the floor with a pistol to his head.

"I want to call my lawyer," Gerry said.

"Who's your lawyer?"

"I have two."

"Who are they?"

"Dan Lyons and my brother Tom."

"You're not calling your brother, but if you want to call Dan Lyons, I'll call him for you," Donovan said.

Gerry gave the detective Lyons's home number, and Donovan dialed it. When Lyons answered, the detective put the phone to Gerry's ear.

"How are you doing?" asked the attorney, who was home with his girlfriend, watching *The Godfather* and sipping a glass of wine.

"Great, except I'm lying on the floor of my garage with my hands behind my back, a gun at my head, and about thirty FBI agents searching my house."

"Let me speak with one of the agents," Lyons told his client.

"We've secured the house," Donovan said, explaining that they were searching for guns and drugs.

"Is he under arrest?" the lawyer asked.

"Not now," Donovan said.

"Is he going to be arrested?"

"That depends on what we find."

Lyons asked to speak with Connolly, who was at a secret location nearby, and Donovan said he'd relay Lyons's number to the prosecutor.

Donovan, leading the raid with the FBI's Alpert, took Capano and his friends into the den and seated them on a couch under the heads of several deer bucks and a moose Gerry had bagged. The detective showed the three men the federal search warrant, then removed their handcuffs. They sat glum-faced, glancing at the television, with an officer, gun drawn, keeping a close watch.

Donovan hit pay dirt in the laundry room between the garage and den.

On top of the washing machine was a rolled-up dollar bill and Gerry's Harley Owner's credit card. Donovan could see white powder residue on the bill and the card. He looked in the cupboard above the washing machine. On the second shelf he found a white plastic sandwich bag with white powder in the corner.

This was exactly what Connolly had hoped—indeed, expected—to find. It was the final piece in the strategic puzzle to get Tom Capano: getting Gerry. If he found guns and drugs, Gerry would be his and, Connolly fully expected, beg to turn his brother in.

Inside a Harley-Davidson motorcycle helmet police found a small bag of marijuana. In the garage, hidden in a red tool chest, they found another small bag of marijuana. In the pockets of Hannig, Gerry's business partner, agents found a small vial of cocaine, a lighter, and a pipe with marijuana stuffed in the bowl. And out in Gerry's pickup, stashed under the front floor mat on the driver's side, was another bag of cocaine.

Upstairs, in a closet in an unused bedroom, police found a large gray safe, unlocked. Inside were eighteen pistols, shotguns, and rifles.

Donovan dialed Connolly. "We found what we were looking for," the detective said.

"Great," Connolly said.

His plan, hatched fifteen months earlier, was coming to fru- ition. The feds had Gerry where they wanted him. Under a little-used federal law, Gerry had committed a felony each time he purchased a gun and signed an ATF form saying he wasn't "an unlawful user of, or addicted to, marijuana or any depressants, stimulants or narcotic drug or any other controlled substance." The prosecutor now could dangle a jail term of up to ten years over Gerry Capano's head.

Connolly then called Dan Lyons, who expressed outrage and demanded that the prosecutor free his client if he wasn't going to be arrested. Connolly said he'd let Gerry go when they were ready and not until then.

Donovan then saw Charles Oberly drive up. The policeman greeted the lawyer in the driveway and explained that he could not go inside but offered to call Connolly, who agreed to come to the house for an impromptu conference.

When Connolly arrived, he explained to Oberly that they were using a federal search warrant. While they spoke, Oberly noticed Gerry's $30,000 truck backing out of the driveway.

"Nice truck, eh," the prosecutor quipped to Oberly.

"Hey, where is Gerry going?" Oberly asked.

"That's not Gerry." Connolly smiled. "That's us."

"You're taking the truck?"

"Damn right," Connolly said.

It was after eleven o'clock when the cops finally left—and Tom Capano arrived. The older brother tried to buck Gerry up, encourage him to "be a man." But Gerry now knew his brother could not protect him.

The next morning, Tom called Louis, who was on a Re- hoboth Beach golf course, playing in a tournament.

"Have you heard the news?" Tom asked.

"No, what's up?"

"They raided Gerry's house and found some drugs. I'm not going to accept responsibility for him using drugs and getting busted. That's not my responsibility."

Once again, Louis urged Tom to turn himself in, but he refused to cave.

Also that morning, an investigator from the raid called the child abuse and neglect twenty-four hour hot line of Delaware's Division of Family Services. Connolly had ordered him to report the conditions inside Gerry's house. The prosecutor was reluctant to alienate Gerry further—he already had Gerry in the palm of his hand, with more pressure in the works— but Delaware law required anyone who "reasonably suspects" child abuse or neglect to notify Family Services. An unlocked safe filled with guns and ammo was a red flag for neglect. Within hours Family Services launched a child neglect investigation of Gerry and Michelle Capano.

Gerry suspected that the feds were only interested in him to get at Tom. He had wanted to talk to them months before— now was the time.

Sitting at the kitchen table of their mother's house the next morning, Gerry glared at his older brother.

"Give yourself up," he begged, one last time, "so they'll leave me alone."

"They don't have anything on you," Tom told him. "They don't have a case against you."

But Gerry now knew better. He was there during the raid. He knew what the cops had confiscated. "I'm going to wave the white flag," he told Tom.

But Gerry procrastinated until, two days later, a social worker called to arrange an appointment to interview them about a child neglect complaint.

"Neglect Case Hits Capanos" was the *News Journal*'s front-page headline the next morning. "Slaying suspect's brother and wife investigated after raid," read the subhead.

Gerry was stunned when he read the article.

"State officials are investigating possible child neglect in the home of Gerard J. Capano, where authorities seized drugs, explosives and an arsenal of weapons last week, officials said Tuesday night," the story reported.

"The state Division of Family Services received a complaint late Tuesday that Capano and his wife, Michelle, are maintaining an unsafe home, said director Kathryn J. Way."

The thirty-four-paragraph article noted that attorneys in Wilmington had speculated that authorities were pressuring Gerry to get to Tom, the murder suspect. It also quoted Joe Hurley, Tom Capano's attorney, scoffing at the notion the cases were linked. "It's totally coincidental," he told the paper.

Gerry blew up—incensed at the paper for printing the story and furious at Tom for getting him into this mess. Now his kids were at stake.

He paid Tom yet another visit at their mom's house, again imploring his brother to end the charade. Once more, Tom turned the tables on Gerry.

"You should sue the state for telling the paper they were investigating you," Tom said. "Go after them."

"I don't want to do that," Gerry pleaded. "I just want this all to be over with."

Gerry went to his brother Louis again, and the two wrestled with their consciences about turning Tom in. Standing near the squash courts in the vacant upper parking lot of the Wilmington Country Club, the brothers commiserated.

"I'm scared to death," Gerry said as tears rolled down his face. "I want to go in."

Louis, also bawling, agreed they both had to tell the truth.

On Louis's forty-sixth birthday, October 24, he met Tom for lunch at Pala's, the pizzeria in Little Italy.

"Gerry's not holding up too well," Louis said. "He's not going to make it. He's just not going to make it."

Unruffled, Tom chided his brother, repeating his well-worn nostrum, "Tell him to grow up and be a man."

Seeing that their pressure had not yet broken Gerry, that same night, October 24, the feds raided 102 Nevada Avenue, the home of Gerry's good buddy Ed DelCollo. The agents seized fifteen guns—two pistols and thirteen rifles and shotguns—several bow-and-arrow hunting licenses in DelCollo's name, and four red fox hides. What the feds were really looking for were the three weapons in the gun case owned by Gerry Capano—specifically, a hunting rifle bought for DelCollo by Capano. DelCollo, a rugged, mustachioed man with a physique sculpted by rigorous weight lifting, was a convicted felon and prohibited from possessing firearms. By buying a gun for DelCollo—authorities had the paperwork with Gerry's signature—Gerry was potentially guilty of a straw purchase and, with the other potential gun and drug charges, was now exposed to a possible dozen years in prison.

Not done squeezing, Connolly didn't arrest either DelCollo or Gerry. But he didn't have to.

The raid on DelCollo's house was the last straw for the youngest Capano, who called his attorney and asked him to arrange a meeting with Connolly.

"It was one hell of a burden," Dan Lyons later recalled. "It was a hell of a secret. A hell of a burden."

But it was also one hell of a prison term for Gerry.

Lyons wanted to make sure Gerry would, in fact, tell the truth this time and told him he had to take and pass a lie detector test before going to Connolly. Before Gerry even took the polygraph, Lyons browbeat his client; he didn't want to be embarrassed if Gerry failed.

"Are you holding anything back?" Lyons asked.

Gerry looked at the floor, silent.

Lyons bore down.

"Did Tom ask to borrow your boat if he killed the people extorting him?"

Gerry looked at his lawyer, sighed, and dropped his head forward.

"Well, I think maybe Tom might have said something like that, that he was thinking about killing someone."

Two days later a polygraph examiner asked Gerry the same questions. He passed.

———

Near the end of October, Connolly met with the Faheys in his office.

"We're making progress," he told them, without revealing that he had decided to arrest Tom Capano soon.

Robert Fahey told the prosecutor his wife had a business trip planned for early in November.

"Should she go away or stay in town?" Bob asked.

"I can't tell you," the prosecutor said.

Susan Fahey canceled her trip.

———

Lyons and Connolly had been conducting a delicate court-ship for weeks. "We might have something to talk about when you're ready," Lyons, who had been waiting for a grand jury subpoena for months, told the prosecutor on one occasion. "But that doesn't mean I do have something. I may and I may not."

"I'm not ready," replied Connolly, who wanted Gerry to sweat as much as possible. "When we make him an offer, it's going to be one he can't refuse."

As November began, Gerry learned that Hannig, Dryden, and other friends had been subpoenaed to testify before the grand jury.

Desperate to save his friends, Gerry, through Lyons, begged Connolly to let him come in for an interview.

But Connolly again resisted. First, he wanted to gather more damning evidence from Gerry's friends in front of the grand jury. On November 6, the day after grilling ten of Gerry's friends, Connolly called Lyons.

"On November 12," Connolly said, "either we're going to indict Gerry or he's going to be on the team. So we're ready if you want to come in." All the pieces were now in place, and Connolly, who knew Gerry had been waffling for months, also knew he had to give the youngest Capano a deadline to prevent any more wiggling. The following Wednesday felt right.

"We're ready to go," Lyons said.

"Let's do it," Connolly said.

They scheduled a meeting for the next day, Friday, November 7, to discuss what information Gerry had and to hammer out a deal. Connolly, fearing Tom would harm himself or someone else if he learned what was going down, warned Lyons to tell Gerry to keep his mouth shut.

When they convened at the IRS building in a suburban office park north of Wilmington, the defense attorney told Connolly about Tom's extortion tale, the boat trip, the cooler, and the shotgun blast through its side. The prosecutor, elated and sickened at the same time, agreed to cut Gerry a deal that would spare him jail time.

Gerry had to swear he didn't kill or conspire to kill Anne Marie Fahey and to cooperate fully with investigators as they tried to corroborate his account. The burden weighed heavily

on Gerry—his words could send his brother to his execution—
but he decided Tom had abused him, leaving him no choice
but to squeal.

Gerry also had to forfeit his expensive white truck and the
twenty-one guns, worth thousands of dollars.

Connolly would not prosecute Gerry for disposing of a
corpse and for the gun and drug charges from the raids; he
would let him plead guilty to covering up a felony, for which
he would receive three years' probation and be eligible for a
pardon.

Though Connolly was sparing Gerry time in jail, he decided
it was a worthwhile bargain, reasoning that Gerry was no different from a drug runner who goes unpunished because he
testifies against a kingpin.

But if Gerry changed the basic facts of his story or reneged,
he would be prosecuted with zeal, Connolly promised.

Though Gerry didn't have much negotiating room, Lyons
told Connolly he wanted to protect the rest of his family.

He asked that his brother Joe be spared from prosecution.
"I didn't want Joe to get in trouble for getting me the anchor,"
Gerry later said. "I just didn't want Joey in trouble." Connolly
agreed.

Gerry also went to bat for his sister. Though he didn't know
what Marian had told the grand jury, Gerry assumed Tom had
pressured her. Connolly agreed to that as well.

Finally, Gerry asked for immunity for his brother Louis and
Louis's son, Louis III. The prosecutor balked. Louis, as an
active participant in the cover-up, was too tainted, Connolly
believed, and decided to play that card separately.

But at Gerry's request, Connolly consented to spare Ed
DelCollo on the weapons possession charge.

Connolly signed the deal and gave it to Lyons to show
Gerry. The prosecutor wanted just one person: Tom Capano.
And he knew Gerry could deliver him.

The next morning, November 8, a cold, gray Saturday,
Gerry, dressed in camouflage pants and a black sweatshirt,
trooped with Lyons at 9:00 A.M. into the same IRS building
where Lyons and Connolly had met the previous day.

Gerry carried the anchor his brother Joe had given him.

Waiting in the criminal division's conference room were Connolly, Donovan, Alpert, and IRS agent Ron Poplos, all eager to hear the eyewitness account of a sea burial, words that could seal Tom Capano's fate. Somber greetings were exchanged, Gerry turned over the anchor, and Connolly directed him to the first order of business, signing the deal.

But before inking his name, Gerry asked for a concession. He had brought a single sheet of paper containing, under the header "TO BE RETURNED PLEASE," a neatly printed list, numbered 1 through 16, of guns and other items seized during the two raids.

Gerry explained that many of the weapons were antiques given to him by his father or which he had bought for his wife and son. Connolly agreed to return nine of the guns to Gerry's mother, and Gerry promised in writing not to retrieve them from his mom.

Then Gerry told his story to Connolly, his former soccer teammate at Archmere, often breaking down in tears. Investigators took notes as Connolly asked dozens of questions, probing for new information or holes in the account from the shaken witness.

"Gerry was distraught," Connolly later recalled. "He cried at times. He felt sick. He was very upset. He felt horrible about what he had done and what was going to happen to his brother as a result of coming in."

They broke for lunch, and Gerry nibbled on a tuna fish sandwich. After a couple more hours of grilling, Connolly turned on a tape recorder and had Gerry repeat everything, for the record.

That Sunday Connolly met Louis's attorney, Katie Recker, at his office. Louis was in Arizona with his wife but had coordinated his cooperation with Gerry. Recker explained that Louis was flying home that night but wanted to start the negotiating process.

Recker told Connolly that Louis would explain how Tom had called him on June 30, 1996, and later told him that Anne Marie Fahey had slit her wrists on his couch and how he had bandaged her up and sent her home, in good shape. Louis would tell how Tom had said that he, with Gerry, had dumped the couch, along with some of Fahey's other personal belongings, in the Dumpster.

Recker said Louis was prepared to tell how Tom had asked him when he stepped out of the shower the morning of his initial appearance to lie to the grand jury and how he agreed to testify that he had Tom for an early-morning business conference on June 28 at his house. The crowning piece, which Recker knew would help Connolly corroborate Gerry's story, was that Louis would tell how a year earlier Gerry had confessed to helping Tom dump a body in the ocean.

And as a bonus, Louis, though he didn't know how Fahey was killed, could offer a clue. Tom had told Louis he had tossed a gun into the Dumpsters, saying it hadn't been fired. Finally, Louis could detail, Recker said, how Tom had resisted his and Gerry's efforts to surrender and repeatedly talked them out of turning him in.

Connolly, once again buoyed by what he was hearing—it was now two brothers, corroborating each other, against one—agreed to cut Louis a deal. The gun story intrigued Connolly. Investigators had checked with area stores and learned Tom hadn't purchased one, but more checking would be needed. Gerry's story of giving Tom a gun and Tom returning it, however, was an indication of Tom's interest in a gun.

In exchange for his cooperation, Connolly told Recker, he would cease all investigations of Louis and promise not to charge him with obstruction of justice or perjury, two crimes he had committed before the grand jury.

Louis would, however, have to plead guilty to harassing a government witness, his mistress Kristi Pepper, by haranguing her during her taped phone conversations a year earlier. He'd get one year of probation. And like Gerry's agreement, Louis's deal would be off if he reneged on any part of his pledge or was found to be lying.

Finally, Connolly instructed Recker to order her client not to tell Tom about any of this conversation—or the deal.

It was a chilly and blustery morning when federal agents sneaked Gerry and Louis into the federal building downtown through a rear basement parking garage to tell their tales to the grand jury. As promised, it was Wednesday, November 12, a day of reckoning for Tom Capano. Connolly wanted to have the brothers actually testifying, proving their mettle, before he made the arrest.

As a precautionary measure, Connolly had ordered twenty-four-hour surveillance of the elder Capano as soon as he had inked the deal with Louis. Agents now waited only for the signal from Connolly and Alpert to make the arrest.

Just after nine that morning, with Gerry in front of the grand jury and Louis waiting in a side room, agents saw Tom pull out of his mother's driveway in his black Jeep. They followed him up Weldin Road, to his brother Joe's house, a half-mile away, and watched as Joe and his wife, Joanne, emerged from their house, carrying suitcases, and got in Tom's car.

"It looks like they're on their way to the airport," the agents radioed to Alpert.

"What's going on?" asked Dan Lyons, who was sitting in the room with Alpert and heard the radio report. Alpert, pumped with excitement, filled him in. "What a fucking asshole," Lyons muttered. Alpert paged Connolly, who was inside the grand jury room questioning Gerry. The prosecutor took a recess and walked out with Gerry.

Alpert told Connolly that Capano's brother and sister-in-law were in his Jeep, with luggage. "They're on I-95 heading north," the agent said.

Connolly was suddenly gripped with a sense of urgency. He had planned to have agents arrest Capano at his mother's home after Gerry and Louis finished testifying. That notion was now out of the question. Connolly didn't want to have to extradite Capano from another state—he would be crossing into Pennsylvania in moments—much less from a foreign country, if indeed Capano was fleeing.

Connolly made hasty calls to his bosses, Greg Sleet and Rich Andrews, and Jeff Troy, who months earlier had become head of the Wilmington FBI office after Tim Munson was promoted to a post in Detroit. They all agreed.

"Have him arrested for obstruction of justice and take him back to the U.S. Attorney's Office," Connolly ordered Alpert, who radioed the agents trailing Capano.

The agents, driving an unmarked sedan, pulled Capano's vehicle over at the Harvey Road exit near Arden—two miles south of the Delaware-Pennsylvania line—and ordered Capano out of the car. Dressed in a dark blue nylon jogging suit, he offered no resistance. The agents cuffed him and led him to their sedan as cars sped north on the interstate toward Philadelphia.

Joe and his wife, who were being driven to the airport to catch a flight to Florida, decided to skip their trip and return to Wilmington in Tom's Jeep. Joe dropped off his wife at home and raced to Hurley's office to inform him of Tom's arrest.

The FBI car headed south into Wilmington, parking outside the freight elevator of the Chase Manhattan building, home of the U.S. Attorney's Office.

They led Capano upstairs in the elevator and hustled him into the small conference room investigators had used as the "war room."

Connolly, with the prey of a lifetime finally in custody after sixteen months, entered the room several minutes later. After Louis finished testifying before the grand jury, Connolly had dashed five blocks from the federal courthouse to his office. He found Capano, pasty-faced and dejected, sitting on a chair handcuffed, as two FBI agents sat across a table.

"We've contacted your attorneys and they'll be here shortly," Connolly said matter-of-factly.

Barely glancing at the prosecutor, Capano said, "OK," and started wondering aloud why his attorneys weren't with him now.

Connolly cut him off.

"You're a lawyer, and you know you shouldn't be talking to me," he said. "Just wait. They'll be here."

Connolly marched out, shut the door halfway behind him, but then cracked it open, paused, and stepped back into the war room.

"By the way, Mr. Capano," the prosecutor quipped, finally ready to even a score from their first meeting, "I sleep very well at night."

14 *Stripped of Privilege*

He was perhaps the richest murder suspect in Delaware history—surely no one with such power and prestige had fallen so far. Tom Capano sat, head slumped forward, nearly motionless, in handcuffs. In an adjoining conference room, Colm Connolly, joined by Greg Sleet and Rich Andrews, talked with the state's top prosecutors, Attorney General Jane Brady and her state prosecutor, Ferris Wharton.

"We believe we've got a first-degree murder case," Connolly said, suggesting the state would have to prosecute Capano, since federal courts didn't handle first-degree murder cases.

Connolly then reviewed the results of the federal investigation for Brady and Wharton, going over the evidence piece by piece, climaxing with Gerry's story about the sea burial.

When Connolly said that Gerry had seen a calf and part of a foot sinking into the sea, Brady interrupted.

"How are we going to prove it was Anne Marie Fahey's foot?" the attorney general asked.

Wharton quickly stepped in, putting everybody's nerves to rest. "I don't think that's going to be an issue," the unflappable prosecutor told his boss.

After a brief discussion with Wharton, Brady told Connolly the state would prosecute Capano for murder.

But Connolly was also working another angle.

He wanted to avoid a costly, prolonged trial, one he knew the state might very well lose. Despite Gerry and Louis and the rest of the damning circumstantial evidence, the government still had no eyewitness to the crime, no body, no weapon, not even a theory about how Annie had died, except that her death was bloody. Only one of twelve jurors would have to waver to get a hung jury. And with the prospect of the cunning Hurley, the king of Delaware cross-examiners, carving up Gerry and the other key witnesses, there was always a chance of acquittal.

Connolly was perfectly ready to offer Capano a deal. If he pleaded guilty to a federal charge of kidnapping resulting in murder, he would get life in a Federal prison instead of risking execution. But first the prosecutor wanted to show Capano just how strong a case they had assembled.

Before bringing Capano and his attorneys into the conference room, investigators placed an Igloo cooler, lock, and chain—the same kind Gerry had described—on the oval conference table, along with the anchor Gerry had relinquished.

Connolly then asked that Capano be brought in. The prosecutor was joined by Wharton, Donovan, Alpert, and Poplos, the IRS investigator. Capano finally entered, escorted by his attorneys Oberly and Hurley.

"Your brothers have signed a cooperation agreement," Connolly opened. "They've given taped statements under oath and testified before the grand jury."

Capano huffed. "You believe them?" he asked with incredulity.

So Connolly played the tapes, handing Capano and his lawyers transcripts.

As his brother's emotional voices filled the room, Capano refused to look at the pages and, becoming annoyed at the sound of Hurley's yellow highlight marker, grabbed his lawyer's hand. "Stop making that noise," Capano scolded.

Hurley capped the marker and took out a ballpoint pen.

When the tapes were finished, Connolly whipped out a Sports Authority receipt for a 162-quart Igloo cooler, with Tom's signature. "We have corroborated your purchase for the cooler," he said. "Here's your credit card bill and the store receipt." The prosecutor waved copies of the documents in front of Capano, saying, "You have no reason to buy this cooler. You're not a hunter or a fisherman."

"Yeah, but my brothers are," Capano shot back, again displaying his willingness to fight.

Connolly and Wharton now offered Capano the plea deal, giving him several days to think about it.

With rumors swirling around Wilmington that Capano had been arrested and reporters and television crews milling around the lobby of the Chase Manhattan building, up in Philadelphia Katie Recker called a news conference to confirm the arrest and explain her client's role.

At three that afternoon Recker read a prepared statement from her office to another press mob, saying Louis Capano had provided incriminating information to the government. She said Louis had first begged Tom to surrender.

"Louis Capano in the past acted out of loyalty to his family," Recker said, "but more importantly he acts now out of concern for doing the right thing."

Television stations preempted afternoon soap operas and talk shows to trumpet the news of Tom Capano's arrest.

Even more reporters, photographers, and news trucks raced to the U.S. Attorney's Office but weren't allowed access to the eleventh floor. They milled around the lobby and on the sidewalks of windy Market Street, finally rewarded, several minutes after Recker had delivered her statement from Philadelphia, with a visit from Joseph Hurley. Wearing a tan trench coat, his white hair perfectly coiffed, Hurley looked uncharacteristically shaken as he waded into the crowd of reporters. But he quickly recouped his composure to insist his client was outraged by the murder charge.

"You can bet every dollar in your pocket and every hair on your head that Tom Capano is going to plead 'not guilty,' " Hurley declared. The attorney said Gerry's story was "bull," called him a "drug dealer," and declared that the Capano family had ostracized the youngest child.

Hurley's remarks, directed by his attorney client, marked the opening salvo in the public war among Capanos. It was the beginning of a long, slow, torturous process by which a family tore itself apart—in public. Some would see it as simply the end of the line for a family that had enjoyed all too much protection from responsibility for years of misdeeds and excesses.

As reporters clamored for details, Connolly was upstairs with Anne Marie Fahey's siblings and their spouses, breaking the news of Capano's arrest and revealing, as gently as he could, the details of how their sister had been dumped in the Atlantic. For the first time in more than a year, Connolly talked openly about the investigation and what his team had discovered.

Tears flooded the Fahey faces as Connolly went over the facts, one by one.

The Faheys' relief and satisfaction at Capano's arrest were overshadowed by the horror and devastation at learning how her corpse was stuffed into a cooler, shot with a deer slug, and then dumped in the ocean like fish bait.

Connolly's eyes teared as he asked the Faheys not to divulge certain details—for example, that Gerry had fired a shotgun blast through the cooler.

They agreed.

His hair disheveled, his complexion pasty, still wearing the sweat suit and black sneakers he was arrested in that morning, Tom Capano stared blankly at Justice of the Peace Rosalie Rutkowski as she told Capano he was charged with "first-degree murder." The suspect stood quietly in the small space of Court 18, just inside the entrance of the Multi-Purpose Criminal Justice Facility, known as Gander Hill prison, the same concrete fortress on Wilmington's dingy northeastern perimeter that Capano had visited not many years before as a respected member of a blue-ribbon gubernatorial commission. Now, with Joe Hurley standing beside him and the state prosecutor watching, Capano listened to Magistrate Rutkowski order him held without bail.

Rutkowski then adjourned the session, which had lasted all of two minutes, and guards led Capano, stripped of privilege and prestige, to his prison cell.

That evening's news shows and the next morning's Wilmington and Philadelphia newspapers dedicated massive space to the arrest. The *News Journal* ran a two-deck banner headline: "Capano Held in Murder of Anne Marie Fahey," with two small headlines: "Louis and Gerard Capano's information implicates Thomas" and "Body allegedly dumped at sea." A series of stories, along with a case chronology, capsules of the major players, and excerpts of Donovan's arrest affidavit, took up three full inside pages of the paper.

Dave Sheppard, an electrical engineer at On-Board Chemical Corporation in Newark, Delaware, put the papers down and shouted at Ron Smith, On-Board's facilities manager, "Hey, Ron! Is that cooler you keep on your boat big enough to put a human body in?"

"What the hell are you talking about?" replied the rugged, gray-haired Smith, whose cooler purchase the previous summer had been the subject of office conversation. Tired of always borrowing the one Chubb had dragged out of the ocean in July of 1996, Smith, during a lunch break, finally just bought his own Igloo. Smith brought it back to work in the back of his Ford Bronco and showed it off to colleagues, bragging about the big fish he would catch and store in the mammoth chest.

"They said Anne Marie Fahey was stuffed in a cooler," said Sheppard.

"I don't know what you're talking about," said Smith, who hadn't followed the case.

"You know, the governor's secretary. They arrested this guy Capano yesterday," Sheppard said. "According to the paper, they said he and his brother used a cooler to dump her body in the ocean. Is the cooler you have big enough to hold a body?"

"I probably could almost get in it," said Smith, who stood a muscular five-foot-ten.

Sheppard said, "OK," and walked away.

But as Smith headed down a hallway, he suddenly realized what Sheppard was saying. *Jesus Christ. I wonder if that cooler Chubb found with the bullet holes and lid missing was the same one.*

Smith called Chubb, the retired submariner and prison maintenance boss, at his home in central Pennsylvania.

"Hey, when did you find that cooler?" Smith asked.

"On July Fourth weekend last year," Chubb said. "Why?"

Smith told Chubb about the news in the papers about the missing secretary. "They've arrested this guy, and the cops

say he put her in a cooler and dumped her in the ocean," Smith
said. "That could be the cooler you found."

Chubb suggested that Smith call the police.

———————

Alpert hung up the phone that morning, astonished at what
he'd just heard. Investigators had purposely held back on the
details, to eliminate crank calls. They expected lots of cooler
calls and so had not mentioned the fact that Gerry had shot
holes in the cooler and removed the top. Even so, no one
expected to find Annie's coffin.

The man on the phone had just described it—exactly.

"That's it!" Connolly exclaimed, after Alpert told him about
the phone call. "That's got to be the cooler."

Several hours later, as the sun was setting, Alpert and Donovan drove into Bay City, on the Delaware shore, following
directions to a trailer park where Ken Chubb had his summer
home. Smith and Chubb didn't need to come; the cooler,
Smith said, was in Chubb's unlocked shed.

That's exactly where Alpert and Donovan found it, bar code
still intact. They looked immediately for the bullet holes and
found them—stuffed with epoxy. Giddy with excitement, the
two investigators loaded the huge plastic container into their
car and drove back to Wilmington.

Connolly greeted the cooler as if it were the Holy Shroud.
It was a miracle, he knew, that Anne Marie Fahey's coffin had
been found and that he should be walking around it now. This
was holy justice indeed.

And when investigators ran a check on the bar code numbers on the side of the container, it matched those on the receipt for the cooler purchased at the Sports Authority on April
20, 1996, by one Thomas J. Capano.

And with an obvious bullet hole in its side, it clearly was,
as Connolly later said, "the ultimate corroboration of Gerry."

The next morning, November 14, Connolly called Hurley.

"Guess what, Joe?" he said. "We found the cooler."

Hurley couldn't believe what he was hearing. "Can I see
it?"

An hour later Connolly ushered both Hurley and Oberly into
a conference room at the Wilmington FBI office. There, sitting

oddly out of place on a shiny wooden tabletop, was an old, bunged white cooler.

Hurley walked around the table two or three times, peering at the epoxy-filled holes, studying the new screws and the replacement lid.

"Oh, well," the hotshot defense attorney quipped. "There goes the 'he didn't do it' defense."

But Capano still wouldn't take a deal.

Despite the explosive impact of Gerry and Louis ratting on their brother and the discovery of the cooler, Connolly and Wharton knew a conviction was by no means a given against a shrewd, well-connected defendant with deep pockets. And Capano showed no signs of wanting to capitulate.

In fact, that Christmas Tom Capano sent out a letter to loyal family and friends. Insisting he was an innocent man being framed, Capano said he would fight the charges and take his chances on the death penalty rather than accept life behind bars.

Was it hubris? Or insanity? Was it the promise of a falsely accused man or of a desperate, cold-blooded killer?

BOOK FOUR

Thomas J. Capano entered this courtroom on trial for his life, a man presumed innocent, and, almost immediately, he embarked on a course of conduct which rebutted that presumption. Intelligent, educated, affluent, accomplished and charming by reputation, he proceeded to negate all of the advantages his life had provided during the harsh confrontation with reality which is a criminal trial and eventually revealed an angry, sinister, controlling, and malignant force which dominated the courtroom for months.

—Judge William Swain Lee, March 16, 1999

15 *Bail Denied*

On January 28, 1998, a cold, miserable winter day, Debby MacIntyre was feeling Colm Connolly's heat. Under oath, sitting in a conference room of the attorney general's office, a few floors below the governor's suite where Anne Marie Fahey once worked, MacIntyre was trying her best to remain Tom Capano's loyal lover.

And the youthful prosecutor who sat opposite MacIntyre was just as determined to turn her into a formerly loyal lover.

The suspect had now been stuck in solitary confinement at Gander Hill for almost three months, and Connolly needed MacIntyre to testify for him at the upcoming bail hearing. Capano had no reason to worry about Debby's loyalty. She had been writing him daily, often disparaging Connolly, whom Capano called a "Nazi" and "weasel."

Through her attorney, Adam Balick, MacIntyre had threatened to fight the subpoenas. But Connolly and Wharton promised not to call her for the bail hearing if she met with them privately.

MacIntyre agreed to the meeting and wasn't particularly worried. She didn't know anything about Anne Marie Fahey's disappearance and believed her boyfriend was merely a scapegoat for prosecutors. She and Balick took seats. Connolly, joined by Wharton, Alpert, and Donovan, turned on the tape recorder and had Debby swear to tell the truth. Then Connolly asked if the transcript of her September 10, 1996, grand jury testimony was accurate.

Debby said she wanted to clarify one thing, then volunteered that her sexual relationship with Capano had spanned ten to fifteen years, not the several months she had told the grand jury about.

Connolly already knew from various sources that she had lied about the affair and changed the subject.

"Has Tom ever told you that he had nothing to do with the

disappearance of Anne Marie Fahey?" Connolly asked in a placid, almost sleepy voice.

"Yes. He has told me that."

"Has he ever told you what he believed happened to Anne Marie Fahey?"

"No."

"He's never suggested that she committed suicide or ran away or anything like that?"

"He—yes, he has guessed at possibilities that maybe she ran away or . . . but no, nothing concrete. He doesn't know what happened to her."

His voice still gentle, Connolly changed gears again, asking Debby if she knew whether Capano had any weapons in his home before June 27, 1996.

She said no.

Connolly then got specific, asking Debby, in a rapid staccato, whether Tom had hunting knives and rifles, firearms, pistols, ammunition, blunt instruments, even a letter opener in his house.

She kept answering no—even to a letter opener.

After asking if any of Capano's friends owned guns or hunting knives, Connolly asked, "Do you own any hunting knives?"

"No, I do not."

"Do you own any handguns?"

"I did," she said softly.

This was the question that all the other questions were leading to. And the prosecutor knew the answer. Connolly had already checked to see if Tom had bought a gun. He hadn't. And Gerry said Tom had returned the nickel-plated 10mm Colt pistol he'd loaned him, a gun Gerry said he had given as a tip to a hunting guide in Alaska. After Louis had told Connolly the previous November that Tom said he had tossed a gun in the Dumpster, agents began checking to see if one of Capano's girlfriends—among them MacIntyre and Susan Louth—had bought any guns.

They hit pay dirt with MacIntyre, Capano's devoted mistress. They discovered she had gone into Miller's Gun Center, the most popular gun shop in New Castle County, on May 13, 1996, just six weeks before Fahey vanished, and bought a .22-caliber Beretta.

"When did you own a handgun?" Connolly now asked.

MacIntyre took a deep breath.

She had been worrying that the police might ask her about the gun. Capano had told her he threw it away, "into the deep." He'd also given her a cover story in case she was ever interrogated about the purchase.

The time had come. But even though she had rehearsed her story, her breath quickened, her voice rose a couple of octaves, and she rambled on, as if hoping to avoid the question.

"Uh, probably I purchased one for self-defense a few years ago," she began. "I hate guns. I've never been comfortable with them, but I was uncomfortable where I lived and I didn't—I thought for some reason that I might be able to use it. I purchased one and never took it out of the box. And, uh, one day I came home at the end of school and my son was walking around my room just looking in my closet and I got nervous. So I took it apart. I don't even know what it was. It was a little, little gun. And I took it apart and I threw it away in, uh, separate bags. Never used it."

Connolly guessed she was lying. Her words made no sense. Her neighborhood, the Highlands, was Wilmington's safest. And people didn't just take apart brand-new guns and throw them in the garbage.

Connolly decided to let MacIntyre hang herself and kept probing, in as kindly a voice as he could muster, about when she had purchased the gun. She finally said that it was the spring of 1995.

"You're certain it's '95."

"Well, maybe '94. No. It was a few years ago. Um—"

"Was it before or after the Anne Marie Fahey incident hit the papers?"

"Well it would be af—it would be before."

"Long before or right before?"

"I don't know," MacIntyre said, flustered. "It could have been a year before; it could have been that year."

MacIntyre said that Tom Capano was the only person who knew she bought the gun, had advised her against doing so, and was delighted when she threw it away.

But Connolly kept pressing, asking MacIntyre to describe the gun and the bullets, tell where she hid the gun, how she took it apart, how many pieces there were, how long it sat in her garbage cans, and, again, explain why she had bought it.

Exhaling heavily now, almost hyperventilating, MacIntyre gave disjointed responses.

"What prompted you to buy this gun that you took apart very soon after you bought it?"

"Because, because I—I guess I was worried about what I was hearing," she stammered. "There's been a lot of robberies and muggings and rapes in my area and I'm home alone a lot. And I have a security system, but I didn't feel like paying the money to upgrade it and I—maybe I tried to talk myself into this and I talked to the man at the store and he said that a lot of people do this and blah, blah, blah, and so I bought it and never opened the box."

Connolly returned to the purchase date, reminding MacIntyre she was under oath.

"When you bought the gun, what season was it?"

"I—winter, spring," the frantic woman replied, struggling to hold herself together.

"And when you got rid of it, you think it was sometime in June?"

After fumbling some more, she said it was the second Friday in June.

"But you're not certain what year it was?"

"Ninety-five or ninety-six."

Connolly had heard enough.

Reaching into his black briefcase, under the desk, he pulled out a plastic bag with a .22-caliber black Beretta pistol and showed it to MacIntyre.

"Was that the type of gun?" he asked.

"Uhh, I don't think it was that big."

Reaching under the table again, Connolly pulled out a store receipt, handed it to her, and asked, "Does this help refresh your recollection as to when you bought this gun?"

"Yeah, it does," she replied. "It was—it was in 1976."

Her lawyer, silent until now, spoke up. "Ninety-six," Balick said, correcting her on her year.

"Nineteen-ninety-six. May," MacIntyre stammered. "I thought it was well before that."

The damage was done. After several more minutes in which MacIntyre swore Capano never touched the gun she bought and insisted Capano never once discussed the gun after Fahey disappeared, Connolly terminated the interview. He had enough ammunition, he believed, to pressure MacIntyre into being a government witness.

After the meeting, MacIntyre went home, sat down at her computer, and typed Capano a letter. She and her "darling" usually wrote or spoke on the phone every day, with Debby filling page after page with upbeat stories about her children, her job at Tatnall, and, their favorite topic, sex. Capano, when he didn't grumble about his captors or his tiny, cold cell, advised Debby on every facet of her life, picking her restaurants and organizing her social calendar. And they made plans to get married after he was acquitted.

But the letter she wrote on January 28, 1998, wasn't upbeat. Describing the interview with prosecutors as "lousy" and "horrible," she spared Capano the details, knowing he would learn what had happened from his lawyers after Balick told them. She complained that the prosecutors "weren't nice" and speculated that the lengthy affair would be "fed to the papers" to smear her.

"Bottom line," she concluded, "they think they have something from me. And I am sure that they had this exercise with me knowing that I will tell you. Adam walked me through their hopeful scenario. So, if they are reading this, Hi. Assholes."

Prison was proving more traumatic than Capano might have imagined. The Gander Hill warden kept him in protective custody—a government euphemism for solitary confinement—arguing that, as a former prosecutor, Capano might be in danger from other inmates. The isolation tormented Capano. Alone all day, except for an hour to shower, shave, walk around, or talk to others in the 1F Pod, Capano had become increasingly dependent on Xanax and other antianxiety drugs. He was depressed, suicidal, and paranoid, his attorneys said, but also intent on finding a way out of the hole.

Also during that last week of January, looking for any advantage, Capano hired another attorney, another old pal, Gene Maurer—affable, skilled, and as respected as Hurley. Maurer, who wore his brown hair almost to his shoulders and resembled Paul McCartney, had defended Steve Pennell, the serial killer Capano's old attorney, Kathy Jennings, had prosecuted. Although Maurer had lost the case, his cross-examination of DNA experts in the trial had won him widespread acclaim.

Capano planned to direct Hurley and Maurer, who would share cross-examination duties, while Oberly would help organize strategy. Local pundits, likening Capano to O. J. Simpson, had dubbed the trio Wilmington's "Dream Team," after the band of attorneys who won Simpson his miraculous acquittal in 1995.

Before falling asleep on January 28, the day Debby testified, Capano wrote her a six-page letter, beginning on a salacious note:

It's 11:57 P.M. and with any luck you're naked right now on all fours with your dinner date making you come like crazy doggy style. Actually, you say something in your Monday night letter—which arrived tonight—about having your period. Okay, so maybe you're naked anyway so he can admire your magnificent body on your knees with his dick in your mouth while he sits in a living room chair giving him the best blow job he's ever had. The thought of these things made me have two relaxation sessions since I found out about your date last night and one of them was in the middle of the day while I was standing in a corner of my cell!

No, I know nothing like that happened and that you are already in bed (alone) if not already asleep. I figure you went out around 7:00 or 7:30 and were home by 10:00–10:30 and he left by 11:00 with a handshake at the door.

Well, it's a start. I hope you had fun and like him enough
to see him again.

On page 2, Capano returned to his own problems. He asked
about her interview that day with prosecutors and repeated his
need to have her testify—on his behalf—at the bail hearing.
His lawyers, he said, thought she was a critical witness:

I'm sorry, darling, but they are right that you should be
there in person. Please forgive me, but I agree with them,
as I will explain, and I freely admit it's purely selfish on
my part. I want to do everything possible to try to get out,
as you know.

Then, trying to give Debby strength for the ordeal, Capano
outlined the "team's" rationale for wanting her to testify, referring to his soul mate in the third person.
"Debby MacIntyre is an important witness for us but, maybe
more importantly, she's an impressive witness," he wrote.
Capano said his lawyers thought she would come across as
a "very honest and credible woman," once she recovered from
initial jitters:

We don't have many witnesses like her who have relevant
and important things to say and are on our side. She comes
across not just as honest but also as level-headed and ma-
ture. That someone of her caliber will say positive things
about Tom while talking about relevant issues helps our
case.

Despite MacIntyre's adamant expressions of love for Capano, her attorney knew she was in trouble. The charges she
might face—perjury, obstruction of justice, accessory to a
murder—flooded his mind, and he told his client he had to
advise her not to testify for Capano.
"If Tom cared about you," Adam Balick told MacIntyre,
"he wouldn't be putting you through this."
It slowly sank in for Debby that she could not help Tom

Capano without sacrificing herself and, by extension, her children.

On February 1, the eve of the bail hearing, after a testy and unpleasant phone conversation with Capano, Debby sat at her computer and wrote: "I am nervous for you and for myself too. But for you it is different, because this is your freedom. I hope I don't disappoint you. You always have high expectations of me, and I am sometimes not sure I can live up to them."

She concluded by promising to testify, with conditions: "I guess the noble thing and caring thing to do is go. I know my not going will not prevent my privacy from being invaded. . . . So you really owe me big time after this is over. I have compromised my quiet, private, boring life for you and will testify, but you will be very busy with me for a long time after this—got it."

But by the next morning, she had changed her mind. She wrote to "My Dear Tom" as he sat in court during the first day of the hearing:

> By the time you get this letter, and well before I think, you will know of my final decision not to testify. I have struggled with my decision since last Wednesday, after my horrible interview. Yes, it was horrible for me, and for a person who is not used to such scare tactics, it hit home.
>
> Possibly I could get myself in serious trouble and I am not willing to take that risk. Deep in your heart, I know you have to agree with me. So my love, this is the first time, in all the years of our relationship, that I have done something for myself, not to sacrifice myself to please somebody else. I know right now you don't believe me and might go so far as to say that my lack of presence cost you your bail if you don't get it.

She wrote that she was praying for him to win and "even tried out a rosary I bought in Rome."

Capano's bail hearing was a high-stakes dress rehearsal for his trial. He had managed to preserve his freedom for sixteen and a half months while under investigation. But now that he was in the clutches of the state and charged with capital murder, Capano would have to fight to be released even on bail. He was risking a lot in the process. Witnesses would be called and cross-examined, and evidence would be introduced. The defense would get a peek at the prosecution's case, but it would also have to expose its own defenses—not an advisable strategy for a defendant who needed every tactical advantage. But Tom Capano, having lived a life of opulence and privilege, conspicuous for its political, financial, and sexual freedoms, was dying in captivity. He was desperate to get out of jail.

Prosecutors often waived bail hearings in death penalty cases because murder defendants, usually of meager means, couldn't afford to post the high bond. Waiving the hearing also spared the state from having to present key evidence so long before trial.

That's what happened in the case of Amy Grossberg and Brian Peterson, the University of Delaware freshmen from affluent New Jersey families who were charged with killing their newborn son in November 1996. In that case, prosecutors waived the bail hearing rather than show the defense evidence so long before trial. But Grossberg and Peterson were each able to post $300,000 bail and gain freedom.

In Tom Capano's case, however, Connolly and Wharton weren't about to waive a bail hearing. They worried that if he were released now, with his financial resources and in his state of mind, he would flee the country or try to tamper with witnesses, including his susceptible brothers. They wanted Capano to stay behind bars.

The pale, graying figure who shuffled into jam-packed Courtroom 301 of the Daniel L. Herrmann Courthouse on February 2, 1998, a rainy Monday, looked gaunt, with sunken cheeks, a much different man from the confident and comfortable lawyer arrested three months earlier. Wearing a charcoal suit, Capano offered wan smiles to his mother, sitting in a wheelchair, estranged wife, two oldest daughters, brother Joe, sister Marian, and several friends. He avoided the hateful glares of Annie's relatives and friends on the other side of the aisle.

William Swain Lee, the lean and athletic Superior Court judge presiding over the case, walked into the cavernous courtroom and called the hearing to order.

The sixty-two-year-old Lee, a good-natured doctor's son and former Marine, was a Duke graduate who grew up in a farming community in central Delaware. Divorced, with four grown children, Lee loved dancing at the clubs in Rehoboth Beach, where he lived. Though he was chief judge of neighboring Sussex County, he was selected to preside over the Capano case because he didn't know the suave Wilmington attorney—unlike most of the judges in New Castle County. Considered fair but tough, Lee was a strong proponent of the death penalty, though he'd never sentenced a man to death. And as he opened the hearing, he cautioned the crowd in the courtroom against any outbursts.

The local press was agog over the hearing since it represented the first time anyone would get a blow-by-blow description of what had happened to Anne Marie Fahey; the first time the public would hear from Capano's turncoat brothers; the first time, it was rumored, they would hear from his longtime mistress, Debby MacIntyre.

One pivotal question was whether Gerry would hold up under a brutal interrogation by Hurley.

Just in case Gerry faltered, Connolly and company had backup: the cooler, the neighbor who had seen Gerry and Tom talking in Gerry's driveway the morning of June 28, bank photos from the ATM at the WSFS bank in Trolley Square that morning showing Tom in shorts and a T-shirt withdrawing $200, phone records from Gerry's beach home indicating calls to MacIntyre's office and Kay Capano's home, the log from the Stone Harbor Marina showing someone paid $138.36 cash for gas that morning, and Tom's own alibi for that day, seized from his office, putting him in Stone Harbor with his kid brother. All were pieces of circumstantial evidence to support Gerry's eyewitness account of a sea burial.

Capano was silent as Lieutenant Daniels, the state police detective who had interviewed him nineteen months earlier, spent the first day of the bail hearing reviewing statements by Annie's friends and therapists. But the defendant's interest— and intensity—increased tenfold the next day, when his brother Gerry took the stand.

Since the plea agreement, Gerry had been spending much of his time at the family's condo in Florida, away from the rest of his family, which, except for Louis, had ostracized him. Tan, wearing a dark sports coat, colorful tie, and khaki slacks, his hair almost in a buzz cut, Gerry emerged from a side room and climbed into the witness-box.

Ashen-faced, Tom rested his palm on his chin and fixed a gaze of cool, clinical contempt on his younger brother. Their mother, sitting in her wheelchair, bowed her head and sobbed.

Avoiding eye contact with Tom, speaking in a barely audible voice, Gerry was led through his story by a friendly Colm Connolly, beginning with Tom's request in February of 1996.

"He asked me if I knew anybody that would—could break somebody's legs or could beat somebody up or, you know, whatever," said Gerry. "And I said I did."

Gerry, guided by Connolly, told of Tom's request in February to borrow $8,000 for extortionists and, weeks later, to use his boat to dispose of a body. Then Gerry described the bizarre events of June 28, from the moment that Tom arrived in his driveway at dawn to the trip to the Dumpsters with sofa and rug.

Gerry told the rapt courtroom audience that he was thunderstruck when Tom asked to use his boat that summer morning. "I never thought he was serious," Gerry, who seemed on the verge of tears, said under the withering gaze of his mother. "I told him I didn't want to go."

"Why did you agree to help him?" asked Connolly.

"He's my little brother," Gerry said, confusing the sibling order as if in unconscious acknowledgment of the role reversal that was then being played out. "He said he needed me."

Connolly guided Gerry through the rest of that day's ghastly events as the two brothers, Gerry said, took a huge cooler to the Jersey shore—then out to sea.

Members of the audience gasped when Gerry said, "I saw a foot sinking into the deep."

"This foot—it was a human foot?" the prosecutor prompted.

"Yeah," muttered Gerry.

"What else did you see?" Connolly asked.

"I saw a little bit of a calf, too."

Gerry then told the courtroom of helping dispose of the sofa with the "basketball-sized" bloodstain and being visited by Tom and his lawyer, Charlie Oberly, two nights later. "They said that a woman was missing and the police may come asking me questions about it," Gerry testified. He also confessed to making up an alibi with Tom, even writing it down on yellow Post-it notes and carrying them with him in his checkbook.

When Joe Hurley stood up, he flashed Gerry a smile. "Did you ever have one of those bad days we all have where you kind of wondered why you're even alive?" Hurley asked.

"Not really," said Gerry.

"You never had a day like that?" Hurley repeated.

"Today," Gerry said.

Hurley quickly proved that he was going to try to make Gerry's day even worse, going immediately after the same vulnerable spot the feds had hit when they raided his house.

"Is it fair to say that you weren't exactly shocked that they found narcotics in your home or your vehicles?" asked Hurley.

"That's correct," said Gerry.

Hurley walked Gerry through his drug use habits as if conducting a seminar. "Snorting it [cocaine], as I understand it, not from personal experience," said Hurley, "is taking some kind of device and putting it up underneath your nose, and then in some fashion sucking in your breath in order to introduce it into the nasal passages?"

"Yes," said Gerry.

"What did it do to you?" Hurley asked.

"Makes you feel good," said Gerry.

"Can you be a little bit more explicit?" asked Hurley. "Is it just a general 'hey, I feel wonderful' feeling?"

"It gives you a high."

"Let's talk about something I'm more familiar with. Have you ever been drunk?"

"Yes."

Asked to differentiate a cocaine high from alcohol intoxication, Gerry said, "I guess you wouldn't black out or get all sloppy like if you were drunk."

"So it's a more refined high?"

"To me it was."

Hurley, aiming to discredit his client's kid brother, jabbed at Capano's memory and his judgment, suggesting that the government's pressure on him—the threat to take his children, for instance—had made him shade his story.

But Gerry stood his ground. And for all his flamboyance, perhaps because of it, Hurley sometimes found himself flailing, at times seeming to dig his client a deeper hole.

"Did you remind Tom, 'Hey, Tom, you remember back on that day you told me you would take care of me and I wouldn't get hurt'?"

"I certainly did."

"I'm sure you did. And what was his response?"

" 'Nothing's going to happen to you.' "

Hurley could not find any certain way to make Gerry's testimony sound unbelievable. He scored points against the rich man's decadent lifestyle, but not the credibility of a man having to help send his own brother to a lethal injection, Delaware's method of execution. Gerry had survived the great Joe Hurley's assault.

Louis followed Gerry to the stand, looking dapper but despondent. His voice cracked as he told how Tom had manipulated him into emptying the Dumpsters and convinced him to lie before the grand jury, how Gerry had confessed to him some fifteen months earlier, and how neither could persuade Tom to surrender.

The prosperous developer's emotional performance was just what prosecutors wanted—testimony that Gerry didn't just make up the story after his home was raided.

But under cross-examination, it took Maurer only seconds

to transform Louis into an irritable, bellicose witness, as the attorney attempted to show that Louis was also fabricating stories and twisting facts. The defense attorney badgered Louis about his criminal liabilities and marital infidelities.

Noting that Louis had been investigated for mail fraud, Maurer asked if the probe had anything to do with his insurance claim for an accident involving his white BMW.

Louis said he didn't know, and Maurer asked if he had told the mechanic Merten fell asleep at the wheel.

"I don't recall," Louis said.

"When you say you don't recall something," Maurer pushed, "does that mean you didn't say it?"

"No," Louis shot back. "It means I don't recall saying it."

"Could you have said it?"

"It happened more than a year ago."

"Could you have said it?"

"I don't know," Louis snapped.

"So when you use the words 'I don't recall,' that means that you could have said it, but you don't know as you sit here today whether you said it."

"That's fairly accurate."

"What does 'fairly accurate' mean?" asked Maurer, relentless.

"I don't recall if I said it or not."

Louis never gave in on whether he ever said Merten fell asleep but acknowledged that the wire fraud probe probably revolved around the insurance claim. Even more embarrassing, Louis had to say publicly that during an argument while he was speeding along a highway Merten had grabbed the steering wheel in an attempt to jerk the car to the side of the road and the BMW had smashed a guardrail.

Louis also had to admit that he was sleeping with Kristi Pepper, and not his wife, on the evening Anne Marie Fahey was allegedly killed.

Scintillating as this testimony was, however, it failed to discredit Louis's damning testimony against his brother. There was, after all, no evidence that Louis or Gerry was anything other than a good brother, loving and loyal, prior to this.

Later, outside court, Louis told reporters he regretted his

actions but didn't know if Tom had killed Anne Marie Fahey.

"This is a very sad situation for our family, the Capano family, and the Fahey family," said Louis. "I recognize I had to do the right thing, the honest thing. I love my brother very much."

That same evening, February 3, Tom Capano read Debby MacIntyre's letter listing the reasons she wasn't testifying. His lawyers had already broken the bad news, but seeing Debby's words infuriated him.

He immediately wrote back:

I am beyond shocked. The one thing I always thought, believed, loved, was that I could always rely on you and your unconditional love. To have that yanked away from me this week is almost too much to bear. And it was done coldly and with finality. I guess I always knew this day would come but that knowledge has not dulled the pain. I am, quite literally, numb with that sinking feeling in my stomach. I've been abandoned in my time of need by most of the people I cared about and who I thought cared about me. I would have bet my life on your unlimited devotion and loyalty.

Capano put down his pen to call. It was his allotted time to use the telephone, make his daily phone calls. He first excoriated Debby for her treason, then begged her to reconsider. Returning to his cell, he continued his written diatribe:

We just spoke 15 minutes ago. I truly wish I could have told you I wasn't hurt by your decision but the stakes are too high to lie about it. I asked if you kept copies of your letters. You said you didn't. I'm enclosing your Sunday night letter because I'd like you to read certain parts again. That is the Debby I always knew and loved. The stranger who wrote the cold and insensitive Monday night letter is not anyone I know. To be very candid, I suppose I'm most troubled by your decision to follow Adam's advice instead of mine. He has been wrong almost every step of the way and I have been right but you have consistently ignored me.

I begged you to avoid the interview last week. . . . If they believe they have a weapon used to commit murder then they will charge you with a crime. It's that simple. But you haven't been charged and won't be charged because they have no proof of any of that because it is not true. Because Connolly is ruthless he will threaten you with charges at some point to get you to change your story and testify against me at trial. He's bluffing. Let's suppose for the sake of argument they can prove that the gun they showed you at the interview was the one you bought and has my fingerprints on it. Juicy, yes. But how can he prove it was used to commit murder? They don't have a body to examine for gunshot wounds. And, taking a huge leap to the next step, how can he prove your involvement in any manner? You've told him about the purchase, the reason for it, and how you got rid of it. But even if I'm wrong, and they somehow are able to connect all these dots, he can't prove that I didn't take it from your garbage, for example, without your knowledge, that you even knew that Anne Marie Fahey—the supposedly intended victim—even existed. I don't know why I'm doing this—arguing the issues. You've made a decision and I'll accept it.

By the end of the long, rambling letter from prison, Capano wallowed in self-pity and tugged at Debby's heartstrings:

Monday's icy letter makes it clear that you are ready to put me behind you and move on with your life. That's good; it's something you should do. As I said, I didn't expect it to be so abrupt or for the ax to fall this week when I'm at my low point. I expect to lose the hearing, remain here 'til trial, be convicted of something at trial and spend the rest of my relatively short life in jail. I would like to die before trial. But you now see the same future—which is no future—and have made the only decision that makes sense for you. I really do understand. You have one and, if you're smart, two men interested in you now so it's perfect timing. Please don't write anymore. Let's just make a clean break.

I do love you but will try to forget. Please tell the kids I
love them. I truly do. I'm so sorry. Forget me.

While Gerry and Louis provided the drama at the bail hearing, MacIntyre—though she didn't testify—contributed the in-
trigue. Through FBI agent Alpert, most of what MacIntyre
would have testified about was introduced, including her
fifteen-year affair with Capano and her purchase of a gun, one
that, prosecutors implied, was probably used to kill Anne Marie Fahey.

As spectators walked out of court on the third day of the
hearing, they all buzzed about MacIntyre and the gun.

The cooler was not shown at the hearing—it was being
tested at the FBI lab in Washington—but Tom Capano's receipt was, and Alpert testified about recovering the cooler
from Ken Chubb's shed.

By the end of the fifth day, no one seemed surprised when
Judge William Swain Lee denied bail.

Capano's shoulders sagged. His head sank, and, as guards
led him away in handcuffs, his lips quivered. Behind him, his
supporters were groaning, hugging one another, and weeping.
His mother leaned her chin on her cane, stared straight ahead,
and sobbed as her son Joe consoled her.

The Faheys marched out, satisfied but stone-faced.

———

On February 27, a drizzly Friday morning, Debby Mac-
Intyre, wearing a black leather jacket, set her jaw and marched
silently past reporters and photographers into the attorney general's office with her new lawyer, Tom Bergstrom of suburban
Philadelphia.

It was exactly three weeks after the bail hearing ended.
Three torturous weeks for MacIntyre.

The *News Journal* had run a front-page profile of her on
February 22, exposing her to more public humiliation. "Capano Mistress' Gun Adds New Twist," ran the headline, with
a subhead: "Though not a murder suspect, Tatnall School official is at the heart of the murder case."

In the meantime, her beloved Tatnall, embarrassed by the

disclosures, forced MacIntyre to resign. And Capano intensified his assault, browbeating her for not testifying at the bail
hearing, questioning her loyalty, and asking her to fire Bergstrom, all the time begging her to remain in his corner.

MacIntyre's ex-husband, David Williams, had urged her to
dump Balick and hire Bergstrom, who had defended John du
Pont, the chemical heir who had killed Olympic wrestler Dave
Schultz on his sprawling estate near Media, Pennsylvania, just
twenty-five miles north of Wilmington.

Bergstrom had advised Debby to come clean with the prosecutors. And on February 26 she wrote Capano to explain her
decision to follow Bergstrom's advice:

> I knew I had lied and they knew I had lied—even the papers
> said I lied, it was that obvious, and I really was not wanting
> to face perjury. You certainly should know me well enough
> to know I can't lie well or at all and could not deal with
> the results. Yes, Adam did not pull through during the in-
> terview, but I believe it all happened for a reason, out of
> my control, and what is going on now is just the same.
>
> Tomorrow will be a big day for me. . . . If I had talked
> with you, I would have told you I was going to be truthful—
> that is the only way. I don't know what the truth will do.
> Will it hurt you? I don't know what the defense case is nor
> do I know what the prosecution case is. A lot of people
> suggest that you should make a deal to save your kids, sib-
> lings, mother, me and you and anyone else who is hurt by
> this case.
>
> Often I wonder why all this tragedy had to happen? What
> happened and why are you involved—will you ever be able
> to tell me? I think not and that will always keep us apart.
> . . . I carry you in my heart always.

That same day, suspecting she was going to cut a deal,
Capano wrote her three letters—a total of sixteen pages of
neat, controlled script.

Haranguing, pleading, waxing nostalgic, Capano mustered
every ounce of strength to keep her from the dreaded clutches
of Connolly and Wharton:

I can feel myself getting angry and again feeling the sense of betrayal I felt when you abandoned me at the bail hearing. Do you love me or not? Do you know what love is, Debby? Giving yourself completely to someone as I have to you. Trusting someone completely as I have you. Protecting someone completely as I have you. I don't want to feel anger. I can't. I don't want to feel betrayal again.

How can you say you love me and in the next breath tell me you won't keep my letters because your new lawyer wants you to give them to him? The obvious message you're giving me is that you may do what he says. What conclusion can I draw from that? That he's more important to you than I am? That perhaps I can't trust you? That you don't care about or love me? As desperate as I am for your love. As much as I adore you. I will not live with that. If you are going to crush me—and perhaps destroy my spirit— it's better that you do it now than later so I can at least try to recover, although I doubt I ever will, now rather than later. You must now prove your love to me.

He offered to fire his entire legal team if she would only come on board:

I will sacrifice the huge amount of money I have already spent, nearly $500,000. I ask only that you give up someone who is a stranger, not a friend, someone you've known for only a few weeks and met only a few times, someone who cannot have cost you much yet, someone somehow connected to Dave Williams, someone who wants you to refuse my calls and turn over my letters so he can do whatever he wants with them, someone who doesn't care and probably didn't ask if you loved me, someone who doesn't care about me as my present lawyers care about you.

But Debby's mind was made up. She knew she could be prosecuted and jailed for her perjury, let alone be considered a murder suspect herself.

So, just like Capano's brothers, she decided to tell the truth, sacrificing Tom to save herself.

When she finally met with prosecutors on February 27, they were ready to deal. They offered MacIntyre a blanket immunity. All she had to do was swear she did not kill or help kill Fahey, admit lying under oath, promise to cooperate fully, and take a lie detector test. She agreed.

Later that wet winter evening, Capano sat in his cell and penned an eight-page letter:

Dearest Debbie:

  My world just ended. It's 7:15. Charlie Oberly just left. He told me you tried to destroy me today.... How could you do such a thing? I've always protected you and would never let any harm come to you because of my love for you. How could you destroy the man you say you love, who has always been there for you, always kept his promise to you, sacrificed greatly for you?. Why? Because you were intimidated. . . .

He ended this letter with a bizarre postscript:

Perhaps it's only fitting that the article about your betrayal and the day I receive confirmation from speaking to you or from some other person (like Joey or Lee Ramunno) who has spoken to you will be on the anniversary of my father's death. We will die on the same date. He died a natural death. I died because you broke my heart, stole my hope, and killed my spirit. I go to my death, knowing that I loved you totally and made the ultimate sacrifice. What would your father think of you now?

———

That February and March, Capano was also corresponding with Susan Louth, who had written him from her new home in the Virgin Islands.

He addressed one of his letters to "Slutty Little Girl," his mother's sobriquet for the attractive legal secretary, and engaged in sexual banter, praising the twin dimples on the backs of Louth's thighs and asking about her friend Charo.

"Don't you wish you had let me do Charo?" Capano asked in one letter.

In another letter to Louth, he asked: "So what did Charo look like in her bikini? Send pictures. God I wish you weren't so inhibited."

Later, in the same missive, he wrote: "I'm getting 'fan' mail from young chicks who want to get together when I get out. Can't wait. One of them will probably send me sexy pictures soon and in her last letter talked about oral sex. Perfect."

Meanwhile prosecutors had asked one more favor of Debby, a favor they hadn't put in writing. Noting that she said she still loved Capano, still believed he was innocent, and couldn't refuse his calls from prison, they asked her to record those conversations when they happened. She agreed.

From February 28 through March 3, MacIntyre taped four of Capano's phone calls from jail. Most of the conversations concerned mundane details of their lives, but Capano also tried to pry information from Debby about what she had told Connolly and Wharton.

"I told the truth," MacIntyre told Capano in their first taped exchange.

"No, no, tell me exactly what happened. Start to finish," Capano demanded in a raspy voice.

After reviewing what led her into the meeting with prosecutors, she said they had asked her about the gun.

"I told them that I bought it and I gave it to you. You wanted it. I gave it to you."

"Why did you say such a thing?" Capano snapped.

"Because you did."

"Why did you, why did you go in there?" Capano began before she cut him off.

"I told the truth, darling; I told the truth," MacIntyre, her voice hysterical, said.

"Why—why did you do that? Why would you do that?"

"Because I don't lie."

"Why would you?"

MacIntyre took a deep breath and insisted, "I can't lie."

In Debby's next, and final, letter, written March 2, she reiterated the need to be truthful and continued professing her love: "There is nothing I can say or write to you that will convince you that I love you now and forever. If you do love me as you say you do, you must trust and believe my words. . . . I want to believe more than anything that we will both go to our eventual destinies in the future knowing that both of us have been loved and have loved completely."

She ended by saying good-bye to her longtime secret lover, the man who, just a month earlier, she was still planning to marry after he beat the murder rap: "I hope and pray you will stand by me. I love you. I miss you. Please be strong."

Debby MacIntyre's betrayal drove Tom Capano into a fury.

While keeping up his steady stream of critical yet pleading letters to Debby in February, Capano began plotting other ways to silence her.

He began confiding in Nick Perillo, the inmate in Cell 2, next door to his. Perillo, a charismatic crook with white hair and goatee, had once been married to a public defender. But he was also a cocaine and heroin addict who had committed burglaries, forgeries, and thefts to support his habit, had spent fourteen of the previous eighteen years in jail, and, after a December burglary, was now facing a possible life sentence as a habitual criminal.

Capano asked Perillo to call Debby and encourage her to keep her mouth shut.

"Tell her to fight the hypocrite bastards and not to change her story about putting the gun in her trash cans," Capano told his prison pal.

Then, on February 27, after Oberly told Capano that MacIntyre had changed her story, Capano changed his request to Perillo.

"Do you have any friends that would burglarize her house and send her a message?" he asked. "It would be easy pickings. I have the alarm code. She's going away soon for about ten days."

Perillo agreed again. All along, however, the veteran con artist had seen an angle in helping Capano. Perillo now figured he could cut himself a deal in exchange for incriminating information about Delaware's most high-profile inmate. And that night he dashed off a letter to his lawyer, Tom Foley, the same attorney who represented Kristi Pepper, offering to become a government witness. "He told me about a gun he had her buy," Perillo wrote. "Jesus, I think the bastard killed her [Fahey] and he's trying to destroy anyone that gets in his way."

When Foley received the letter, he blew it off, thinking prosecutors would never want to use someone with Perillo's shady past.

But Perillo was determined. On March 4, he wrote Wharton a letter, identifying himself as an inmate in Capano's unit. "I have some information pertaining to Mr. Capano and his dealings with Debby MacIntyre that I'd like to discuss with you," he wrote.

A few days later, Foley was visiting another client at Gander Hill when, almost as an afterthought, he stopped to see Perillo. The inmate repeated his story, even promising a map of MacIntyre's house that Capano had said he'd draw.

"Bring it with you when you meet the prosecutors," Foley said, thinking it would never happen.

But on March 11, when Wharton and Connolly met with Perillo and Foley, the inmate stunned everyone by pulling out a detailed four-page diagram of MacIntyre's house, with security alarm code and copious instructions for the burglary—all written by Capano:

MUST SHATTER FLOOR TO CEILING MIRROR ON WALL IN MASTER BEDROOM. ABSOLUTELY REQUIRED.

MUST LOCATE AND REMOVE PLASTIC BAG WITH SEX TOYS AND VIDEOS IN A CLOSET IN MASTER BEDROOM SUITE OR UNDER BED.

ALL ART IS ORIGINAL AND VALUABLE. MUST REMOVE ALL OR SLASH AND DESTROY.

JEWELRY IN TOP DRAWERS OF FURNITURE IN DRESSING ROOM OR MASTER BEDROOM BUT MAY BE HIDDEN IN CLOSETS OR BUILT-INS.

Connolly and Wharton were astonished by what they were reading. Trying to intimidate a prosecution witness was known in the trade as "consciousness of guilt." Not as good as landing an eyewitness to the crime, but pretty incriminating nonetheless. "I couldn't have drawn that detailed a map of my own house," said Wharton. They thanked Perillo, took the papers, and promised to help him get moved to another jail.

Prosecutors then informed Capano's attorneys and also told Bergstrom, who filled MacIntyre in.

Capano wrote MacIntyre on March 17, apologizing for his actions, explaining that he had hatched the plan in a weak moment. But he also blamed Perillo. "A con man who befriended me—I'm certain he was planted here for the purpose of getting close to me—took advantage of my rage and got me to do something terrible," Capano wrote.

MacIntyre didn't read Capano's explanation. Instead she gave the letter, unopened, to her attorney, who turned it over to the prosecutors.

The burglary scheme became public on March 21, after Bergstrom told Jerry Hager of the *News Journal*. "Capano Plots to Frighten Ex-Lover," a front-page headline screamed. But even after his plot was exposed, Capano continued writing MacIntyre, castigating her for turning on him, trying to persuade her back to his side, tugging at every heartstring he could—pledging his undying love and devotion, lamenting the pain he was causing his daughters, and reminding Debby how a decade earlier he had helped her deal with her parents' deaths.

MacIntyre, on Bergstrom's advice, had stopped opening Capano's letters. Instead she turned them over to the lawyer, who gave them to prosecutors. Capano also stopped calling Debby.

And in a letter to Louth, Capano belittled MacIntyre and began planting the seeds of a defense. Noting that an older female cousin had seen MacIntyre's photo in the paper, he wrote that the woman said Debby "looks like a shrew and a backstabber. Pretty perceptive? You think I should tell her that she swallows and loves it?"

And in response to suspicions being talked about in the

media, Capano tested another defense. He wondered if Louth had heard that a couple of Philadelphia television stations "reported that I was going to say Debby killed Anne Marie and I covered up for her. I can't tell you or anyone where I'm headed, but if you talk to anyone, why don't you say it makes a lot of sense for a lot of reasons. Maybe you avoid talking about it at all. Well, at least she loved blow jobs and swallowing—couldn't get enough of it. If only I could have found someone else with the same qualities, maybe none of this would have happened."

Late in March, after Capano's plot with Perillo became public, another Gander Hill inmate contacted Connolly and Wharton, promising to reveal a much more sinister scheme by Capano. The prosecutors agreed to meet with Wilfredo "Tito" Rosa, head of a Wilmington cocaine ring, who was awaiting sentencing for conspiracy and money-laundering convictions. The story Rosa told was even more startling than Perillo's.

"He wanted me to look into, uh, what the cost and what the details were about having Gerry, um, killed," Rosa told the prosecutors.

Rosa, an intelligent, bespectacled man, explained that he had no intention of carrying out a hit on Gerry but planned to lead Capano along in order to get $100,000, the balance of the mortgage on his house.

By March, Rosa continued, Capano had added Debby to the hit list. "He went from killing Gerry, his brother, to now killing Deborah," explained the convict. "And he wanted it done as soon as possible."

Rosa said Capano had described MacIntyre's house, written down her address, and provided photos of her. "He said no one would be around during the day and there was a good possibility that someone could just walk up to her door like a delivery flower guy and just whack her."

Rosa told Connolly and Wharton he strung Capano along but contacted them in hopes of cutting a deal for a reduced sentence. He faced thirty years to life in jail.

The prosecutors, once again amazed at what they were hearing about Capano's behavior in jail, told Rosa they couldn't make any promises. They instructed him to let Capano keep talking about the plot but ordered him not to talk about Anne Marie Fahey. That could jeopardize the murder case, they warned.

16 *A Liar, a Junkie, a Stone-cold Bum*

Defending Tom Capano—the client who insisted on calling every shot—was finally more than Joe Hurley wanted to handle, professionally or emotionally.

So, on April 6, 1998, the lawyer who had proclaimed, "I have arrived," upon joining the defense team fifteen months earlier quit without comment. "I'll take the reasons to my grave," he promised with customary hyperbole.

Tom Capano immediately began interviewing high-profile out-of-state attorneys to lead his team. He was in a hurry, since Judge Lee had scheduled jury selection to begin on October 6 and had indicated that he wasn't about to delay the trial because Capano had lost one of his three attorneys.

After celebrity attorney Roy Black of Florida (who had successfully defended William Kennedy Smith against rape charges) turned Capano down and he interviewed Manhattan lawyer Jack Litman (of Preppy Murder fame), Capano talked to Joseph Oteri, a gregarious and successful Boston attorney best known for representing accused drug traffickers. Black had recommended Oteri, the man so busy in 1990 that he turned down an offer to represent Gen. Manuel Noriega, the deposed dictator of Panama.

Capano took a liking to the bearded sixty-seven-year-old grandfather, former Marine, and fellow Italian-American. Oteri had grown up on Boston's rough Irish South Side and had become something of a legal legend in his hometown when, emerging from court in 1959, he was shot in the head, back, and thigh by a city cop who had just lost a child support case to Oteri. He survived. And over the years, if anybody asked about his close brush with death, Oteri took great relish in exclaiming, "Every day since has been a free one!"

When Capano attended Boston College in the late 1960s, he'd sat in on a guest lecture by Oteri, who was then also a regular guest on *The Advocates,* a PBS program on legal issues. For a time Oteri even hosted *The Joe Oteri Show* and was the first attorney in America to raise post-traumatic stress disorder as a defense, in the case of a former Vietnam War helicopter pilot caught importing 8,000 pounds of hashish from Morocco. Because of the pilot's illness, Oteri argued, "he was driven to seek out action. He was addicted to it." Oteri won an acquittal for the pilot.

Oteri accepted Capano's offer and later quipped, "I may be his third choice, but I charge first choice prices." The fee was more than five hundred thousand dollars, plus the use of a car and condominium in Wilmington.

Oteri arrived in town on June 11, one day after the *News Journal* published a story about Capano's alleged plot to kill his brother and mistress from jail.

"Capano Linked to Murders-for-Hire," blared the headline, over the blurb: "Defendant wanted brother, lover slain, attorneys say."

Capano dashed off a long letter to MacIntyre that morning: "PLEASE, PLEASE DON'T BELIEVE ANY OF THIS NON-SENSE. I am so angry I won't say anything here because I'm enraged by this horrible bullshit. . . . I recently wrote you a love letter because I miss you so much. I meant every word of it and I still do. You've got to believe that. . . ."

Debby again turned the letter over to her lawyer unopened.

Oteri, trying to establish himself in Wilmington as a take-no-prisoners fighter, immediately went on the offensive, blasting Rosa as a "fraud" and insisting witnesses from Gander Hill "will prove, as much as you can prove a negative, that this never happened."

The new chief of Capano's legal team also began telling any reporter who would listen—as did his predecessor, Hurley—how despicable Gerry was. "They're making him out to be a family man," Oteri said of Gerry, "and he's nothing but a liar, a junkie, and a stone-cold bum."

Privately, however, Oteri confided to friends that Gerry's story was a hard one to refute. "I'd love to argue reasonable doubt," he confided to one man. "But every avenue I take runs right into that damn cooler. This is 'The Cooler Case.' "

With the deadline for filing a wrongful death civil suit against Capano approaching—two years from the time of death—the Faheys were in court on May 20 trying to have Annie declared legally dead. If they waited for a murder conviction, they would lose the right to sue for damages in civil court.

Kathleen and Robert Fahey thus stood before Delaware Chancery Court judge Myron Steele having to insist that the only explanation for their sister's disappearance was that she was dead. They told the judge that Annie wouldn't have abandoned family, friends, or coworkers.

"She was fine," Kathleen said, her voice choked with emotion, as she described having dinner with Annie on June 26, 1996, the night before her dinner with Capano at the Panorama. "I have not seen or heard from her since."

Kathleen also described the gut-wrenching evening when she had gone to Annie's apartment and found the rotting vegetables in her kitchen and the disarray in her bedroom. She told of the vigil her family had kept on Annie's porch, praying she would miraculously return.

On June 18, almost a month later, Judge Steele decreed Anne Marie Fahey dead. The ruling was no cause for celebration. It merely "brought back all the emotion and the heinous way she was murdered," Kathleen said. "These are going to be some difficult days."

On June 25—two days shy of the second anniversary of Annie's presumed death—the Faheys filed a nine-count lawsuit against the four brothers and the five Capano business entities, alleging Tom had killed their sister and his three brothers had participated in an elaborate cover-up and seeking unspecified damages. "Someone must make the Capanos understand," Annie's siblings said in a prepared statement, "that when you purposely hurt people, you must answer for your actions."

The Faheys got some bad news at the end of the month, when the U.S. Navy reported the results of its search for Annie's remains in the Atlantic.

A few weeks before, a sonar scan of the ocean floor, near the spot Gerry said Annie's body was thrown overboard, had detected a metal device. Investigators had suspected it might be the anchors and chain from the *Summer Wind*.

"Our hope was that they would find Anne Marie's remains and we would have some semblance of a burial," Robert Fahey told the *News Journal*. But the navy could only find a clam trawl. "Now we're denied that burial forever."

And the search for Annie was abandoned.

As the trial date approached, it was clear to the attorneys on both sides that the blood in Capano's home had become a major pretrial issue.

Despite the positive match for Fahey's blood, Capano insisted that the blood specks were probably from his daughters. "It could be from one of the four kids," he told his loyal friends. "They're always running all over the house and the backyard, getting scraped up and bruised."

In police interviews with the two oldest girls, both under oath, Christy said she had "probably" bled at Grant Avenue and Katie was sure she had cut herself there, "almost positive" she had left blood in the house.

But Capano wouldn't allow his daughters to take blood tests. Kay Capano, who had filed for divorce after the bail hearing, had made arrangements to have the blood drawn after Christy's June 8 graduation from Archmere. Connolly also agreed to let the samples be drawn at Kay's house or any location she chose. But Kay changed her mind, saying the daughters would not surrender the samples.

Again forced to played hardball, Connolly secured search warrants ordering the girls to surrender blood.

Only at the eleventh hour, with prosecutors ready to draw blood from his daughters, did Capano cave, agreeing in writing that the girls, ages twelve to seventeen, did not bleed on his radiator or woodwork.

In another pretrial maneuver, the defense moved to suppress the tape recordings MacIntyre had made of conversations with Capano. The drama around the tapes had intensified because Capano's mistress was planning to testify for the prosecution.

Capano wrote her twice in the days preceding the August 18 suppression hearing. He rambled about a history book he'd sent her, wished her a happy birthday, and told of his deteriorating physical and emotional state.

Had she opened the August 8 letter, she would have seen, in handwriting that appeared to be that of a drunk author, a Capano she didn't recognize. Her former lover babbled about losing track of days, saying he just realized the hearing was looming.

"I've decided that I will not attend," he said. "Although I admit part of the reason is selfish—seeing you would hurt me—my main reason is to make it easier for you."

Capano said he'd ordered his attorney to treat Debby "kindly and gently" or else be fired. "I love you with all my heart, Deb, and I know I always will. That is why I have been a zombie this weekend and have experienced such terrible anxiety. My love, I have also been told that I am a colossal fool for loving you."

Days before the hearing, Capano lawyers asked the judge to let their client be "voluntarily absent." But Lee rejected the proposal, ruling that Delaware law does not give a defendant the right to skip a hearing about the admission of evidence he wants to suppress. Lee also said he wanted to observe Capano's physical condition.

So on August 18, a surly Capano shuffled into court. He looked emaciated. The judge asked Capano if he wanted to plead his case to be absent. Capano stood up and approached the podium, which would become his lectern.

In a clear, scolding voice, Capano began:

"I find it very paradoxical that you would not accept the representations of my counsel or any other alternative other than to force me here against my will, to tear me from the routine which I have, which is one of the only things that keeps me together."

Not many prisoners, especially ones who had begged prison officials to move them from solitary confinement, would characterize a coveted breath of freedom as a burden.

But glancing down at notes he had prepared on a yellow legal pad, Capano lectured on.

"I also find it paradoxical that you would so blithely ignore the opinions of three highly competent mental health professionals in what appears to be a slavish deference to the Department of Corrections, a department that, in its wisdom, which you appear to find infinite, chooses to deny me the medications that I so desperately need to function, notwithstanding the order of the government's doctor just yesterday that those medications accompany me to this building today. They're not here. I've not had them.

"As a result, I speak the way I do. I have a shaky voice, I tremble, and I'm also going through withdrawal. Further, as a result, I will not have them this afternoon. The medical consequence of that is that I will be worthless. I will be a wreck.

"I know that is of no consequence to the Court, but I will further be worthless to my attorneys for the next several days because it is not easily resolved by doubling dosages later on. That does not happen. And I think that is something the Court should have been mindful of. I will not use the word *sympathetic* since I know that does not exist.

"There's more I have to say, but I don't think I can go further. I would please like to be removed from this courtroom as promptly as possible so that I am not subjected to the additional strain which has been inflicted upon me without necessity."

Judge Lee, seeming to ignore the unprecedented diatribe from an accused killer, one who was also a member of the Delaware Bar, responded in a soft, respectful voice.

"I understand why you don't want to be here," the judge told Capano. "And while I don't feel the need to respond to your comments, I will."

Exercising cool judicial restraint, Lee calmly corrected the defendant.

"You're wrong to say I'm not sympathetic to your needs," Lee said. "I certainly have no reason to see you treated other than as a worthwhile human being who needs, for very practical reasons, to be in good health, needs to be able to assist counsel. But I'm also not going to treat you any different than I would any other prisoner in your situation."

But Capano, showing no signs of regret for his remarks, shot back, "I've not asked for that. And I am being treated different. And Your Honor is well aware of it. And if Your Honor thinks nine months in solitary confinement is not designed to break me, in concert with the government and the department, Your Honor is sadly naive. And it has worked, by the way."

"Well, I'll deal with my particular problems personally," the judge replied, almost mocking his adversary, "as you're dealing with yours personally."

Still, Lee granted Capano's request to leave the courtroom and return to his cell.

With Capano gone, his lawyers proceeded to the task at hand: to prevent the playing of taped phone conversations between Capano and Debby MacIntyre in open court—neither at trial nor on this day.

They insisted that the government, with the surreptitious tapes, had violated Capano's constitutional right to have an attorney present during any questioning. But prosecutors countered that MacIntyre was not acting as a "secret agent" for the government and had been instructed not to elicit incriminating information. The tapes had been made, they argued, because Capano might later try to twist MacIntyre's words.

"This is not a criminal trial," said Oberly, referring to the hearing. "The problem with playing the tapes in open court is there is a potential for damage in this case."

Lee was inclined to agree. "I don't need to hear these statements on my ride home tonight," he said.

But Connolly and Wharton insisted on playing the tapes, and the judge didn't stop them.

So for the first time, the media heard Debby's voice, crying and sighing as Capano berated her for telling prosecutors about the gun. The judge could hear the tapes on the radio during his ride home that night but did ultimately rule that they could not be played at trial, unless Capano himself took the stand. The judge ruled that MacIntyre had interrogated Capano, violating her explicit instructions not to act as a cop, by asking Capano, "What about the gun?" during one of the taped calls.

Lee issued several more pretrial decisions, rejecting what amounted to efforts by the defense to suppress almost all of the evidence. Everything the FBI gathered was legal, the judge wrote, also ruling that inmates Perillo and Rosa could testify and that the time-line alibi seized from Capano's law office could also be introduced.

Capano added a fourth lawyer to his crew—Jack O'Donnell, a curly-haired former football player Capano had met at Boston College and socialized with over the years. O'Donnell, who lived in Fort Lauderdale, Florida, was the attorney Capano had hired to help Gerry out of a drunken driving case more than a decade earlier.

As autumn began, prosecutors filed even more charges against Capano—three counts of criminal solicitation, for asking Perillo to arrange the burglary of MacIntyre's house and for trying to hire Rosa to bump off Gerry and Debby.

Tom Bergstrom began telling any reporter who asked that Capano would likely blame his client, MacIntyre, for Fahey's death. Prosecutors filed court papers saying they too suspected Capano would finger Debby.

Oteri, who was playing his cards close to the vest, wouldn't say what defense he had in store for Capano. The man from Boston had a good reason for not doing so—Capano wouldn't tell him.

17 *To Tell the Truth*

The line to Courtroom 302 on Monday, October 26, 1998, snaked down the circular marble staircase of the three-story building. Dozens of people were angling for a chance to get one of the hottest tickets in town—a seat to the opening day of Tom Capano's murder trial. Some of the spectators had arrived at dawn, content to wait in the cool autumn air in front of the gracious limestone walls of the neo-Gothic Daniel L. Herrmann Courthouse, knowing they were first. They watched the television news vans shimmy up to the sidewalk on King Street and shoot their antennae twenty feet in the air while sleepy-eyed cameramen rolled out of the trucks, clutching their Starbucks eye-opener coffee cups.

Across King Street, where morning traffic was moving, city buses were also picking up the pace, rolling up along Rodney Square, one after another, unloading their rush-hour clients. And in the center of the square-block park, looking as if he were going to charge the massive courthouse, was the twenty-foot-high statue of Caesar Rodney, on horseback. The monument commemorated Rodney's famous ride from Dover to Philadelphia, from July 1 to 2, 1776. "Despite ill-health," the inscription at the base of the statue read, "Rodney rode through thunder and rain to cast the deciding vote in the Delaware delegation for Independence." Behind him, Terence McNally's *Master Class* had played its last performance at the Playhouse—"Wilmington's Little Broadway"—the day before, next to the luxurious Hotel du Pont, where Anne Marie Fahey and Tom Capano had their first lunch together.

For the next several weeks—or longer—the best theater in town would be on the other side of Rodney Square, at the Herrmann courthouse, where Capano was on trial for murdering Fahey.

At the rear of the massive building, out of sight of the gawking public and most of the curious media, a white prison van rolled slowly up to a metal garage door. A handcuffed Tom Capano, dressed in a white prison jumpsuit, stepped out of the vehicle, sporting a fresh fade haircut and clutching a brown accordion folder. He strode quickly and confidently past several photographers, with a prison guard on each elbow, and into the bowels of the building.

At 8:00, the outside crowd was allowed to move indoors, through a first-floor metal detector, and up to the third floor, to settle in for another wait, outside Room 302, in front of another metal detector. By 8:45, the line of public court watchers—including parents of the lawyers, friends of the Fahey and Capano families, retirees from New Jersey, and tourists visiting the trial before going to the Winterthur Museum— stretched halfway to the second-floor landing.

"Everyone knows you go up against the Capano family," said an unemployed black truck driver, waiting in line, "and you float." Other people in the line nodded, having heard the rumors; all were anxious to share their opinions about whether Capano did it or not.

Carrying a box of legal documents, Colm Connolly moved through the crowd just before nine, looking relaxed, nodding respectfully at members of the Fahey family, who stood in a large group just outside the courtroom.

Members of the Capano family huddled several yards away, standing around the wheelchair-bound matriarch of the family, Marguerite Capano, Tom's mother. Reporters began arriving a little after nine, taking their places just beside the metal detector, gabbing with one another, looking up whenever a new face appeared.

When Joseph Oteri, smiling broadly and easily, pushed a small handcart loaded with boxes through the crowd, one of the reporters called, "Hey, Joe, who's your first witness?"

Oteri flashed a mischievous smile. "C'mon; don't ask stupid questions."

In the few months Oteri had been on the Capano team, he had established an easygoing relationship with the press, encouraging reporters, some of whom had put as much time in on the case as he had, to call him Joe and to ask stupid questions.

A little after nine Kathi Carlozzi, the court administrator, began ushering the families—Faheys first, then Capanos— then the press, finally the public, into the cavernous courtroom. Each person passed through the arched "Friskem" and surrendered his or her cellular phone and tape recorder. Carlozzi also passed out red "Admit One" tickets, the kind sold at traveling carnivals, to the public, telling them they couldn't get back in without a ticket. Dozens of people were turned away after the courtroom swelled beyond its 122-person capacity. The fortunate ones squeezed into several of the high-backed pews not reserved for members of the press and families of the victim or the accused. Three sketch artists, wielding colorful palettes and chalky pastels, took their reserved places in the front row and immediately began to work, drawing at a furious pace the scenes no other person could record. There would be no television cameras in this courtroom. That was the law in Delaware.

It was finally D-day for Tom Capano, who had spent his forty-ninth birthday in jail just fifteen days earlier.

Over the weekend, the defendant had finally hammered out a trial strategy with his increasingly frustrated lawyers. For months he'd only spoken in theoretical terms about what had happened to Annie. But on the eve of the trial Capano had begun to realize that his original story—that he had dropped Annie off at her apartment, unharmed—seemed desperately weak. He and his attorneys had gotten a good glimpse of the arsenal the prosecution had gathered at the bail hearing: Gerry's testimony, Louis's testimony, the cooler, the receipt for the gun, MacIntyre's testimony, and a slew of people who would describe Tom and Annie's tumultuous affair.

Connolly and Wharton knew the case was no slam dunk. The media pundits, their numbers seeming to grow with each thrust and parry by prosecution and defense, had theories about every conceivable scenario. But the prosecutors were taking nothing for granted. They knew the state still didn't have a body, a weapon, or an eyewitnesses to a murder. And in Delaware prosecutors had never won a murder conviction without a body. The only time it was attempted—in 1990, while Charlie Oberly was attorney general—the accused was acquitted.

At exactly ten o'clock that morning, perfectly on schedule, as befitted a former Marine, Judge William Swain Lee emerged from a door to the side of the courtroom and strode quickly to the bench. "All rise!" came the voice of the red-headed female bailiff in uniform in the well of the court.

There was a noisy rustle of clothes, paper, and shuffling feet as the 150 people—125 of them jammed into the nine rows of benches and the dozen wooden chairs stuffed in the side aisles in the back half of the otherwise spacious room—rose.

The defendant turned briefly, as if to inspect the crowd, and offered wan smiles to his family—his mother, her wheelchair in the center aisle, siblings Joe and Marian, even his estranged wife, Kay, who was with their three youngest daughters.

But no sooner had everyone stood than the loud crack of the gavel brought them down.

"Please be seated," said Lee, immediately directing a court officer to bring the jury in. At 10:05, twenty ordinary men and women trooped into the courtroom through a side door and took their seats in two rows of chairs, raised slightly, facing the well of the court. The group, which included twelve jurors and eight alternates, had been selected over the previous three weeks from a pool of 259 prospects. The panel was almost exactly what Capano and his team wanted—no highly educated engineers, chemists, accountants, or doctors, which the town was full of. Only two of the jurors—a social worker and an incorporation associate—even had college degrees. Among the rest were a pipe fitter, a few factory workers, secretaries, a retired phone company manager, a lab technician, and a traveling salesman. The eight alternates, four men and four women, would sit through the same trial, in the same jury box, with no deliberative powers unless one of the regular jurors had to be excused. As the twenty jurors and alternates sat down, they exuded a communal expression of fright, a herd of deer caught in the headlights.

If they were Tom Capano's perfect jury, however, they didn't show it. To a person, they kept their eyes glued on Judge Lee, sitting in front of them and slightly to their right, as if afraid to gaze to the left and see the table of prosecutors and, behind them, the table of defense lawyers—with the accused man, in a pale gray suit and cheap prison haircut, sandwiched between the attorneys and looking much like them—and the crowd of family, press, and other onlookers.

"Good morning," said Lee, giving a broad and relaxed smile to the jurors.

"Good morning," said the men and women who would be judging Tom Capano. The vocalization broke the spell. Some of the jurors now allowed themselves to look to their left as Lee, without fanfare or even introduction, as if he were presiding at Small Claims Court, directed the prosecution to begin.

"Thank you, Your Honor," said Ferris Wharton as he pushed back his chair. The state prosecutor walked behind Colm Connolly, the federal prosecutor; the two men had decided that Wharton would deliver the opening statement and Connolly the closer. They had also divided up the witness examination duties—Connolly, the altar boy with a pit bull temperament, would get Gerry Capano; Wharton, the warhorse, would get MacIntyre.

The six-foot-three, forty-six-year-old Wharton, eighteen years in the attorney general's office, only had to take a few steps to get to the slender podium in the well of the court, a few feet from the jury, his back to the audience. But he faced the judge, who sat elevated behind a mahogany rampart, between U.S. and Delaware flags, twenty feet in front of him.

"Good morning," said Wharton to the jurors, then began a methodical, precise, and thorough presentation of the case. Though Wharton had really only been involved with the case at its inception and during these last several months of trial preparation, when he quoted from Anne Marie Fahey's last diary entry he stepped away from the podium and spoke slowly and loudly, enunciating each word, without notes: " 'I finally have brought closure to Tom Capano. What a controlling, manipulative, insecure, jealous maniac.' "

Wharton stopped and looked at the jurors. "Not even two weeks later," he said, that same man "walked into a Sports Authority on Route 202 and made a curious purchase. He bought a cooler. This wasn't a cooler you'd put your lunch, a few beers or sodas in. It was a 162-quart cooler. Huge."

Wharton left the podium, took a few determined steps toward the jury box, and, as if taking them into his confidence, whispered, "It was a curious purchase for the defendant, because although he could well afford it, he didn't have a boat and he had no interest in fishing."

Over the years Wharton had won plenty of cases with his preacherlike bearing and relaxed verbal style. He knew how to walk jurors through a complex circumstantial case in calm baritone. In a 1985 case, the prosecutor had won a conviction against Christie Shipley, a former Baltimore police officer who had shot her husband and sawed his body into pieces. Wharton had called more than seventy witnesses over several weeks, overwhelming a high-priced out-of-state defense attorney.

Wharton now spent ninety carefully orchestrated minutes laying out the case against the man seated at a long table to his left. Capano, scribbling on a yellow notepad and whispering into the ear of one of his attorneys, gave the impression of being only mildly interested in Wharton.

Only three weeks after buying the cooler, Wharton continued, Capano had his girlfriend, Debby MacIntyre, buy him a gun. "Now that's curious," Wharton said, "because Tom Capano, the defendant, was a lawyer, not a felon. There's no legal prohibition on him buying a gun himself, but, yet, he got someone else to buy a gun for him, which is a crime. It's a federal crime."

And six weeks after the gun was bought, Wharton asserted, Capano used it to kill Anne Marie Fahey.

"And the cooler that he had bought in April," Wharton said, "became what he had always intended it to be. It became Anne Marie Fahey's coffin." Wharton removed his glasses and stared directly at the jurors.

In her seat in the second row Kathleen Hosey felt her face tighten. The backs of her brothers Brian and Robert, on either side of Kathleen, stiffened. They had lived with these details for many months; they knew the scenario; they understood that their sister was dead and were convinced that the man who had killed her was sitting in the courtroom. But living with pieces of the puzzle was different from seeing the full picture all at once.

It was painful listening to Wharton take the jurors on the journey to sea with Gerry and Tom, hear about the shotgun blast through the cooler and through their sister's body, listen to a description of a bloodstain "about the size of a basketball"—their sister's blood.

The Fahey siblings also had to listen to Wharton describe Annie's harsh childhood—which was also their own—her insecurities, her eating disorder, and, tragically, her falling for the charming, wealthy lawyer who was sitting just ten feet away.

"She wanted to end it, but she couldn't," said Wharton, walking slowly in front of the jury box, weaving a tale of love, sex, and murder that had the packed room silent. " 'I left my wife for you,' he would say. 'Don't do this to me. I can give you everything.' He threw money at her. He bought her things, clothes."

When that didn't work, said Wharton, Capano got angry. He threatened to expose their affair; he took the gifts back. "Sometimes he got volatile. 'You're nothing but white trash. You should feel lucky I'm even interested in you.' "

While admitting that her body had not been found, after everything was out on the table, Wharton promised his audience, there would be only one possible explanation for what had happened to Anne Marie Fahey.

"The evidence will show you, ladies and gentleman, that the man she described as 'a controlling, manipulative, insecure, jealous maniac' would not allow her to decide with whom to spend the rest of her life. The evidence will show you, ladies and gentleman, that Tom Capano murdered Anne Marie Fahey."

Wharton finished at 11:45 and the judge, after consulting the attorneys at his bench, called for a short recess. Marguerite Capano, Tom's mother, sat blankly for several seconds after the judge gaveled for the adjournment. She stared ahead, a cane lying across her lap like a saber, as people filed around her, saying nothing.

Joseph Oteri was a good foil for Ferris Wharton. The self-described "old fart" was as glib as the Wilmington prosecutor was unadulterated. While Wharton wore a boxy black suit, plain shirt, and solid dark tie, Oteri strode to the podium in the manner of a don, with a starched two-tone shirt and bright yellow rep tie and soft-leathered loafers. Oteri, the former marine, moved his compact five-foot-eight body around the room as if he were born there.

As he paced back and forth in front of the jury, Oteri smiled, frowned, whispered, yelled. Though the jurors refused to reveal their reactions to this dramatic white-haired, bearded orator, almost no one moved during his forty-five-minute defense of Delaware's most infamous accused murderer. It was ridiculous, Oteri told the jury, to suggest that his client was anything but a gentleman who loved Anne Marie Fahey.

Oteri then attacked the presumption that Fahey was naive or gullible. "She had been with Tom Capano on and off for approximately two or three years," he said, "so she wasn't a kid starting out with some older guy. And further, she was not a person who was insular. She had lived in Spain. She had lived in Washington, D.C.—that cesspool—and she had been down there working."

Oteri was taking a risk—belittling the victim, a dead woman—but he had to shade the image of innocence if he were to save his client. "Anne Marie Fahey knew what was happening."

Anticipating the testimony of Annie's friends and therapists, Oteri claimed that Annie wasn't always forthcoming or honest: "Anne Marie Fahey tells things a little bit off center when they suit her purpose."

None of the Faheys in the audience registered a reaction to the smear. They had been prepared for the tactic. And as difficult a ride as this roller coaster was, they knew it was the final circuit. They just had to hold on.

So, too, did Marguerite Capano, who gripped the sides of her wheelchair as Oteri ripped into her youngest son.

Gerry is a "typical screwed-up rich kid, who never had to earn anything in his life," said the defense attorney, with a knifelike edge to his Boston accent. "He has a brain like a fried egg" from all the drugs he had ingested, Oteri charged, and he suffered from "confabulation." The word was dropped into the courtroom as if from a B-52. Members of the audience looked at one another; reporters looked up from their notebooks. Everyone knew that the words of Gerry Capano, if believed, would be Tom Capano's ticket to lethal injection. Court watchers had been speculating for weeks about what the dream team would pull out of its sleeve. Confabulation?

"Confabulation," said Oteri, "is a process where a drug

user's mind starts to have black holes in it, little black holes where they remember something about conversations, but not the rest of it, and they make it up." Like any assertion made in opening statements at trial, it would remain to be seen whether this would be proved in later testimony.

Oteri then went after Tom's other brother, accusing Louis of being a pathological liar who once before had cooperated with the police to save his neck. "Louis is hardly worthy of belief," Oteri scoffed.

Finally, it was Debbby MacIntyre's turn for roasting. She had already changed her story several times, said Oteri, but still "gets a deal where she gets total immunity. She doesn't get charged. The other two boobs who got charged, they cut a plea to something. She doesn't get charged."

But there was still one question that everyone in the courtroom knew Oteri would have to address if he were to save his client's neck: What did happen to Anne Marie Fahey? Even if the two brothers and the lover were not believed, a mess of circumstantial evidence smelled of guilt: How did the cooler get in the ocean—with bullet holes in it? What happened to Capano's sofa? How did Fahey's blood get on his wall?

Speaking as if he were in their living room, Oteri strolled back and forth in front of the jurors, twirling his glasses in his right hand, inviting the twenty men and women to follow him. "Tom Capano is a bright guy," he proposed. "If Tom Capano is buying a coffin with this big cooler, would he go to a store a couple of miles from his house? Would he buy it with his credit card? Would he leave it with the bar code on it that puts it right to that store? That's insanity. He wouldn't do a thing like that."

He returned to Gerry with the same bewildered air, mocking the story he knew Gerry would tell about a blackmailer as "a figment of his fevered, drug-burned-out brain."

Not only that, scoffed Oteri, but "the local rag," the *News Journal,* "had tried, convicted, crucified Tom Capano without a trial."

But Oteri had been talking for more than thirty minutes and still had not suggested what had happened to Annie or what his client might have been doing the night she had disappeared.

"Now, ladies and gentlemen, you are going to hear testimony that Anne Marie Fahey is dead. You're going to hear testimony that Tom Capano did not murder Anne Marie Fahey—premeditated or any other way, he did not murder her—that Anne Marie Fahey died as a result of an outrageous, horrible, tragic accident that only one other person, who was there, knows everything that happened that night, and that Tom Capano and his brother, Gerry, disposed of Anne Marie Fahey's body by placing it in a cooler and taking it to sea and sinking it."

Many people in the jammed courtroom seemed not to hear the bombshell Oteri had just dropped. Reporters glanced at each other's notebooks. Those who had heard correctly realized that Oteri had just admitted that Tom Capano, after twenty-seven months of denials, had indeed dumped Anne Marie Fahey's body in the ocean. Spectators were still whispering to each other as Oteri raced ahead.

"You're going to hear that Tom Capano is not the least bit proud of that.

"You will hear that it was motivated, the conduct was motivated, by fear for himself, by a desire to protect himself, by a desire to protect others."

In his rhetorical mode, Oteri stayed close to the podium, glancing toward his yellow pad from time to time, shuffling several steps to the right and back again. But now he moved to the low barrier in front of the first row of jurors and touched his hand to it. "You will hear about what happened to Anne Marie Fahey's body," he continued, looking intently up and down the two rows of jurors. "How did she die? Was it murder or was it not? Was it an accident? Was it something else?"

With the impact of the revelation still settling over the courtroom, Oteri brought his forty-five-minute statement to a close, making one final patriotic plea, his voice rising sharply. "We remain innocent," Oteri thundered, "wrapped in a cloak of innocence, until that prosecution can rip that cloak from you by proof beyond and to the exclusion of all reasonable doubt. And until that's done, Tom Capano's innocent. And please, I beg of you, don't forget that."

Judge Lee called a lunch recess, and spectators left the courtroom, all wondering the same thing.

What kind of accident?

And who, besides Capano and Fahey, had been inside the house?

Oteri, like all the lawyers in the case, walked out the same double doors at the entry to the courtroom as did family, friends, press, and spectators. But he was immediately mobbed by reporters in the third-floor vestibule. "Was Debby the other person?" someone asked. "Joe, let me introduce you to a columnist from the local 'rag,' " laughed another.

Oteri smiled back, at ease in the spotlight, grinning slyly as he refused to answer the questions.

"Did she kill herself?" another reporter asked.

"That's a no," Oteri said, then excused himself, leaving, for now, more questions than answers about Tom Capano's role in the death of Anne Marie Fahey.

The apparent 180-degree turn in Capano's defense seemed to deflate the importance of Gerry's testimony and focus the trial on another key question, one that the prosecution had no witness for: Just what had happened inside the Grant Avenue house that night?

But it also left the defense with a heavy obligation. By claiming Fahey had died in an accident at Capano's house, with one other person present, Oteri had created the expectation that the defense would offer a believable account of what had happened. And if MacIntyre, who almost everybody suspected was the mystery person, denied being there, the defense gambit could force Oteri to put Capano on the stand—a move that no self-respecting defense attorney would support. In more than ten murder cases over his career, Oteri had never let a defendant testify.

Huddling during the lunch recess, Connolly and Wharton weighed their options. Capano's admission to the sea burial, through Oteri's opening, seemed to have scotched the need to have Gerry Capano tell every detail of his story. But the prosecutors also knew that Capano's lawyers might be setting a trap—perhaps they wouldn't offer a defense at all—and decided they had to keep to their script. They would show jurors every piece of damning evidence that they had compiled over more than two years of investigation and use Annie's family, friends, and therapists to paint a sympathetic picture of a good-hearted, decent yet troubled woman who had fallen in love with a demented older man she couldn't shake.

And they anticipated Oteri and his team would fight them every inch of the way.

———

Brian Fahey, a fifth-grade teacher, the most articulate and relaxed of the six Fahey children, was chosen to introduce his missing sister to the jury. Wearing a blue blazer and gray slacks, Brian strode confidently through the double doors when his name was called, marched down the gallery's carpeted center aisle, brushing Marguerite Capano in her wheelchair, and kept his head straight as he passed within six feet of the man who he believed had murdered his sister, veered right around the podium in the well of the court, then continued along the row of jurors—a long walk, of nearly eighty feet to the witness-box. Raising his right hand, the rumpled teacher swore to tell the truth and nothing but the truth, then climbed into a chair to the left of the judge's bench.

Ferris Wharton immediately rose and began the process of leading Brian through the story of his little sister's traumatic upbringing.

In spare and unadorned prose, Brian described the pitiful tale of their mother's premature death and their father's descent into alcoholism.

"It was complicated," said Brian. "You know, we couldn't go and ask the neighbors for food or money, so we just tried to get by as best we could, and you know the siblings, we all just sort of hung in there together."

He was equally candid when talking about Annie's later battles with depression but also talked about their enjoyable trip to Ireland in 1994.

But at 2:35, after just thirty minutes on the stand, Brian's testimony was interrupted by Judge Lee, who called the lawyers to a sidebar. This was peculiar, since these private conferences were usually the result of a dispute between attorneys that needed to be resolved out of earshot of the jury. But there had been no quibbles.

Tom Capano, now alone at the long table, turned in his seat and calmly surveyed the crowd, gently stroking his chin. When he saw his mother, he winked, then turned his back to the gallery and continued his writing.

A few feet away, in the front-row gallery seat on the right side of the center aisle, Susan Schary motioned toward the tall uniformed woman who stood constant guard at the low wooden barrier separating the gallery from the courtroom well. Schary, a Philadelphia artist contracted by several television stations to sketch the trial's heroes and villains, had been drawing feverishly all morning, juggling a half-dozen pastel sticks in her hands as she sketched on the large pad on her lap the drama in front of her as if racing the clock. Schary's shoulder-length red hair was frizzled, her black-aproned lap was littered with pastel dust, and her fingers were the color of a rainbow; she looked distinctly out of place among the smart suits and pressed skirts of the rest of the trial watchers. "Would you mind moving the podium a bit to the left?" she now whispered to the court officer. "It's hard to see the witness." The officer smiled and obliged.

Judge Lee, meanwhile, was leaning into the crowd of six lawyers standing at the right edge of his large elevated desk.

"I wanted to inform everybody," Lee whispered, "that at about two o'clock we received a phone call saying Capano was 'going down' in an hour, whatever that means. Clearly, at that time, it means whoever was making the phone call wasn't in the courtroom."

Lee assured the attorneys that there was ample security, "but I thought everybody ought to be aware of this and I don't know whether you have any suggestions. I'm inclined to just go on and figure it's a crackpot call."

Oteri, always looking for a laugh, tried to lighten up the caucus: "May Mr. Capano be moved up to the prosecution table, please?"

Lee enjoyed the exchange but was determined to keep focus. He told the group that a second officer from the Capital Police, the courthouse force, would be stationed outside the doors and reminded the lawyers that that all visitors to the courthouse, not just those entering Room 302, passed a metal detector at the first-floor entrance.

Gene Maurer, Capano's long-haired contemporary, wasn't satisfied. "I did have a client one time that got in through a security system with a loaded .25-caliber," he told the judge.

"I'm not telling you it can't happen," Lee responded. "I'm telling you, under the circumstances, I didn't feel like interrupting the trial. On the other hand, I thought all of you were entitled to know that."

The lawyers agreed. The trial continued. And the public was never notified of the death threat.

Resuming his story, Brian Fahey now told jurors about the Fahey family's hopeless vigil for their missing sister.

"During this entire time," asked Wharton, "when your family was there at 1718 Washington Street with this vigil and you were pleading in the media for any information about Anne Marie, did Tom Capano ever come by?"

"No."

"Were you hiding from him?"

"No."

Wharton paused, then said, "I don't have any other questions, Your Honor."

Throughout Brian's testimony, Tom Capano had busied himself writing on his yellow legal pad, tugging on either Jack O'Donnell's or Gene Maurer's sleeves, and passing his pad over to Joe Oteri, who sat on the right end of the long rectangular defense table, looked intently at the pad, always nodded, then passed it back.

Oteri, after inviting Brian to "call me Joe," wasted no time trying to shatter Brian's sister's image as innocent victim.

"Now, did you, sir, ever have occasion to see Anne Marie Fahey when she lost her mind, when she was screaming and punching your father for stealing her tip change?" Oteri asked. "Did you ever see that?"

"No," Brian replied in an unruffled voice. "I heard about it, but I didn't see it."

"Did you ever see Anne Marie Fahey when she hit your father with a hockey stick?"

"No."

"But you heard about it?"

"I did."

"On more than one occasion?"

"Well, once from her."

Oteri dug for more. "And would you characterize your sister as having a pretty good Irish temper?"

Brian wasn't biting. "What do you mean by that?"

"Well, Irish men sometimes have a temper?" fished Oteri.

Brian retorted calmly, "I've never known one to have a temper."

Oteri smiled. "Well done," he said.

But the defense attorney, who hadn't earned his formidable reputation by being a softy, even with victims' families, kept pressing, reminding Brian that his sister had talked about her temper in a note to Capano.

"I don't think she had a bad temper," Brian said, calm but unyielding. "I know that at certain times things in our house got extremely overwhelming."

Oteri also attempted to undermine the perception of closeness between the siblings. "You didn't know that your sister called Tom Capano from Ireland, did you?" he queried.

"No," said Brian.

Brian began to show his frustration when Oteri zeroed in on the family's hiring of an attorney the Monday after Annie disappeared. "You were already preparing a civil suit against Tom Capano and his family!" Oteri yelled.

"That's incorrect," Brian protested.

But Oteri seemed to win his point when Brian confirmed that David Weiss had indeed filed a civil lawsuit against the Capano family.

Ferris Wharton helped resurrect Brian on this point during his redirect examination.

"Why did you file the lawsuit?" asked the prosecutor.

"We were very mad," said Brian, "and believed that they were responsible for causing my family a great deal of pain, for killing my sister and being perfectly content to see us live out the rest of our lives without ever knowing what happened to our sister."

Brian stepped down from the stand at 3:30 that afternoon, after nearly ninety minutes of testimony, and Judge Lee immediately called for a recess. Lee knew that at a big trial, as with a long ocean voyage, it would require time to get one's sea legs. And the audience seemed to appreciate the recess. There was a rush to the exit, and the bathrooms around the corner of the vestibule were immediately jammed.

The lawyers seemed to disappear except for Oteri, who allowed himself to be mobbed by reporters just beyond the metal detector outside the courtroom. "How we doin'?" the attorney said, smiling.

"Not confabulating yet," a reporter laughed back.

"So, Joe, who's the other witness to the death?" Trying to take advantage of the light moment, one of the journalists had slipped in the subject that everyone knew would lead the six o'clock news that evening and grace the front pages the next day.

Whether caught off guard or simply playing with them, Oteri flashed his toothy grin, said, "We'd all like to know," then walked off.

The final hour of the first day of the trial was taken up by a succession of witnesses who knew Anne Marie Fahey and told of their last meetings with her. Sue Campbell-Mast, a middle-aged secretary whose desk was five feet from Annie's in the governor's office, recalled playfully exchanging E-mails with Annie on Thursday about messages and pedicures after the younger woman reminded her she wouldn't be in on Friday. "I thought, *Oh my, I won't be seeing her until Monday,*" Campbell-Mast told the court.

"You were close to Miss Fahey?" asked prosecutor Wharton.

"Very," said the woman.

Diane Hastings, another aide to the governor, recalled how happy Annie was that Thursday. "She was really looking forward to her day off," Hastings said. "She was going to the park, read a book, get a pedicure."

Though defense attorney Jack O'Donnell attempted to elicit testimony from the women to show Fahey was unstable, it was largely a futile effort, and their cross-examinations were brief.

By 4:30 that afternoon, fatigue had begun to take its toll. An elderly white-haired juror in the front row had dropped his chin to his chest. Reporters were looking at their watches.

But when Colm Connolly called Jackie Dansak to the stand, the room seemed to come alive. People whispered to one another. Those who didn't know the name were quickly told by those who did that Jackie Dansak was the waitress from the Panorama—the last person, notwithstanding what Tom Capano or the promised witness might add, to have seen Anne Marie Fahey alive. People were still sharing their knowledge of the witness with one another when the double doors swung open and a slim woman wearing a long dark dress walked into the room and down the center aisle. Tom Capano, hand on his chin, watched closely as the stunning dark-haired young woman strolled to the witness stand.

Under examination by Connolly, Dansak quickly showed herself to be a self-assured witness. She described the Panorama as upscale but "one step below fine dining" and said she remembered serving Fahey and Capano the night of June 27 because they were so unfashionably dressed. "Most of the patrons were Main Line and very fashionable," said Dansak, referring to Philadelphia's most exclusive neighborhood. Fahey, however, instead of trendy black, was wearing a brightly patterned dress. And the man she was with looked equally out of place. "His glasses were odd," said Dansak, referring to his tortoiseshell two-tones. Most noticeable, however, said Dansak, was the couple's behavior. "They didn't speak to each other," she said. "And he ordered everything without consulting her." The woman looked "haggard, gaunt, tired," and her hair was "unkempt." They only "picked at their food."

Dansak painted a picture of a troubled couple. And the detail of her recollection was so good that it was hard to see how Charlie Oberly, who stood to cross-examine the pretty waitress, could do anything to change the impression that if this was Anne Marie Fahey's last meal, Tom Capano had known it.

But Oberly attacked, using the standard arrow of a defense's quiver: questions. He asked Dansak enough questions about the night that Capano and Fahey ate at the Panorama that she was bound to slip up on something. How many people did she wait on that night? How many tables did she serve? Where was the table positioned?

But Dansak proved unassailable. And when she left the stand, a little after five, her credibility was intact.

On the broad steps outside the courthouse on King Street, as prosecutors filed past the press mob without comment Joe Oteri strode to the microphones. Facing Rodney Square, cocky, almost self-absorbed before the cameras, Oteri seemed anxious to elaborate on his opening statement. Fahey had not committed suicide, he asserted.

Why then, one of the reporters asked, was the body dumped in the ocean?

"Well," Tom Capano's attorney quipped, "he couldn't keep her in the house?"

A few reporters smiled. Others grimaced.

Prosecutors kept the case moving at a steady, meticulous pace, bringing in Annie's sister, her friends, and her therapists to testify.

But Oteri, used to calling the shots in nearly a half-century as a defense attorney, was becoming more and more disgusted with his client, who injected himself in the trial by shoving questions across the table at his attorney, demanding that Oteri ask them.

When Kim Horstmann was on the stand, she told the jury she had named her new baby Anne Marie and Capano quickly scribbled: "Ask her if Annie told her about our trip to Homestead." Oteri knew better than to ask a question he didn't have the answer to, but Capano insisted.

"Yes," Horstmann said, she knew about the trip Annie and

Capano had taken to the resort in Virginia the summer of 1995.

That was just the opening Connolly wanted, on redirect.

"What did Annie tell you about that trip?" the prosecutor asked on redirect.

"She said it was kind of a disaster."

"She said they fought, didn't she?"

"Yes."

"And that was right before, as far as you knew, the relationship ended?"

"Correct."

Oteri leaned toward Capano's ear. "Do you see now," he whispered with disgust to his client, "why I didn't want to ask that fucking question?"

Several days later, on November 11, Siobhan Sullivan, the state trooper on Governor Carper's security team, told the jury about the conversation she had with Annie after Annie returned from her Memorial Day weekend with Scanlan in New England.

Asked by Wharton what Annie said when told by Sullivan that Capano had called that weekend, Sullivan leaned toward the jurors and replied in a loud voice, enunciating each word, " 'He's fucking stalking me.' "

The chilling words reverberated through the courtroom.

When Michael Scanlan was on the stand, Oteri tried to portray Annie's affluent paramour as a cheapskate who wouldn't loan or give his girlfriend the money to replace her windshield or air conditioner—and emphasize that his client, Tom Capano, had paid for them. The defense lawyer also suggested that Scanlan only dated Annie to please Governor Carper and benefit his company.

"The governor's pretty important to your bank, isn't he?" Oteri charged.

"I wouldn't have any knowledge of that," Scanlan countered.

"OK," Oteri said, trying to make the point another way.

"The fact is that you called Anne Marie part out of curiosity and part to placate the governor, right?"

"Not at all," Scanlan shot back, staring hard at his former rival's attorney.

"Mr. Oteri asked you some things about gifts," Connolly asked during his redirect. "Did you offer to buy Anne Marie a Lexus or any other kind of expensive car?"

Scanlan leaned into the microphone and spoke forcefully. "Mr. Connolly, I had the means to take her to fancy dinners, to buy her a Lexus, to move her out of the apartment that she was in.

"The relationship I had with Annie wasn't based on money and never at any time did I have any reason to think that she was with me because of my money. Our relationship was based on each other, on spending time with each other, and she never gave me any indication that she was seeking a material status."

Scanlan paused for a second, then resumed his soliloquy.

"She was interested in becoming a teacher, so she was interested in going from one job that paid a relatively low salary to one that probably paid a similarly low salary, and it was clear to me that she was seeking things, to do things that made her happy, and to be in relationships that made her happy.

"The kinds of gifts that she got from me were when I went on trips, I would bring her something back. It could be a sweatshirt from someplace we were. It could be a birthday gift. Things that were modest.

"But I never judged the value of the relationship upon the gifts you give somebody, and I've never bought a girlfriend, and I don't ever intend on buying a girlfriend."

Scanlan's long uninterrupted speech left the courtroom silent.

Annie's therapists—psychologists Michele Sullivan and Gary Johnson and psychiatrist Neil Kaye—detailed Fahey's shame about the affair with Capano and her reports of his stalking and how his controlling behavior exacerbated the patient's anorexia.

They said her accommodating nature and desire to please, rooted in her awful childhood, contributed to Annie's inability to break away.

"It was clear to me," testified Sullivan, a petite gray-haired woman who said she had seventeen fifty-minute sessions with her patient, "that Anne Marie was spending time [with Capano], I think, in her movement from a love relationship. She really hoped that she could maintain a friendship."

Oteri, cross-examining Sullivan, seemed to score some points. He forced the therapist to admit that Annie's word wasn't always reliable. For example, while she said during one session that she had told Scanlan about Capano, Scanlan had testified that he was never informed. And while E-mails showed that Capano gave her $500 to pay for treatment, Annie never used the money to pay the therapist. The checks she got—one for $1,000, another for $1,500—came from Robert Fahey.

"So you were treating her without really knowing all that was going on between her and Mr. Capano?" Oteri charged.

But Sullivan didn't flinch. "That's one way to describe it," she said. "Another way I would describe it is that a person doesn't tell me all the details. What I did know was she was still spending time with him at dinner and she was still trying to maintain a friendly relationship."

The state's twenty-ninth witness took the stand on Monday, November 9, the beginning of the trial's third week. And still sensing a trick from the defense, the prosecution continued to consider Gerry Capano their most important witness.

But the months had taken a toll on Gerry, as he tried to come to grips with the fact that his words, if believed, would likely spell his brother's execution. Gerry coped by drinking and taking drugs. Wharton and Connolly had told him to stop, saying they wouldn't protect him if he got busted again, but Gerry, feeling his life was a mess anyway, continued to smoke pot, snort cocaine, and drown his sorrows in booze. Prosecutors were well aware that Gerry carried baggage to the witness stand. But he was the government's star witness—he had helped his brother dump a body and had finally decided to turn him in.

Connolly guided Gerry through the same territory he had covered at the bail hearing nine months earlier. Court observers were anxious to see what the defense would be; everyone wondered if Gerry could survive a concerted attack, especially by Oteri, the man who loved referring to criminals-turned-government-witnesses as "rat bastards."

The witness covered all the bases Connolly wanted him to, from the mysterious extortion story in early 1996 to the hair-raising events on the Atlantic Ocean on June 28 of that year.

Connolly finished by having Gerry address the new "accident" defense.

"Now, did your brother tell you at any time on June 28 that that human foot you saw that was in the cooler was there because of an accident?"

"No."

"At any time has he ever told you that you were put on that boat with him and you emptied a cooler because of an accident?"

"No."

Gerry went on for the entire day methodically retelling the story that he had recounted, now, many times.

Oteri, the master, finally began his interrogation of Gerry at almost four o'clock that afternoon.

"May I call you Gerry?" he asked sweetly.

"Yes."

"Call me Joe, OK?"

"OK."

It was an Oteri trademark, the disarmingly friendly salutation. And the more congenial it was, the quicker and harder Oteri pounced.

"Now, Gerry, do you remember the first time you used cocaine?"

As advertised, Oteri went right to the drugs—and stayed there. "What was the first illegal drug you ever did?"

"Probably smoked marijuana in high school," said Gerry.

At times the interrogation seemed more like a drug education seminar than a murder trial. Drug names, drug effects, drug use. It was much the same territory covered by Hurley at the bail hearing—but in almost unendurable detail.

At Oteri's prompting "Did you use any other drugs in high school?" Gerry also admitted using "crank."

"Crank is a form of methamphetamine, a speed, is that correct?" asked Oteri, who noted that students use it for studying.

"Any other drugs?" continued Oteri.

"Maybe occasionally some mushrooms," said Gerry.

Oteri turned toward the jurors. "You don't mean to say mushrooms served up at home?" he asked with feigned disbelief. "You mean psilocybin mushrooms that you eat?"

Gerry, not the type to study *The Physician's Desk Reference* before putting mind-altering chemicals in his body, wasn't sure. "I don't know the name."

Oteri wanted to know how Gerry ingested the drugs, how they made him feel, about the mood swings cocaine could cause. With Oteri steering, Gerry discussed the proper method of snorting cocaine and of making crack, the pure, highly addictive form of the drug. "You cook it in a microwave and then smoke it," Gerry said of the primitive method he used.

It might have gone on like this for days if Connolly had not, finally, objected. "Judge, could we get some time frame on this?"

The lawyers went to a sidebar.

"May I presume you're trying to establish a foundation for your expert?" the judge inquired, speaking of the confabulation specialist the defense had promised.

"Exactly, Your Honor," Oteri replied.

But Lee chided the defense attorney for discussing drug use that was not closely related to the events that the trial was concerned with.

Oteri said he would try to limit his questions, "but I can't be committed."

"That's not good enough, Judge," Connolly protested. "I mean, the prosecution could go play this game big-time, to the defense's detriment."

Still the saga of Gerry Capano's drug and alcohol abuse

continued. But could Oteri bring all the talk of chemicals to the point at hand? Could he make the jurors believe that Gerry's drug use had caused him to imagine that his brother had talked of killing people and borrowing his boat months before showing up at Gerry's door on June 28, 1996?

In case not, Oteri tried to toast Gerry on the question of whether the threat of going to jail had made him lie. And Oteri zeroed in on Gerry's drug use after the plea agreement and the fact that the prosecutors knew about it.

"You told Mr. Connolly and Mr. Wharton that you had committed six, seven, eight, nine felonies by doing drugs?" Oteri said. "You knew they weren't going to have you busted, right?"

Gerry hemmed and hawed.

"Let me ask you the key question," Oteri charged. "Have you been arrested since you told them?"

"No, sir."

"Has anybody searched your house since you told them you were doing drugs?"

"No, sir."

All Gerry could muster was, "Trying my best to stay away from it, sir."

"I understand that, Gerry," Oteri said, taking the tone of an exasperated parent. "I'm not fighting, but you're doing them, right?"

"Occasionally."

"And nobody is busting you, right?"

"That's fair to say."

"And the government knows it, because you've told them, right?"

"I did."

An amazing series of admissions by the prosecution's most important witness. And Oteri knew it. He asked for a recess for the day.

The next day Oteri came right back at Gerry, grilling him about his testimony against his brother, suggesting that he was high or drunk whenever his so-called conversations with Tom took place. Gerry held his ground and Oteri went after Gerry's pampered lifestyle, his expensive homes, antique Corvettes, and Harley-Davidson motorcycles, his boats, his guns, his extravagant hunting expeditions.

———————

As everyone moved to the exits for a recess, Tom Capano lingered at the defense table, searching, he told the two prison guards who were ordering him to move, for a copy of his brother's testimony at the bail hearing.

The tension between Capano and the guards had been building for weeks. The officers were supposed to make sure the prisoner never left their sight; when he wasn't sitting at the defense table, he was quickly hustled out of the courtroom to a basement cell or prison van. From the outset of the trial Lt. Carl Meadwell, Capano's chief guard, had his hands full with a murder suspect who acted as if he were one of the lawyers. Capano constantly challenged the rules, insisting on chatting with family and paralegals in the gallery during recesses. With a death threat against Capano, the guards, also charged with protecting Capano, were especially edgy about their charge ducking authority.

With Capano now ignoring the guards' entreaties to move, Meadwell finally grabbed his arm and pushed him toward the courtroom door. Capano resisted, threatening, "If I didn't have my cuffs on, I would beat you upside the head."

Meadwell responded by shoving the former assistant attorney general, former city solicitor, former counselor to the governor out of the courtroom and into the hallway. It was a rude reminder of the fact that Capano was no longer a master of the universe.

Still, the defendant bitched about the guards and wrote an account of the incident, which Oberly read to the judge during a sidebar before court resumed.

"Another incident with Meadwell as I was leaving the table area cuffed and holding my file," Capano wrote. "I saw my mother in tears in her wheelchair. I paused for a second and they started to push me, manhandled me all of the way out of the courtroom. Once they got me in the hallway, they squeezed me up against the wall as I was trying to walk."

Capano wrote that he told Meadwell and the other guard, who wasn't identified, "that the next time they manhandled me I was going to fight back. The judge does not have enough heart to understand why I was momentarily stopped by my mother's condition, but it was natural and very brief."

Capano also threatened to boycott the trial. "I'm not going to put up with this nonsense and degradation," he concluded in the note. "They can go ahead with this farce without me."

Lee, who had witnessed part of the altercation, wasn't impressed. "I don't want him mistreated," the judge told Oberly and the other attorneys. "I certainly don't want him to leave the courtroom. On the other hand, as I mentioned before this incident occurred, he continues to act like a practicing member of the bar in here, chatting."

Oteri then passed on another complaint.

"Your Honor allegedly shows facial motion," he said, with a straight face, "facial motions, to indicate displeasure, disbelief, or some such things, at certain parts of the testimony. The interpretation is that you are showing disbelief or incredulity, or whatever it is, at my questions. My response to them is if he is, it's at the answer, not the question, and I don't see it. But I'm pointing it out for you for the record because I have been ordered to do so. That is the complaint."

"Of who?" Wharton asked.

"Of my client," mumbled Oteri, embarrassed by what Capano was making him say.

Lee, who had invited the lawyers out for drinks after court that day to toast the birth of the Marine Corps 223 years earlier, didn't want to spoil the evening.

"Pardon me, because I hope that's not the case," Lee said. "I'm not someone who's inanimate. But have any of the other lawyers noticed that?"

"Not at all," Connolly said.

"No," Wharton added.

Even Oteri agreed. "If you were doing anything I thought was in the least bit indicative of displeasure with me, I would have been up here to find out why, Judge. Believe me."

When Gerry returned to the stand after the lengthy recess, Oteri concluded his cross-examination with another blow at Gerry's moral character.

"Now, Gerry, do you remember making a phone call and leaving this message on February 9, 1998, to your mother?"

February 9 was three days after the bail hearing had ended. Oteri acted as if he were reading, though he knew the words by heart. " 'Mom, this is your son, Gerry. I called you but Katie hung up on me. You have ten minutes to call me back. If you don't, you can go fuck yourself.' "

Oteri enunciated every syllable in a booming voice. The lawyer now walked up to Gerry. "Do you remember making that call to your mother?" he asked calmly.

Gerry seemed rattled by the disclosure. "I was drinking that day," he stammered, "and I remember apologizing afterwards."

"But you did make the call?"

"I'm not saying I didn't."

But Oteri wasn't done.

"How about the second call, Gerry? Do you remember this? Do you remember saying this? 'Mom, this is your son. Mom, your son Gerry. You better fucking call me. I'm tired of being the bad guy. If you don't fucking call me, you'll never fucking see me or my wife or my kids again. What? Are you pissed because I told the truth? Because Joe fucking Hurley couldn't break me down? As far as I'm concerned, you have three sons. One is a murderer in jail for fucking life, one you hate, and that's Louie, and Joey. Like I said, you can go fuck yourself. Did you really think that I would go to jail for twelve fucking years? If you thought I was bad on the stand, God fucking help you if this goes to trial. I'll think up even more shit to keep my ass out of fucking jail. And I'll make up fucking shit as I go along to keep Tommy in there for fucking life. I hate him. You got ten fucking minutes to call me back or you'll never see my kids again. I'm not threatening you, but if you don't call me back in ten minutes, you can go fuck yourself.' "

"Did you make that call and make that statement, Gerry?" Oteri demanded as members of the gallery whispered in disbelief.

"I'm sure I did, if you have it on tape."

"Thank you. I have no further questions, Your Honor."

While the revelation of Gerry's phone calls was unsettling, it bothered Wharton and Connolly that they didn't even know that the tapes existed—if there were tapes. The defense was required to turn over any such materials, but the prosecutors decided not to make an issue of it until closing arguments and pressed on with their redirect questioning of Gerry after lunch.

"Do you recall leaving those messages?" Connolly asked.

"I remember calling and yelling at my mother," said Gerry. "I don't exactly remember what I said. I had been drinking, I was very upset, and I just don't remember exactly what was said."

Seeking to gain some sympathy for the witness, Connolly probed. "Why were you upset?"

"I don't think that my mother is taking a fair position with what's going on."

Marguerite Capano listened from her wheelchair, as if from the grave. From where she sat, in the center aisle of the gallery, she could see both Tom and Gerry without moving her head. Now, her gaze fixed straight ahead, she barely blinked.

"What kind of relationship have you had with your mother since you signed the plea agreement?"

"None."

"Why?"

"I just told you."

"Have you tried to contact your mother?"

"She talks to me on occasion, but it's nothing like it used to be."

"Were you close with your mother before this?"

"Very close."

Tom Capano stared at his brother, occasionally looking down to write on his legal pad.

Connolly then had Gerry quickly reaffirm his story, to expunge any doubt that Oteri had gotten to him.

"Are you making up anything here today?"

"No, sir."

"Are you making up that your brother said that if he killed somebody could he use your boat?"

"No, sir."

"Are you making up that you shot a hole through that cooler?"

"No."

Sticking with their plan of presenting all the elements of their theory of the case, prosecutors next called Louis Capano to the stand. They needed Louis to corroborate Gerry's testimony about dumping the body and the sofa and to tell the jury about Gerry's emotional confession and confrontations with Tom. And that in all their conversations Tom had never mentioned anything about "an accident."

As Oteri had done with Gerry, Gene Maurer, who had harangued Louis at the bail hearing in February, again hammered away at his less-than-sterling past: his lies, his previous brushes with the law, his infidelity to his wife, and what was at stake if he didn't testify against his brother. But unlike during the bail hearing, this time Louis didn't lose his cool but calmly answered Maurer's questions. "I'm telling the truth today," he insisted.

Just as he had with Gerry, Tom looked straight at Louis while he testified.

Both brothers, though bloodied, held up under the expected assault. The defense did not score a knockout on either one.

Knowing he faced public humiliation, Keith Brady walked ramrod straight to the witness stand on the morning of November 18. The tall, black-haired chief deputy attorney general of the state of Delaware had admitted to prosecutors that he had a sexual dalliance with Debby MacIntyre and had confessed his infidelities (there were others) to his wife. But once he took the stand, *everyone* would know. If nothing else, this march to the witness stand was like a trip to the political career gallows.

Wharton and Connolly didn't want to humiliate their colleague—Brady, after all, was Wharton's boss. But anticipating that Capano would blame MacIntyre for the killing, they needed all the ammunition they could muster in order to show that Tom had manipulated her into buying the Beretta. They needed Brady to prove that Capano had controlled her sexually.

Brady told jurors that Capano was a longtime friend and golfing buddy and had confided in him about his affair with Anne Marie Fahey. Connolly then asked if Brady knew Debby MacIntyre.

"My recollection," the handsome lawyer replied, "is that Tom told me that they had a long-term relationship."

"Did you ever have a sexual encounter yourself with Debby MacIntyre?"

"Yes," Brady said, his sad eyes downcast, as a few spectators gasped.

"Who arranged that sexual encounter?"

"Tom did."

Connolly did not dig deeper. The prosecutor had the information he needed.

But on cross-examination, Oteri was merciless. After getting Brady to say he and Capano had been confidants, Oteri reached for the jugular.

"And you confided in him the fact that you had adulterous relationships, correct?"

"I confided in him that I had committed adultery."

"On numerous occasions with three different women at least?"

"No."

"How many women have you committed adultery with?"

"More than one."

"More than two?" Oteri shot back. If his witness wanted to be coy, Oteri would play rough.

"I have committed adultery with three different women, not including Debby MacIntyre."

"Not including Deborah MacIntyre?"

"Yes."

When the defense attorney asked Brady if he engaged in "one-night" stands, Connolly jumped to his feet.

"Objection." The prosecutor asked for a sidebar.

At the bench Lee directed Oteri to limit his questions about infidelity to MacIntyre.

Oteri came back, now determined, it seemed, to expose

Brady and, by extension, MacIntyre as despicable human beings, well aware that the information would not exactly en-
hance his client's image with the jurors.

"In fact, sir, you did what's known as a threesome with
Deborah MacIntyre and Tom Capano, did you not?"

"No."

"You didn't?" Oteri asked, wide-eyed.

"No."

"Wasn't Tom on the floor watching pornographic movies
with you and Deborah at the same time, all three of you naked?"

"No, that is not my recollection."

"In fact, you had oral sex with Deborah, she had oral sex
with you, while Tom was there watching you, was he not,"
Oteri said, not so much a question as an accusation.

"That's not correct."

"Now, did you have sex with Deborah?"

Brady paused, then spoke robotlike into the microphone.

"Deborah MacIntyre attempted to arouse me physically by
performing oral sex on me, and I could not achieve an erec-
tion."

Oteri spent a few minutes on some other subjects before
returning to sex.

Later that day, as word of Brady's disclosures spread
through Wilmington, the attorney general issued a statement
saying her top aide was taking an open-ended leave of absence
to "address his personal life."

Debby MacIntyre, a daughter of privilege, with the blue-
blazer life of a proper girls' school administrator, came to the
witness stand with her reputation already tattered. From a strategic point of view, her testimony was crucial on two levels:
she tied Tom Capano to a gun, perhaps *the* gun, and she was
a witness, a participant even, in Capano's vulgar life.

Even though her story had been told by others, Debby in
the flesh was different. By virtue of her reclusiveness, she had
become one of the trial's major celebrities, and the gallery was
filled to capacity for her testimony, which began on November
18, immediately after Keith Brady left the stand. She was not

only the "other woman"; she was also about to be, everyone assumed, blamed for the "horrible accident" that had killed Anne Marie Fahey.

Ferris Wharton led MacIntyre gently through the story of her affair with Capano. Her short, matronly haircut seemed at odds with her story, that of a sexually robust woman who had carried on a fifteen-year affair with a friend's husband. MacIntyre periodically glanced at Capano, who kept his gaze on the legal pad in front of him.

She told the jurors about buying a gun for Capano in the spring and about leaving a message on Capano's machine the night that Anne Marie disappeared. MacIntyre had been watching David Letterman on the television when her phone rang.

"I said hello, and he said, 'Don't you ever leave a message on my voice mail,' " MacIntyre now told the jury.

"What was your reaction to that?" asked Wharton.

"I was puzzled because I had done that many times before. I didn't understand why I couldn't leave a message on his machine."

"What was his tone of voice?"

"He was very irritated," MacIntyre said.

MacIntyre also reviewed Capano's strange behavior that weekend, popping over to her house to drop off X-rated films and ranting about the police setting him up. She also recounted how, on the following Tuesday, Capano had called her at work to say he was the last person to see the governor's secretary, the woman who was missing. "I was devastated," she told the jury. She had never heard of Anne Marie Fahey before.

Trying to preempt what was sure to be a hard-nosed cross-examination, Wharton had MacIntyre acknowledge her lies to police and the grand jury but also had her read some of Capano's pleading letters before the bail hearing, the missives in which Capano insisted she was a credible witness.

Leaving the courthouse that day, clutching the stuffed accordion file folder that he now carried everywhere, the handcuffed Capano looked toward the news cameras and lamented, "She broke my heart." The next day, with speculation building about how Capano's team would blame MacIntyre for the "accidental" killing, Gene Maurer stood up. A casting director could not have found a person more different from Wharton. The slightly built, long-haired Maurer moved about the courtroom with the kind of quick, lightning-fast moves that had made him a five-foot-nine high school basketball star in Philadelphia, a breeding ground for NBA players. When he asked a question, Maurer's body seemed to be in a different place by the time his words reached the witness-box. A hostile witness would turn mushy just trying to follow Maurer.

His challenge now, facing an articulate middle-aged woman, was daunting. But Maurer, with a quick series of questions, forced MacIntyre to acknowledge dozens of untruths she had told, in grand jury testimony and in interviews with investigators, including one with Connolly just two weeks before Capano's bail hearing. Maurer mocked her attempts to explain the difference between "intentional" and "unintentional" lies.

Turning to the lengthy affair with Capano, Maurer exposed MacIntyre as a shameless vixen. He had her tell the jury about the day Capano had tried to fondle her in his office.

"I assume then," Maurer said, "since you're not being controlled by him, you went to Kay [Capano] and said, 'I don't like what's going on here. You better talk to your husband'?"

"No, I did not," MacIntyre said.

"You never did that, did you?"

"No, I didn't."

When MacIntyre insisted her deceptions were over—"I'm telling the truth today"—Maurer fired back. "Today, November 19, you used the word *truth*. Does it mean the same as it means when you used it on January 28 of 1998?"

"I was not telling the truth then."

"Does the word *truth* mean the same then as it does now to you?"

"Yes," the exasperated woman answered.

Maurer, who shuffled stacks of papers as he assailed the witness, closed the day's inquisition by asking Debby if she'd ever added up the lies she had told under oath, just during the January 28 interview with Connolly, when the prosecutor had shown her the gun receipt.

"I told a lot of lies under oath."

When Maurer suggested the number was between sixty and seventy MacIntyre nodded in assent. "Correct, yes," she said quietly.

Maurer's hundreds of queries were all designed for only one purpose—to so discredit MacIntyre in the jurors' minds they wouldn't believe her on the only issue that mattered: where she was and what she did the night of June 27.

But that crucial encounter would have to wait, as Judge Lee adjourned the proceedings for a three-day weekend. When MacIntyre resumed the stand, her former lover, at the defense table, was suffering a colitis attack. He was hunched over in pain as MacIntyre was made to review once again her version of the events from June 27 through July 2, 1996, the date, MacIntyre said, she first heard the name Anne Marie Fahey.

Maurer suggested she had learned about Fahey earlier.

"No, Mr. Maurer, I never heard of Anne Marie Fahey until July 2."

"Didn't you go to 2302 Grant Avenue on June 27 or 28 with a firearm to visit Tom?" The gloves were off.

MacIntyre, who had been bracing for the assault, suddenly became aggressive. "Mr. Maurer," she answered in a forceful, defiant voice, "I never left my property from the time I returned home from the Arden Swim Club until the next morning when I went to the Tatnall School."

"Very strenuous about that, aren't you?" Maurer said.

"I am."

But that didn't stop the inevitable accusation.

"Didn't you have your firearm at Tom Capano's house on June 27, 1996, where you first learned about him and Anne Marie Fahey?"

"No, I did not."

"And you deny that your firearm discharged that night inside that house, striking her?"

"I don't know what happened with that firearm. I gave that firearm to Tom Capano on May 13."

"You deny that you discharged that firearm?"

"I deny that I discharged that firearm."

"Are you absolutely certain about that?"

"I'm absolutely certain."

Though Gerry Capano and Debby MacIntyre had taken a thrashing, the two star witnesses for the prosecution had absorbed the blows of defense attorneys without losing their cool or, it seemed, their credibility. Next came Nick Perillo to tell jurors about Capano asking him to arrange the burglary of MacIntyre's house; Susan Louth to say Capano had asked her to lie under oath; Tom Shopa, Capano's Archmere classmate, to tell the jury that Capano, after his arrest, had asked him to have sex with MacIntyre because she was lonely. An FBI agent verified that it was Fahey's blood in the den. And Capano's housekeeper, Ruth Boylan, said she noticed that the nice new rug and sofa in Capano's house had been replaced right after Fahey disappeared. Even Kay Capano, whose divorce was granted during the third week of the trial, took the stand for the prosecution.

The state had done so well, prosecutors believed, that they decided they didn't need Wilfredo Rosa, the inmate who told of Capano's plot to kill Gerry and Debby.

The state finally rested, on December 2, just as Connolly and Wharton had planned it, after Ken Chubb pointed to a huge white cooler sitting on a table in well of the courtroom and said, simply, "As far as I can tell from here, it looks like it."

The defense was scheduled to begin its case on December 7, Pearl Harbor Day; instead, that was the day the case blew up in its face. At 10:05 that morning, in the judge's chambers, Charlie Oberly broke the news to Judge Lee and the prosecutors that Tom Capano had fired his legal team. The defendant would defend himself.

Lee had feared such a fiasco. "Obviously it changes the way we would proceed with the latter part of the trial," he said, with some understatement.

"Your Honor," Wharton offered with a smile, "you mean not meeting in chambers?"

Lee smiled. But having Capano join their morning gab sessions and sidebars was the least of his worries. He was more concerned that Capano would transform the trial, which Lee had worked so hard to control, into a farce. Capano had already tested the judge at every turn. If he now tried to mount his own defense, Lee foresaw all his efforts at order unraveling.

"Why don't we go and let the bomb drop," offered Lee, deciding to quiz Capano on the subject, "and then we'll take a recess and see where we are?"

Ten minutes later, with no jury in the courtroom, but with spectators in the gallery anxious to see how the defense would begin its case, Joseph Oteri stood up—and asked Lee's permission to let all four defense attorneys withdraw from the case.

There was an audible collective gasp from the courtroom audience, which immediately understood why the jury had not been brought in.

"We have a serious strategic difference with the defendant as to how the case is to be tried," said Oteri, his voice heavy with resignation. "The difference is deep."

Oteri explained that Capano wanted to pursue one defense strategy, but his lawyers "are committed to a different course."

Lee ordered Capano to explain himself.

"I don't want to relieve them," Capano said, and asked to clarify the reasons.

"You have the floor," Lee said.

Capano took a deep breath. "I think that anyone in the position that I'm in should use every legitimate weapon available to him. I'm on trial for my life," he said. "And it's not a very good analogy, I know, but if I were a soldier in a foxhole, and I had ten grenades available, I'd use all ten of them if I was surrounded by the enemy rather than using, say, five."

Spectators and members of the Fahey family cringed at the accused killer's use of military terminology.

Capano continued. "My counsel collectively believes that— these are Joe's words, in particular—that it's better to proceed with a scalpel. His approach is 'less is more.' I believe, again, that someone in my situation should proceed with a chain saw."

Again there was a collective flinch from the Fahey family at Capano's choice of metaphor.

Capano asked for permission to address the jury to explain his decision. But prosecutors objected immediately, arguing that Capano shouldn't be allowed to make any statement without being subjected to cross-examination.

Lee asked Capano to be specific about what he wanted. A "hybrid" defense, said the defendant, in which his attorneys would present their case and then he would cover areas they had skipped.

Oteri jumped up, saying he opposed such a strategy. "I can only consider it would be a Pinocchio show in front of a jury here," the Boston attorney argued. "We would all look like fools." Worse, Oteri said, "it would convict him immediately."

Capano stressed that he wasn't delighted with the circumstances.

"I'm torn to pieces," he told the judge. "I haven't slept all weekend. I never expected this to reach this point."

Lee called for a short recess to research Capano's request and asked the attorneys to meet him in his chambers at one o'clock. When they reconvened, Lee announced that he thought it was too late for Capano to defend himself. "It's insane," he said, then corrected himself. "I hate to use that term."

Capano could proceed *pro se,* said Lee, meaning he could defend himself. But the jury would not be told why—no reason at all—and Capano couldn't make a statement. Lee gave Capano until the next morning to make a decision.

That night, at Gander Hill, Capano's attorneys and his attorney brother-in-law Lee Ramunno all screamed at Capano to listen to them. Reluctantly, he agreed. The next morning, he told the judge the differences had been revolved. "There were some misunderstandings on my part," he said sheepishly.

18 *The Greater Evil*

That crisis past, the defense began wielding Oteri's "scalpel."

The first days of its case produced a few jabs, but no hard punches. Prison psychiatrist Carol Tavani, a short, chatty redhead, said Capano and Fahey's E-mails showed "genuine caring and fondness" on Capano's part. Tavani also described Capano's deterioration in solitary confinement, saying he was at a low point when he drew up the MacIntyre burglary plot.

Tavani, it turned out, was the defense's confabulation expert. The psychiatrist testified that Gerry's drug and alcohol abuse, based on transcripts of his testimony, clearly indicated that he suffered from confabulation.

But Wharton, on cross-examination, quickly got Tavani to admit that she had never examined or even met Gerry Capano, conceding "there is no substitute for an actual face-to-face interview."

A handful of prison inmates—among them Robert "Squeaky" Saunders, a murderer Capano had prosecuted in 1976—told jurors that prisoner Nick Perillo bragged about preying on Capano, calling him a "free ticket" out of jail. "He said Capano was a mouse trapped in a corner and he was a snake," David Lawhorn, a felon with a menacing goatee and a history of violence, told jurors.

But Lawhorn's allegiances were also clear. Escorted to a prison van after testifying, he pumped his fist in the air and bellowed to photographers, "Capano rules!"

Capano's secretary, Denise Frawley, told the court she had received up to six calls a day from Fahey during June of 1996. Dr. Barbara Wingate, a friend of Capano, said he had approached her about getting help for an unnamed friend with an eating disorder. And Joe Capano took the stand for his older brother. The tanned, curly-haired builder and former wrestling champ, who was awaiting heart bypass surgery, said he had suggested that Tom buy a cooler for Gerry. Joe also said that Gerry's drinking affected his memory: "He tends to get things twisted."

A surprise witness was Mattie Coleman, a former housekeeper for Tom and Kay Capano and for Marguerite Capano. Coleman repeated a story she swore she heard from another client—that Michael Williams, Debby's son, told the client's son that he had seen a gun in his mother's bedroom. The prosecutors, believing Coleman's thirdhand story was too absurd for questions, didn't ask any. Instead they put Michael Williams and Sharon and Joe Purzycki, the Coleman clients who reportedly had told the story, on the stand. All of them denied any knowledge of the Coleman story; Michael also said he never saw a gun in his mom's house.

At 11.45 A.M. on December 16, 1998, after more than a week of defense witness testimony, Judge Lee leaned over to the witness stand to his left and addressed Tom Capano. "Mr. Capano, it's my understanding that we have reached the stage in the proceedings where it is necessary for you to make an election as to whether you choose to testify in this trial or whether you elect to stand on your constitutional right against self-incrimination and refuse to testify. Have you made that decision at this stage?"

"Yes, I have, Your Honor," Capano replied in a soft, clear voice.

An air of excitement reverberated around the courtroom. Capano's attorneys, with the jury out of the room, had said they were calling the accused as a witness. And Lee had decided to quiz Capano to make sure he realized the possible consequences.

"All right," said Lee. "And what is that decision?"

"I wish to testify," Capano said without hesitation.

Lee probed some more, to make certain Capano understood the potential downside and was making the choice voluntarily.

"How long have you discussed this with your attorneys?" Lee asked. "Give me a rough guesstimate."

"Probably for six months," said Capano. "On and off."

"And you're satisfied that they have fully informed you of the pluses and minuses of any decision you make?"

"Yes, Your Honor—mostly the minuses," said Capano, who went on to praise his legal team for their fine service.

As the spectators leaned forward in their gallery pews, desperate to hear Capano's words, at the defense table his lawyers wore expressions of forlorn resignation. Of the four, only Oberly thought Capano should testify. He reasoned that his client had to give some explanation of the accident that had killed Fahey in order to have any chance of acquittal or a lesser conviction.

But Oteri, who had never let a murder defendant speak before a jury, was fed up with his client. Never before had a client been so resistant to his advice. "If he asks me to ask a question, I don't complain anymore," Oteri confessed to a reporter during one break in the trial. "I just ask it."

And when the cameras weren't on, Capano's lawyers let reporters see them roll their eyes, shake their heads, and murmur obscenities. Now at least three of those attorneys were begging Capano not to testify—certain his arrogance and haughty temperament would erase what little empathy they'd managed to muster on his behalf.

Connolly and Wharton meanwhile were rooting for Tom Capano; they couldn't wait for him to climb into the witness-box. The banned MacIntyre phone calls could be played, and if he slipped and said he would never hurt a woman, jurors would learn about Linda Marandola, the woman he had run out of town nearly two decades earlier. Connolly couldn't wait to grill the man he'd come to loathe.

As the clock struck noon on December 16, calmly explaining that he had weighed the risk and benefits, Capano affirmed his decision to testify.

The defendant did provide his lead attorney some solace, assuaging the attorney's fears of a Capano lawsuit over his representation.

"I love him," Capano said of Oteri. "I'm happy with him." And Capano again asserted his recognition of the risks. "I want to testify. And I understand all the garbage that's going to be thrown at me during cross. And to cover Mr. Oteri and anybody else sitting at that table, this is all me, not them."

Lee sent Capano back to the defense table, then summoned the jury to their seats.

"The defense calls Thomas Capano."

It was an emaciated, speckle-gray-haired man in a dark gray suit who walked to the witness stand just after noon on December 16, 1998, placed his hand on the Bible, and swore to tell the truth.

As he took his seat, Capano accidentally brushed the Bible, which the bailiff had placed on the cornice shelf surrounding the witness-box, and the book fell to the floor.

"Thirty seconds and you wreck things," Joe Oteri remarked, trying to defuse the tension.

"Yeah," Capano said with a sigh. "I know."

"How are you feeling?" Oteri asked. "Are you all right?"

"No," Capano said. "I don't mean that in any way. I'm perfectly competent to testify. I'm just—I just mean I'm nervous."

As if wanting to communicate to the jury that "nervous" was an understatement, Oteri immediately had Capano list his current medications—Xanax, Wellbutrin, Lomotil, and Tylenol—and had him explain he was having trouble concentrating.

"I ramble," he explained.

In a grandfatherly voice, Oteri asked Capano to describe his background. "As a kid, growing up, what was it like?"

Capano jumped at the chance. "This part is pretty important to me because I've been portrayed as a spoiled rich kid born with a silver spoon in my mouth."

But the words were barely out of Capano's mouth when Connolly jumped to his feet. "Your Honor, we're going to object. We're not going through his life history."

Oteri countered, "The defendant is on trial for his life. The government has painted a saintly picture of Anne Marie Fahey and a demonic picture of the defendant."

The judge gave Capano some latitude but added a warning. "I'm not interested in a complete life story," Lee said. "Take that information that you think is relevant. I would expect Mr. Capano's responses to be in answer to your inquiries, rather than simply an unimpeded presentment to the jury."

Capano, taking liberties with Lee's ruling, began a glowing self-portrait, talking about his "blue-collar background" and explaining that his grandfathers, his uncles, his cousins, his father were all in the building trades. "I come from a background of people who worked with their hands," he said.

Capano skipped the part about growing up on a comfortable estate, having a summer house at the beach, and going to private schools. He did say, however, that of the four brothers, he was the only one to graduate from college.

"Just like the typical Italian family," quipped his Sicilian attorney. "The rest go out and make money and one goes for an education."

"That's exactly right."

Oteri started to ask a question about Capano's marriage, but the witness stopped him.

"I was going to mention about working."

"Go ahead," Oteri said, realizing his client wanted to connect with the working-class jury.

Capano then described his work, during high school, on his father's construction sites, digging ditches and mixing concrete.

"You didn't sit in an office with an adding machine?" Oteri asked helpfully.

"No. Not hardly. If you knew my father you would know that."

The self-portrait was a convincing description of a man who worked for what he got. And as Oteri led Capano through the rest of his biography, he didn't miss an opportunity to highlight Capano's financial sacrifices in order to take on public-service jobs and his dedication to his family.

"The most important thing in your life?" Oteri asked Capano about his daughters.

"Nothing else comes close," he responded forcefully.

Over Connolly objections, Capano was allowed to list the names of school, church, government, and legal groups in which he served, including his stint as a board member for the National Conference of Christians and Jews.

Then, almost as an afterthought, Oteri asked Capano about his purchase of a cooler at the Sports Authority. He didn't wear a disguise, Capano said, and he paid with his credit card, affirming Oteri's earlier statements that these were hardly the actions of a man plotting murder.

"Now, sir, why did you buy—why did you buy this cooler?"

Capano said it was a gift for his brother Gerry, who had been very generous to Tom's kids while they were at the beach. But the problem, Tom suggested, was what to get someone who has everything, someone who is "an overgrown kid" himself. And he took the first of many swipes at his youngest brother. "We lamented the fact that Gerry's a spend-thrift, and buys toys nonstop." He was a family spectacle. "We all preached to him, 'Stop this. Stop this. You don't need eight or nine Jet Skis or a collection of six antique Corvettes. Just stop it.' "

A cooler?

"As my brother Joey told me, you can't have too many coolers," said Tom, who explained that Gerry "was really into fishing."

Not for nothing had Tom Capano been counselor to mayors and governors. His political savvy had been legendary in Delaware before he was charged with murder; it was now on full display as he shrewdly picked apart his little brother, the "overgrown kid" whose testimony could send Tom to his execution.

Oteri had Tom explain the $8,000 loan from Gerry in February 1996 by suggesting that Gerry "was being nosy." It was Gerry, in his "tough-guy mold," who proposed, said Tom, "all sorts of possibilities," including a blackmailing scheme. "Finally, just to make him stop," Tom explained, "I said, 'Yeah, yeah, yeah.' "

And it was Gerry who said, "If somebody is bothering you, I'll get somebody to break his legs," said Tom. "It's like a line out of a movie."

"He said that *that* day?" Oteri asked, speaking of the day in February 1996 that Gerry had replayed endlessly.

"Yeah, but he said it all the time," said Tom.

"What did you do when he said it?"

"I laughed."

Tom also said it was Gerry who had offered him a gun for security—one night when Gerry was drunk on "dago red." Tom himself was afraid of guns. "I'd probably shoot myself with it rather than anybody I was aiming at," Capano told the jurors. Though he accepted his brother's offer, he immediately felt uncomfortable having a gun around the house when his daughters were visiting and returned it.

"I figured my baseball bat would do," explained Capano.

Calmly providing his account, Capano was doing better than Oteri had expected. But he then blurted something that confirmed why defendants shouldn't be put on the stand.

"I should mention," Capano offered, "if I may, that I did have the conversation with him about my children that he described."

"What conversation?" asked Oteri, not exactly sure where Tom was going.

"Gerry testified that we had a conversation about my kids that, you know, if anybody hurt them I would kill them?"

"Tell us about that," Oteri said, now worried.

"Well, we had that conversation. I mean, I said that frequently. If I've said it once I've said it a thousand times. I mean it. Anybody hurts my kids I kill them."

Though Oteri tried to shut his client up, the damage was done, his killer instincts fully aired. "When he said that, I almost shit my pants," Oteri later recalled.

Oteri then had Tom spend a lot of time criticizing Gerry and Debby. Gerry had concocted the stories about blackmailers, and it was Debby, not Tom, who wanted an affair. "She was very aggressive with me," complained Capano.

During a morning recess on Capano's second day on the stand, defense attorney Jack O'Donnell emerged from the courtroom, an angry scowl on his face. "How long do you think he'll be on?" a reporter asked.

"That motherfucker," O'Donnell grumbled about his law school buddy before he grabbed a pack of cigarettes, dashed outside, and stuck a cigarette in his mouth.

"If he'd just have kept his fucking mouth shut, we had either an acquittal or a hung jury," O'Donnell muttered, puffing furiously. "But he has to talk."

But Capano had just begun to talk. He spent most of Day Two talking about MacIntyre, usually in unflattering terms, continuing to portray himself as innocent victim of her feminine powers: "She made all the moves and I couldn't control myself."

And the more he talked, even in defending each specific act, the more jurors could see that Tom Capano was probably not like them. Even while married and with a mistress, he admitted, he had other affairs. And attempting to show his compassion toward his wife, he said, he took his girlfriends away from Wilmington in order to protect Kay from humiliation.

"I had friends who knew other people who were having affairs and were indiscreet about it, and I don't judge people and I didn't judge them, but I would raise hell," Capano said, in an apparent attempt to take the high road. "I said, 'Look, I don't care what you do, it's your business, but she's the mother of your children and you do not go around town embarrassing her.' I mean, Wilmington is such a small gossipy place and so I never, *ever,* ever did anything around here that would have caused embarrassment to Kay."

Oteri seemed almost dazed by his client's performance but could do nothing to stop it. Whenever Oteri tried to cut him off, Capano insisted on finishing his answer. He also insulted Oteri on occasion, ridiculing his Boston accent when Oteri said "kah" instead of "car."

So Oteri, his tolerance tank on empty, let Capano blather, trying only to keep him on track.

Turning to the gun MacIntyre had bought, Capano claimed that he had nothing to do with it. She had invited him to lunch at Arner's that day, and when he walked up to her car in the parking lot to say hello, Debby reached in a bag and "showed me the gun she had purchased at Miller's."

Over lunch, Capano said, Debby explained that with the spate of shootings in Wilmington, she felt she needed some protection. A week or two later, Capano said, Debby showed him the gun again, pulling it out of her bedroom closet, where it had been hidden.

"When was the next time you saw the gun?" Oteri asked.

"June 27," Capano said.

"Did Debby MacIntyre ever give you the gun?"

"No," he said emphatically. "She did not."

But Oteri wasn't ready yet for an explanation of the "tragic accident" that was the cornerstone of the defense. Instead he changed gears, turning to the letters his client had written Debby from jail. Capano said he was emotionally destroyed after learning she hadn't destroyed the letters, as promised, calling her act "a monstrous lie."

Oteri then, knowing Connolly would play them if he didn't, played the four phone calls MacIntyre had secretly recorded for the jury.

Oteri asked if there was any reason he never mentioned to MacIntyre during the phone calls "what happened at your home on the twenty-seventh of June 1996."

"Well, two reasons," Capano said. "I wasn't sure of the security of the phones. And secondly, I wanted to reassure her, just as I needed to be reassured of her feelings. I wanted to reassure her, as I had done in writing earlier, that I was going to protect her at any cost."

After his arrest, Capano said, he had told Debby he'd "make sure she was protected and no harm came to her. I promised that. I vowed it melodramatically, as I can sometimes. That's what I did."

"You keep saying 'protect her,' " Oteri observed.

"Yes."

"Protect her from what?"

"Well, from—I wanted to protect her from any involvement at all in what had happened, but what I meant primarily was I was going to protect her from having any charges, any legal results or legal consequences against her."

"As a result of what?"

"As a result of the—what happened on that evening."

Spectators, aching to hear Capano's story, thought the moment had finally arrived—nearly thirty months after Annie's death.

But it was only a well-planned tease. Despite Oteri's advertised lack of control over his client, he still held some rein. And he now changed channels and began asking Tom about Annie. Capano said he had flirted with her at the governor's office and explained how casual chats had turned into lunches and then a love affair. But it wasn't fair to Anne Marie, Capano said, to continue, and toward the end of 1994 he broke off the relationship.

"We were both falling in love and I finally said, 'This is nuts. Look at the age difference.' And you know, 'I'm married. I have four children.' There was just very little in common other than our feelings for each other. And I really tried to end it in a very nice way."

As he had done with Debby, Capano portrayed Annie as the sexual aggressor. He even tried, he said, to cut off all communications with her early in 1995—just as Annie's diary indicated—but she pestered him with phone calls. "So when she called back, you know, we gradually resumed the relationship."

The name Scanlan surfaced, Capano said, in late fall of 1995, when a friend told him that Annie was seeing someone from MBNA. Capano said he was disappointed, not angry.

"I don't like being lied to," he recalled telling Annie. " 'Just tell me what's up. Tell me what's going on.' And she said, 'You know, at this point we're just friends and it's no big deal.' "

Attempting to show that Capano wasn't jealous, Oteri asked if his client had dated other women during that period. "Probably eight or nine," Capano said. "Not simultaneously."

Asked to describe his relationship with Fahey after she began seeing Scanlan, Capano said it was "excellent," that he was content to be a father figure or "fifth big brother" and confidant, and they even had sex on a few occasions in the spring of 1996, as late as June 18—nine days before she vanished.

He said the stories about his begging to buy her a Lexus were ridiculous. The luxury sedan was simply her favorite car, and they often talked about her desires. Then, in an odd attempt to appeal to jurors—two of whom worked for General Motors—Capano stressed that he only bought American cars for himself.

The closest to tumult in the relationship that he would admit to was the previous Christmas, when "our biggest fight occurred." It began when he bought her a round-trip ticket to Spain, he said.

"She refused it, but she refused it in a very hurtful way," he said, not elaborating. "And one word led to another and that's the famous incident of when I threatened to take back everything that I had given her, in which—it was almost funny in a way. I mean, she, we were yelling. She says, 'Fine, I don't want any of this stuff.'

"And I said, 'Fine.' And I unplugged the big television and I took it off the stand and put it on the floor. She started pulling clothes out of closets and throwing them on the floor."

They both cooled down a few minutes later, he said. Annie went to the pile, picked up a heating pad he'd bought her, and clutched it to her chest, grinning. "I actually spent the night that night," Capano concluded, clearly satisfied with his having turned a linchpin prosecution anecdote into a touching lovers' squabble.

"Did you come up the fire escape and keep her in the room and take all the gifts?" Oteri asked.

"No. Absolutely not," Capano said firmly. "I would have had to break the door down and there was a dead bolt and I didn't."

In hour after hour on the stand Capano gave similar twists to every story about his jealousy and possessiveness and insisted that he and Annie remained close friends. He took credit for referring her to therapist Michele Sullivan, adding, sarcastically, that the piece of paper on which he jotted the psychologist's name "has apparently disappeared."

In fact, the $8,000 he borrowed from Gerry, he said, was to help Annie—not hurt her. He added the money to $17,000 he had already withdrawn from the bank—then gave the $25,000, in cash, to Annie, beseeching her to use the money for inpatient treatment of her disease.

"And what did Annie do with the $25,000?" Oteri asked.

"Threw it in my face," Capano said, again dismissing the incident as an innocent spat between friends.

After the afternoon break on Day Two of Capano's testimony, the court was again thrown into confusion when defense attorneys requested a private hearing with the judge. The public, press, and prosecutors would be barred from the ex-parte meeting.

Capano, who sat alone at the defense table after learning what his lawyers planned, shook his head violently and muttered to himself. Veteran court observers immediately speculated that Capano's lawyers were informing Lee that they suspected their client was prepared to lie on the stand and, bound by strict ethical rules, they wanted to alert the judge. But the transcript from the session was sealed, and no one, not Lee or any of the attorneys, would reveal what was said in the meeting.

But it didn't seem to matter, as the proceedings resumed and, nine weeks after first floating an alternative theory, four days before Christmas, on his third day on the stand, Capano finally told the world his version of what had happened on the night of June 27, 1996.

The Fahey family and friends, who had loyally filled two and three rows of pews in the gallery every day of the long trial, expected him to point the finger at Debby MacIntyre.

As he had done with most of the other stories about his relations with Annie, Capano admitted most of the facts while spinning their meaning. Yes, Annie was in a sullen mood that night, Capano said, but it was about "getting gouged" on prescription medicine she had just bought. And the reason she seemed morose at dinner, said Capano, was because they talked about a sobering topic, her anorexia. And Annie wasn't really "glum" until the waitress "brought the wrong calamari dish." Capano even had an explanation for giving a 20 percent tip for what he now said was lousy service. "We would be punishing the other people"—busboys and servers—who shared the gratuity.

After dinner, Capano said, he drove straight to Annie's apartment, but they decided to watch *ER* on television at his place, because her third-floor unit "was hot as blazes." They dropped off the doggie bag from the Panorama and some soups and grains he had bought for her earlier, then drove to Grant Avenue, arriving just after *ER* began.

Capano spared no detail in his story, including the fact that Annie took off her panty hose and sat on the sofa in front of the television "with her knees pulled up." Checking his phone messages, he told the jurors, he found a call from Debby MacIntyre and dialed her. She asked to come over.

"I said, 'Not right now. I've got company. It will have to

be later,' or something like that. And I just hung up," the calm, composed defendant recounted.

He returned to the den, he said, and stretched out on the love seat next to Annie.

"All right," Oteri said in a comforting voice. "What happened next, sir?"

"Well, the next thing I knew Debby MacIntyre was in the room. She must have entered the front door. She had a key to my house as I had a key to her house. I even had a garage door opener for her house. And she was pretty ballistic."

Capano said the noise of his air conditioner had prevented him and Annie from hearing Debby enter.

When Debby saw him and Annie on the sofa, she became enraged, Capano recounted. "She was yelling, 'Who's this? What is this all about? Is this why you couldn't see me?' "

Capano said MacIntyre became hysterical about finding another woman, and Annie said she wanted to leave. As Annie began putting on her pantyhose, he said, Debby pulled a gun from a small, straw case she was carrying. Annie actually laughed, then returned to her nylons.

But Debby, he said, began ranting about suicide and raised her arm as if she might kill herself. Capano said he instinctively grabbed her arm.

Capano finished the story with the exquisite—and excruciating—detail and drama of a practiced storyteller, finally saying, "Debby shot Anne Marie."

The statement sailed through the courtroom as a giant anticlimax. The hush in the gallery was the quiet of exhaustion.

But Capano continued, explaining how he had slapped Annie, who had a bullet hole near her right ear, trying to get her to "come to"; how he and Debby "became wrecks"; how they had tried CPR and shined a flashlight in Annie's eyes.

"Did you call 911 or anybody else?" Oteri asked, wanting to give Capano a chance to explain a particularly odd part of the "accident" story.

"No," Capano said, shaking his head, grimacing. "Most cowardly, horrible thing I've ever done in my life."

"What did you do after you determined that Anne Marie was dead?"

"It was like my whole life flashed before me. If you're in a situation like that you just start—everything is, 'Oh my God.' " Capano said he and Debby couldn't believe what had transpired. "Debby is crying and she's hysterical, and I want to calm her down, and I'm thinking of, as I said, my own life flashed before my eyes, and I always thought I was a guy with some guts and I wasn't. And I'm just being selfish, too, to protect myself and also to protect Debby. And so, since I knew the paramedics could not do anything, I knew Anne Marie was dead, I chose not to call the paramedics or the police but to protect myself and to the extent that I could to protect Debby."

This was, perhaps, the most important speech Capano could give. The failure to report the "accident" was the black hole of the story that sucked everything into it. All explanations about all things meant nothing if this scene was not credible. Would the jurors believe it?

Capano continued. "I break down. I fell apart, and I cried and I screamed at myself, and I punched the wall, and after about five minutes of that, I did something I'm capable of doing. I compartmentalized. And then I just said I have to do something. What am I going to do? What am I going to do? And the first thing I have to do is take care of Anne Marie's body."

As Kathleen Fahey fought back tears in the gallery and her brothers clenched their jaws, Capano pushed on, a madman in gray flannel, articulately describing the complete lack of control that explained his "panic" and, in the next breath, the coolheadedness with which he "compartmentalized" the situation.

The grains of truth that his fevered genius gathered were then sprayed about like the disconnected pellets of a shotgun blast. It was a story that seemed to emerge as if from a dream, everything about it real—except the dream itself. And he pushed on, explaining what he did with the body and how he cleaned up the house and stashed the gun, a glibly demonic narrator, worthy of Dostoyevski. Capano even recognized his dilemma—and had an explanation for that too. He wasn't getting emotional about Fahey's death, he said, because he was taking stronger doses of the tranquilizer Xanax. "I'm certainly not the person I used to be."

At the prosecution's table, Connolly and Wharton were taking notes, knowing that as preposterous as Capano's tale was, they would have to make sure the jurors didn't buy it.

The only question prosecutors had—and they would probably never know the answer now—was whether Capano merely sneaked up behind Anne Marie and fired or held the gun over her head, making her beg for her life.

Reporters called Thomas Bergstrom, Debby MacIntyre's attorney, who laughed at Capano's account. "It makes no sense," he said, "that she was hysterical, accidentally killed her, and, after talking with Capano for a few minutes, was composed enough to drive home and go to work the next day."

The next morning, Oteri wanted to quickly wrap up his questioning, but Capano insisted on reading dozens of E-mails, claiming he needed to offer his explanation to the jury. He made his attorneys take his request to the judge.

Lee, wiping his brow, couldn't resist a dig at the defendant during the sidebar conversation.

"I'm certainly not going to tell the defense how to run its case—but then again you already have somebody to do that for you," Lee remarked, but warned that Capano might "bore this jury to death."

But the defense team also recognized a more strategic reason to drag out Capano's examination. It was December 22, the final trial session before a six-day Christmas break. If they could keep Connolly away from Capano today, the jury would have more than a week to consider their explanation of what had happened to Anne Marie Fahey.

And so Tom Capano read E-mails between himself and Annie, offering turgid and self-serving explanations at every turn. The real show, everyone knew, would begin when Colm Connolly, who had been listening patiently as Capano droned on, attacked.

The big moment arrived at 11:30 A.M. on December 29, when the earnest whiz kid from Duke Law stood before "the monk" charged with murder and asked, "Since June 28, 1996, how many crimes have you committed?"

Unlike Oteri, Connolly made no pretense of collegiality with a witness he wanted to eviscerate. He didn't introduce himself, didn't call the defendant by any name, and had nothing but derision in his voice from the first question out of his mouth.

And Capano—who already looked disheveled, with a thick stubble on his face that he attributed to Gander Hill's having run out of razors over the holiday weekend—was momentarily disoriented by the abrupt and unadorned mathematical problem presented, one whose answer would no doubt leave him imprinted as a rotten criminal. He fumbled for something to say.

Connolly knew that Capano had crafted his defense to fit as many of the obvious facts as possible. It didn't surprise the prosecutor that Capano admitted being with MacIntyre when she bought the gun, because a call on his cell phone had been made in the area of the gun store that day. Nor was Connolly surprised that Capano confessed that Annie had died in his den— he couldn't dispute the fact that it was her blood splattered on the radiator and woodwork. And the sea burial, Connolly knew, because of the cooler and Gerry's testimony, was an indisputable fact.

Capano's only gambit—Connolly was sure he was lying— was turning those facts on their heads by offering a plausible alternative explanation. If he could plant enough doubt in the jurors' minds, he could win conviction on a lesser charge, a hung jury, or even an acquittal. The alternative theory was simple enough: Debby did it. After all, MacIntyre's signature was on the gun receipt. Sure, he had had arguments with Annie—but who didn't have arguments with his lover? And the bad things Annie told her friends about him, Capano argued, were simply part of the pattern of an unstable young woman in therapy.

But in response to Connolly's first question, Capano gathered himself and admitted he had committed a number of crimes since June 28, 1996, including desecrating a corpse, multiple counts of suborning perjury, and obstruction of justice.

Connolly's next question left Capano even more exposed: "How many lies have you told related to the disappearance of Anne Marie Fahey since June 28, 1996?"

"Well," Capano replied, gaining a measure of equilibrium and with it a tone of contempt toward his younger inquisitor, "I certainly don't have a number, but I know that I never told the truth. I lied to everyone."

But that wasn't good enough for the prosecutor, who had decided to never let Capano off the hook. Standing erect at the podium, Connolly squared his shoulders and bore down on Capano.

"Approximately how many lies did you tell?"

"I have no idea, Mr. Connolly."

"Too many to count?"

"Sure," Capano conceded.

Colm Connolly knew he had to somehow break Capano but also recognized that he was questioning a master manipulator, whose verbal sleights of hand were as dexterous as those of any magician. Connolly planned to do it fact by fact, to slowly, methodically, topple Capano's carefully constructed house of cards.

How, for instance, was Capano going to dispose of the body himself, as he said he had planned to do, if he also had needed Debby, as he had said he did, to help him carry it downstairs because of his bad back?

"So you were going to lift that cooler into the back of the Suburban by yourself?" Connolly asked in disbelief.

"I was going to try," Capano said, pointing out that if he failed, he "had materials where could try to slide it up" into the truck's rear.

Within an hour of beginning his cross-examination, Connolly had sliced a dozen small Capano assertions to pieces, in the process exasperating the defendant.

Pushing Capano's buttons was what Connolly most wanted to do, to get under the haughty defendant's skin so badly that he'd reveal a simmering, explosive temper.

Next calling attention to Capano's handwritten notes, the ones stashed in his law partner's office that detailed his last dates with Annie and his actions after she had vanished, Connolly pointed to the defendant's mention of a pleasant phone conversation with Laura Kobosko, Keith Brady's secretary, just nine hours after Annie died.

"It's significant to you, isn't it, that fact, that it was a pleasant or friendly conversation," Connolly accused.

"Not particularly."

"Well, it was your intention to convey to your lawyers the character, the tenor of the conversation, wasn't it?"

"You are capable of doing a lot of things, Mr. Connolly," Capano said harshly. "But I do not believe you can read my mind, so I don't—if you say what my intention is, I don't necessarily agree with that."

When Connolly persisted, Capano interrupted. "I'll play your games, but not that one. I did deeply love Anne Marie Fahey. You never even knew her."

Connolly, who also realized Capano was trying to rattle him and reveal him as an overzealous and mean-spirited prosecutor, didn't react but simply pressed on. He spent hours forcing Capano to give precise, graphic details of the shooting, the disposal of Fahey's body, and the cover-up, attacking Capano's rendition of reality at every turn.

He mocked Capano's claim that Annie wasn't frightened, even put on her panty hose and chuckled, while a hysterical woman she'd never met was five feet away with a gun. "No, she wasn't frightened," Capano protested. "You didn't know Anne Marie. The gun wasn't aimed at her anyhow."

Asking about Annie's fatal wound, Connolly spent ten minutes pressing Capano to give exact detail about how many inches the bullet hole was from the ear, whether there was an exit wound, the amount and color of blood, the size of the hole.

Connolly realized that besides pinning Capano down and infuriating him, he was also forcing the jury to focus on the gunshot wound in Annie's head. And every once in a while, Capano stumbled into a contradiction. When he told Connolly he took the gun from Debby's hand, Connolly pounced, pointing out that Capano had told the jury in his direct testimony that Debby dropped the gun.

"Well, now I'm telling the jury that yes, I got it out of her hand or she handed it to me," stammered Capano. "These are not things that were burned into my memory."

"Shootings occur in your living room all the time?" the prosecutor asked, his voice dripping with disdain.

Playing up Capano's inability to remember certain details, Connolly highlighted his criticism of Gerry's memory. "Are these kind of like the Swiss cheese holes that you have referred to on numerous occasions in describing Gerry's testimony?"

"No," Capano said, proving his debating mettle. "I think my word was like *mush*."

Stuffing Annie's five-foot, ten-inch frame into a three-foot, eight-inch cooler was another act Connolly made Capano describe with numbing precision. The point, again, was that no matter how Capano answered, the image of him cavalierly cramming a dead woman's body in a cooler built for tuna would be emblazoned in the jury's mind. Connolly then changed course, asking why, if the shooting was an accident, Capano had gotten rid of the corpse. The forensic evidence alone surely would have exonerated MacIntyre and himself.

"The forensic evidence wasn't important," Capano asserted.

But Connolly reminded him that Squeaky Saunders had just testified on his behalf in the trial; that Capano had prosecuted Saunders for murder, and that, in that case, a firearms expert, questioned by Capano, had established the trajectory of the bullets and proved that Saunders fired the first of three shots that killed Joseph "Spoon" Johnson. "You knew because of your involvement in the Squeaky Saunders case that forensic evidence is critical to determining the cause of death," Connolly drilled. "Isn't that right?"

Capano shot back, "I can't believe you're asking me to remember a case I did in 1976."

"Well, the case has interesting similarities to this case, doesn't it?" Connolly retorted, pointing out that Saunders had shot his victim "about two inches from the ear."

"I'm not going to talk about the Saunders case," Capano growled. "I'm not going to talk about it."

"The victim was shot in the head—one lethal shot about five inches from the top of the head. Correct?"

"I'm not talking about it."

But Connolly talked about it. The prosecutor now told the jury how Capano, in his closing arguments at the Squeaky Saunders trial, had made a big deal of how Saunders and his accomplices dumped Johnson's body in a creek near Delaware

City, thinking it would flow into the river and then the Atlantic, only to have the corpse caught by floodgates.

"Will you remember closing arguments twenty-two years from now?" the incensed defendant interjected.

But Connolly ignored the protests, pointing out that, just like Saunders, Capano knew exactly how important the forensic evidence was and had taken great pains to get rid of all such evidence, even scrubbing the room where Annie had died—missing, of course, the two drops of Annie's blood that helped break the case.

Connolly even recited from Capano's closing argument in the Saunders case. " 'We don't have the gun. If we had the gun, it would be a lot easier case, but we don't,' " Connolly said, repeating Capano's words from twenty-two years earlier. " 'Why? Because once again, Robert Saunders shows us how bright he is. Get rid of it. Get rid of the murder weapon before you do anything else.' "

———

The next morning, Connolly returned to Capano's account of Annie's death.

"So there was no way to corroborate or to disprove your account of the relative positions of Debby MacIntyre and Anne Marie Fahey, correct?"

"Other than my testimony and Debby's testimony."

"So you, as a prosecutor, got rid of all the evidence that could have corroborated your testimony?"

"Yes, I did," Capano said. "And I was in a panic."

"And that's the same evidence that could have corroborated your testimony?"

"No, it couldn't have."

"Well," Connolly said, folding his arms at the podium, "it couldn't disprove it if we didn't have it."

"Correct. You don't have it."

Satisfied that he had made the point, Connolly moved to other topics.

He spent most of the second day of his Capano cross-examination grilling the defendant about his relationship with Annie. Using the E-mails and letters as props, Connolly was able to show the jury how Capano had manipulated Annie with money and gifts and even curried her sympathies with a bogus story about his daughter's brain tumor.

Capano bristled under the assault, becoming flustered and quarrelsome, denying almost everything Connolly charged, and firing back his own questions.

Judge Lee, growing more disenchanted with the witness each minute, admonished Capano several times.

"Mr. Capano knows the rules," Lee told the defendant and the jury, his voice stern. "Mr. Capano must abide by the rules."

Connolly continued to probe Capano about his manipulation of others, working the defendant into a rage when he accused Capano of using his daughters to elicit sympathy from his mistresses.

"With Debby MacIntyre, when things got really bad and you needed her to stop cooperating, you would reference your kids?"

"Don't go there," Capano snapped.

"Did you or not?" Connolly repeated.

"No. I spoke of my children, but not in the way you would have it, that you would try to convince this jury or any civil human being."

"And you, with Anne Marie Fahey, in the spring of '96, when she would not return your romantic overtures, you told her that one of your daughters needed brain surgery, didn't you?"

"That is an outrageous lie."

"You told Kim Horstmann the same thing, did you not?"

"Kim Horstmann got it confused."

Turning to the jury, Connolly folded his arms and shook his head. "Kim Horstmann is confused. Anne Marie Fahey is lying to her psychiatrist. And you are to be believed?"

Capano, even more infuriated now, said, "I don't necessarily believe anything that that particular psychiatrist wrote down," and that Kim had probably misunderstood his account of a medical procedure his daughter had several years earlier.

When Capano denied calling Debby MacIntyre "stupid," the prosecutor had him read from one of his own letters. When he denied calling her "submissive" and "slow-witted," Connolly again asked Capano to read from his own writings, di-

recting him to the page and paragraph. The prosecutor left
Capano flustered as he raced from letter to letter, showing with
cutting precision exactly where the words came from, having
the defendant read them himself.

The prosecutor seemed to surprise Capano when he played
the tape of his February 28 phone conversation with Mac-
Intyre. Capano and MacIntyre's scratchy voices were projected
through the courtroom's public-address system.

"I told the truth," says the woman, MacIntyre.

"No, no, tell me exactly what happened. Start to finish," says
the man, unmistakably Capano, his anxious voice on the tape
echoing across the courtroom. Connolly flicked off the tape.

"You didn't jump for joy?" he asked Capano.

"No."

"You weren't happy when she told you she had told the
truth?"

"No, I was extremely emotional during that call."

"She told you the truth. Do you say, 'Thanks, Debby'?"

Capano, caught by a comment he couldn't spin to his advantage, finally sputtered that he "didn't know what she
meant."

And on the part of the tape where MacIntyre said she bought
the gun, Capano had asked simply, "Why did you say such a
thing?"

The prosecutor pressed his point. "You didn't deny it [buy-
ing the gun]. In fact, you never denied it in any of these phone
calls."

Capano, backed into a corner, said he thought the calls
might be taped and didn't want to incriminate Debby.

"I never trusted any of these phone calls," the defendant
said, "and as it turns out, I couldn't trust Debby, either."

Capano finally detonated on January 4, 1999, at the conclusion of his third day of cross-examination.

Connolly had assailed Capano all morning and into the
afternoon, bouncing from topic to topic, about lies he had
told—to cops, friends, and his own attorneys, when he said
that Annie had been sighted at Newark Airport; to psychiatrist

Joseph Bryer, whom he told that Annie got a bloody nose on the night she died after she punched him and he tried to restrain her; about his affinity for high-risk sex in parking lots, law offices, and his estranged wife's house during a Christmas party; about diagramming MacIntyre's house so it could be robbed.

Capano's courtroom discomfort was made worse by a malfunctioning air-conditioning system. The temperature in the room had been rising all day until, by midafternoon, spectators in the gallery had shed coats and were waving newspaper fans in front of their faces.

To help keep the heat down, Judge Lee ordered the lights turned low, and light spilled in through the high arched windows thirty feet above the floor, glinting off the dust that swirled around the cavernous room like incense drifting through a medieval cathedral. And on the distant altar "the monk" held his pale vigil.

The grand inquisitor, Connolly, bore down on the wan silhouette at the far end of the room as if chasing a mouse into its hole. Marching from the table, where he would pick up a document, to the podium, where he had other documents, to the witness stand, where he thrust the papers at the defendant, Connolly kept challenging Capano to explain.

He had Capano read from a letter he wrote to MacIntyre March 17, 1998, saying: "I love you with all my heart and beg you to give me another chance."

Then, as if to make the defendant eat his words, Connolly read the letter Capano had written to Susan Louth the same day, in which he quoted a female cousin about MacIntyre: "She looks like a shrew and a backstabber."

Capano, unable to defend the remark, could only offer, "It was later in the day."

By 4:30 that afternoon, despite the heat and the many hours of strenuous verbal jousting, the two combatants showed no signs of fatigue. But Connolly had one button he had yet to press.

"Now, notwithstanding what you've told us about your deep love for your daughters," Connolly began, "you used your daughters in this investigation, did you not?"

"Do you really want to get into this?" Capano almost spit the question out. He focused a hard and hateful gaze at the young prosecutor who was moving toward him.

"Did you use your daughters to impede the investigation?" Connolly repeated.

"You tormented my daughters. You tormented my mother!" Capano shouted.

Though Capano was clearly violating Lee's order to only answer the questions, not argue with counsel, the judge held his tongue. Capano's attorneys had long before forsaken efforts to protect their client—from himself.

"All right," said Connolly, as if snapping his fingers in prelude to a back-alley brawl. "Let's talk about your daughters."

"No," Capano said forcefully. "No, we're not."

Connolly ignored him. "You were given an opportunity to make it so that your daughters would not have to be interviewed by the government," he said. "All you had to do was agree to submit to an interview yourself. You didn't do that, did you?"

"That's not a choice."

"You had a choice," Connolly said.

"No, no, and you, as this unethical—"

Oteri finally stepped in. "Your Honor! May we approach?"

Capano swatted the microphone, muttering obscenities about Connolly.

At the bench, Oteri asked for a mistrial, claming Connolly had commented unethically on Capano's refusal to be interviewed, a violation of his Fifth Amendment right against self-incrimination. Lee quickly denied the request, pointing out that Capano had already waived that constitutional protection by testifying.

Oteri had hoped to buy Capano some time with the sidebar, let him settle down. But as Connolly returned to his podium, Capano followed him with an icy stare.

"Now, you had the opportunity to prevent your daughters from undergoing any trauma associated with an interview, correct?" Connolly would not be denied.

"Absolutely incorrect!" Capano exploded, as if the sidebar

interlude had only fanned his flames. "You heartless, gutless, soulless disgrace of a human being!"

Connolly didn't flinch. His face betrayed no emotion. "You not only had the opportunity by agreeing—" he said, before Capano, only beginning his histrionics, cut him off.

"Why don't you explain what you did to my mother! Let's include that as well."

Connolly looked at the judge. "OK, Your Honor. I mean, we did nothing to his mother."

"You did nothing to my mother?" Capano screamed. "That's a lie right there in front of the Court."

Lee glanced at the guards. "Please take Mr. Capano out of the courtroom," he ordered.

As Capano was hustled out of the side door, in front of the jury, he looked back to the courtroom and hollered, "He's a liar!"

Lee paused to collect his thoughts and said in an exasperated voice, "Well, it just got a little warmer in the courtroom, so we're going to quit early today."

As astonished spectators filed out of the courtroom, the lawyers adjourned to Lee's chambers.

"Anybody have any suggestions about how we recommence the festivities?" the judge quipped.

O'Donnell suggested a mental exam for the volatile defendant.

Lee remarked that while he understood Capano's disdain for questions about his kids, "I was surprised that he totally lost it up there."

Connolly said he wouldn't take long the next day to conclude but asked the judge not to let Capano apologize.

Lee agreed, over the protests of Capano's counselors, and at 10:25 the next morning, with the jury out of the courtroom, Capano resumed his familiar seat in the witness-box for his eighth and, presumably, final day of testimony.

Looking down at the defendant, Lee told him to pay attention so he wouldn't misunderstand his marching orders.

"There will be no apologies to the Court and the jury for yesterday's outburst," Lee commanded. "You are simply to answer questions directed to you by Mr. Connolly. He will be permitted to ask questions on cross-examination subject only to your attorneys' right to object. When I have ruled on objections, those rulings are not subject to your final approval."

Lee's dressing-down of Capano was highly unusual—but so was the defendant, who sat glowering in the witness box.

"If you refuse to accept the responsibilities of cross-examination, there are draconian sanctions which can be imposed and they will be considered," Lee continued. "You're to stop trying to manipulate the state's questions to serve your purposes with unresponsive answers."

Lee was not through.

"I have attempted to give you every consideration because of the position you find yourself in, but I will do my job. Do we understand each other?"

Capano hesitated, then asked, "Does that mean you want a response from me?"

Lee's eyes blazed with fury at Capano's defiance. But he refrained from responding. "Please bring the jury in," he snapped to bailiffs.

Connolly picked up where he had left off—with Capano's daughters—but the defendant now restrained himself. And the battle now moved to territory that the two Catholic-school-educated lawyers were very familiar with: the question, What is a lie?

Connolly decided to grill Capano on his lecture, delivered under friendly questioning by Oteri several days earlier, about lying.

"I mean a lie is only when it's based on evil intent," Capano had lectured. "I mean, we all lie every day. You might see your great-aunt, for example, who really doesn't look so good, she missed her makeup that day or her lipstick, and of course, you're going to tell her, 'Oh, you look beautiful.'

"I mean, from that insignificant lie to a serious lie. I mean, if those people in World War II who harbored Jews, when the Gestapo came to their doors and said, 'Are there any Jews in your house?' people said, 'Of course not,' that's a lie. But that's not considered a sin in the eyes of the Church. I mean that's a valid, OK lie."

Oteri had asked his client how he justified all the lies he'd told about the death of Anne Marie Fahey.

"I felt I had given my word to protect someone I loved, and I had to protect her," Capano replied. "It's a good thing to be loyal to your family and those you love. That's a very good thing. It's also a good thing to be loyal to the truth. But you know, sometimes those things collide, and, you know, figuring your way out of—when those two things collide, figuring your way out of it and making a decision is not nearly as easy as the prosecution would suggest to you."

What the Church's moral theologians would have said about Capano's teachings was anyone's guess—what Colm Connolly said was, "Now, you've talked about virtuous lies."

Capano took offense, saying correctly that he never used the word *virtuous,* only said that it was OK to lie under certain circumstances.

But Connolly persisted, and Capano relented. "Do you want to call it virtuous lies? Go ahead; call it virtuous lies."

"Was it necessary to tell Dr. Bryer you had no involvement in the disappearance of Anne Marie Fahey?"

"Well," Capano said with a sigh, "we'd have to spend about an hour with a Jesuit, but since there was no evil intent there, I was—my overriding concern was to protect Debby."

"Was it necessary to ask Kim Horstmann to come to Stone Harbor so you could put your heads together to think about where Anne Marie Fahey could be?"

"Yeah, because by reaching out to Kim in the only way I could possibly try to get her in person so I could try to unravel all of this much larger evil. Yeah, that way, there was nothing wrong with that. There was no evil intent there. It was just the opposite. It was a good intention."

Connolly then asked Capano to explain how that convoluted logic made the lie "necessary."

"I figured it was the only way I could try to get her to attend in order to—again, move against the greater evil."

"The greater evil being?"

"What happened to Anne Marie."

Connolly let Capano's statement hang in the air, then moved on, directing the defendant's attention to the news release he

had Oberly send out in January 1997—some five months after
he had dumped Annie's corpse in the Atlantic—saying he was
"devastated by Anne Marie's disappearance and like everyone
else hopes she will be found safe."

Capano insisted it was a necessary truth to say he was "devastated" and that once Connolly got involved, "we had no
alternative left" but to conceal Annie's death.

"So it was necessary not only to say that you were devastated but to also say you hoped Anne Marie Fahey would be
found safe?"

"No," Capano conceded. "Just sitting here thinking about it,
I take back my prior answer. That was not necessary. That
should not have been in there."

"But it was," Connolly asked.

"Yes, it was."

And with that last exchange, Connolly walked away. "No
further questions, Your Honor."

That night, when Connolly got home, his wife, Anne, had
a surprise for him. She'd had been saving it for eight days—
since December 29, the day Capano's cross-examination began.

"Colm," she said, smiling. "I'm pregnant."

The prosecutor embraced his wife. It would be their fourth
child. Their second and third sons had been born during the
investigation of Tom Capano.

BOOK FIVE

It's a black hole without boundaries, and it is as black as it gets. There is no light. And we, collectively, not only siblings, but spouses, infant children, cousins, friends, uncles, aunts, have been trapped in that hole for the last thirty-one months.
—ROBERT FAHEY,
at Tom Capano's sentencing hearing

19 *A Verdict*

After twelve weeks of shuttling in and out of the Wilmington courthouse, sitting together for hundreds of hours but forbidden from discussing what they had seen or heard, the six men and six women of Thomas Capano's jury got their first chance to talk about Capano on Thursday, January 14, in a hospitality room of the Christiana Hilton.

Judge Lee had sent them to the hotel, seven miles south of Wilmington, just across the street from the Home Depot where Anne Marie Fahey was once rumored to be buried, with the admonition that they make their judgment based solely on the evidence, not on sympathy for the victim. "Proof beyond reasonable doubt is proof that leaves you firmly convinced of the defendant's guilt," Lee told them, defining the crucial standard of guilt in American criminal jurisprudence. "If you think there is a real possibility, or, in other words, a reasonable doubt that the defendant is not guilty, you must give the defendant the benefit of the doubt by finding him not guilty."

The end of the trial, after the exhaustive battle between Connolly and Capano, had been anticlimactic, despite a surprise witness sprung by the defense. Kimberlee Lee Johnson was marched to the witness box to say she lived across the street from Debby MacIntyre and recalled her neighbor screeching into her driveway late one night in June 1996. "She stumbled out of her car in a real quick motion," Johnson said. "I heard her issue a terrible kind of anguished sob and then she quickly ran to the side door of her house." Though Johnson couldn't recall what night it was, the message that the defense was clearly sending was that this was the night Debby had killed Annie.

Gene Maurer exuded confidence about Johnson's testimony. "She is within a very close period of time of this incident," the defense attorney told reporters on the courthouse steps. "It is up to the jury to decide how many times you come home at night like that."

The rest had been housecleaning—necessary but not, perhaps, crucial. Prosecutors landed a couple of witnesses who contradicted key elements of Johnson's story. A firearms expert said it was highly unlikely that a gun like the Beretta Debby MacIntyre had bought would fire accidentally. Bud Freel told of his futile efforts right after Annie disappeared to get Capano to help find her. And Robert Fahey stepped into the witness box to read the letter that his family had sent to Capano in July of 1996, begging him to help.

"Do what your father Louis would expect of one of his sons, come forward and share all you know about Anne Marie's disappearance," the Faheys had pleaded in that letter. "Imagine, if you will, that this case involved one of your four daughters, not our sister. We know you would expect the last person to be seen with your children to come forward and be helpful."

On cross-examination, Joe Oteri asked Robert if his family wasn't just trying to manipulate Capano with this letter.

"I'm attempting to motivate him to come forward and tell what he knows about my sister, yes," Robert said coolly.

Oteri pressed, however, suggesting that the family, when it wrote the letter, was only interested in its own needs and couldn't have known if Capano was protecting anyone.

"I believe," Robert said, setting his jaw and fixing his stare on the old man from Boston, "the only thing I wanted was my sister back."

During the dark days of the trial, even as he displayed his vain, controlling personality on the stand, Capano often tried to buck up the lead attorney's spirits. "You'll win it at closing," he would exhort Oteri.

The day to win had arrived on January 13. Oteri would have to wait until Colm Connolly, wearing a crisp black suit, finished his summation, a calm, methodical three-hour recitation of fact, heaping scorn on Capano's "lies," the most glaring of which, Connolly said, was the "ludicrous" story he finally told on the witness stand: that Annie's death was an accident.

The prosecutor asked why Capano waited two and a half years to say she had died in an accident. "The answer," Connolly said, looking solemnly at the jury, "is because the defendant thought he could get away with murder."

Joe Oteri stood up to deliver what most court observers knew would have to be the speech of a lifetime. But as with everything else he attempted to do in this case, he moved about the podium shackled not just by his client's reported deeds but also by his client's trial demands. Oteri hoped to speak for not much longer than an hour, but Capano insisted he read volumes of E-mails between the defendant and the dead woman. In the end, Oteri's strongest argument, like Connolly's, was a question: "If Tom Capano planned to kill Anne Marie Fahey, what kind of moron would kill her in his home?"

Finally, as the big white-faced clock on the wall over the courtroom doors clicked toward nine on this cold winter's night, Ferris Wharton had risen to deliver the prosecution's rebuttal. The state, which had the burden of proof, always gets the final word. He spoke for nearly an hour, issuing this syllogism to the jurors: "When you lie, when you lie to everybody, when you lie to your lawyer, when you lie to your psychiatrist, when you lie to your family, when you lie to everybody, you lie for one reason." Wharton paused, his deep baritone still ringing around the courtroom. "You lie because you're guilty."

At almost nine-thirty that night the jurors were led out of the courtroom with just one question to answer: Was Tom Capano guilty of murder? All or nothing. The judge had considered but rejected offering jurors the chance to consider lesser charges—second-degree murder, manslaughter, criminally negligent homicide. It was now up to twelve ordinary people to judge. All or nothing.

The jurors were driven through the Wilmington night in two vans, still forbidden from speaking about the case, not knowing whether they would need the several days of clothes and toiletries that Judge Lee had instructed them to pack. They would not be permitted to leave the hotel, Lee had told them, until they finished their deliberations. In fact, Judge Lee broke with tradition when he decided to keep the group at the hotel for deliberations. He reasoned that it would waste an hour or more each day traveling back and forth, not to mention what would be saved by not subjecting them to the media hordes waiting outside the courthouse almost around-the-clock. At the sprawling suburban hotel, isolated in a second-story wing, the jurors would deliberate in pampered privacy.

They ate dinner that night at eleven o'clock and went to bed. And the next morning, after their communal breakfast, they were at work in their large conference room by mid-morning. The foreman, a solemn-faced middle-aged General Motors pipe fitter, quickly emerged as the group's leader, even though, by Delaware law *foreman* was only a ceremonial title, bestowed on the first juror chosen. But he had been on juries before and knew the ropes. He had also served as a father figure for some of the younger jurors and already on numerous occasions acted as adviser and counselor. He was once seen consoling a teary colleague while leaving the courthouse.

The jurors' task, if they were to take the judge's admonition about weighing the evidence seriously, was daunting. More than four hundred exhibits had been introduced at trial; more than one hundred witnesses had sworn to tell the truth. Boxes of documents were wheeled into the conference room. In them were thousands of pages of transcript testimony and evidence, including confessions, police interviews, secret phone tapes, Annie's diary, her appointment calendar and psychological reports, E-mail transcripts, dozens of long letters written by Capano—even Capano's handwritten map of MacIntyre's home, with marginal notes about how to burglarize it. Nevertheless, they were not permitted to study transcripts and hadn't been allowed to take notes. So when it came to the testimony, the jurors could only rely on their memories.

In another corner of the room, stark and vivid reminders of what the case was really about, were crates containing a cooler, chain, lock, anchor, shotgun, and black .22-caliber Beretta pistol.

The jurors informally divided up some of their duties, depending on which questions loomed largest. Erin Reilly, an upbeat twenty-eight-year-old customer service representative for an incorporation company, decided to scrutinize anything involving MacIntyre. Like many other jurors, Reilly had serious problems with the mistress's credibility, especially with her claim that she never figured out the gun might be connected to the investigation of her boyfriend. If she was lying about that, Reilly figured, she could be lying about everything—including what she was doing on the night of June 27. Even if she didn't kill Fahey, maybe MacIntyre had helped clean up Capano's home, Reilly thought. And what of the anguished sob reported by MacIntyre's neighbor?

"I could see her coming into Capano's home and doing it," Reilly later recalled. "The prosecution made her look like a weak, fragile person and I don't think she's that. Part of me also could see why Capano wouldn't want everything about him coming out, everybody knowing he was such a sleazeball. And you know the old saying, 'Hell hath no fury like a woman scorned.' "

Other jurors also had doubts about MacIntyre. But there seemed to be early consensus about Tom Capano. Reilly found him pompous, arrogant, and disgusting, especially after watching Connolly spin him in circles with his lies and seeing him erupt. She had serious doubts about his story, especially the part about Annie calmly putting on her panty hose.

Still, Reilly and others thought the accident scenario described could have occurred. They surely weren't going to convict anybody without being absolutely certain.

By contrast, almost everyone believed Gerry's story, despite the defense's claims of confabulation. "I told myself during the trial, and I wasn't the only one, that if I heard that word one more time I was going to scream," Reilly said later. Even heavy drug and alcohol users, the jurors reasoned, could remember death plots and sea burials.

The jurors quickly realized that, stripped to its essence, the case boiled down to whether they believed Debby MacIntyre or Tom Capano, the two longtime lovers now pointing the finger at each other.

Heavy snow fell on northern Delaware that Thursday, icing highways and forcing several downtown offices to close early. But the jurors kept talking, kept looking through documents, kept walking around the room and engaging one another in private discussions. They broke for a hearty meal in the main dining room—alcohol was not allowed—and returned for more pondering.

While the attorneys stayed close to their office phones and pagers that day, Judge Lee had left Wilmington in the afternoon for his home in Rehoboth Beach, ninety-five miles south of Wilmington. Lee had stayed in a Wilmington hotel on trial days, going home on weekends. He now told reporters he'd stay at home until the following Tuesday unless there was a question or a verdict.

Tom Capano, meanwhile, complained, through his attorneys, about having to wait in a cold, damp holding cell in the courthouse. By that afternoon, Gander Hill officials relented, deciding they could let the defendant wait in his more commodious jail cell near the Delaware River.

The next day, Friday, several jurors made it clear they would vote guilty. Others were uncertain and one or two leaned toward acquittal. Spirited arguments dominated the day, but without the rancor they had witnessed over the previous twelve weeks in the courtroom.

Kimberlee Lee Johnson's story was debated, but in the end, most agreed that MacIntyre's neighbor had heard something, some night, but who knew when it occurred?

The jurors finally decided to reenact the shooting as described by the accused, as Wharton had suggested, to see if it seemed believable.

Two jurors sat on a small couch in their deliberation suite. Another walked up, held the Beretta at his side. The juror closest to the gun stood up and attempted to grab the gun as it was raised in the air. Just as Wharton had told them, it couldn't be done, unless the person raised the gun at a snail's pace.

Several jurors also tried to load the ammunition clip in the gun and were shocked by how much strength it took. Others were amazed by how much pressure was needed to cock the trigger. "A few of the women couldn't even do it," Reilly said. "It hurts your fingers."

By Saturday afternoon, there seemed to be a consensus and jurors decided it was time to vote. It was 3:30, but some jurors said they needed time to think and so the group recessed for dinner, where they were not allowed to deliberate.

"Before the vote, I went back to my room and thought about some things," Reilly said. "I just totally had to be 100 percent certain. I couldn't have any doubt. In my mind I went over things to make sure there was absolutely no doubt."

She thought about Oteri's words of warning. "I have to look in the mirror every day. And more than anything, I wanted to do what was right for Annie."

At 7:50 that evening, Capano's jurors reconvened—and voted. It would be their only vote. It was unanimous.

The foreman informed a bailiff, who called Judge Lee. Lee immediately scheduled the announcement for 9:30 the next morning.

Though an elaborate phone tree had been devised to inform attorneys, court personnel, and family members of a verdict, the press seemed to be the first to know. Doug Shimell, a reporter for Channel 10, the Philadelphia NBC affiliate, got wind of the momentous decision and called the judge at his home. Lee confirmed that a verdict had been reached, and Shimell went on the air with the news about eight-thirty. Dominic Desderio, a Wilmington FBI agent who lived in Philadelphia, saw the special report and was stunned. Nobody expected a verdict until Tuesday, after the Martin Luther King Jr. holiday.

Desderio called Colm Connolly, who was home with his wife and children, sipping wine with another married couple while Anne prepared shrimp scampi. Connolly hadn't heard a thing, but figured that a verdict this soon could only mean one thing. There could be no way, Connolly thought, that twelve people who heard all that evidence could unanimously vote to acquit Capano this soon. And a hung jury, a distinct possibility in a case like this, was not considered a verdict. So it was either guilty or not guilty—and Connolly was guessing guilty.

The federal prosecutor, juiced to be only hours from the moment of truth, paged Wharton, who was at a restaurant. Wharton knew nothing.

"If you get paged, will you call me?" Connolly asked his partner.

Not one to get excited, Wharton, the erstwhile veteran, said sure. "But I'm going to wait until after dinner."

When Joseph Oteri got the call, he, too, was at the shore, two hours away. The defense attorney rushed back to Wilmington.

I spent that Saturday working around my house, playing with my three-year-old son, Luke. My wife, a nurse, was working on the weekend. And I checked in with Terry Spencer, my reporting partner at the trial, who was spending his day at the courthouse. Spencer reported no action and went home at five. Both of us were certain there would be no verdict this day.

I took Luke out for pizza, did some errands, and returned home at nine. As my son was brushing his teeth and putting on his Power Rangers pajamas, my mother, Bernie, called.

"Did you hear there's a verdict?" she asked.

"Mom, what are you talking about?" I exclaimed in an annoyed voice. This was, after all, the same woman who had told me, during the summer of 1996, that she had it on high authority that Anne Marie Fahey was being kept in the Christiana Hospital morgue.

"It was on television."

"Let me make a few calls."

I called my paper and, sure enough, someone on the news desk had heard the report on television. Spencer was on his way into the office.

I knew it was no use trying to contact the Capanos; they never offered any comment or returned calls. I called Connolly, who said he assumed the report about a verdict being in was accurate but was still waiting for official word. I then called Charlie Oberly, who said the same thing.

"It's got to be bad news for you guys," I offered.

"You know," Oberly said in a resigned voice, "it's been bad news for us ever since this thing started."

The crowds began gathering at the courthouse not long after the sun rose on Sunday, January 17, 1999, which turned out to be an unusually warm, pleasant winter morning.

By 8:30 a dozen television trucks, and three times as many reporters, were milling around the stone steps and circular columns, waiting for the major players to arrive. By 8:45 nearly three hundred spectators had gathered, lingering on the sidewalk in front of the closed courthouse, sipping coffee, reading the paper, chatting excitedly. The rest of downtown was eerily quiet, as it always was on a Sunday morning.

Shortly before nine, Judge Lee, dressed in his gray wool coat, with his trademark scarf wrapped around his neck, ascended the steps to polite applause as the throng parted. Minutes later the mob became silent, reverent, when Wharton and the Faheys arrived, marching in tight, solemn formation through the glass double doors.

Next came Marguerite Capano, pushed down King Street in a wheelchair by a niece. "My son is innocent!" barked the family matriarch, waving a cane. Referring to MacIntyre, the old woman added, "She's a drunk."

Cheers greeted Connolly as he walked through the path created by well-wishers.

Capano's ex-wife and three youngest daughters showed up—Christine, the oldest, was away at college in New York—along with his sister, Marian. Oteri and the rest of the defense team avoided the spectacle by entering a back door, where they met with their client in a dank basement holding cell.

Once the principal players were in the courthouse, the media and spectators passed through metal detectors. Once the reporters were seated, fifty members of the public, as usual the first to arrive, were allowed to enter. The others, dozens of them, simply waited outside the room in the third-floor rotunda, content to be this close to the biggest news event of the year.

Inside the courtroom, the atmosphere was tense as reporters argued over seats and spectators whispered expectantly. Connolly, Wharton, and Detective Donovan, thinking they had won the war against Tom Capano, smiled as they leaned on the jury box, chatting.

But all the noise ceased at 9:54, when Thomas Capano, wearing his charcoal suit, shuffled in with his guards. He offered a slight smile to his family and sat down.

One minute later, a buzzer announcing his arrival, Judge Lee entered.

"All rise!" the bailiff shouted one more time.

Lee warned the gallery he would tolerate no outbursts, then addressed the Capano and Fahey families.

"Some group of people is going to be very upset," he said somberly. "I understand that. But I want you to control your emotions until you get out of the courtroom."

Lee then summoned the jury. Just as they had done on over a hundred occasions, the four remaining alternates marched in first, followed by the dozen official jurors.

None looked at Capano. Oteri knew what that meant.

The judge ordered Capano to stand. Capano rose slowly, looking pessimistic yet stoic.

Lee asked for the verdict. The pipe fitter stood and now stared hard at the defendant.

"Guilty as charged," he said in a strong, serious voice.

While Tom Capano, now flanked by his attorneys and surrounded by six armed guards, stared straight ahead, showing no emotion, his family behind him sobbed. They embraced one another. Across the aisle, Robert, Kathleen, Brian, Mark, and Kevin Fahey did the same.

Colm Connolly and Ferris Wharton both stood and turned toward the gallery, subdued grins creasing their faces. FBI agent Eric Alpert walked from the gallery to the prosecution table and slapped Donovan on the back. The crew-cut detective, chewing his ever-present paper clip, beamed with jubilation.

———

After the foreman read the verdict, Kathi Carlozzi, the courthouse clerk who acted as gatekeeper to the courtroom, turned and opened the heavy doors. She uttered a single word—"Guilty"—and shut the door again.

Cheers erupted in the rotunda. Outside, under a blue, sparkling sunny sky, a man with a radio to his ear yelled, "Guilty!" and the crowd burst into boisterous applause. A carnival atmosphere pervaded the courthouse steps as the Faheys, prosecutors, and investigators were greeted by ovations. Cars driving down King Street honked with joy.

The Capanos, their eyes red, faces distraught, filed past the onlookers without a word.

Then a familiar face seemed to appear from nowhere. It was Deborah MacIntyre. Her attorney, who had been in the courtroom and heard the verdict, had driven to her home and picked her up, figuring she could deal with the certain media onslaught with one dramatic news conference. Wearing a conservative violet suit, she now met the swarm of reporters and, for the first time in nearly two years, answered every single question fired at her.

She wasn't surprised to be accused of firing the fatal shot, she said, and expected as much after Capano hatched plots to burglarize her home and then have her murdered. "I have nothing to say to Tom," she said. "I do not love Tom Capano at all."

Colm Connolly, accompanied by Ferris Wharton, stepped outside into the winter sunlight. As spectators applauded, Connolly, his face placid, stepped up to a bank of microphones on the marble courthouse steps to take questions from the media for the first time in thirty months.

But even with a triumphal glow, the young prosecutor neither smiled nor gloated. Instead, magnanimous to the end, he shared credit with Wharton, Donovan, Alpert, and a host of other investigators who had brought Tom Capano to justice.

"They gave of themselves. They suffered. They didn't spend as much time with their families," said Connolly, the father of three young boys. "Without them we wouldn't be where we are today."

The case, he said, was a "roller coaster, full of times of desperation, times of elation." But they had executed the plan, "and it worked."

As cheers kept ringing out, echoing around the crowded courthouse steps in an otherwise-deserted city, Connolly reminded the gathering that the verdict was no cause for celebration.

"Tom Capano," the prosecutor said, "put a lot of people through a lot of distress, suffering, and pain."

20 *A Malignant Force*

On January 20, three days after the verdict was announced, court reconvened for a hearing to determine Thomas Capano's fate—life in prison without parole or death by injection with sodium pentothal.

In Delaware, the ultimate decision rested with the judge. But by law he was required to give the jury's recommendation "great weight."

Until 1991, jurors in Delaware had made the final decision about sentencing. But that year citizens had became outraged after a jury gave life sentences to four bandits who had shot two armored car guards to death in broad daylight. So the Delaware General Assembly, reacting to public outcry, passed a law that gave the final say to the judge.

Over five court sessions, Capano prosecutors and defense attorneys laid out their cases. To execute, the state had to convince jurors that Capano had engaged in "substantial planning," one of twenty-two aggravating circumstances needed to impose the death penalty.

On the first day, jurors got to hear from Linda Marandola, now forty-four, the woman Capano had stalked nearly two decades earlier. Prosecutors were forbidden from calling her during the trial but had no such restriction during the penalty phase.

Marandola, wearing a mint green dress, appeared petrified on the stand, trembling and clenching a pack of tissues as she recounted her brief fling with Capano and his relentless attempts to keep it going and ultimately run her out of town. Capano stared at her for the entire hour she testified.

Spectators looked at each other in amazement when Marandola revealed the contents of one letter: "He said he wished it had been me who gave birth to his child, not Kay."

Three of Annie's siblings—Robert, Kathleen, and Brian—also told of their heartache at losing Annie, the trauma of learning what had happened piece by painful piece, the rage at knowing they would never learn the whole truth.

"It's a black hole without boundaries, and it is as black as it gets," Robert said in a somber voice. "There is no light. And we, collectively, not only siblings, but spouses, infant children, cousins, friends, uncles, aunts, have been trapped in that hole for the last thirty-one months. It is boundaryless. You never know how deep it is. You never know when you're going to get out of it. It is the most inhumane treatment that could ever be inflicted upon human beings."

Robert also expressed his melancholy at not being able to give his sister a proper burial.

"Rather than Anne Marie being buried in a family plot next to her grandmother and her mother, my image is that Anne Marie, instead of being surrounded by her family when she died, and her friends, Anne Marie was surrounded by her killer and the killer's brother. And she was thrown over the side of a boat, wrapped in chains and an anchor and rope, rather than in her finest dress."

Kathleen, describing her kid sister as her best friend, said her own children had been deeply affected.

"My sons are afraid the bad man is going to come and get them. Kevin is afraid to go on boats. We went down to the shore and went on a boat, and he said, 'Mom, is that where the bad man put Aunt Annie?' These little triggers, and they happen all the time."

Brian spoke about how he feared his sister might have died cowering in a corner, with a gun at her head. But he also recalled the vibrant, outgoing sister he adored.

"I want to tell you how great she was. That's all. I mean, if you don't hear anything else, she was outstanding, you know, and she had—she just had a great vitality and spirit, and the world is going to miss her."

Defense attorney Jack O'Donnell had the job of trying to save his old college and law school buddy's life. He lined up all of Capano's siblings, including Gerry and Louis, who wanted to testify, against Tom's wishes, as well as his mother, ex-wife, and children. Three priests, two from St. Anthony's and another from Archmere, along with a handful of old pals, including former Wilmington mayor Tom Maloney, also agreed to make an appeal for Capano to live.

Louis and Gerry, whose testimony was punctuated by sobs, whimpers, and sniffles, begged jurors and Judge Lee to spare the brother they had helped convict.

"This is horrible. Horrible for the Faheys. Horrible for us," Gerry said as tears streamed down his tanned face. "I miss him," he said of his brother. "This is not the Tom I knew. He's not the Tom I grew up with, who I went to for advice. I don't know what happened to him, but something happened."

Gerry dabbed his swollen eyes with a handkerchief as he left the stand. Some spectators cried.

Kay Ryan, whose ex-husband had betrayed her for so many years and then subjected her to unimaginable humiliation, said she spoke for her daughters.

"I am not here to stand by my man. I am as repulsed by his vile acts as anyone here," she said, crying as she apologized to the Faheys. "But for everything he has done, he has been a loving father."

Kay also said her children should decide if their dad lived or died. "That should not be decided by the jury, not by the judge, and not by the government," she said, defiance in her voice.

On the final day of Capano's sentencing hearing, a day after what would have been Annie's thirty-third birthday, attorneys convened in Judge Lee's chambers at 9:30 in the morning.

"Are you waiting with bated breath?" O'Donnell asked the judge.

"We got fired yesterday," Oberly added.

"Anybody keeping count?" the judge quipped.

"What's the tally?" Maurer joked.

Wharton couldn't resist one more crack.

"Is that why Joe [Oteri] is not here? He accepted?"

The defense attorneys explained that their client was upset that they weren't calling enough witnesses on his behalf. Lee told the lawyers it was within their rights not to call certain witnesses and said that if Capano wanted to fire them when they were finished, so be it. But, for now, they would finish this.

Once court was called to order, Marguerite Capano, seventy-five, rolled up to the witness stand in her wheelchair, pushed by Oteri.

"My son is not a murderer," she said in an anguished voice. "He is not guilty of killing Anne Marie. I feel sorry for her, but he didn't do it. He's too good a person to hurt anybody. He did wrong by not calling 911 when she was hurt, but he didn't do it. I don't care what anybody says, and nobody will ever convince me that he did. I love him. I need him. . . . Please don't kill my son. Please spare my son for me and for his family and for his daughters."

Lee let Capano's mother finish and thanked her before Oteri pushed her wheelchair back to the gallery.

Then the judge turned to the jury.

"I must again instruct the jury that while Mrs. Capano's belief in her son and his innocence is understandable, that question has been resolved and that was an improper comment and you're to disregard it."

Allocution, a right derived from English common law, lets a man facing the possibility of capital punishment plead for his life before the jury without disputing the facts of the case or comment on the trial. Capano chose to exercise his legal right, again against the advice of his legal team. And at 11:40 that morning, he stepped back up to the witness stand.

Lee issued a stern warning before Capano began.

"Allocution is extended only to acceptable expressions of remorse, pleas for leniency, statements about his own good person, and plans or hopes for the future," lectured Lee. "It is not to dispute the evidence or the verdict, to attack the investigation or the prosecutors. Those limitations are to be strictly enforced. And if in fact they are violated, I will terminate the allocution."

Capano told the judge he didn't hear him clearly.

"The acceptable things," the annoyed judge responded, "are expressions of remorse, pleas for leniency, statements about your own good character and person, and plans and hopes for the future."

Capano, with a stack of papers in front of him, immediately stretched the limits of the judge's order.

"I hope you can appreciate it is pretty difficult for me to speak to people who have already rejected me," he told the jury. "In your mind you say to yourself, *What's the use?* You've made your decision, and I'd be less than honest if I didn't say we're still reeling from it."

Capano reminded jurors that when he testified, he didn't "use a lot of phony baloney stuff, saying, 'I can't recollect,' or, 'That is correct,' or those other things that trained witnesses do."

He called the case a tragedy and said that despite what had been said, he loved his victim. "If I could do anything, anything, to undo it, I would. If I could trade places with Anne Marie, I would."

Over the next fifty minutes, he quoted the Jesuits, Greek philosophers, Hubert Humphrey, and the Beatles in a rambling, disjointed monologue. At times he wept. He called himself a good father, loyal friend, dedicated public servant, and responsible Catholic who had been maligned by the media and wrongly described during the trial.

"I don't know the guy that's been betrayed—portrayed— portrayed in this courtroom. And I don't even know the guy now that stands before you. . . . I was never a big Beatles fan. They killed Motown. That's why I didn't like them. I like their ballads and particularly, 'Yesterday.' There's a line in there that friends sent me. It says, basically: 'Now I'm half the man I used to be.' And that lyric is going around in my mind so many times. I'm even less than half the man I used to be."

Judge Lee raised his eyebrows several times during Capano's confused peroration but refrained from interrupting until the convicted killer revived the argument with Connolly over his daughters' treatment.

"My kids were harassed," Capano said. "They were lied to—"

"We're done," the judge declared. "Please take Mr. Capano out of the courtroom."

Capano begged for one more chance. "Can I take it back, Your Honor, and finish?"

The judge said no, then changed his mind.

"Sort of blown my rules apart here ... but the next time you make such a blatant attack on the rules that you're forced to operate under I will remove you. There won't be taking back anything. You will not be present for the rest of the trial," he told Capano.

Capano droned on for another twenty minutes, with Lee issuing periodic warnings.

Capano asked the jury to spare him, but only for his daughters, so he could stay involved in their lives.

"I don't beg," the killer said. "I'm not going to sit here and beg for my life."

He ended with one more meandering discourse:

"We all seem able to deal with our mortality, even though we seem to be the only creatures on earth who can realize what is happening. We give little thought to that ride on a pale horse because we don't know when it will come, always confident it won't be today. But still, while the world may wonder or even envy the success or failure of any particular man or woman, rare indeed is the life without trial: the loss of a loved one, as the Faheys have experienced; perfidy of a trusted friend, I've learned that in spades; the savaging of one's reputation; the pain of ignored effort; the lonely awareness that youth and health are receding. So many dark moments in our lives that make our private world stand still. What is to sustain us through those things, all those little dents, all those little cuts? It is only faith, it is only moral strength, it is only those attributes nurtured by the study of those things that I was taught, and those things Jack O'Donnell was taught, Joe Oteri was taught, and my kids were taught; that's what's important. That's what gets us through."

The convicted killer wiped his nose with a tissue, paused, and said softly, "Sorry if I broke the rules." Then he left the stand and, shoulders hunched, shuffled back to his seat at the defense table.

Colm Connolly now stood up and reviewed Capano's privileged life, his crime, cover-up, abuse of the Faheys and his own loved ones.

"He put his mother in an untenable, horrible position to

choose amongst her sons. He did it in a heartbeat," the prosecutor told the jury.

"You know, Robert Fahey talked about being in a black hole. Mr. Capano talks about the Church, Fathers Aquinas and Augustine, the Jesuits. You know there's a Catholic teaching that evil is not in existence in and of itself. Evil is the absence of good. Like a vacuum. That's what the defendant is. He's a black hole. He's a vacuum of evilness, and he's sucked all those different people into a black hole, and he's ruined their lives—from his daughters, to his ex-wife, his mother, the Faheys, Keith Brady, Susan Louth, Louis Capano, Gerry Capano, Anne Marie Fahey."

Ferris Wharton, who did the prosecution rebuttal, warned that Capano was a danger even from behind prison walls. "You will have an opportunity to do more than to simply confine this evil that Tom Capano has become," the prosecutor told the jury, "because that type of evil is relentless and will not be confined. You will have an opportunity to end its presence in our lives, ladies and gentlemen, because that type of evil must be ended."

At 3:30, jurors retreated to a room off the court. Again their deliberations were without rancor. After only three hours of discussion, they voted.

At 7:00 P.M., Lee called the court back to order. The jury filed in as both families waited along with press and spectators.

The foreman handed a piece of paper to a bailiff, who turned it over to Judge Lee.

He read the vote—11–1 in favor of substantial planning and 10–2 for death.

The ball was now in Lee's court. Only once had a Delaware judge overruled a 10–2 or better vote for execution. But Lee would have several weeks, months if he wanted, to decide Capano's fate.

Lee thanked the jury for their yeoman service—"You're underpaid and overworked. Welcome to state employment"— and ordered the guards to "remove the defendant."

I'll be all right, Capano mouthed to his mother as he was handcuffed and led away.

Then the judge turned to the gallery and his voice softened.

"I would also like to express my thanks to those of you who were in regular attendance as members of the working press and as members of the Capano and Fahey family," he said.

"It's been a long and trying ordeal. I particularly respect the restraint that the Capano family has shown at the announcement of the verdict. God bless you all."

On March 16, 1999—not quite seven weeks later—the families, reporters, and spectators gathered one more time at the Herrmann Courthouse. The scene took on the atmosphere of a reunion as trial regulars, almost in withdrawal from the fourteen weeks they had spent together, hugged and exchanged warm greetings.

Inside the courtroom, on this grave occasion, only Judge Lee spoke. Capano's attorneys had twice requested the chance to make even more comments, but the judge disparaged their plea as "ludicrous."

"There comes a time," Lee wrote in a letter responding to the Capano team's requests, "when the presentation of facts and argument cease and the time of decision arrives. That time has come and gone."

The courtroom went quiet instantly when Capano entered at 1:15 P.M., escorted by two armed prison guards. Dressed in a dark suit, Capano carried the cardboard accordion file that was his daily companion throughout the trial.

He smiled at his family, raising his eyebrows, and mouthed, *I love you,* as he was led to the defense table. Daughters Katie and Jennie looked forlorn, as did brother Joseph and sister Marian. Absent were daughters Christy and Alex.

Speaking forcefully, the judge didn't mince his words. Capano scribbled on a notepad, periodically glancing up at the judge.

After completing the process [of reviewing the jury's deliberations], I was left with a feeling that the legal and intellectual exercise required by our law was inadequate to describe what occurred in this trial. For that reason, I have chosen not to read from my opinion but to supplement it with my remarks today.

I believe that it is important for any reviewing court to understand what occurred in the courtroom that cannot be reflected in a transcript. The gradual revelation of the personality and character of the defendant clearly was a factor in both the verdict of the jury and its recommendation concerning appropriate sentence. It is a significant factor in sentencing and decision today.

Thomas J. Capano entered this courtroom on trial for his life, a man presumed innocent, and, almost immediately, he embarked on a course of conduct which rebutted that presumption. Intelligent, educated, affluent, accomplished and charming by reputation, he proceeded to negate all of the advantages his life had provided during the harsh confrontation with reality which is a criminal trial and eventually revealed an angry, sinister, controlling, and malignant force which dominated the courtroom for months.

From the beginning, he systematically and contemptuously degraded all of those who participated in the proceedings: the prosecutors, witnesses, prison personnel, the Court, and his own attorneys. From direct insults to the prosecutors to withering stares at witnesses, continuous claims of privilege from correction officers, constant violation of the rules of the Department of Correction and the limitations established by the Court and suborning perjury to the constant undermining of the efforts of the excellent lawyers he assembled to represent him, Thomas Capano needed to show everyone that he was in charge and that he held all those he viewed as adversaries with contempt.

In spite of imposing his will on his attorneys in matters where, by law, the decision was rightfully theirs, the possibility remained that he would be acquitted until he insisted that they adopt his unsupported theory of the case in the defense opening statement, which all but required his testimony once a promised credible witness failed to materialize. Again, against the unanimous advice of his counsel, the defendant insisted on testifying and solidifying the remaining area of weakness in the state's case by presenting a story of Anne Marie Fahey's death which the jury found incredible.

Having sealed his fate on the question of guilt or innocence, he displayed the malevolence of his nature, which
became crucial in determining sentence. The defendant insisted on a 'chain saw' approach, attacking, maiming, and
destroying the character and lives of lovers, friends, and
family who had, in his eyes, been disloyal to him in his
time of need, a practice that extended to his allocution even
after instructions by his lawyers and the Court that such
statements were improper and impermissible in exercising
the limited right he claimed.

The defendant fully expected to get away with murder
and, were it not for his own arrogance and controlling nature, may well have succeeded. He raged at federal intervention in his case when he was certain that things could
have been worked out if only the police department of his
city and his friends had been exclusively in control. He
ranted about the intrusive investigation in a missing person,
possible kidnapping, and possible homicide case where he
was an uncooperative suspect. 'Gestapos' and 'Nazis' harassed him and his family in a desperate search for a woman
whom he had killed and whose body he had disposed of.
What was all the commotion about? If the virtuous Tom
Capano had ever existed, he no longer did at this time.

He chose to use his family as a shield, make his brothers
and his mistress accomplices, use his friends and attorneys
for disinformation, attack the character of his prosecutor,
make his mother and daughters part of a spectacle in an
effort to gain sympathy, chide his brother to 'be a man'
when the weight of the investigation fell upon him, rely on
character assassination when that brother is compelled to
testify, and insist that the family ostracize him for telling
the truth. How glibly he finally acknowledges that everything Gerard had said was true, with one exception, and that
one exception was verified by his 'loyal' brother, Joe. When
his mistress is trapped by the lies he has told her to tell and,
like Gerry, is forced to tell the truth, her 'disloyalty' is rewarded by attempting to terrorize her and blaming her for
the killing. He even bullied, berated, and undermined the
efforts of his own attorneys who believed they could gain

his acquittal. The defendant has no one to blame for the circumstances he finds himself in today except himself.

In the end, the defendant claimed the right of allocution, the ancient avenue of a convicted criminal facing death to accept responsibility, express remorse, and ask for mercy relying upon his good and contrite character to gain that mercy. As a lawyer specifically instructed by his own lawyers on the limits of allocution and further admonished by the Court before and during allocution, he specifically refused to ask for mercy, showed no remorse, and continued to attack the decision of the jury, the disloyalty of those who testified against him, and the tactics and character of the prosecutor and investigators who assembled and presented the case against him, all specific violations of the right of allocution.

The selfishness, arrogance, and manipulativeness of Thomas Capano destroyed his own family as well as the Fahey family. He did not hesitate to use his family to commit and suborn perjury, or to ask for the mercy he specifically refused to ask for himself. His only remorse is for himself.

The most powerful mitigation presented does not involve the defendant. Rather it is the impact of his remarkable daughters and a brother he involved in his criminal activities and then ridiculed and excommunicated from the family when guilt and circumstances forced him to tell the truth. Tom Capano does not face judgment today because friends and family failed him. He faces judgment because he is a ruthless murderer who feels compassion for no one and remorse only for the circumstances in which he finds himself. He is a malignant force from whom no one he deems disloyal or adversarial can be secure, even if he is incarcerated for the rest of his life.

No one, except the defendant, will ever know exactly how or why Anne Marie Fahey died. What is certain is that it was not a crime of passion but, rather, a crime of control. By all accounts, she had ceased to be the defendant's lover but had never escaped his sphere of influence, control, and manipulation. Anne Marie Fahey could not be permitted to end the relationship unless he said so; she could not be allowed to reject him. The defendant's premeditation and planning for a contingency that, perhaps, he hoped would never happen, but did on the evening of June 27, 1996. He chose to destroy a possession rather than lose it; to execute an escaping human chattel.

Considering and weighing all of the evidence, the verdict and recommendation of the jury was just.

After court was adjourned and the crowd dispersed, Lee told a reporter that Capano's crimes baffled him.

"When I drove into Wilmington today," the judge said, shaking his head in exasperation, "I thought, *This was his city. How could he throw it all away?*"

Thomas Capano had indeed thrown it all away. And with it, many lives, including one cut short at just thirty years, that of Anne Marie Fahey.

Epilogue

After Tom Capano was sentenced, Joe Oteri bid good-bye to his new friends in Wilmington, expressed despair at not being able to save Capano's life, and headed back to Boston, where he was defending a man accused of smuggling five tons of marijuana into the country. Jack O'Donnell flew back to Fort Lauderdale, Florida, to resume his own criminal practice. Charles Oberly and Gene Maurer returned to their practices in Wilmington, which they had neglected during their defense of their old buddy.

Colm Connolly, meanwhile, who had planned on leaving the U.S. Attorney's Office before Anne Marie Fahey disappeared, took a job with a private Wilmington firm six weeks after the sentence was pronounced. Ferris Wharton, the veteran state prosecutor, continued to do the same thing he'd been doing for nearly two decades, putting Delaware's violent criminals behind bars.

Bob Donovan, the Wilmington police detective, returned to the streets, hunting down robbers, drug dealers, and gunmen.

Eric Alpert, the FBI agent who helped crack the case, went back to Washington, D.C., where he had been transferred after Capano's arrest and promoted to supervisor.

William Swain Lee, the judge who had run a difficult trial with such diplomacy and patience, pondered a run for governor.

Friends and colleagues of Annie Fahey tried to pick up the pieces of their lives. Kim Horstmann doted on her new baby, named Anne Marie. Michele Sullivan, the victim's therapist, took a sabbatical.

Keith Brady, Ferris Wharton's old boss, whose reputation took a beating with the revelations of his sexual escapades with Deborah MacIntyre and other women, returned to the attorney general's office after his leave of absence in a lesser post. Susan Louth, Capano's girlfriend, tried to start a new life in the Virgin Islands.

Debby MacIntyre, the mistress Capano had tried to blame for the killing, kept a low profile in Wilmington but appeared on ABC's *20/20*, saying of her former soul mate, "Right now, I'm afraid of him; I'm afraid that he might do something to me."

Kay Capano retook her maiden name, Ryan, and with her daughters stayed in Wilmington, despite persistent rumors that they might move away.

Louis, Joe, and Gerry Capano moved to another court fight, defending their fortune against the Faheys' civil suit, on which a court-imposed stay had been lifted. On June 8, 1999, Louis and Gerry were sentenced to probation for the crimes in protecting their brother to which they had pleaded guilty.

Tom Capano had promised interviews to a host of television reporters on the day after his sentencing—but reneged on all of them and refused all further requests for interviews. A few days later he was shipped to the state prison outside the rural town of Smyrna in central Delaware, once again put in solitary confinement, this time limited to one phone call a week and one visitor a month. He planned his appeal, hiring a New Jersey lawyer to handle the case. Looming, five or so years into the twenty-first century, was his execution.

And the Fahey siblings, now five, struggled to get on with their lives, without their youngest sister, Annie.